STRATEGIC
SURVEY 2003/4

AN EVALUATION AND FORECAST
OF WORLD AFFAIRS

Published by

OXFORD
UNIVERSITY PRESS

for

The International Institute for Strategic Studies
Arundel House, 13–15 Arundel Street, Temple Place,
London WC2R 3DX, United Kingdom

STRATEGIC
SURVEY 2003/4

Published by

OXFORD
UNIVERSITY PRESS

for

The International Institute for Strategic Studies
Arundel House, 13–15 Arundel Street, Temple Place,
London WC2R 3DX, United Kingdom

Director: ....Dr John Chipman
Editor: ....Jonathan Stevenson

Assistant Editor: ....Jill Dobson
Map Editor: ....James Hackett
Editorial Manager: ....James Green
Designer: ....Simon Nevitt
Cartographer: ....Jillian Luff

This publication has been prepared by the
Director of the Institute and his Staff, who
accept full responsibility for its contents,
which describe and analyse events up to
12 April 2004. These do not, and indeed
cannot, represent a consensus of views
among the worldwide membership of the
Institute as a whole.

Cover images © The Associated Press

First published ....May 2004

ISBN 0-19-853019-6
ISSN 0459-7230

Strategic Survey (ISSN 0459-7230) is published
annually by Oxford University Press.

Payment is required with all orders and
subscriptions. Prices include air-speeded delivery
to Australia, Canada, India, Japan, New Zealand
and the USA. Delivery elsewhere is by surface
mail. Air-mail rates are available on request.
Please add sales tax to prices quoted. Payment
may be made by cheque or Eurocheque (payable
to Oxford University Press), National Girobank
(account 500 1056), credit card (MasterCard, Visa,
American Express), direct debit (please send for
details) or UNESCO coupons. Bankers: Barclays
Bank plc. PO Box 333, Oxford, UK, code 20-65-18,
account 00715654.

Claims for non-receipt must be made within four
months of dispatch/order (whichever is later).

Please send subscription orders to the Journals
Subscription Department, Oxford University
Press, Great Clarendon Street, Oxford, OX2 6DP,
UK. *Tel* +44 (0)1865 353907. *Fax* +44 (0)1865 353485.
e-mail jnl.orders@oup.co.uk

Strategic Survey is distributed by Mercury
International, 365 Blair Road, Avenel, NJ 07001,
USA. Periodical postage paid at Rahway, New
Jersey, USA, and additional entry points.

US POSTMASTER: Send address corrections to
Strategic Survey, c/o Mercury International,
365 Blair Road, Avenel, NJ 07001, USA.

Abstracted and indexed by: Reasearch Base
Online, PAIS.

Printed in the UK by Bell & Bain Ltd, Glasgow.

Contents

List of Maps

Strategic Survey Online

Members of the IISS can access *Strategic Survey 2003/4* online
via the Members area of www.iiss.org. The address for
subscribers is http://www3.oup.co.uk/stsurv, where they
will first need to register using their subscriber number.

Perspectives

Throughout 2003 and into 2004, the US-led intervention in Iraq dominated the full spectrum of world affairs. Indeed, its primacy has crystallised a kind of ongoing strategic culture shock. In counter-terrorism terms, the intervention has arguably focused the energies and resources of al-Qaeda and its followers while diluting those of the global counter-terrorism coalition that appeared so formidable following the Afghanistan intervention in late 2001. Politically, it split the US and major continental European powers, leaving the United Kingdom uncomfortably in the middle, and induced uncertainty in other governments about the extent of any contribution to the post-conflict effort. In political-military affairs, the high-maintenance character of the intervention has set a forbidding precedent that even the Americans will find difficult to meet. In the state-building arena, the US effort initially marginalised the United Nations and, in effect, provisionally broadened the criteria for international intervention beyond humanitarian concerns or imminent threats to strategic transformation. The Iraq war and its aftermath have also raised serious questions about pre-emptive and preventive war as a means of counter-proliferation, and about the uses and abuses of intelligence as a basis for military action.

For all of these jolts to the international system, by early spring 2004 state-building in Iraq finally appeared to be taking hold, and the diplomatic relationships and international institutions that the dispute over intervention had damaged so severely seemed to be regaining some of their integrity. Whether the Iraq enterprise had increased global security overall, however, remained hotly debated.

Net assessment: terrorism

Overall, risks of terrorism to Westerners and Western assets in Arab countries appeared to increase after the Iraq war began in March 2003. With the military invasion and occupation of Iraq, the United States demonstrated its determination to change the political status quo in the Arab world to advance American strategic and political interests. Al-Qaeda seeks, among other things, to purge the Arab and larger Muslim world of US influence. Accordingly, the Iraq intervention was always likely in the short term to enhance jihadist recruitment and intensify al-Qaeda's motivation to encourage and assist terrorist operations. The May 2003 attacks in Saudi Arabia and Morocco, the gathering of foreign jihadists in

Iraq, and the November 2003 attacks in Saudi Arabia and Turkey confirmed this expectation.

The Afghanistan intervention offensively hobbled, but defensively benefited, al-Qaeda. While al-Qaeda lost a recruiting magnet and a training, command and operations base, it was compelled to disperse and become even more decentralised, 'virtual' and invisible. Conservative intelligence estimates indicate that al-Qaeda is present in over 60 countries, and that at least 20,000 jihadists have been trained in its Afghanistan camps since 1996. Although half of al-Qaeda's 30 senior leaders and perhaps 2,000 rank-and-file members have been killed or captured, a rump leadership is still intact and over 18,000 potential terrorists at large, with recruitment accelerating on account of Iraq. Al-Qaeda's cells still appear to operate semi-autonomously, maintaining links through field commanders to leaders who are probably in the cities of Pakistan or its 'tribal areas' near the Afghan border. Now with few military point-targets, the US and its counter-terrorism partners must depend for immediate self-protection mainly on homeland security and law-enforcement and intelligence cooperation. This has proven qualifiedly effective where mature governments, robust security institutions and longstanding bilateral security relationships prevail: since 11 September, one major attack – in Madrid on 11 March 2004 – has taken place in Europe while none have occurred in North America. But where security institutions are weak (as in Kenya) or constrained by anti-Western domestic sentiment (as in Indonesia, Pakistan and Saudi Arabia), vulnerabilities arise that are easier for al-Qaeda to exploit. Such countries have become soft targets of opportunity.

The US remains al-Qaeda's prime target. A dominant al-Qaeda theme is Islam's alleged historical humiliation at the hands of the Judeo-Christian West, and al-Qaeda spokesman Suleiman Abu Ghaith has cited four million American dead as a prerequisite to any Islamic victory. Unlike those of ethno-nationalist or ideological terrorist groups, al-Qaeda's complaints have been transformed into religious absolutes and cannot be satisfied through political compromise. Further, Christian nations' forcible occupation of Iraq, a historically important land of Islam, has more than offset any calming effect of the US military withdrawal from Saudi Arabia completed last August. Thus, al-Qaeda has added Iraq to its list of grievances. With Osama bin Laden's public encouragement, up to 1,000 foreign jihadists have infiltrated Iraq. They have now had time to establish operational relationships with Baathists loyal to Saddam Hussein who initiated the ongoing insurgency. Furthermore, the substantially exposed US military deployment in Iraq presents al-Qaeda with perhaps its most attractive 'iconic' target outside US territory. The capture of Saddam Hussein in December 2003, while a boost to the domestic popularity of US President George W. Bush, did not immediately dampen the Iraqi insurgency.

On a tape broadcast on 21 May 2003, al-Qaeda second-in-command Ayman al-Zawahiri indicated a new focus on the Arab world, branding Saudi Arabia, Kuwait, Qatar, Bahrain, Egypt, Yemen and Jordan as collaborators in the war against Iraq. By twice striking hard in Turkey in November 2003, however, al-Qaeda widened its operational purview beyond the Arab world. The synagogue attacks reflect the group's customary enmity towards Jews. Bombing the British consulate and a UK based bank in Turkey suggests an intention to punish the United States' close strategic partners, especially those who would assist US-led efforts in Iraq. Subsequently, in the London-based Muslim newspaper *al-Quds al-Arubi*, bin Laden cited Italy, Japan and Australia (along with the US) as potential targets. Targeting Turkey has additional, if secondary, significance. Turkey is the West's ranking model of secular Islamic government, the only largely Muslim country in NATO, and the only one with smooth diplomatic and defence relationships with Israel. In the Islamist leanings of Turkey's Justice and Development Party – in power since November 2002 – al-Qaeda might sense better political traction for radical Islam there. Al-Qaeda may have been sending Ankara the message that impious government and partnership with Western countries and Israel will not be tolerated. This could backfire: security priorities are likely to yield the Turkish military – guardian of Turkey's resolutely secular Kemalist creed – more leeway in suppressing both Islamism and terrorism.

On account of its offensive limitations, al-Qaeda must now relinquish substantial operational initiative and responsibility to local talent. Still, experienced al-Qaeda middle managers can provide planning and logistical advice, materiel and financing to smaller groups, as they did in Saudi Arabia and Morocco and probably Indonesia and Kenya. The Turkish Sunni Muslim group Great Eastern Islamic Raiders' Front claimed joint responsibility with al-Qaeda for the Istanbul bombings, and the main perpetrators were apparently Turks. Nevertheless, al-Qaeda is the common ideological and logistical hub for disparate local affiliates, and bin Laden's charisma, presumed survival and elusiveness enhance the organisation's iconic drawing power. Galvanised by Iraq if compromised by Afghanistan, al-Qaeda remains a viable and effective 'network of networks'.

Through regime change in Iraq, the US and the UK partly intended to usher democracy into the Gulf region to advance a salutary long-term political convergence between Islam and the West. But insurgency and other state-building problems have raised doubts about the project's ultimate political benefits, while costs in terms of increased terrorism have materialised. Imparting positive spin, some US officials have observed that the jihadist influx brings more terrorists into a smaller killing zone. But as a flat, multi-nodal network reliant on local talent, al-Qaeda is unlikely to appreciably concentrate forces: the 1,000 estimated to be in Iraq is a minute fraction of its potential strength. The November 2003 attacks in Riyadh and

Istanbul and ongoing planning activity in the US and Europe occurred as jihadist infiltration into Iraq intensified. Lack of progress in securing and stabilising Afghanistan also permitted a resurgence of al-Qaeda and Taliban operations there. This varied activity attested to al-Qaeda's resilient capacity to conduct operations in multiple 'fields of jihad'.

While the organisation and its affiliates and friends do not enjoy the financial fluidity that they did before the post-11 September counter-terrorism mobilisation, neither do they appear shorn of resources. Moreover, terrorist operations are asymmetrically inexpensive. The Bali bombing cost under $35,000, the *USS Cole* operation about $50,000 and the 11 September attacks less than $500,000. Moving large amounts of cash therefore is not an operational necessity. Furthermore, since the Afghanistan intervention forced al-Qaeda to decentralise and eliminated the financial burden of maintaining a large physical base, al-Qaeda has needed less money to operate. Its increasing use of hawalas has prompted new laws in the US, Hong Kong and elsewhere requiring remittance houses to register. Compliance has been low, however. There are some indications that al-Qaeda has converted its assets to gems (including 'conflict diamonds'), gold and other commodities that are susceptible to bartering and hard to trace. Finally, the local affiliates on which it has come to rely more and more since the Afghanistan intervention sometimes have their own local funding sources.

Since 11 September, to be sure, mainstream Western banking has become subject to substantial vigilance. Big strides in financial surveillance, however, will now be difficult to make. Al-Qaeda's post-Afghanistan decentralisation allows it to leverage atomised local sources that are harder to monitor. Informal hawala remittance systems – based on trust rather than a paper trail – are very difficult to regulate. Though some Arab governments have shown grudging cooperation, Muslim banks and their regulators tend to be averse to the application of heavy scrutiny. Private citizens, particularly Saudis, continue to contribute heavily to charities and schools (madrassas) that serve as fronts and training grounds for terrorist organisations. Perhaps the most important measure that Western governments can yet take is to add such charities to official lists of terrorist organisations and, correspondingly, freeze their assets.

Overall, risks to Westerners and Western assets in Arab countries have increased since the Iraq war. The Madrid bombings in March 2004 suggested that al-Qaeda had fully reconstituted, set its sights firmly on the US and its closest Western allies in Europe, and established a new and effective modus operandi. While al-Qaeda remained a generally flatter and less hierarchical organisation than it had been prior to the Afghanistan intervention, US agencies developed intelligence suggesting that certain functions – in particular, bomb manufacture – may be more centralised and therefore potentially more efficient and sophisticated than earlier believed.

Al-Qaeda will keep trying to develop more promising plans for terrorist operations in North America and Europe, ideally involving weapons of mass destruction (WMD). Meanwhile, soft targets encompassing Americans, Europeans and Israelis, and aiding the insurgency in Iraq, will do. Given the group's absolutist objectives and transnational ubiquity and covertness, stiff operational counter-terrorist measures, inter-governmentally coordinated, are still acutely required. Progress will come incrementally. It is likely to accelerate only with currently elusive political developments that would broadly depress recruitment and motivation, such as the stable democratisation of Iraq or resolution of the Israeli–Palestinian conflict.

Net assessment: rogue regimes and WMD

The failure of the US to find significant chemical or biological agents or elements of a military nuclear programme in Iraq de-emphasised the counter-proliferation dimension of the Iraq intervention. Certainly, denying al-Qaeda a potential state supplier of WMD was a genuine justification of coercive regime change, but the deeper strategic objective – changing the political status quo in the Middle East and Gulf – loomed larger in early 2004. Insofar as Iraq's presumed WMD capability was the strongest justification for self-defence, its apparent absence made the intervention appear all the more like a war of choice. Politically, scope narrowed for unilateral American action – even when the stated purpose was to neutralise WMD. Nevertheless, the demonstrated willingness of the US to move militarily against perennial rogue regimes appeared to have a suppressive effect on two of them: Syria, which by late 2003 had stopped assisting Iraqi insurgents and foreign jihadists and sought renewed dialogue with Israel; and Libya, which abandoned its nuclear programme and settled claims for airliner bombings. More broadly, though, it became clear that Iraq had posed an exceptional case – in terms both of US threat perceptions and the legal, political and military circumstances that led to war. Subsequently, Washington's decidedly diplomatic approach to Iran and North Korea – the other two members of the 'axis of evil' delineated by Bush in his January 2002 State of the Union address – demonstrated that pre-emption and prevention were, as the September 2002 US National Security Strategy indicated, extraordinary remedies of last resort and not the primary chosen means of counter-proliferation.

In early 2004, military pre-emption was infeasible with respect to both Iran and North Korea. In regard to North Korea, it was too late, as the country posed a significant regional missile threat and artillery threat to South Korea and may already have one or two nuclear bombs. As to Iran, it was too early for pre-emption, since it was not yet capable of producing weapons-grade uranium or plutonium. Washington's preferred non-proliferation option of traditional multilateral diplomacy thus was clearly re-established with respect to these two countries. Neither diplomatic track looked easy, but neither appeared implausible. Although North Korea had the leeway to threaten nuclear or missile tests pending the 2004 US presidential election, it was more dependent on outside assistance than it was in 1994, when the now-obsolete Agreed Framework was signed, and constrained by the risk of alienating China, Russia and other governments sponsoring multilateral talks. Assuming continuous operation of its 5-megawatt reactor at Yongbyon, North Korea could produce one nuclear bomb per year; under the worst-case scenario, if it completed its 50 MW reactor within two years, annual output could jump to 8–13 nuclear bombs in the second half of the decade. Both sides thus had strong incentives to negotiate. These dynamics made it likely that Washington could eventually strike a bargain involving enhanced verification and early North Korean disarmament measures.

While Iran played a more subtle hand than North Korea, nobody was fooled by its dubious claims – given its indigenous oil resources – that its civilian energy requirements necessitated its nuclear fuel cycle activity. Accordingly, the US and its allies – including Russia and the European Union (EU) – have mobilised international pressure on Iran, culminating in a tough International Atomic Energy Agency (IAEA) Board of Governors resolution on 12 September 2003 demanding that Iran satisfy IAEA concerns; suspend uranium enrichment-related activities at its Nantanz facility until the IAEA determines that Iran is in compliance with its existing safeguards obligations and has implemented the Additional Protocol; and accept the Additional Protocol unconditionally. While Iranian officials warned that undue international pressure could strengthen hardliners in Tehran calling for withdrawal from the Non-proliferation Treaty (NPT), Iran actually chose to cooperate with the IAEA to defuse international pressure, divide the opposition and buy time to complete the Nantanz facility under IAEA safeguards. This course preserved its nuclear breakout option, but also bought the US and its partners time to formulate a deal whereby Iran would relinquish its fuel cycle programme in exchange for economic and political incentives. Calculations were complicated by the political struggle within Iran between the reformist government and the conservative religious establishment. Divisions became more acute when a third of the Iranian Parliament quit in February 2004 to protest the clerics' barring over 2,000 candidates from standing for election to the 290-seat assembly later that month.

Whereas counter-terrorism quite clearly did not receive a boost from the Iraq intervention, it appeared to yield benefits in terms of counter-proliferation and state sponsorship of terrorism. North Korea remained a singularly sticky problem, but a negotiating process had at least been established through dogged diplomatic efforts of several nations – China, in particular. Syria became less provocative. Libya's now thoroughgoing transformation is not directly attributable to Iraq. The conversion began with the second Clinton administration's measured law-and-order approach to Libya's involvement in the Pan Am 103 bombing, and was nurtured by carrots dangled by the Bush administration before intervention in Iraq. These included quiet US and UK pledges to end UN sanctions if Tripoli changed its tune on Pan Am 103 and American indications that US sanctions could be dropped if Libya forswore support for terrorism and WMD programmes. But while Libya probably would have dropped its nuclear programme in any event, US-led intervention in Iraq might well have hastened it, as Libyan President Muammar Gaddafi requested a key meeting with British officials as the US initiated leadership strikes on Baghdad in March 2003. By late 2003, Iran, which voiced express concerns about the increased salience of US pre-emptive military action after the Iraq intervention, was both negotiating with respect to its nuclear programme and restraining Shi'ite insurgent provocations in Iraq despite having agents in place. While there were violent Shi'ite provocations as of April 2004, there was no evidence of either active or passive Iranian involvement.

A damaged UN, under repair

The US-led invasion of Iraq in March 2003, undertaken without the most explicit Security Council authorisation for the use of force, generated a spate of gloomy predictions about the lasting damage that the war was likely to inflict on the United Nations (UN). Suffice it to say that reports of the UN's death were greatly exaggerated. A fraught year of US-dominated occupation revealed that even the United States needed help rebuilding a religiously divided, politically fragmented and economically weak country emerging from decades of oppressive and despotic rule. With US casualties exceeding 500, no sign of an early reduction of US troop levels and the financial costs of occupation mounting, by October 2003 members of the Security Council agreed that the Iraqis themselves need to be given a much greater role in restoring stability and in running the country. Accordingly, the dynamic within the Council was sharply different from the one that prevailed in March 2003. To satisfy Iraqi Shi'ite leader and cleric Grand Ayatollah Ali al-Sistani, the Bush administration solicited UN certification of its plan to hand over sovereignty to the Iraqis.

Moreover, UN Security Council Resolution 1511, drafted by the US and passed unanimously in October 2003, urged member states to provide troops for a 'multinational force, under unified command to take all necessary measures to contribute to the maintenance of security and stability'. By 'unified command' Washington meant US command and control. But significant contributions from the member states the administration had in mind – India, Pakistan, South Korea and Turkey –

were not forthcoming. None of these governments were able to overcome powerful domestic opposition to dispatching troops. Yet other countries did not question the idea or importance of providing extra troops. Indeed, in a much-publicised interview with the *New York Times* on 21 September 2003, French President Jacques Chirac, the fiercest official critic of the occupation, was careful not to rule out the possibility of France providing troops. Subsequently, French officials openly confirmed the possibility of France's deploying troops in Iraq. Member states also accepted that overall military command-and-control would continue to rest with the US. A donors conference in Madrid in October 2003 raised over $33 billion for Iraq's reconstruction over the ensuing four years. There was a US preference for alleviating the acute security problems caused by the Iraqi insurgency and possibly foreign jihadists before handing over sovereign authority to the Iraqis, which a number of other countries – notably France – questioned. On 15 November, Paul L. Bremer, the US administrator heading the Coalition Provisional Authority, announced that sovereignty would be transferred to a transitional Iraqi assembly by 1 July 2004.

The UN's principal inhibition with respect to Iraq was more practical rather than philosophical. On 19 August, less than a week after the UN Assistance Mission to Iraq was established, insurgents attacked the UN compound in Baghdad, killing Sergio Vieira de Mello, the UN Secretary General's Special Representative for Iraq, along with 21 others. Questions were raised within the Secretariat about the security of UN personnel in Iraq and, by implication, the risks involved in becoming too closely associated with the US-led occupation regime without being given comparable political and administrative influence.

With the media's attention so firmly fixed on Iraq, other, arguably more significant, news about the UN's expanding role in the field of international peace and security have almost escaped attention. On 19 September, the Security Council unanimously passed Resolution 1509, establishing a 15,000-strong stabilisation force for Liberia to assist in the implementation of the peace agreement signed following the departure of former president Charles Taylor, under international pressure, in August 2003. The United Nations Mission in Liberia (UNMIL) was set up under Chapter VII of the UN Charter for an initial period of 12 months and formally replaced an Economic Community of West African States (ECOWAS) force on 1 October 2003. UNMIL's mandate was extraordinarily ambitious, involving detailed provisions for the disarmament, demobilisation, reintegration and repatriation of former combatants. It also envisaged a role for the UN in monitoring and restructuring the Liberian police force, and it will assist the transitional government in re-establishing 'national authority throughout the country'. Success in this venture would be central to the stabilisation of West Africa, which has been chronically unstable substantially on account of Taylor's provocations.

Perspectives

When the Liberian deployment is complete, the number of troops and civilians deployed on UN missions around the world will be close to 50,000 – a figure historically surpassed only for a brief period in the early 1990s. The figure may climb still further if a UN mission deploys to Sudan. The UN Security Council approved two additional new operations after the formal end of hostilities in Iraq – the UN Mission in Cote d'Ivoire (MINUCI), authorised on 13 May, and, a few weeks later, the deployment of a French-led Interim Emergency Multinational Force to eastern parts of the Democratic Republic of Congo. In some respects, the Secretariat was never busier. It looked set to get more involved in Iraq with key tasks such as assisting in the drafting of a new Iraqi constitution and supervising the first general elections. The extent of its involvement would, it seemed, be determined by how much administrative control the US would yield to the UN in post-transition Iraq. But Washington appeared increasingly open to a more prominent UN role – not least because it could facilitate greater military and diplomatic burden-sharing and thus alleviate the appreciable overstretch that the US was experiencing on both the military and the diplomatic front.

Partners of concern
In the critical non-military arena of law-enforcement and intelligence, the US and its Western counter-terrorism partners continued to rely – non-optionally – on the cooperation of three crucial largely Muslim countries: Saudi Arabia, Pakistan and Indonesia. Each government was subject to domestic Islamist influences that made cooperation a fraught proposition. In Saudi Arabia, the Wahhabi religious establishment to which the ruling House of Saud substantially owed its legitimacy was suspicious of geopolitical American motivations, and did not rein in private support for jihadist causes and Islamic terrorist groups around the world. The al-Qaeda-linked bombings in May and November 2003 (in which over 30 Saudi Muslims were killed), as well as the US military withdrawal from Saudi Arabia following the removal of Saddam Hussein from power, gave the Saudi counter-terrorism apparatus greater motivation to act and more political room to manoeuvre. But neither robust counter-terrorism cooperation, nor broader sympathy with a deepened US–Saudi relationship, could be counted on.

Pakistani President Pervez Musharraf's secular vocation appeared to be genuine, but it was constrained by a rising (if still relatively small) radical Islamist movement and the presence of Islamists in both the security services. Illuminating the gravity of the former problem were two serious attempts to assassinate Musharraf, probably by Islamist groups. Reflecting the latter problem was the government's revelation in January 2004 that the founder of Pakistan's nuclear weapons programme, Abdul Qadeer

Khan, had over the course of 15 years covertly sold nuclear secrets and technology to Iran, Libya and North Korea – to advance political Islam and to divert attention from Pakistan's nuclear programme, he said. While Pakistani cooperation has yielded a substantial number of arrests of al-Qaeda members – some of them major players – the Islamist and anti-American cast of its Inter-Services Intelligence organisation was perceived to have inhibited joint US and Pakistani efforts to capture bin Laden and Mullah Omar.

The terrorist bombings in Bali and Jakarta – carried out by al-Qaeda affiliate Jemaah Islamiah – resulted in ramped up capacity-building assistance from the US and Australia, better enforcement on the part of Indonesian authorities, severe judicial punishment of the perpetrators and official recognition of an indigenous terrorism problem. But Indonesian Prime Minister Megawati Sukarnoputri was, to an extent, politically beholden to Islamists. Accordingly, it appeared probable that the government lacked the will and the clout to mount a sustained effort to dismantle terrorist networks in Indonesia. Reinforcing this suspicion was the Indonesian Supreme Court's reduction of the subversion conviction of Abu Bakar Bashir – widely believed to be Jemaah Islamiah's spiritual leader – from three years to 18 months, resulting in his release from prison in March 2004 ahead of parliamentary and presidential elections slated for April–September 2004.

Elsewhere...

With Iraq and the political and demographic centres of Islam in the Gulf and Asia, respectively, absorbing so much attention and so many resources, it was easy to forget about other areas of strategic importance. Sub-Saharan Africa, for example, acquired renewed strategic resonance. While similar expectations – centring on the need to save failed states and strengthen weak ones to prevent terrorist co-optation à la Afghanistan – arose immediately following 11 September, they did not pan out owing to the higher and consuming priority of the West's self-protection. With more robust counter-terrorism postures consolidated, circumstances in early 2004 seemed more propitious for sustained Western interest.

The United States' risky venture in Iraq placed a higher premium on Washington's cultivating non-OPEC oil supplies to ensure its energy security, for which sub-Saharan Africa is key. There were also signs that preventive counter-terrorism in the continent – especially east Africa – was not enough to contain transnational threats emanating from anarchic locales like Somalia. Further, the Iraq war's perceived lack of legitimacy put pressure on the Bush administration to apply US foreign policy in ways that do not involve the unilateral use of force, and to find a common cause through which transatlantic relationships could be rehabilitated and

Atlanticist institutions – NATO and the EU in particular – reinvigorated. The international consensus that Africa is the neediest continent in humanitarian terms and a potential staging area for transnational Islamic terrorist operations, coupled with the fact that most major international actors have or have had substantial economic or colonial interests on the continent, makes it an ideal stage on which to achieve all of these objectives. Another important factor is that regional powers in Africa – notably, South Africa and Nigeria – from late 2002 adopted more energetic and assertive foreign policies that held promise for ameliorating poverty and political dysfunction and resolving conflict. (They had not, however, passed the litmus test of effective regional diplomacy in sub-Saharan Africa: dislodging Robert Mugabe's brutal and decadent regime in Zimbabwe.) Democracy and good governance, against many expectations, were slowly advancing in Africa. Notwithstanding Rwandan President Paul Kagame's old-style 95% victory in August 2003 elections, Kenya's competitive December 2002 elections boded well for the future, and Nigeria's April 2003 polls were less problematic than many anticipated. Finally, in early 2004, prospects for conflict resolution in Somalia and Sudan and stabilisation in west Africa appeared brighter than they had for years.

The close involvement of China and Japan with the US in dealing diplomatically with North Korea's brinkmanship augured guardedly well for key great-power relationships in Asia. China itself adopted a threatening posture in reaction to the Taiwanese government's plan to hold a 'defensive referendum' on 20 March 2004 on independence-related issues – even after Taipei narrowed the question to whether Taiwan should acquire more advanced anti-missile weapons and negotiate with the mainland to establish a peaceful and stable framework for interaction. Beijing's alarm showed that China's relative quiescence in foreign policy – though anchored in the domestic challenges attending its economic transformation and leadership change – was fragile. Beyond these standout issues, Asia's wider strategic importance was never really in doubt, but it was unclear how long it would take the US and other major powers to elevate their concerns – save for those about North Korea – above counter-terrorism. It started to happen in south Asia in 2004, when Washington acted as a facilitator in India's promising initiative to engage Pakistan on Kashmir. In southeast Asia, however, outside powers had enough on their hands with ongoing terrorist threats and more energetic but still questionable enforcement institutions – especially in Indonesia mainly for political reasons, but also in Thailand due to institutional incapacity. The resurgence of the Taliban in Afghanistan and surrounding areas kept the 12,500 American troops deployed in central Asia from operating much beyond their counter-terrorism remit – though US commanders felt in early 2004 that they were drawing closer to capturing or killing bin Laden and Taliban leader Mullah Omar, both of whom are believed to be hiding, inside several layers of protective fighters, in the 'tribal areas' near the Afghanistan–Pakistan border.

Latin America broadly retained its post-11 September sense of being neglected by the US, and was increasing less acquiescent. It was not that the US was uninterested in the region. Its involvement in Colombia's civil conflict and related Andean problems had expanded from counter-narcotics to counter-insurgency. The complaint was rather that Washington was too narrowly focused on security, and had procrastinated on its Western Hemisphere economic agenda for helping emerging-market economies and on once central bilateral issues such as immigration normalisation with Mexico. Latin American dissatisfaction came to a head at the Future of the Americas Conference in Monterrey, Mexico in January 2004, when the Argentine and Brazilian presidents criticised a perceived American default solution of free trade as a panacea for problems of poverty and social exclusion. Hemispheric security concerns also intensified in February, when anti-government unrest in Haiti moved Washington to force the resignation of President Jean-Bertrand Aristide and prepare, with others, to deploy peacekeeping troops. Despite the United States' many distractions elsewhere, in early 2004 ripening economic challenges, insecurity in Haiti as well as ongoing instability in Venezuela and President Hugo Chávez's increasingly anti-American behaviour kept more of Washington's high-level attention on its own hemisphere than it might have preferred.

US grand strategy

The United States' problems 'elsewhere' – not to mention those in the areas of its strategic focus – show that even the lone superpower cannot easily maintain stable and attentive policies in all areas at once. The ongoing terrorism crisis has of course amplified the problem. In the two-and-a-half years following 11 September, the first priority was understandably and correctly self-protection via improved homeland security and enhanced law-enforcement and intelligence cooperation. Advances have occurred, particularly transatlantically, since 11 September. Given the continued viability of al-Qaeda, none of the many potential targets can afford to relent, and these two areas must continue to receive primary attention. Nevertheless, because the US and Europe have a better grip on the transatlantic terrorism than they did in late 2001, they may now have the opportunity to devote greater efforts to the medium- and long-term challenges of eliminating the root causes of such terrorism. Arguably, the Iraq intervention was a bold first step in that direction: it extended counter-terrorism into counter-proliferation, and sought aggressively to export US-style democracy to the Middle East and Persian Gulf region by means of a catalytic state-building effort that would serve as an exemplar. But the considerable post-conflict slippage between vision and reality in Iraq made it unlikely that any dramatic political catalysis would arise. Iraq created plenty of shock but not enough awe, and in the process engendered a US image problem at home and abroad.

The Iraq intervention represented an entrepreneurial foreign policy – the Bush administration wanted to sell America to the Arab states and then the larger Muslim world. But it also put a great many eggs – the Israeli–Palestinian peace process, political and economic reform of Arab governments, and potentially American primacy in international politics – in the single basket of Iraq. This dispensation made the reputational risks to the US prohibitively high. To spread and manage them more effectively, US Secretary of Defense Donald Rumsfeld, in a memo artfully leaked in October 2003, said: 'Does the US need to fashion a broad, integrated plan to stop the next generation of terrorists? The US is putting relatively little effort into a long-range plan, but we are putting a great deal of effort into trying to stop terrorists. The cost-benefit ratio is against us! Our cost is billions against the terrorists' costs of millions'. These remarks reflected some recognition of the need for a comprehensive American grand strategy – that is, a clear vision of what kind of world the United States wants to promote and of how to apply its military, economic and political power to realise that vision.

Such a strategy would not logically discount the long-term goal of the Iraq intervention: political and economic reform in the Middle East, and a corresponding warming of the relationship between Islam and the West. Nor would it counsel, against the inclinations of the post-11 September Bush administration, an introverted US foreign policy or even a substantially less entrepreneurial one: the United States' Middle East allies – Arab states as well as Israel – generally favour a strong and assertive America. But in April 2004, it was clear that moving beyond hard counter-terrorism towards achieving a political accommodation between Islam and the West would require, at once, policies that were more affirmative and less reactive and persuasion that was more measured and less strident. For a second Bush administration – which seemed the most probable outcome of the November 2004 US presidential election – these requirements appeared to dictate several specific policy adjustments. First, the US had to engage more deeply in conflict resolution in the Middle East, which was likely to be at least as catalytic, in terms of West–Islam relations, as political reconstruction in Iraq. Second, the US need to embrace state-building more fully as a central element of foreign policy. Third, continued increases in US foreign assistance through the Millennium Challenge Account looked increasingly desirable.

There were also broader considerations. Since the end of the Cold War, US grand strategy had pivoted on maintaining overwhelming military, economic, and political dominance. It did not appear in early 2004 that

Washington should discard that basic objective. It did appear, however, that the Bush administration had not fully appreciated that the 11 September attacks were a violent reaction to America's pre-eminence – or at least the implications of that reality. The point was that the manner of US preponderance had to change. If there was to be any reasonable expectation of winning hearts and minds, and cancelling out the asymmetric terrorist advantage identified by Rumsfeld, the appearance of American unilateralism needed to be tempered. Strategic ends had to be more adeptly coordinated with tactical means. The necessary tools included more nuanced public diplomacy, which could portray a less parochial and chauvinistic society while emphasising religious pluralism; less doctrinaire political and economic conditionalities attached to foreign assistance, which were liable to alienate Muslim governments and populations alike; and an approach to international law that – after more than two years' delay – openly admitted that the old standards of intervention and the laws of war that applied to state-based security problems and standing armies did not easily fit new security problems, and that these required systematic, collegial reconsideration on a multilateral basis. A highly critical White House-commissioned study of US public diplomacy, numerous criticisms of foreign-assistance criteria and a federal judiciary increasingly concerned about the erosion of due-process in the name of counter-terrorism indicated that American officialdom was, to varying degrees and at varying levels, seized of these problems.

Strategic Policy Issues

Transforming US Nuclear Strategy

On 8 January 2002, the George W. Bush administration, responding to a congressional requirement contained in the FY2001 National Defense Authorization Act, submitted a comprehensive review of US nuclear forces, including a plan for their long-term sustainability and modernisation. Although the Nuclear Posture Review (NPR) remains classified, shortly after its issuance major excerpts were leaked. These reflected a departure from the traditional US approach to deterrence.

During the Cold War, US nuclear strategy was more diverse than its popular characterisation of mutual assured destruction implied, but nevertheless emphasised the delivery of a devastating second-strike attack against the Soviet Union. By contrast, the NPR calls for a transformation of US strategic deterrence, to develop credible doctrine and capabilities that respond to a wide range of threats that have emerged in the last decade. These new threats will require better integration of the entire range of US offensive and defensive weapons and doctrine, and the potential development of new types of nuclear weapons designed to destroy deeply buried underground facilities. The NPR also states that Russian–American strategic relations should be based on cooperation, and that US nuclear force planning and doctrine no longer contemplates Russian nuclear capabilities as the primary threat. Critics charge that the NPR simply turns a new page in the arms race by calling for the development of the next generation of nuclear weapons, and that it lowers the nuclear threshold by calling for the integration of US nuclear weapons into a strategic deterrent intended to respond to a wider range of circumstances than those set forth during the Cold War. Others note, more positively, that it lays the groundwork for a further reduction in the overall size of the US nuclear arsenal, and contend that it raises the threshold for the use of nuclear weapons by calling for increased reliance on conventional precision-strike capabilities to hold at risk facilities and forces once targeted by nuclear warheads.

The NPR is not merely a description of capabilities available to today's policymakers but more importantly a road map for the future. It will take decades to implement the strategic vision depicted in the NPR, as significant technical, doctrinal and operational hurdles must be overcome to develop the required capabilities. But the objective is a new strategic deterrent and war fighting capability.

The new strategic vision

The authors of the NPR have determined that the United States has been getting by with a Cold War surplus nuclear arsenal that is becoming increasingly obsolete and ill-suited to twenty-first century security challenges. They cite three international trends that influenced their thinking about nuclear deterrence: the collapse of the Soviet Union, the continued proliferation of weapons of mass destruction (WMD) and the emergence of asymmetric threats. They believe that today the possibility of a massive nuclear exchange between the United States and another nuclear-armed state is virtually non-existent, while it is likely that US forces will face opponents armed with nuclear, biological or chemical weapons. They also identify an increase in the number of state and non-state actors that are difficult, and perhaps in some cases impossible, to deter, which places a premium on the ability to conduct counterforce attacks against opponents before they can strike the United States, its allies or its forces deployed overseas. The operative fear among US planners is that no one really believes that the US government would use against current adversaries large nuclear warheads that were once destined for counterforce or counter-value missions against Soviet military, political and economic targets.

In response, the Bush administration has worked to shift the focus of US strategic planning away from a rapidly fading Russian threat towards emerging challenges. US withdrawal from the Anti-Ballistic Missile Treaty and the force reductions outlined in the 24 May 2002 Moscow Treaty reflect the move toward cooperation; both diplomatic initiatives reduced the role played by nuclear deterrence in Russian–American relations. Administration officials even resisted the idea of undertaking arms control with the Russians – they announced publicly their willingness to cut the US nuclear arsenal unilaterally – in part because they believed that negotiations represented a counterproductive vestige of a bygone era of hostility. While the reductions required by the Moscow Treaty reflected Russia's diminishing ability to afford a large nuclear arsenal rather than traditional concerns about nuclear parity or even crisis stability, the treaty facilitates the transformation of US strategic forces by reducing the number of legacy systems that will remain operational.

By 2007, the United States will have deployed 3,800 nuclear warheads, which will be further reduced to between 1,700–2,200 by 2012. The planned 'legacy triad' will eventually consist of 14 *Trident* ballistic-missile submarines, 500 *Minuteman* III inter-continental ballistic missiles (ICBMs),

76 B-52H bombers armed with cruise missiles and gravity bombs, and 21 B-2s armed with gravity bombs. Four *Trident* submarines, the MX ICBM and 18 B-52Hs will soon be retired. These force reductions also simplify nuclear stockpile life extension plans: only three warhead refurbishment programmes – for the W-80 cruise missile warhead, the W-76 submarine-launched ballistic missile (SLBM) warhead and the B-61 bomb – will be undertaken by the end of the decade.

To meet the challenge created by the proliferation of chemical, biological and nuclear weapons, the NPR calls for the creation of a 'new triad' of (1) non-nuclear and nuclear strike capabilities including systems for command-and-control, (2) active and passive defences, including ballistic-missile defences, and (3) research and development (R&D) and industrial infrastructure needed to develop, build, and maintain nuclear offensive forces and defensive systems. Administration officials believe that the new triad will eventually provide policymakers with a range of strike capabilities that will bolster deterrence by creating credible strike options to replace what they consider to be the non-credible threat of retaliation with high-yield nuclear weapons to less than catastrophic provocation. They also believe that strategic war planning itself must change to meet the proliferation challenge. Gone are the days when a deliberate planning method took about two years to produce a nuclear war plan (that is, the Single Integrated Operations Plan). Instead, planners are beginning to employ a capabilities-based adaptive planning system to increase their ability to respond to unforeseen circumstances.

Although the first two legs of the new triad have received the most attention, the administration has probably made the greatest progress in laying the groundwork for revitalising the R&D and industrial infrastructure. It has enhanced nuclear-test readiness, revived nuclear warhead advanced concepts efforts at the national laboratories, and accelerated planning and design for a modern weapons-grade plutonium production facility. Given the end of the design and testing of nuclear weapons in the aftermath of the Cold War, prompt action was deemed necessary to prevent an accelerating deterioration in the ability of the United States to maintain its nuclear arsenal.

A key step in strengthening nuclear infrastructure was the passage of the FY 2004 National Defense Authorization Act. This law repealed Section 3136 of Public Law 103-160 (1994), which had barred the Secretary of Energy from conducting R&D that could lead to the production of a new low-yield nuclear weapon, defined in the statute as a weapon with a yield of less that five kilotons. With this decade-old restriction on precision low-yield weapons design (PLYWD, or 'plywood' for short) repealed, the Bush administration moved quickly to launch an R&D programme to investigate future applications for low-yield nuclear weapons. It has earmarked $7.5 million to continue assessing the feasibility and cost of a Robust Nuclear

Earth Penetrator and $6m to begin other advanced-concepts work to determine whether existing nuclear warheads could be adapted – without nuclear testing – to hit hardened, deeply buried targets. The administration also has committed $25m to continue the process begun in FY 2003 to reduce the time it would take to conduct an underground nuclear test from 36 months to 18 months.

Administration officials have been quick to stress, however, that they have no plans to develop new nuclear weapons or to conduct nuclear tests. Instead, they state that they are hedging against the possibility that the United States may someday need to conduct a test to confirm a problem or verify that a problem has been solved with respect to a weapon critical to the nation's deterrent. The 18-month test readiness target was chosen because they believed it was the minimum time needed, once a problem had been identified, to assess the problem, develop and implement a solution, and plan and execute a test that would provide information needed to confirm that the 'fix' was successful. Advanced-concepts design work and engineering development of selected designs is also essential to counteract the gradual deterioration in US scientific nuclear research and engineering that has resulted from the nuclear testing moratorium. The idea is that undertaking real design work that leads to an engineered system will ensure that there is a succeeding generation of capable nuclear-weapons designers and engineers in case threats calling for nuclear capability continue or arise in the future.

If additional congressional approval is forthcoming, administration officials are prepared to develop programmes to modify or repackage existing warheads within two years of a decision to restart engineering and development. Similarly, they are prepared, following congressional authorisation, to launch programmes to design, develop and produce new nuclear weapons within about four years of a decision to commence engineering and development. Although no new nuclear weapons are currently under development, the capability of refurbishing and building them will become increasingly important as existing warheads approach the end of their planned life expectancy.

Implementing the NPR

As a vision of future US nuclear strategy, the NPR reflects the multiple challenges facing policymakers. Yet in doing so, it advances contradictory policies. The contradictions flow essentially from the familiar paradox of nuclear deterrence: that the threat and capability of visiting nuclear destruction makes it less likely to be necessary. Thus, the NPR justifies nuclear arms reductions and seeks to eliminate nuclear deterrence as the basis of Russian–American strategic relations, while giving young scientists and engineers the task of improving the nation's ability to develop and test the next generation of nuclear weapons. It greatly reduces the number of deployed operational nuclear weapons, but it retains a large stockpile – the so-called 'responsive force' – of surplus weapons as a hedge against emerging threats. It attempts to reduce the likelihood that WMD will be used on some distant battlefield by developing plans to integrate nuclear and conventional weapons into a 'seamless' strategic deterrent. Nevertheless, the NPR is vulnerable to criticisms similar to those levied at nuclear strategy during the Cold War. Some critics say that the NPR is not ambitious enough in transforming the US nuclear arsenal to meet new threats. But the most forceful opponents of the NPR argue that it is actually too ambitious, and constitutes a dangerous and provocative turn away from deterrence that in fact makes nuclear use more likely.

The most controversial element of the Bush administration's vision of a new strategic deterrent is its active study of a new generation of earth penetrating, low-yield nuclear weapons that are intended to hold at risk hardened underground targets that can serve as command-and-control centres as well as storage and manufacturing facilities for nuclear, chemical and biological weapons. Criticism of the so-called 'mini-nuke' raises questions about both the feasibility and the desirability of the programme. Many believe that it is simply impossible to devise a way to contain nuclear weapons effects by burrowing incoming warheads underground. Even when they are made of the hardest steel, earth-penetrating warheads can only survive an impact of about one kilometre per second, giving a three-metre long warhead the ability to penetrate about 12 metres of steel-reinforced concrete. A penetration this shallow probably would not contain the explosive blast produced by the smallest nuclear warheads currently available, creating the prospect that nearby areas would be heavily contaminated by radioactive fallout. Weapons capable of penetrating materially deeper than 12 metres, then, would be needed to contain nuclear weapons effects and to better concentrate blast energy on the ground to attack deeply buried targets. Given the limits of existing materials and technology, it isn't clear that the engineering challenges of solving this problem can be met.

Furthermore, even if effective ways to bury incoming nuclear warheads so as to contain their effects could be devised, critics believe that the whole mini-nuke concept is strategically flawed and likely to imperil a nearly six-decade epoch of nuclear non-use in battle. Integrating earth-penetrating, low-yield nuclear weapons or other types of exotic nuclear devices into deployed forces and operational plans, they argue, will lower the nuclear threshold because nuclear weapons will simply be 'conventionalised' and easier to use in combat. They also claim that development of a new generation of nuclear weapons would trigger a new arms race. What they tend to ignore, however, is that proliferation trends shape US nuclear strategy and the status of the nuclear threshold. If proliferation slows or reverses, then the threshold for US nuclear weapons use will rise and the pressure to develop new nuclear weapons will decrease. If, on one hand, other states begin to integrate WMD into operational units or deterrent forces, it would seem imprudent for the US to give them a 'free ride'. If, on the other hand, the US does deploy or demonstrate an intent to deploy low-yield nuclear weapons that would constitute a more credibly limited response to adversaries' use of WMD, WMD proliferation itself would be deterred and a higher nuclear threshold maintained. Thus, administration officials emphasise that they do not intend to lower the nuclear threshold or to blur the distinction between nuclear and non-nuclear weapons; that the president would authorise the use of US nuclear forces only in the direst circumstances; and that increasing the range of nuclear options will increase the credibility of the US deterrent, reducing the possibility that chemical, biological or nuclear weapons would be used against US forces or allies, and therefore decrease the likelihood of nuclear use.

Debate about the feasibility and wisdom of developing a new generation of nuclear weapons and the threshold for using nuclear weapons will continue, but two aspects of the current strategic setting will pressure US officials to develop new nuclear and non-nuclear counterforce options. First, US policymakers are likely to face international crises that are extremely unstable, which may present strong reasons for using nuclear weapons first to prevent opponents armed with relatively small nuclear, chemical or biological arsenals from using their weapons in a crisis or in war. Unless opponents themselves develop secure second-strike capabilities, incentives to pre-empt in a crisis are a matter of strategic reality. Second, the distinction between US deterrent and war-fighting forces and commands, maintained during most of the Cold War, has already collapsed. The US Army, which spent most of the Cold War deterring attacks along the inter-German border and the 38th parallel, has been fully engaged in high intensity conventional combat, counter-insurgency and peacekeeping operations since the early 1990s. The B-2 bomber, designed for what would likely have been a single mission in a superpower nuclear exchange, now routinely flies conventional bombing runs. The Strategic Air Command has been transformed into a new US Strategic Command that has embraced the nuclear transformation mission of developing operational concepts and doctrine for the new triad. Interest in developing new types of nuclear weapons is thus only part of a larger trend towards an integrated national military that functions as both a strategic deterrent and a war-fighting force.

Beyond nuclear threshold issues, some doubters about the NPR, hoping for deeper and so-called 'irreversible' cuts in US nuclear forces and the curtailment of the legacy triad and the reserve force of nuclear weapons, have noted that bombers, SLBMs and ICBMs can be uploaded with additional warheads from the reserve force, and that the cuts outlined in the

Moscow Treaty could be reversed in a matter of months. For diametrically different reasons but to similar effect, advocates of the new triad have resisted spending on the existing force structure at the expense of programmes intended to develop the new strategic deterrent. Traditionalists, for their part, are anxious about compromising the legacy systems. Maintenance of the legacy triad is very expensive because it requires the Air Force and Navy to maintain three distinct career and training paths to supply officers and enlisted personnel to serve a diminishing force structure of bombers, SLBMs and ICBMs. Yet, probably because the traditionalists enjoy the heaviest political backing, the Bush administration has decided to forego an opportunity to save additional funding by eliminating one or even two legs of the legacy triad. The administration also has not pushed the development of new delivery systems that can be used to destroy high-priority targets quickly once they are identified.

In addition, administration officials have justified the opportunity and financial costs involved in retaining the legacy triad and a substantial reserve force of nuclear warheads in terms of the overall strategic goals listed in the NPR: to assure allies about the US commitment to them and the US ability to make good on that commitment; to dissuade potential adversaries from trying to match US capabilities; to deter any threats that emerge; and to defend and defeat threats that cannot be deterred. They note that a large reserve force should assure allies that the United States possess sufficient nuclear capability to meet any current or future contingency and a large reserve of nuclear weapons guarantees that any potential 'peer competitor' would lose a nuclear arms race by ensuring that the US could move existing nuclear weapons from the reserve force into the operational force faster than a competitor could build new weapons. The administration also has set several goals for the responsive force to achieve its assurance and dissuasion objectives. For example, efforts have been ramped up to make certain that no part of the nuclear infrastructure – for example, warhead transportation or tritium production – creates critical bottlenecks in any future effort to expand the size of the US arsenal.

Anxious allies

The United States' fellow NATO members have had mixed reactions to the NPR. They have generally welcomed the Moscow Treaty as a reassuring sign that Russian–American strategic relations are improving, despite the US withdrawal from the ABM Treaty. The reductions in strategic nuclear forces called for by the Moscow Treaty also mirror favourable trends in Europe, and the Bush administration's commitment not to treat Russia as a strategic military threat is supported by the rest of NATO. No concerns about US extended deterrence, or decoupling the US nuclear deterrent from

Strategic Policy Issues

NATO, have emerged in the aftermath of the Moscow Treaty. Following one of the objectives of the NPR – to maintain deterrence at the lowest possible nuclear force levels – NATO has reportedly relaxed alert requirements for its dual-capable aircraft, further reducing the day-to-day role played by nuclear weapons in allied strategy. At the same time, European NATO members are more reticent about the new triad and US efforts to refurbish its nuclear infrastructure. They do not share the Bush administration's determination to develop deterrent and war-fighting strategies to respond to the proliferation of chemical, biological and nuclear weapons. Instead, they are more concerned about the large numbers of non-strategic nuclear weapons that still exist inside Russia and the general failure to address this issue either through arms control or confidence-building measures.

Furthermore, a number of European commentators expressed profound concerns that changes in US nuclear strategy would further weaken an already shaky non-proliferation regime. They are troubled by the United States' failure to take 'irreversible steps' to make the corresponding reductions permanent, and by its decision to maintain a reserve force, believing that it is a ploy to avoid reducing the US nuclear arsenal to Moscow Treaty levels. They are concerned that the plan to integrate nuclear and conventional weapons into a single strategic deterrent/war-fighting posture sends the wrong message about the apparent military effectiveness and usability of nuclear weapons. In their view, efforts to revitalise the US nuclear R&D and industrial infrastructure – especially activation of a new facility to overhaul plutonium pits – violates the sprit of the international effort to halt the production of fissile material. They also believe, more broadly, that the deterrent impact of a shift in US strategy towards countries that are seeking to gain chemical, biological or nuclear weapons is open to doubt. Some noted that harsh rhetoric and the US attack on Iraq probably reinforced Libya's inclination to abandon its clandestine efforts to acquire nuclear weapons, but exacerbated an already tense situation vis-à-vis North Korea.

Aspiration vs. implementation

Although the policies outlined by the NPR are revolutionary, much of the planned transformation of US nuclear policy still only exists on paper. In the realm of nuclear strategy, the Bush administration has achieved two objectives during its time in office. First, withdrawal from the ABM Treaty and the signing of the Moscow Treaty has helped to further delegitimise mutually assured destruction as the basis of Russian–American strategic relations, creating a framework for the further reductions in increasingly obsolete nuclear weapons and delivery systems. Second, the revitalisation of the US industrial and scientific infrastructure has halted a further deterioration of the US capability to maintain a credible nuclear deterrent in the face of a shifting threat environment. Achievement of these objectives reflects the Bush administration's effort to achieve 'strategic deterrence' at the lowest possible nuclear force levels while maintaining a hedge to meet unforeseen threats and to dissuade others from engaging in a nuclear arms race.

The controversy over the development of a new generation of nuclear weapons, and the dire predictions of what will follow in their wake, seems premature. The Bush administration has only launched concept studies on how nuclear weapons could be adapted to penetrate deeply buried underground targets. The Bush administration's policy has been to remove congressional restrictions on the study and development of the next generation of nuclear weapons, but to leave restrictions on the development of the weapons themselves intact. It is by no means certain that these new weapons will actually be developed, or indeed if they can legally be developed, given the current moratorium on nuclear testing. The Bush administration, it is true, is attempting to remove legal obstacles to preserve the option of actual development for future US administrations.

How the administration will advance the transformation of US nuclear deterrence doctrine remains uncertain. The United States' new nuclear posture is meant to be part of a larger denial strategy that meets the challenge of denying potential enemies – especially WMD-armed ones – their military objectives by establishing a global conventional strike capability. In a revolutionary way, this would reduce reliance on nuclear weapons and raise the threshold for their use. For it to work, however, the US will need greatly enhanced non-nuclear strike forces as well as refined nuclear capabilities and effective missile defences. For example, the capacity to deliver conventional weapons over global ranges in times comparable to those achievable by current nuclear strike forces needs to be developed. Beyond that, it is not clear how nuclear and conventional strike options will be combined in operational force planning as part of the capabilities-based approach to adaptive planning. Little mention has been made of how offensive and defensive forces will be integrated for deterrence and war-fighting purposes and the new types of command-and-control that will be needed to make the new triad a reality. US Secretary of Defense Donald Rumsfeld, in his foreword to the NPR, also predicated the success of a denial strategy on 'exquisite' intelligence. In light of the recent failure of US and allied intelligence services to assess accurately the state of Iraq's unconventional arsenal and industrial infrastructure, there are also salient doubts about the ability of the intelligence community to support the revolutionary transformation of US deterrence policy outlined by the Bush administration. But the reconsideration of US nuclear doctrine that the Bush administration has commenced, in light of the new threats facing the US and its allies, appears to have sufficient power and appeal to compel the next US administration to take it seriously.

Strategic Policy Issues

Human Intelligence and 11 September

The war on global terrorism has focused new attention on one of the oldest forms of intelligence collection – namely, intelligence drawn from human sources, or, as it is often called, 'HUMINT'. In part, HUMINT has attracted special interest because some experts believe that human-source intelligence is uniquely effective against terrorist targets. In part, this interest derives from the view of some critics that Western HUMINT capabilities have suffered because officials have favoured 'technical intelligence' – e.g., communications intercepts and satellite imagery – in the almost certainly erroneous belief that it could provide sufficient information for combating terrorists and rogue states. And in part, the attention HUMINT is now receiving reflects the conviction of some that Western intelligence organisations have been ineffective in conducting HUMINT intelligence operations and need to adopt new techniques.

HUMINT sources

The public often equates HUMINT with spying, where an agent disguises his true identify to penetrate a targeted organisation to collect information first-hand. In fact, this kind of activity constitutes only a small portion of HUMINT operations. HUMINT is generated by a wide range of actors, including:

- Recruited 'assets', or people who are enticed or coerced into providing information, either knowingly or surreptitiously;

- 'Walk ins', or assets who, for personal, ideological, or financial reasons volunteer to provide information about their countries or organisations while remaining in place and concealing their cooperation;

- Defectors and émigrés who provide information about their countries or organisations after leaving and finding sanctuary with an intelligence service; and

- Liaison services, or members of foreign intelligence organisations that knowingly agree to exchange information.

Arrangements with such actors are usually made secretly, but it is important to note that much, if not most human-source intelligence is collected by officials who are openly posted abroad and who do not conceal their identities. These include Foreign Service Officers and military attachés who, according to US officials, were the largest source of HUMINT during the Cold War, accounting for 80% or more of the total.

Although the public usually identifies human-source intelligence with spies, HUMINT is often collected by uniformed military personnel (albeit concealing or camouflaging themselves or their activities). HUMINT combat support activities relevant to counter-terrorist operations may involve, for example, support to direct action (e.g., sabotage and raids) and the provision of targeting data to missile, artillery and aviation units. Indeed, the difference between a 'spy' and a 'combatant' providing HUMINT for military operations is largely a legal one, deriving mainly from the 1899 Hague Convention on the Laws and Customs of War on Land. The Hague Convention drew a line between armies, militia and volunteer corps (who were part of a chain command and wore recognisable uniforms) and spies (who disguised their identity and operated secretly within a country's territory). Despite the difference – and the fact that combatants had greater rights than spies if captured – the Hague Convention recognised that both spies and combatants could collect information while concealing their presence.

Moreover, the distinction between human-source intelligence and technical intelligence is often less distinct than press reports and commentary might suggest. The connection between technical and human-source intelligence has become increasingly tight. Today HUMINT operations are often crucial, for example, in facilitating access for the collection of intelligence from telecommunications networks. Unlike older analogue systems, in which a link between two communicants usually required a dedicated telephone line that could be tapped, digital communications make it possible for many data streams to occupy the same link, and are inherently easier to encrypt than analogue systems. Packet communications, such as those used for the Internet, increase the volume of data further. Overcoming the volume and encryption challenges usually calls for intercepting a message close to its source, and often a clandestine penetration – that is, a HUMINT operator – is required to place the tap.

Because terrorists are making greater use of computers, the Internet and the full range of available electronic communications technologies, such devices have become critical targets for intelligence operations. These devices often contain large amounts of data – e-mail, electronic copies of letters produced via word processing software, voice mail files and imagery. Some of these devices can be penetrated with HUMINT assistance, others can be recovered in raids and through the cooperation of liaison services.

Finally, one other source of HUMINT that has become especially important in the war on terrorism is intelligence provided by the interrogation of prisoners. Most clandestine HUMINT depends on the ability of a case officer to understand and exploit interpersonal dynamics. It also requires structuring situations so as to influence and, ideally, dominate an intelligence asset. These basic skills are directly applicable to the interrogation, where one has even greater opportunities to structure circumstances so as to make a subject dependent and cooperative. Prison conditions also make it easier to use techniques that are the stock and trade of HUMINT operations, such as the use of 'honeypots', the exploitation of personal vulnerabilities, and rewards and punishment. However, effectiveness is often dependent on the competence of the interrogator, and limited by the conduct-after-capture techniques that the captive may have been taught.

Winding down HUMINT

HUMINT collection against terrorist targets has been a concern of the Central Intelligence Agency (CIA) at least since the late 1970s, when Western countries were threatened by both radical groups in Europe such as the Red Brigades in Italy and the Baader-Meinhof gang in West Germany. By the 1980s, US intelligence services faced these threats and, in addition, the first wave of radical Islamic terrorist groups, such as Hizbullah and Islamic Jihad. At that time, concerns about terrorism were closely linked to the Cold War. Many Western experts believed that the Soviet Union sponsored these groups, although it was also clear that many were sponsored by the Islamic regime in Iran, which had taken power in 1979. In addition, several countries, such as North Korea and Libya, were themselves believed to use terrorism as an instrument of national power. At about this time, then-Director of Central Intelligence (DCI) William Casey established within the CIA the Counter-terrorism Center (CTC), an organ specifically devoted to the collection and analysis of intelligence against terrorist targets. Public assessments of the CTC are mixed. Some observers give the CIA credit for creating the centre; critics claim that the CTC lacked resources and was a stepchild to the agency's regional offices. These critics also claim that, rather than serving as a means of engendering cooperation among agencies, the CTC merely served as a battleground for those agencies to play out their bureaucratic rivalries.

The belief that the Soviet Union was a key sponsor of terrorism proved ironic. By the end of the Cold War, US and Soviet intelligence services began to cooperate on what was often seen as a common threat. According to the memoirs of Milt Bearden, a former CIA operations officer, the CIA and the KGB established a hotline between the two agencies called 'Gavrilov', named after the nineteenth-century Russian poet and probably also a play on the Russian word 'gaverit' ('to speak'). According to Bearden, the CIA established the link generally to exchange information on terrorist threats, and more specifically because the CIA believed the Soviets could assist in recovering William Buckley, a CIA officer who had been kidnapped by Hizbullah in Lebanon. By the early 1990s, Gavrilov and the meetings held to support it had turned into larger conferences in which CIA and KGB (later, SVR) officers exchanged data on common terrorist threats. In addition, Gavrilov was used to exchange information on international narco-trafficking and proliferation threats – the latter of which, of course, are closely related to terrorism owing to the possibility that terrorists may use nuclear, chemical or biological weapons.

As the Cold War drew to a close, CIA HUMINT capabilities were frozen or drawn down as national security budgets were cut. According to the account given in Bob Woodward's *Bush At War* – apparently written with the cooperation or acquiescence of top US officials – the CIA virtually halted its training of new case officers. Current DCI George Tenet has since confirmed this fact in a public address delivered in February 2004. Other published reports have cited CIA offices as having been downsized or eliminated in countries that, at the time, seemed unimportant. In retrospect, these actions can be viewed as mistakes, as they included CIA HUMINT operations in countries with weak governments that later proved to be operations bases and manpower pools for terrorist organisations. In 1994, however, HUMINT operations were drawn back further. At the time, several high-profile cases had emerged in which the CIA had foreign agents on its payroll who were, according to one press account, implicated in 'murder, assassination, torture, terrorism and other crimes'. These agents were recruited assets, not intelligence officers. Nevertheless, critics of the CIA in the media and in Congress argued that ties to such individuals were unacceptable, and the agency was compelled to begin a 'scrub' of its assets. According to then-DCI John Deutch, the agency had sometimes recruited agents 'blindly, without thorough vetting and established procedures for accountability'. Under the new guidelines, the cost of having such assets on the CIA payroll was more carefully weighed against the benefits, or the possibility of collecting the information through other means. According to reports, as many as 1,000 agents, said to be one fourth to one third of its total, failed to meet the test.

The region most heavily affected by the 'scrub' was Latin America, where many foreign assets who were government officials had particularly voluminous records of human-rights violations. These guidelines also had a significant effect on the CIA's abilities to pursue terrorists in other regions. Obviously, a member of a terrorist cell would himself often be guilty of terrorism, and so might be unacceptable as a recruited asset. But the guidelines also had the effect of making it harder for the CIA to enlist foreign officials guilty of human-rights violations, which included many police and intelligence officers in the Middle East and Asia. Even if intelligence services were not engaging such officials in mutually acknowledged liaison relationships, the guidelines could preclude other options, such as recruiting them as paid assets.

In the 1990s, HUMINT activities undertaken by the US military services were cut or curtailed, along with other defence and intelligence functions. At the same time, the Department of Defense tried to make HUMINT efforts directed at al-Qaeda and other terrorist targets more concerted. Its efforts were concentrated primarily in its Defense HUMINT Service, which was created in 1992 as a subunit of the Defense Intelligence Agency to consolidate the various disparate military HUMINT operations. The Defense HUMINT Service's clandestine HUMINT operations have been described as being similar to those of the CIA's Directorate of Operations (DO), though on a smaller scale. Whatever its intent, according to some observers, this reorganisation had the effect of diminishing rather than enhancing US military HUMINT capabilities. The US Army, which among the services had been the most active supporter of military-related HUMINT, appeared to lose much of its discretionary power to develop HUMINT. Also, after the Defense HUMINT Service became the 'owner' of the Pentagon's HUMINT operations, individual services had less interest and incentive to expend their own capabilities to serve what was then, in effect, a separate organisation. Further contributing to this decline was the limited use of HUMINT and special-operations forces in the 1991 Gulf War. According to most accounts, the commander of the coalition forces, General H. Norman Schwarzkopf, favoured conventional military operations over the kinds of special operations for which HUMINT was especially important. Given the unequivocal operational success of the Gulf War, it was natural for the Defense Department subsequently to favour the development of precision-guided munitions and networked communications, which had proven key to the decisive victory over Iraq, and to disfavour areas like HUMINT that had not proven vital.

Reviving HUMINT

After restricting its HUMINT efforts in the 1990s, the CIA reportedly modified its policies. Beginning in late 1990s, the press began to quote US officials who said that the agency was hiring 'more than five times as many' case officers as it had in 1995, when the agency's recruitment reached a post-Cold War low. The same officials said that the hiring effort would accelerate in the following years. In addition to bringing in more case officers, the CIA reportedly planned to reopen some of the operations bases it had closed a few years earlier. The top mission of these bases had previously been to recruit local Soviet officials. Now, however, US officials realised that these bases were important for recruiting counter-terrorist assets. By February 2004, Tenet was saying publicly that 'rebuilding our clandestine service' had been his 'highest priority'. Nevertheless, there have been many critics of the CIA not only on account of its sporadic HUMINT efforts, but also for its methods. These critics claim that the CIA's approach of relying on case officers under official cover is ineffective against the current terrorist threat.

One such critic was Reuel Marc Gerecht, who, writing under the nom de plum Edward Shirly identified himself in 1999 as a former CIA case officer. Gerecht asserted that the CIA lacked personnel with the language skills and cultural insight to collect HUMINT effectively. In 2001, just before the 11 September attacks, Gerecht published an article in *The Atlantic Monthly* portraying the CIA DO as being inordinately conservative and risk-averse. Gerecht's criticisms were echoed and elaborated by Robert Baer, also a self-identified former CIA officer. In recounting his own career, Baer described the DO as overly bureaucratic and, prior to 11 September, insufficiently interested in the rise of Islamic fundamentalism in the Middle East. According to Baer, collecting intelligence on targets other than the Soviet Union were a low priority for the CIA, and its operators lacked the training and organisational support to do so.

After 11 September, the House and Senate Intelligence Committees together created a committee (the 'Joint Inquiry') that provided additional details on US HUMINT operations, and specific findings about its efforts prior to the terrorist attacks. According to the Joint Inquiry's report (completed in December 2002 and released with redactions in unclassified form in July 2003), the CIA began trying to collect HUMINT on al-Qaeda in the mid-1990s. The CTC, which had survived the post-Cold War drawdowns, created a special team to pursue Osama bin Laden in early 1996. This unit initially had fewer than 20 staff members, and primarily used case officers assigned to the DO's regional offices to collect intelligence. Tenet testified to the Joint Inquiry in public session that the CIA did penetrate al-Qaeda. But the Joint Inquiry's report rejected this claim. It said that, despite many creative attempts to obtain access to bin Laden's inner circle, former CTC officers had testified that the CIA had no penetrations of the al-Qaeda leadership prior to 11 September 2001.

Because the al-Qaeda target was so challenging, the CTC relied mainly on liaison services to develop sources. These relationships provided valuable intelligence that allowed the United States to avert at least one terrorist attack. However, the Joint Inquiry also found that, because the CIA depended so heavily on liaison services, there were regions of the world for which it lacked adequate information on the terrorist network. If the liaison services did not wish to help there was, said one US official, little that the CIA could do. Although the problem of relying too much on liaison services has become more widely appreciated in recent years, some experts and US officials believe the CIA and other agencies have been too slow to develop unilateral alternatives. For example, in July 2002, the US House

Permanent Select Committee on Intelligence observed that 'the Committee is not confident that the [HUMINT] rebuilding effort that the Committee has been calling for and now sees beginning is headed in the right direction. The Committee is concerned, for example, that there is an over-reliance on assistance from allies to collect information'.

One reason that CIA HUMINT was so stressed during this period was that US intelligence spending either declined or remained constant during the 1990s. Although US intelligence devoted more resources to terrorist targets, overall the intelligence community (and, by extension, HUMINT) was under-resourced. HUMINT operations require significant support for logistics, maintaining reports and counter-intelligence, and these were apparently in short supply. Further, US intelligence had to devote significant HUMINT resources to operations in the Balkans. HUMINT was essential to 'force protection', which itself becomes more important as troops are required to expose themselves for prolonged periods in peacekeeping operations. In addition, the CIA depended so heavily on liaison sources because their predilection for placing case officers under 'official cover' did not lend itself to generating useful counter-terrorist intelligence. When operating under official cover, intelligence officers merely posed as US officials assigned to overt activities abroad. They didn't hide the fact that they worked for the US government – only the fact that they were working for the CIA. Former CIA Deputy Director Bobby Inman has written that this practice developed in the 1960s, when 'a vogue for systems analysis and cost-benefit tradeoffs swept through government' and 'it was decided that non-official cover – in most cases, posing as businessmen – for clandestine officers was too expensive'. Unfortunately, while case officers using official cover may have been effective for recruiting Soviet bloc targets – in particular, Soviet military, diplomatic and intelligence personnel whom case officers might encounter posted abroad – it is virtually useless for achieving direct, unilateral penetrations of terrorist organisations. The kinds of people who are likely to join or affiliate with terrorist cells are not prone to warm to people who do not hide the fact that they are officials of the US government.

Case officers working under official cover were also effective in attracting, recruiting, or luring Soviet bloc officials who might defect. Because professionals can often see through official cover, potential defectors could be encouraged by the knowledge that there was someone on the Western side who could receive an offer of defection and provide safe haven. Many Soviet military, diplomatic and intelligence officials became disillusioned with the Soviet system and communism after Khrushchev exposed Stalin's excesses in 1956, and certainly as the Soviet regime became more ossified, bureaucratic and corrupt in the 1980s. Present-day terrorists, on the other hand, are volunteers from highly motivated constituencies whose ideological fervour has not yet worn thin.

Thus, a HUMINT model that relied heavily on encouraging and facilitating defection is often ill-suited for the religious zealot who is likely to be a target today.

As in the case of using liaison services, there is public evidence both that US intelligence is seeking alternatives to official cover – and that critics are not satisfied with the pace of these changes. In May 2003, for example, the Senate Select Committee on Intelligence said in the report accompanying its authorisation bill that 'various Committee Members expressed concern about the need for more vigorous HUMINT collection – especially unilateral collection – under non-official cover and from non-traditional HUMINT platforms.... [T]he Committee attaches the highest degree of importance to far more aggressive and sustained non-traditional HUMINT collection program'. According to the Joint Inquiry, the Defense HUMINT Service increased its efforts against al-Qaeda after the 1998 US embassy bombings in Kenya and Tanzania, but there is no evidence that their HUMINT operations have been any more successful than those of the CIA. But several press reports in 2003 and early 2004 suggest that the downward trend for HUMINT in the US military services – like that at the CIA – is being reversed, largely owing to the need for enhanced counter-terrorism capabilities. Further, the Joint Inquiry report noted that Defense HUMINT Service sources were 'extremely useful' in the air campaign undertaken as part of *Operation Enduring Freedom*. This observation reflects an important trend that has arisen since the end of the Cold War: the tighter integration of HUMINT into military operations. According to some US officials, however, US military forces lacked adequate human-intelligence assets in Afghanistan prior to *Operation Enduring Freedom*. Although the CIA would retain the lead role in HUMINT there, military forces had specialised needs – such as locating targets inside hostile territory and obtaining targeting assistance – and could not allow themselves to be totally dependent on another agency for HUMINT support. The military capability to hit terrorist targets also called for detailed information about the local environment and political conditions, which is hard to attain through any means other than HUMINT.

Away from the battlefield, the Federal Bureau of Investigation (FBI) has also undertaken clandestine HUMINT operations against al-Qaeda. Prior to 11 September, the FBI had full field investigations underway against 70 individuals that had been linked to al-Qaeda. Not as well known, but equally important, were the FBI's efforts overseas. Since the late 1980s, the FBI has increased its foreign presence as part of the campaign against international organised crime and narco-trafficking, in addition to terrorism. The Joint Inquiry reported, however, that FBI representatives outside the United States were required to get approval from FBI headquarters to allow potential sources to engage in illegal activity, which hampered their ability to recruit and run them. In effect, the prevailing policy appears to have

Strategic Policy Issues

required a terrorist to stop being a terrorist before the FBI could use him for HUMINT collection. In addition, FBI HUMINT activity was fragmented, so that operations in different regions could not coordinate effectively.

One area of HUMINT that has received special attention in the war on terrorism is the interrogation of prisoners captured abroad, which the US government has controversially deemed 'unlawful combatants' or 'battlefield detainees'. During the Cold War since the United States and Soviet Union were not actually engaged in a 'hot' war, there were relatively few detainees to interrogate, which made the enterprise relatively unimportant. It has become of substantially greater importance in the war on terrorism, though, precisely because so many detainees have been captured and because other sources of HUMINT, such as unilateral recruits and defectors have been harder to come by. Also, because of the nature of terrorist campaigns, the adversary is often within one's own territory and likely to be captured. Suspected terrorists captured within one's jurisdiction are usually considered criminal suspects and are accorded the rights of the accused. (There are some exceptions, as the case of Jose Padilla illustrates. Padilla, an American citizen, had travelled abroad and was apprehended while re-entering the United States after allegedly training with al-Qaeda. Padilla was deemed to be an unlawful combatant and detained in a military brig.) Suspected terrorists captured abroad fall into a grey area – not quite prisoners of war, as they do not comply with the rules and customs of war, but still entitled to some legal protections. Once in custody, these prisoners can be subjected to a variety of interrogation techniques. US officials firmly insist that they do not use torture; in any case, usually such extreme measures are both unreliable and unnecessary. Because captors can almost completely control the environment of a prisoner, they can use rewards, limited punishment and creating confusion to manipulate a prisoner into providing much information. In addition, Western governments can often deport or 'render' prisoners to other governments that may use more robust methods of interrogation. US officials, however, have rejected claims that such governments use torture, commenting only that renderings are more effective or appropriate in some circumstances.

The US government has not released much official information on detainees out of concerns that doing so could afford terrorist organisations tactical advantages – for instance, by confirming that one of their members has, in fact, been killed or captured. Even so, press interviews with US officials at the detention centre at Guantanamo Bay, Cuba indicate that 610 detainees have been held from 44 countries. Of these, over 100 have been released, and approximately 50 have been determined to be hardcore terrorists who would present a significant danger if released. Intelligence elicited from detainees has often proven critical in obtaining the most current plans and tactics of terrorist groups. US officials have said publicly that al-Qaeda detainees, and especially leadership figures such as Khalid Shaikh Mohammed, Abu Zubeida and Ramzi Binalshibh, are crucial both in averting planned terrorist strikes and in unravelling additional parts of a terrorist network. But some detainees who have been released from the US detention centre at Guantanamo Bay have told reporters that they were mistreated, subjected to beatings and isolated for long periods. The interrogation of detainees will likely remain controversial because of fears that government authorities might use excessive force to elicit information, not to mention legal issues – so far inadequately addressed – concerning the extent of the prisoners' due-process rights.

Future trends

In executing a general strategy of denying weapons of mass destruction (WMD) to rogue states and non-state actors, the Bush administration's National Security Strategy notes that pre-emptive or preventive war may occasionally be necessary. Establishing a firm casus belli for such a war may turn on intelligence – as indeed it did in the case of Iraq in 2003. The non-discovery of WMD in Iraq reflected a critical failure of intelligence that has compromised the credibility of the global counter-terrorism coalition. The technical intelligence – satellite imagery and telephone intercepts – that US Secretary of State Colin Powell presented at the United Nations in February 2003 that strongly suggested an active Iraqi WMD programme were real enough. US underestimations of the extent of Iraq's nuclear programme in the 1980s and early 1990s also conditioned an alarmist interpretation of the technical indicators, and Saddam's haughty resistance to inspections supported the conclusion that he had something to hide. Thus, US and other intelligence agencies made a crucially incorrect inference. Supporting this bad inference was bad HUMINT provided by Iraqi exile Ahmed Chalabi – head of the London-based Iraqi National Congress and hardly a presumptively objective source. Yet in a world that is technologically increasingly complex and 'dual-use', technical intelligence is likely to become more, not less, ambiguous. Accordingly, even if HUMINT may be inherently less reliable, it is more important than ever as a partial gauge of the accuracy of technical intelligence. Good HUMINT could have prevented the intelligence failure on Iraq.

Closer and more effective integration of technical and human intelligence collection therefore should be a priority. Additional needs include developing cover and tradecraft that permit greater access to terrorist organisations, and balancing the tight security traditionally accorded to HUMINT sources with the utility of sharing intelligence among a larger population of users. HUMINT will remain critical to US counter-terrorism and non-proliferation efforts, but will require considerable additional effort to keep up with the new challenges that new

Strategic Policy Issues

targets present. It remains unclear whether existing American intelligence organisations, which are strongly committed to their current tradecraft and operational methods, can address these issues effectively. If not, it may be necessary to create a new organisation that can develop the required capabilities and integrate their implementation into the national security agenda.

However it improves its HUMINT capabilities, the US government may be able to draw on the greater experience of its European partners in countering terrorist threats. For the British government, for instance, penetrating the Provisional Irish Republican Army (IRA) via HUMINT assets was a key aspect of a 25-year effort that succeeded in weakening the IRA and at least tentatively pacifying the group to a manageable degree. The IRA, to be sure, is very different from al-Qaeda: it had far more limited objectives and proved amenable to non-violent political negotiations, and was composed of members whose racial and cultural similarity to their adversaries made them presumptively easier to co-opt and the organisation easier to infiltrate. Nevertheless, the likelihood that a hobbled post-Afghanistan al-Qaeda is seeking to enlist 'clean skins' from outside the Arab world – in part among nationals of the United States and European countries – suggests that al-Qaeda's recruits may collectively become less religiously absolute in mindset, closer to their enemies in background and therefore more susceptible to tried-and-true HUMINT techniques. Thus, the counter-terrorism experiences – which emphasise HUMINT – of European authorities against 'old' ethno-nationalist terrorist groups like the IRA or ideological ones like the Red Brigades may become all the more relevant to the war on transnational Islamic terrorism.

US Military Doctrine and Counterinsurgency

After nearly three decades in obscurity, counterinsurgency has re-emerged as an urgent priority for the US armed forces. The campaign against the violent opponents of the coalition occupation in Iraq, the hunt for al-Qaeda and Taliban remnants in Afghanistan, and the global campaign against terrorism has placed new pressures on the military – in particular, the army – to defeat non-traditional threats to American security. For the US Army, deeply scarred by its experience in southeast Asia, counterinsurgency – defined by the Defense Department's Dictionary of Military Terms as 'those military, paramilitary, political, economic, psychological, and civic actions taken by a government to defeat insurgency' – was seen as an aberration, and as a distraction from its central task of preparing to fight and win conflicts against modern, conventional armed forces. Until recently, mainstream strategic studies journals also were dominated by discussions of topics like the 'revolution in military affairs', national missile defence and emerging 'peer competitors' of the United States. Today, however, both the army and the broader national security policy community are trying to develop approaches for countering violent irregular forces and movements that threaten important US and broader Western interests. Understanding both the past and the present strengths and weaknesses of American approaches is essential, as insurgencies that threaten the United States and its allies are likely to remain part of the international security environment indefinitely.

Early approaches to counterinsurgency

Campaigns to suppress irregular forces were a regular feature of nineteenth-century US Army life. During the Civil War, army units fought Confederate 'raiders' and other unconventional units; cavalry were used throughout the West to suppress Plains Indians; and army forces battled against local opponents of the US occupation of the Philippines in the wake of the Spanish–American war. However, despite the frequency with which the army was engaged in such missions, suppressing bandits, guerrillas and other irregulars was widely seen by the officer corps as a secondary mission. By the late 1800s, preparing to fight and win conventional armed conflict had emerged as the service's central organising principle. Before, during, and after the Second World War, army leaders typically saw operations against guerrillas, occupation duty and assistance to foreign security forces – elements of what would later be termed 'counterinsurgency' – as at best a distraction from preparing for and conducting large-scale combat operations.

The US Marine Corps, on the other hand, looked upon such 'non-conventional' missions as part of the service's raison d'être, and was institutionally more enthusiastic about suppressing rebellious locals, establishing indigenous militias and conducting assorted state-building activities. During the so-called 'Banana War' period of 1915–1934, the US repeatedly sent marines to restore order in unruly and unstable countries like Haiti, Nicaragua and the Dominican Republic. These operations served as the raw material for an early statement of US counterinsurgency doctrine, the marines' *Small Wars Manual*. Published in 1940, the manual was a distillation of pragmatic lore intended to guide marines preparing for duty in turbulent and unstable political and operational environments. *Small Wars* has stood the test of time, and like all true classics, the manual remains remarkably fresh. For example, its authors conceptualise small wars as complex politico-military activities, in which diplomacy and armed force serve complementary roles. These conflicts are characterised by uncertainty and are marked by an absence of clear-cut authority, thus requiring the full use of a marine's individual initiative. Victory, such as it is, can only be brought about by undercutting support for rebellion by addressing its underlying social, political, and economic sources. Addressing these 'root causes', in turn, requires an understanding of the language, culture and history of the country in question.

The *Small Wars Manual* has a decidedly contemporary feel. It is little wonder that the marines reprinted the manual in 1987, when ambiguous 'low-intensity conflict' loomed as a serious US national security challenge in central and south America. Given the Bush administration's new emphasis on waging unconventional conflicts in countries like Afghanistan, Pakistan and Iraq, it is perhaps unsurprising that the marines have once again dusted off the manual. A new draft of *Small Wars*, intended to be more accessible to today's military audience, is considerably shorter, and no longer contains discussions of supposedly arcane topics such as the use of pack animals (*pace* the use of horses in *Operation Enduring Freedom* in Afghanistan). The army never produced anything comparable to the marines' manual. Army doctrine in the 1940s and 1950s focused on preparing its forces for large-scale conventional combat operations. For the remainder of the Cold War, central Europe would remain the service's most important foreign front. Although the army was engaged in substantial advisory efforts in the Third World, supporting a friendly nation's counterinsurgency activities, or engaging in counterinsurgency operations directly, was at most a secondary and 'lesser included' mission easily handled by regular troops.

The army, counterinsurgency and Vietnam

The army's lack of interest in counterinsurgency revealed itself most dramatically in South Vietnam, the recipient of the army's largest Cold War-era defence advisory operation. The United States assumed a steadily larger advisory role after the defeat of the French in 1954, and the emphasis until the late 1960s was on creating an indigenous army capable of resisting a conventional attack by the North Vietnamese armed forces. By the late 1950s, the US Military Assistance Advisory Group (MAAG) succeeded in turning the Army of the Republic of Vietnam (ARVN) into a mirror-image of the US army – complete with a divisional structure more appropriate to waging war on the North German plain. Drawing on the institutional experiences of the army during the Second World War and the Korean conflict, MAAG advisers shaped the ARVN using what military analyst Andrew J. Krepinevich terms the 'Army Concept' – that is, a force oriented primarily toward 'mid-intensity' conventional conflict involving the lavish application of firepower.

American military advisers in South Vietnam did not completely ignore the problem of guerrilla warfare. But irregular forces were not seen as key tools in revolutionary struggles, as they would be by later counterinsurgency theorists. Instead, the MAAG conceived of guerrillas in essentially Second World War terms, as auxiliaries that conducted raids, sabotage and other behind-the-front-lines operations in support of conventional military forces. For senior US army personnel in Vietnam, the communist Vietcong guerrillas were a diversionary tool used by Hanoi to divert the ARVN to the southern and western parts of the country so that they would not be trained or be in position to repel an invasion from the north. The ARVN did prove useful in disrupting guerrilla operations, at least initially. But by the early 1960s, when the Vietcong, supported vigorously by the Hanoi government, launched a major insurgency, the ARVN was ill-prepared. MAAG commanders paid lip-service to the importance of developing a capable counter-guerrilla force, but remained wedded to creating an army capable of resisting, at least temporarily, a cross-border invasion from North Vietnam. President John F. Kennedy, shortly after assuming office in January 1961, reportedly asked his senior advisers, 'What are we doing about guerrilla warfare?' Kennedy and his civilian aides eagerly spread the gospel of counterinsurgency, but the military had little enthusiasm for the president's programme for defeating communist subversion in the developing world, which it did not see as requiring much military innovation.

By the late 1960s, the inability of the South Vietnamese government and its American sponsors to defeat the Vietcong insurgency led to a shift in strategy. Rather than using the military to conduct large-unit 'search and destroy' missions to eliminate main-force Vietcong units, the new approach stressed 'pacification' – that is, combined military political, and economic activities aimed at securing the countryside by addressing fundamental sources of the insurgency as well as its violent manifestations. In 1967, the US established the innovative Civil Operations Rural Development Support (CORDS) programme, which drew together in a single organisation all of the previously inchoate support activities aimed at strengthening South Vietnam's military, police, intelligence and economic development activities. Although part of the US Military Assistance Command Vietnam, CORDS officials recognised the importance of the non-military dimension of what was termed 'the other war'. With CORDS came an increased stress on improving the ability of the South Vietnamese to target, disrupt and dismantle the so-called 'Vietcong Infrastructure' (VCI) – that is, the underground political apparatus that lay at the heart of the insurgency. The notorious Phoenix Program, misleadingly branded as an 'assassination' campaign by the war's opponents, was one important facet of the anti-VCI struggle. Phoenix was in essence an intelligence programme that helped the Vietnamese security forces identify, apprehend and draw

Strategic Policy Issues

useful information from Vietcong cadres. Some were killed, and historians remain divided as to the effectiveness of this approach; but there is a consensus that Phoenix marked a significant improvement over the feckless search-and-destroy operations of the mid-1960s.

After Vietnam

By the end of the Vietnam War in 1975, the US Army's leadership was eager to forget a war that most officers considered a disaster – destructive of morale, strategically and operationally unsuccessful, and unpopular at home. Although the service had engaged in a wide variety of missions in southeast Asia, including direct combat operations, the army's leadership identified its counterinsurgency role as particularly fruitless. Thus, the service quickly shed an important symbol of a counterinsurgency orientation by reducing the size of Army Special Forces – the 'Green Berets' who embodied for many Americans the country's ill-fated adventure in southeast Asia. During the remainder of the 1970s, the service devoted almost no official attention to what was now termed 'low-intensity conflict' (LIC). Special Forces, always (and necessarily) small in relation to the conventional army, were widely perceived as a backwater, a career dead-end for officers hoping to rise to general officer rank. Army schools such as the Command and General Staff College at Fort Leavenworth devoted almost no classroom time to 'foreign internal defence' (FID), the new and presumably less politically charged term for counterinsurgency. Army doctrine, such as the 'capstone' field manual, *Operations*, virtually ignored what was perceived to be the grubby and thankless range of non-traditional military missions.

Yet for all its eagerness to forget counterinsurgency, the service was never able to entirely banish it, and like a bad dream, counterinsurgency returned during the 1980s. The Reagan administration, like the Kennedy administration, identified insurgency and subversion as instruments of Soviet statecraft in the developing world, and it sought to rebuild American capabilities for conducting FID. LIC and special operations received new emphasis at service schools; new Special Forces groups were created; a new institutional home for special operations, the Special Operations Command (SOCOM), was established; and within the Pentagon, a new bureaucracy, the Office of the Assistant Secretary of Defence for Special Operations and Low-Intensity Conflict (OASD SO-LIC) was given responsibility for developing policy and overseeing programmes.

The most vivid example of the Reagan administration's commitment to fighting communist-backed Third World insurgencies was in El Salvador. The tiny central American country, dominated by a near-feudal social structure, was racked by political turbulence and a formidable insurgency mounted by the Frente Farabundo Martí para la Liberación Nacional (FMLN).

The US response entailed the full array of FID instruments, including economic aid, intelligence support, police assistance and military equipment, advice and training. Domestic and international opposition to US involvement in El Salvador, and the desire to avoid the mammoth 'footprint' that marked the US presence in South Vietnam, led Washington to limit the number of advisers allowed in-country at any given time to 55, most of whom were Special Forces personnel. In El Salvador, the United States encountered persistent challenges familiar from its Vietnam experience: a greedy and tyrannical ruling elite, fearful of losing its power, and thus unwilling to undertake reforms needed to undercut the insurgents' base of popular support; a corrupt and incompetent military leadership; and an army woefully unprepared for the demands of counterinsurgency. Yet by some accounts, the small group of advisers performed remarkably well. The El Salvador armed forces grew far more effective during the 1980s, the country took on at least the trappings of liberal democracy and by the early 1990s, the FMLN was demobilised and integrated into the country's political order.

That said, the US Army as an institution never fully embraced the FID mission in El Salvador. In *American Military Policy in Small Wars: The Case of El Salvador* (1988), a scathing critique of the service's response to the conflict in central America, four serving officers highlighted the army leadership's unwillingness to commit what it defined as its best personnel to the advisory group in El Salvador. Much of the US-provided advice and training, according to the authors, reflected the US Army's conventional mindset, stressing the use of firepower rather than the patrolling and small-unit operations favoured by counterinsurgency theorists and practitioners. For many senior officers, El Salvador had the scent of Vietnam. As with Vietnam, the army was eager to leave El Salvador behind after the conflict was over. But while the service's Center of Military History had devoted considerable effort to assessing the army's performance in Vietnam, sometimes in sharply critical terms, there was no comparable systematic attempt to critique the army's role in El Salvador, or to apply lessons learned during that conflict to the development of strategy, doctrine, training or equipment. The first Gulf War buried El Salvador even more deeply in the army's institutional memory. A high-technology and occasionally high-intensity conflict, the Gulf War was a brilliant victory for the US armed forces that reinforced the army's belief that 'fighting and winning the nation's wars' was far preferable to intervening in messy and ambiguous Third World insurgencies.

Counterinsurgency doctrine today
In the decade following the end of the Cold War, counterinsurgency doctrine in the US military atrophied. Although the United States and its

allies conducted unconventional military operations relatively frequently in places like Somalia, Haiti and the Balkans, these activities were viewed by the military as second-order and essentially discretionary. Preparing for conventional conflict in southwest Asia and on the Korean Peninsula remained 'first-tier' national security priorities for both civilian and military leaders. Despite the existence of SOCOM and OASD SO-LIC, in the Pentagon's lexicon 'low-intensity conflict', never a particularly satisfactory term, was replaced but hardly improved upon by the tortuous phrase 'military operations other than war' (MOOTW). In the military's service schools, special-operations 'proponency offices', established during the 1980s to ensure that unconventional forces and doctrine were represented in the academic curricula, were disbanded. During both the Clinton administration and in the first years of the George W. Bush's presidency, Pentagon officials attempted to eliminate OASD SO-LIC; although Congress thwarted the move, only one OASD SO-LIC official had day-to-day responsibility for FID-related policy. FID-related instruction, even at the Special Forces' John F. Kennedy Special Warfare Center at Fort Bragg, formed a minuscule part of army education.

The army has provisionally remedied this deficit, at least with respect to counterinsurgency doctrine. Although the most recent version of *Operations*, published in June 2001, devotes only two of its 313 pages to FID, subsidiary manuals such as *Stability Operations and Support Operations* (February 2003) cover it in substantial detail and capture some of the lessons the service derived from Vietnam and El Salvador. While there is no suggestion that the service embraces FID with anything that could be called institutional enthusiasm, *Stability Operations and Support Operations* promulgates a sensible and sometimes sophisticated set of counterinsurgency tenets. Counterinsurgency, in the army's present view, is essentially a political task aimed at 'neutralising' the insurgent organisation by reducing its ability to conduct operations, discrediting its propaganda and addressing those underlying conditions that contribute to the insurgency's strength. The army conceptualises FID as an effort to help friendly nations protect themselves from 'lawlessness, subversion and insurgency'. In other words, the United States typically plays a supporting role in defeating these internal threats by supplying a 'host nation' with political, economic, intelligence and military assistance.

Reflecting an American cultural tradition that resists anything smacking of heavy-handed colonialism, the US expects threatened nations to defeat the insurgents on their own, albeit with appropriate aid from American government institutions. Military support, in turn, 'cannot be conducted in isolation from other aspects of US policy in the host nation'. Most of the US Army's role will be in the background – providing defence equipment, carrying out joint exercises, intelligence sharing, and providing healthcare and other support to local populations. Direct combat operations by army forces are intended to be rare, since such operations 'undermine the legitimacy of the host government and [risk] converting the conflict into an American war'. But when American interests are deemed high, and indirect support is insufficient, US combat forces may 'conduct strike operations to disrupt and destroy insurgent combat formations'. However, the use of force must be kept to a minimum, and always be tailored to the environment. Specifically, 'military operations designed for war must be modified for counterinsurgency' and 'must complement and reinforce political, social and economic reforms'.

Counterinsurgency in Iraq

In Iraq, and to a lesser extent Afghanistan, the army has been compelled to revisit a subject it has embraced fitfully over the past century. Initially, the US high command was unwilling to concede that anything as structured as an insurgency was underway in Iraq, choosing instead to characterise the unrest as largely criminal and unfocused. American military and civilian leaders have since referred to the conflict as an insurgency. The depth of the insurgency's strength was revealed on 4 April 2004, when violent uprisings broke out in Baghdad, Najaf and Basra, leading to the death of American, Spanish and Salvadoran troops, and scores of Iraqis. To date, however, little of the army's FID doctrine appears to have been applied in Iraq, at least not in any systematic way. Indeed, the service's performance during its first year in Iraq has been reminiscent of the army in Vietnam during the mid-1960s.

Operations such as *Soda Mountain* (July 2003) and *Iron Mountain* (December 2003) – large-unit sweeps designed to pulverise 'former regime loyalists' (FRLs) and foreign jihadists – recall Vietnam operations like *Junction City* (March 1967), a four-division search-and-destroy mission along the Cambodian border. Occupying forces, such as the First Armoured Division, and the Third and Fourth Infantry Divisions, arrived in Iraq with no counterinsurgency training. One army colonel candidly told a reporter in October 2003, 'We are not trained to fight a war like this'. Force protection has been a paramount goal. While admirable, it has prevented troops from conducting necessary foot patrols, which are seen as too dangerous. Forces move about in high-speed Bradley fighting vehicles or 'Humvees' down the centres of streets, thus preventing troops from gathering potentially valuable information from the local population. A single-minded determination to root out FRLs has led to overly aggressive raids, which have needlessly antagonised Iraqi civilians. Vast US bases, complete with Pizza Huts and other modern trappings, are heavily fortified. While helping to ensure that US forces are comfortable and protected from terrorism, such cantonments also further isolate troops from the local population. Physical isolation, a lack of awareness of Iraqi customs and culture, and heavy-handedness may prove to be cardinal errors. Even with

Strategic Policy Issues

elaborate imagery and signals intelligence, it is unlikely that US forces will be able to find insurgents without tip-offs from Iraqi citizens.

For the mainstream US Army, the application of force remains the principle tool for achieving military objectives. As a result, the army has had a difficult time in Iraq making the transition from war-fighting to stability operations. The continuing lack of public order in Iraq highlights this shortfall in dramatic terms. Since the fall of Saddam Hussein, robbery, rape, murder and other serious crime have increased greatly, and few Iraqis feel secure in their homes or on the streets. Absent public security, the political, social and economic reconstruction of Iraq is all but impossible. However, a longstanding aversion to anything smacking of police work and a chronic lack of military policemen has kept the army from performing a law-enforcement function. The US has placed the full burden of public order on the nascent Iraqi police service, a force crippled by a lack of equipment that will not be remedied anytime soon. This is in marked contrast to the British approach, which has benefited from long experience in containing and diminishing an urban low-intensity terrorist insurgency in Northern Ireland. Recognising the need to rapidly re-establish an Iraqi police presence, British forces began joint patrols with Iraqi police in Basra and Maysan provinces. This entails smaller units and lower force-protection standards, but tends to pay dividends in terms of winning hearts and minds. While British troops too have come under fire and suffered casualties, they also appear to have gleaned more probative intelligence and drawn less hostility from Iraqis.

Looking ahead

The escalating insurgency in Iraq and the demands imposed by the global campaign against al-Qaeda have forced the United States to reconsider the way it organises, trains and equips its military forces. Slowly, but perceptibly, the army leadership is moving the service from an industrial-era enterprise into a leaner, more flexible instrument capable of conducting not just traditional war-fighting missions, but also counter-insurgency, urban combat, state-building and related activities. The pressures of Iraq, together with the demands of hunting down al-Qaeda cadres and strengthening the capabilities of 'front-line' states like Afghanistan, Pakistan and the Philippines, has moved the army to stress previously outré capabilities like Special Forces, military policing, intelligence collection and analysis, and foreign-language skills. US Army Chief of Staff General Peter J. Schoomaker has proposed moving thousands of troops in assignments with air-defence and artillery units into positions as military policemen, combat engineers and civil affairs specialists.

The army is also proposing to increase the size of the Special Forces over the next five years by 20% to 30,000 men. Since 11 September 2001, the

Special Forces have had a prominent role in training indigenous security units to control borders, disrupt terrorist operations and carry out other counterinsurgency and counter-terrorist operations. Given the demands placed on Special Forces groups in Africa, Latin America, and central and southeast Asia, it is inevitable that the Pentagon would plan to expand the force. However, there is a danger in increasing the force too rapidly. To meet the manpower demands of the Vietnam War, the army lowered Special Forces standards, and took in thousands of under-qualified personnel.

Although the army is likely to be in Iraq for a long time to come, ramping-up measures are unlikely to take effect quickly enough to have much impact on the insurgency there. Even so, despite setbacks in the US-led counterinsurgency campaign, there are signs that progress is being made, at least on the conceptual level. Junior field-grade officers, like Army Major John Nagl, a guerrilla-warfare expert serving with the 82nd Airborne Division, has been widely quoted in the press and has served as an articulate spokesman for an approach to countering the insurgency that stresses winning public support, building local institutions and strengthening the capabilities of Iraqi security forces.

Another potentially encouraging sign has come from the marines. In spring 2004, in one of the largest troop rotations since the Second World War, thousands of marines began replacing army units in Iraq. Based on their experience in suppressing insurgencies in Latin America and the Philippines, the marines' approach calls for restraint and an emphasis on building local relationships. The Marine Corps also intends to revive the Combined Action Platoons, small units that lived in villages in Vietnam and trained the local population to defend itself against communist insurgents.

On balance, the US military has made progress in recasting its military effort to fight low intensity conflict. But it is far too early to be sanguine about the success of the military's programme to establish a counterinsurgency capability that is up to meeting new challenges. The marine approach appears promising, although the service, with 174,000 active-duty personnel, remains small in comparison with the army, which has 485,000 on active-duty and another 700,000 reserves. The army will necessarily remain *primus inter pares*. If the United States is to achieve success in its current missions, and in future counterinsurgency and counter-terrorist operations, it is essential that the army is properly organised, trained and equipped. The stiffest challenge is not likely to pivot on the service's FID doctrine, which appears more than sufficient for providing the framework for responding to insurgent threats. Rather, the challenge is likely to involve the army as an institution, which has long resisted the grubby, protracted and politically messy arena of counterinsurgency. Schoomaker, a former SOCOM commander, and Secretary of Defense Donald Rumsfeld are clearly committed to reorienting the service. But when they leave office, or if the demands posed by Iraq and al-Qaeda abate, the pressures to transform the service may wane as well. Absent these pressures, the service may revert to its preferred roles and missions – fighting and winning the nation's wars.

Getting Homeland Security Right

Ever since the 11 September attacks debunked the myth of America's invulnerability, the Bush administration has conducted a two-front war against global terrorism. While the offensive elements of the administration's strategy – intelligence and law-enforcement cooperation, the proactive military pursuit of terrorists, and the military elimination of actual and potential state sponsors of terrorism – have been executed with relentless energy, resolve and determination, the same cannot be said about the defence of the American homeland. Most experts acknowledge some progress being made by Secretary of Homeland Security Tom Ridge. Yet unlike its efforts overseas, the administration's implementation of an ambitious homeland security agenda – generally characterised as vulnerability- or capabilities-based, and contemplating the minimisation of all vulnerabilities to ill-defined threats as well as responses to emergent ones – has been slow, inconsistent and under-resourced. Vulnerabilities in transportation networks and border security remain, and intelligence shortfalls have continued.

The US strategy

The breadth of the challenge facing the United States – an open society with myriad potential vulnerabilities – calls for a clear and wide-ranging strategy. This strategy should be the product of a deliberative process by which ends are related to means, policy aims to distinct objectives and programmes to resources. Yet President Bush's National Security Strategy provides little guidance on how the subordinate National Strategy for Combating Terrorism or National Strategy for Homeland Security fit into the overall US security plan, which embraces foreign policy, intelligence, international trade, threat reduction and non-proliferation. In effect, homeland security has been relegated to a supporting role in an broader counter-terrorism strategy that seeks first to defeat terrorists, then to deny them sponsorship or sanctuary, then to diminish the causes or conditions that they exploit, and only last, to defend US citizens. This '4 D' strategy is based on the notion that 'the best defence is a good offence'. Bush has stated that the US 'must take the battle to the enemy, disrupt his plans and confront the worst threats before they emerge'. Such an approach fits America's strategic culture and the proclivities of the personalities at the apex of its government. However, the underlying strategy and the manner in which it is being conducted may only worsen the problem.

The newly salient strategic threat of non-state actors using asymmetric means has highlighted a world in which traditional organisational boundaries and institutional borders have less relevance. Yet the Bush administration has segregated homeland security from the strategy development and crisis management processes of the National Security Council (NSC). The Homeland Security Council has been largely cut out of the NSC loop. Furthermore, the Homeland Security Advisor (HSA) has provided little overall guidance to the Department of Homeland Security (DHS). Instead, the HSA has conducted an end-to-end assessment of bio-defence – certainly a useful guide for long-term research and resource allocation, but not consistent with a strategic coordinating role. Thus, the United States' counter-terrorism and homeland security strategy appears to lack clarity and definition as to precisely what threats and what vulnerabilities need to be addressed, and in what order. Numerous terrorism experts, notably Bruce Hoffman of The RAND Corporation, have stressed the need to develop a comprehensive net assessment that has not yet materialised. In this light, the Bush administration may ultimately admit that it erred in allocating policy responsibility for homeland security outside the NSC.

Bush's homeland security spending plans have not met the expectations of Congress or America's 50 state governors. Given the offensive thrust of Bush's grand strategy, military spending has snared the lion's share of increased US security spending. Of an estimated $240 billion in federal spending for security since 2001, more than 80% has gone to the Pentagon. An even larger share of homeland security funding is earmarked for military bases and cyber-security initiatives for the Defense Department. Funding for law enforcement, intelligence, countering bio-terrorism, border management, emergency management, airport security, computer defences and transportation security compete for the rest. Numerous homeland security analysts, including Stephen Flynn of the Council on Foreign Relations, find the logic behind the administration's spending priorities counterintuitive. Flynn has noted that 'modern terrorists attack soft targets and key elements of our infrastructure, which places our entire economic system and way of life at risk. The policy and resources should reflect this reality'.

The FY2005 homeland security budget was a nominally generous $40.2bn, ostensibly reflecting a 10% increase over FY2004. But this rise was shown to be an accounting gimmick that included increased port user fees and taxes, and incorporated the multi-year $2.5bn BioShield Program as a single year's appropriation. Ridge admitted that discretionary spending for his fledgling department was less than 4%, which would barely cover inflation and expected pay rises for his 180,000 employees. Spending for port security programmes like Operation Safe Commerce, and for local first responders was actually reduced, raising the ire of numerous Congressmen who have pressed for funding levels reflecting the greater mission load and poor capitalisation of the DHS. Despite 11 September, the government has continued to put more resources into farm subsidies and the federal highway programme – notorious repositories of special-interest 'pork barrel' funding – than homeland security.

Critical infrastructure

With the release of The National Strategy for The Physical Protection of Critical Infrastructure and Key Assets in February 2003, the US government signalled its resolve to securing critical infrastructure. But issuing a strategy with the president's signature was only the first step of an excruciatingly slow process. Only a year later did the DHS begin to outline initiatives to support the new strategy, announcing in February 2004 that it would begin to build a National Database of Critical Infrastructure. The DHS also said that by May 2004 it would create a National Infrastructure Coordination Center that would include representatives from private industry, which is estimated to own 85% of the telecommunications, banking, energy and transportation networks that comprise the most critical components of America's infrastructure.

These initiatives, though useful, fall short of establishing wholesale federal regulatory oversight over the protection of critical infrastructure. The dominant government assumption has been that the interests of private industry in maintaining commercial viability will lead significant efforts in self-protection that government need only complement with prescriptions of best practices and relatively thin supervision. Unfortunately, this does not appear to be the case. Despite the two-and-a-half years of intensive interest in domestic security since 11 September, America's infrastructure remains substantially exposed. Numerous exercises continue to highlight multiple openings for an attack. For example, in October 2003, a think-tank exercise called Silent Vector simulated terrorist attacks on critical infrastructure assets, and demonstrated the broad vulnerability of chemical plants to a plane or bomb attack. According to one government study, there are 123 chemical facilities in the United States that each could produce one million casualties if attacked. Chemical plant controllers are not generally trained to respond to an attack against a facility and do not know what measures to implement to reduce contamination. Another internal government report noted that security training at most nuclear facilities had been reduced or outright eliminated since 11 September due to resource constraints.

Federal authorities have not mandated additional security measures, nor sought grant money to improve security in the chemical industry. Oversight of nuclear site security also remains weak. A power outage in Canada and the northeastern states in September 2003 demonstrated the cascading effects of seemingly inconsequential faults in the electronic grid. More than 50m people were without power for more than a day.

Cybersecurity

Computer-network security is perhaps the most important element of critical infrastructure protection. The Bush administration issued a glossy strategy document to promulgate its approach to closing shortfalls in this area. But instead of providing clear guidance, goals and oversight, top homeland security officials merely reinforced their immediate post-11 September exhortation to the private sector to join with government in a partnership, rather than drive towards more robust federal regulation. Cyberattacks and criminal intrusions increased more than 40% in the United States in 2003, with several billion dollars of damage to US companies caused by a number of malicious 'worms'. In August 2003, hackers released two of the most virulent computer viruses in history. The Blaster virus, which infected at least 500,000 computers, forced CSX Corporation to stop train services after the virus brought down the company's rail signalling system. The virus also disrupted computer check-in services at some major airlines. The following week, the SoBig virus, one of the quickest spreading viruses ever, infected over 570,000 computers. It is not difficult to envision the potential threat either virus could have posed if the infiltrators were intent on imperilling national security. Computer experts agree that the SoBig virus could have been programmed to launch an Internet-wide attack, which would have had far-reaching ramifications for the government and private sector ranging from economic trauma to hindering consequence-management operations.

The Bush administration has been slow to address the cyber-security threat and information warfare. Richard A. Clarke, the first Director of the National Security Council's Office of Cybersecurity appointed after 11 September, resigned in January 2003 because he felt not enough attention was being paid to the issue. The NSC cybersecurity position was eliminated and the White House delegated responsibility for cyberterrorism issues to DHS. Without White House backing, DHS is unlikely to forge the more muscular public/private relationships needed to protect critical infrastructure, especially the computer networks that drive much of modern commerce and society. Nor is the private sector likely to implement security measures in the absence of extraordinary market pressures that may come too late – after rather than before the next attack – or White House intervention. The DHS' new cybersecurity director,

Robert Liscouski, is attempting to institute new programmes, including a computer attack alert system, but these steps do not address the most critical issues facing the country. The DHS itself was one of seven federal agencies that received a failing grade on its network security for 2003 in an annual Congressional assessment.

It is understandable that Washington is loath to micromanage a significant portion of the private sector. But its inability or refusal to recognise the gaps in market-based approaches and their inconsistency with vulnerability-based security and unwillingness to substitute guidance, standards and accountability will only ensure that a gap between strategic rhetoric and security remains.

Preparedness for biological attack

Two years after the anthrax letter attacks, a large-scale exercise called TOPOFF II simulated a biological and radiological attack in several American cities. The exercise exposed continuing deficiencies in first responder communications, hospital preparedness and vaccine distribution. Although most of the conclusions of the exercise are classified, its broad results have been promulgated. On balance, the simulation showed that progress has been made at detecting attacks but that the country was not as prepared to respond. TOPOFF II intensified government concerns about anthrax, which were already quite high given that the 2001 attacks showed that the terrorist production of high-grade anthrax was apparently possible, and that studies of possible distribution modalities indicate that a deadly mass-casualty attack is quite feasible. The fact that intelligence reports from captured terrorists indicated al-Qaeda's interest in anthrax was also discomforting.

Hospitals are the weakest link in the biological response chain. Currently, hospitals cannot handle the thousands of people – both infected and healthy – who will demand treatment during an attack. A Government Accounting Office report concluded that hospitals do not have enough equipment such as ventilators, isolation beds and protective suits to handle an influx of infected patients. Only half of the hospitals surveyed in the study even conducted bio-terrorism response drills. Other studies have arrived at similarly dismal conclusions. Most hospitals lack basic equipment to handle even a small biological attack, and most communities do not have staffs of state and local public health officials that have been properly vaccinated and sufficiently trained workers to handle a biological attack.

The US also needs to develop sensors capable of detecting and identifying a disbursed biological agent. Most state and local hospitals rely on 'passive' surveillance to detect an outbreak. State and local officials are consigned to waiting for nurses, doctors and emergency technicians to report suspicious illnesses. Even when they do, timely reporting from public health officials – who often do not have the time or inclination to note trends in symptoms – may not be forthcoming. Infected victims might not show symptoms for up to 14 days after the attack, depending on the agent, and by that time the attack will have hit in full force. The Bush administration is supporting a number of important research initiatives to create chemical and biological detectors. It has put significant resources behind Project BioShield, a $6bn programme to enhance the development of sensitive detection devices and to encourage bio-defence research by the American pharmaceutical industry. While some biological agent detectors have been deployed in urban areas and in some transportation networks, sophisticated systems will probably not be deployable for five to ten years.

All in all, the US may not be any better off than it was on 11 September 2001 in terms of its capacity to respond to a major emergency. The administration's own internal assessment after the TOPOFF II exercise was damning, identifying many of the same critical deficiencies that plagued pre-11 September drills, including poor communications capability, a lack of interoperable systems, confusing command chains and inadequate training. Throw in the limited availability of medical supplies and the inadequate surge capacities at US hospitals, and a recipe for disaster in any US metropolis comes into view. The results of this exercise echo other external studies. One, commissioned by the Pentagon's Defense Threat Reduction Agency, was conducted immediately after the anthrax attacks in late 2001 by the Center for Strategic and International Studies (CSIS), a Washington DC-based think-tank. The CSIS study, based mainly on discussions with about 40 government and private experts on public health, national security and law enforcement, identified weaknesses in virtually every aspect of US bio-terror preparation and response. Although the study was unclassified, the Pentagon did not see fit to release parts of it until March 2004. Similarly, a June 2003 Council on Foreign Relations (CFR) report concluded that American emergency responders were 'drastically underfunded and dangerously unprepared'. The CFR Task Force urged DHS to cut red tape, streamline grant programmes and procedures, and establish national emergency standards. Reinforcing demands by the country's governors and mayors, the CFR report also urged a substantial increase in first-responder funding, detailing how current funding levels barely scratch the surface and yield a nearly $100bn shortfall in resources over the next five years.

The CFR's findings do not incorporate existing state and local assets and assume that the whole problem is Washington's responsibility. But this methodological skew also shows that a division of labour between federal and local capabilities has not been systematically worked out and that this failure has produced confusion in the resource debate. It remains unclear what the federal role should be for funding first responders. Washington is reluctant to allocate scarce resources to regular community policing and

Strategic Policy Issues

emergency medical services. Yet state officials, faced with depleted revenues and overburdened law enforcement and emergency personnel, would like the federal government to assume most of the burden. In any event, as of early 2004, the administration's efforts had not adequately addressed either the large funding deficiency or the problem of balancing federal, state and local responsibility. Indeed, in February 2004, Ridge admitted that as much as $8bn previously appropriated by Congress had not yet been distributed to state and local officials. While this delay is of course frustrating to local communities shouldering a high and unwarranted burden, the silver lining to the administration's slow approach may be an inadvertent opportunity to target authorised funds intelligently. Given the absence of a comprehensive risk or vulnerability assessment, Ridge might be applauded for his discipline but criticised for his sense of urgency.

Border and transportation security

US border and transportation security officials face a two-way challenge: preventing terrorists or weapons of mass destruction (WMD) from entering while also facilitating America's interaction with a fast-paced global economy. This means maintaining an open society with a porous membrane that seeks to filter out dangerous actors from the 80m visitors, 11m trucks and 2.5m rail cars, 30m automobiles and 7m cargo containers that enter the United States annually. Despite the inherent tensions involved in meeting this challenge, DHS's border activities can claim some measurable successes by virtue of several innovative programmes and strong leadership by Undersecretary of Border and Transportation Security Asa Hutchinson. But implementation and resources remain limited. For example, Congress has not provided enough money to help port authorities meet the mandate from the Maritime and Transportation Security Act to assess vulnerabilities in ports and vessels, and address the gaps. The US Coast Guard estimated the first year of the plan alone will cost $1.25bn ($7bn over ten years), yet the administration proposed no funding for port security and Congress added only $125m to the 2004 budget. At the current rate, the United States will finish assessing weaknesses in port and maritime security by the end of the decade without materially investing in additional security. The Coast Guard's Deepwater Project is another case in point. Designed to upgrade its fleet of Second World War-era cutters and increase maritime awareness along the country's borders and key ports, Deepwater remains substantially under-funded even on a 20-year timescale.

Customs security is critical to a nation that relies on international trade. DHS is advocating 'smart border' technologies to single out high-risk containers, trucks, automobiles or persons for inspection. Its Container

Security Initiative seeks to 'push back the border' and identify high-risk cargo overseas before it hits America's shores. These initiatives, while important, have not been complemented by sizeable increases in funding for manpower and technology. With as many as 7m containers passing through US ports annually, and concerns that al-Qaeda is targeting maritime systems for attack, the Customs and Border Protection Bureau has started a number of programmes to enhance the ability to detect and inspect suspicious cargo containers. But they are not getting substantial help from a cash-strapped international shipping industry. 'Smart' container technology to better secure and track cargo shipments in transit is available, but resisted by industry as an additional cost. Customs officials have received nuclear detection technologies, but are still hampered by limited or outdated information systems. Data from various shipping and commercial sources is now being collected, but analysis and full maritime domain awareness are far from thorough.

The Customs–Trade Partnership Against Terrorism (C-TPAT) is hailed as a breakthrough initiative. Developed in cooperation with major supply chain companies, this programme commits businesses to adhere voluntarily to certain standards and to provide the government access to data about personnel, practices and cargoes. In return, the government offers expedited inspections and easy access through border stations. Such 'fast lane' procedures offer a carrot to the private sector, but with more than 5,000 companies signed up, only 141 have been screened and approved for participation. But between major ports of entry, security is also receiving renewed attention. The US Border Patrol has ramped up its hiring and now has 9,800 agents covering 12,000km of land border, up from 3,600 agents a decade ago. Still, illegal border crossings occur hourly, and the backlog of illegal aliens in the country has not got any shorter.

Much of America's focus since 11 September naturally has been centred on airport security. The Transportation Security Administration (TSA) – benefited by better screeners, updated information systems and a raft of new technological investments – remains one of the few unequivocal structural achievements in homeland security. Still, numerous security failures emerged, and flights from Europe to the United States have been cancelled due to intelligence tips that they would be subject to attack. One of the open dirty secrets in the airport industry is that, despite spending tens of billions to screen passengers and personal baggage at major airports, air cargo on the same planes is rarely inspected and on many cargo flights is not inspected at all. To improve security and screening of travellers, DHS in January 2004 implemented the US Visitor and Immigrant Status Indicator Technology (VISIT) programme by which visitors have their photographs and fingerprints taken to confirm their identify and validate their entry into and exit from the United States. As of March 2004, more than 2m visitors had been documented. VISIT is in place in 130 airports and seaports, and is set to expand. Yet, few resources are available to go after those who do not leave and join the estimated 8m illegal aliens circulating inside the United States. The programme also has a gaping statutory hole, since visitors from 27 allied countries are exempt from participation. A number of potential terrorists have travelled to the United States from or via these countries.

Another new tool is the second-generation Computer Assisted Passenger Screening System, or CAPSS II. This system, scheduled to be implemented in late 2004, matches routine passenger information against government databases to pre-screen flight lists and identify 'high-risk' travellers. The TSA plans to collect this data from airlines to score passengers, and assign a colour code to passenger boarding passes. High-risk passengers with high-threat indicators could be barred from flying or subjected to intensive searches. DHS, however, has not yet satisfied its critics that this programme is cost-effective or that privacy and due process concerns are being addressed.

American intelligence agencies continue to believe that foreign terrorists are targeting transportation networks as the most likely venue for an attack. In November 2002, an attempted – and nearly successful – surface-to-air missile attack against an Israeli airliner exposed a new vulnerability of commercial airliners. Perimeter security at airports was bolstered following the attempt and lawmakers called for more funding for countermeasure research. Protecting the US commercial fleet with current technology is expensive – roughly $10bn – and neither the airline industry nor the government is willing to fund it. DHS is putting $60m towards countermeasure research, but the country may be years away from deploying an affordable comprehensive system. Other transportation networks, including the regional rail system and most urban light-rail lines, remain open to attack. More than 10m Americans use trains each day, and the US rail system includes nearly 225,000km of track and hundreds of commuter rail stations. Security measures, including more surveillance cameras and biological/chemical sensors have been deployed in anticipation of some form of WMD attack, but the Madrid bombings in March 2004 show how vulnerable most urban ground transportation networks are.

Intelligence

It has been noted that domestic al-Qaeda cells have little trouble coordinating with the global transnational terrorist network. Unfortunately, the same cannot be said for US domestic law enforcement and the wider US intelligence community. The ease with which the 11 September terrorists entered and travelled through the United States illuminated major fault lines within and between American intelligence and law-enforcement organs. For instance, two of the 11 September hijackers, previously identified by the CIA as terrorists, entered the United States, applied for visas, purchased airline tickets and used a credit card – all in their own name. A congressional inquiry looking into the attacks found that 'prior to September 11, the Intelligence Community was neither well organised nor equipped, and did not adequately adapt, to meet the challenge posed by global terrorists focused on targets within the domestic United States. Serious gaps existed between the collection coverage provided by US foreign and US domestic intelligence capabilities. The US foreign intelligence agencies paid inadequate attention to the potential for a domestic attack'. The report added that 'at home, the counterterrorism effort suffered from the lack of an effective domestic intelligence capability'. The report withheld judgement as to whether or not the FBI should perform domestic intelligence collection and analysis or whether a new agency was needed.

The Bush administration believes that the current intelligence and law enforcement structure is sufficient. The FBI continues to be the nation's domestic collection agency, and under the USA PATRIOT Act has greater authority to collect and act on information on suspected terrorists. The CIA retains primacy over foreign intelligence, strategic analysis and threat warnings. The administration established the Terrorism Threat Integration Center (TTIC) as an interagency analysis unit to bridge the gap between FBI and CIA. This move effectively pre-empted proposals to create a new entity that would have competed with the CIA's dominant role. DHS provides additional personnel for this new centre. Though it lacks authority and capacity for raw intelligence collection, there is still considerable congressional pressure to situate central responsibility for raw data collection and analysis with respect to domestic threats in the DHS. There is no consensus that the reforms taken to date are adequate. Many intelligence professionals believe the FBI is incapable of collecting and analysing domestic intelligence on foreign terrorist threats within the United States. There is a substantial basis for this assessment. The FBI has been an investigative agency, its agents trained and charged mainly to gather evidence to solve crimes after they have occurred. This 'prosecution first' mentality is not the best conditioning for identifying terrorist rings and preventing attacks. The FBI's analytic capabilities also are not designed to penetrate and identify terrorist networks. Its culture does not view analysts as integral to the FBI's mission. FBI Director Robert Mueller's attempts to modify this entrenched culture do not appear to have taken root.

Intelligence and law enforcement information sharing remains a challenge. Sharing information between two agencies as culturally distinct and historically competitive as the FBI and CIA does not come easy. It is unclear whether TTIC will be able to overcome the cultural and historical obstacles. TTIC remains dominated by the CIA. Its staffing and experience levels remain limited. Furthermore, while the CIA had attempted, with the creation of the Counterterrorism Center in the 1990s, to improve information flow between the foreign intelligence and domestic law-enforcement elements of government, 11 September revealed its basic failure. At some levels, the failings persist. The US government still has not produced a common terrorist database and watch list to assist consular, immigration and border patrol agents with some means of separating tourists from terrorists.

Intelligence sharing between the federal government and state and local authorities is limited. Improving federal to state/local information sharing has been tasked to Joint Terrorism Task Forces (JTTFs), sponsored by the Justice Department, which bring together local, state and federal authorities to share information on potential threats in major cities, and federal agencies have promised to accredit state officials for clearances. But non-federal investigators remain uncertain as to where they should send locally sourced information since both the JTTFs and DHS have a mandate to improve information flow to state authorities. Moreover, the multi-layered system of information sharing established by the TTIC will not provide real-time transmissions from federal to local officials or vice-versa. DHS has reacted to this criticism by announcing yet another information network.

Transatlantic security interdependence

It became clear very soon after 11 September that there was an organic connection between US and European homeland security: improved American homeland security would make the US less vulnerable and Europe a commensurately more attractive target, and vice-versa. Indeed, the targeting primacy of the US as Islam's 'far enemy', combined with the relative freedom of action afforded Islamists in Europe, made it most useful to al-Qaeda as a recruitment, planning and staging ground, rather than a direct target, before 11 September. Certainly following 11 September, Europe and the US were more secure than any other regions, owing to their superior counter-terrorism institutions and heightened alert towards transnational Islamist threats. Given the high political value of European targets, the fact that Europe was not hit until 30 months after 11 September suggests that, relatively speaking, it was not a soft target. Nevertheless, European jurisdictions – the UK most emphatically – have held that a major attack in Europe was a matter of 'when' rather than 'if'.

Madrid proved them ruefully correct. European security organisations – which are generally geared to act on emergent threats on the basis of current intelligence – may now have to move closer to the US vulnerability-based conception of homeland security, under which law-enforcement and intelligence agencies seek through preventive measures to minimise unspecified threats by denying terrorists access to territory and opportunities to act. Success in this enterprise is difficult to achieve under any circumstances, and has become more elusive as al-Qaeda has come to recruit from and operationally rely on local talent. In Europe, the homegrown pool appears to be getting richer. These circumstances paint a daunting picture of inchoate terrorist cells already in place.

The fact that Europe is now a target for Islamist terrorist attacks should not obscure its ongoing usefulness as a platform for attacks against the US, and certainly will not blind Washington to this reality. Although transatlantic law-enforcement and intelligence cooperation has become durably more robust since 11 September, European governments should expect more pressure from the US with respect to the pursuit and apprehension of suspected terrorists within Europe. Europe's proactive national law-enforcement and intelligence efforts as well as homeland-security measures are likely to become more vigorous and risk-averse. This could mean, for example, broader, possibly European Union-wide, implementation of security standards akin to those reflected in the USA PATRIOT Act, according police greater detention powers and intelligence agencies access to pooled immigration data, and better coordination of border security. Only two or three national European governments, most prominently Britain, have enacted laws comparable to the USA PATRIOT Act. But they are constrained in applying them – for instance, by detaining large numbers of terrorist suspects – by legitimate legal and political considerations that are more salient in Europe than the United States. Despite the domestic civil-libertarian condemnation of the British government's power to detain foreign terrorist suspects indefinitely, it has been applied to fewer than 20 people.

Nevertheless, European perceptions of the terrorist threat have broadly converged with American ones. The UK in particular, perhaps owing to its singularly close strategic alignment with the US, is hypersensitive to threats of WMD or so-called 'weapons of mass disruption' such as radiological dispersal devices, or 'dirty bombs'. It has mobilised the military to guard against risks from surface-to-air missiles. The UK government emphasises civil defence and national resilience, having simulated a chemical attack in central London to sharpen its preparedness. In light of transnational Islamist terrorists' preference for mass casualties, British law-enforcement agencies are more inclined than they were when the Irish Republican Army (IRA) was the main terrorist adversary to arrest suspects preventively, as are authorities elsewhere in Europe – France in particular. Since the Madrid bombings, British authorities have reiterated that a terrorist attack in the UK is 'inevitable'. They are probably as ready to deal with such an attack as any jurisdiction in Europe, having emphasised and bolstered civil defence and national resiliency since 11 September.

Yet local and regional British officials – through the Emergency Planning Society – have criticised the UK's level of civil-defence preparedness,

Strategic Policy Issues

noting that its first responders could handle a limited IRA-style operation but not a no-warning mass-casualty attack on the order of the Madrid bombings. Although the UK's civil-defence budget has increased by 35% over pre-2001 levels, it is still only £35m per annum. Comprehensive preventive means do not appear to be in place to compensate for any first-response deficiencies. For instance, the UK's 17,700km, 2,500-station rail network, which is used by five million people a day, is vulnerable. Metal detectors and baggage scanners are used only on the Eurostar service running between London and Brussels and London and Paris. Universal airport-style security checks would be impractical and forbiddingly expensive. Notwithstanding a generally more pronounced emphasis on homeland security in the United States, security for land-based transportation there before the Madrid attacks did not appear to be markedly better than Europe's. This reveals a more general truth: while the European threat-based and intelligence-driven approach to counter-terrorism is somewhat at odds with the American vulnerability-based approach, American invulnerability remains only an aspiration.

Still a non-strategic enterprise

Homeland security is not a government function that can be easily stuffed into a single bureaucratic box. In many respects, both Ridge's title and organisation are misnamed. Many other skill sets contribute to an aggregate national capacity to thwart catastrophic terrorism. Homeland security is a composite of many capabilities, including diplomacy, financial controls, intelligence, law enforcement, public health and military muscle. By and large, the federal agencies that provide these capabilities are beyond Ridge's control. In other words, homeland security has yet to be fully integrated into the United States' national security strategy. While the DHS has made progress in harnessing the collective efforts of many heretofore disparate pieces of a stove-piped structure, much more needs to be done. Most of the attention has been deflected to the DHS. But the DHS is a fledgling institution, and its mere creation did not guarantee that the synergies sought among under-resourced constituent institutions – like the Immigration and Naturalization Service and the Coast Guard – would automatically be realised. There remains a need for focused reform and improvement within these constituent institutions and, beyond that, a focused, cohesive and proactive strategy, intelligence reform, greater cooperation from the Defense Department and sustained attention to institutionalising international cooperation and coordination.

The Americas

Much as they did during the previous year, the United States' foreign-policy travails elsewhere crowded out its engagement in its own hemisphere in 2003–04. The increasingly problematic state-building effort in Iraq, combined with the demands of countering transnational Islamic terrorism and containing the proliferation of weapons of mass destruction, preoccupied Washington and barred any serious reinvigoration of the hemispheric trade agenda that President George W. Bush had counted as a key element of US foreign policy before 11 September 2001. A reasonably stable US economy and relatively buoyant US stock indices afforded the Bush administration the freedom to be somewhat relaxed on global economic issues. The fifth ministerial meeting of the World Trade Organisation in Cancún, Mexico in September 2003 produced no agreement, thus spreading pessimism about the future of global and regional trade negotiations. What it did yield was a unified position between Brazil and Argentina against the US and EU's intentions to impose their views on WTO members – particularly those in the developing world. American and European expectations of easy access to the markets of developing countries, at least through multilateral arrangements, were discouraged, and favourable conditions were created for the emergence of a durable consensus among developing countries with common interests in agriculture. It appeared that the United States' strategic distractions outside the hemisphere were encouraging a new assertiveness of regional powers within it. But Brazil's new political leadership continued to be less radical than originally feared, and Argentina remained constrained by its substantial financial dependence on the International Monetary Fund.

If there was a looming geopolitical crisis closer to home that had any potential to compete with Iraq and Afghanistan for Washington's attention, it involved Venezuela. There President Hugo Chávez continued to resist democratic change, flirted with anti-American partnerships with Cuba and Colombian rebels, and imperilled a paramount US interest – diversifying oil supplies – by allowing his country's production capacity to degrade. Even so, as of April 2004, ongoing legal and political processes that could lead to a salutary change of regime in Venezuela had yet to play out. Thanks to Chávez's recklessness, domestic economically based tensions in Bolivia that had arisen to threaten its political stability, and the resurgence of the Shining Path guerrilla movement and the ineffectual government of President Alejandro Toledo in Peru, Colombia may, by default, be the most successful government in the Northern Andes. While the US maintained

Map The Americas

close operational involvement in counter-narcotics and counterinsurgency in Colombia, in 2003–04 the Colombian government itself carried the labouring oar in repelling the Revolutionary Armed Forces of Colombia. Terrorist attacks decreased from 1,645 in 2002 to 850 in 2003. Some 6,967 suspected leftist rebels were arrested in 2003, an increase of 85% over the previous year.

An armed uprising in Haiti against the presidency of populist priest Jean-Bertrand Aristide did force the US to divert its attention to crisis management in its own backyard in February 2004. Aristide had been democratically elected in 1990, overthrown by a military coup in September 1991, restored to power via a US-led intervention in 1994 and re-elected by a dubious 90% majority in 2000. But that mandate was highly suspect, and Aristide had shaped up as a corrupt and incompetent leader in a country that suffered chronic poverty. Fearing that rebels would overrun the Haitian capital Port-au-Prince and trigger mass bloodshed, Washington urged Aristide to leave the country and arranged for his comfortable exile to the Central African Republic, though he subsequently decamped to Jamaica and has accused the US of forcing his exile. By Resolution 1529, the UN Security Council on 29 February authorised the three-month deployment of a Multinational Interim Force to Haiti. Starting on 1 March, the US sent nearly 2,000 troops, France more than 800, Canada over 400 and Chile over 300 to establish security. Looting, sporadic violence between anti- and pro-Aristide Haitian factions and between Haitians and peacekeepers, and large-scale humanitarian deprivation persisted. Within a few days, however, the insurgents, led by Guy Philippe, proved amenable to standing down in deference to Interim President Boniface Alexandre and Interim Prime Minister Gérard Latortue, pending new parliamentary and presidential elections scheduled for 2005. In a visit to Haiti on 5 April, US Secretary of State Colin Powell announced US pledges of $55 million for emergency aid to Haiti, and $9m to the Organization of American States for promoting democratic practices.

With the situation in Haiti thus contained, Washington quickly refocused on military deployments farther afield and counter terrorism. As Shi'ite and Sunni insurgencies coalesced in Iraq, warlordism persisted and the hunt for Osama bin Laden and his inner circle was frustrated in and around Afghanistan, and the transnational Islamic terrorist movement increasingly targeted close US allies, the problems in these areas were only becoming more acute. More broadly, Bush's heightening political vulnerability over Iraq, serious public controversy over the Bush administration's alertness to terrorist threats before 11 September and fundamental disagreements between the two main US political parties about Bush's grand strategy held out a real possibility of a significant shift in the tone, if not the substance, of US foreign policy starting in January 2005.

The United States: Four Wars

On 1 May 2003 President George W. Bush alighted, in full flight suit, from a S-3B *Viking* jet that had just landed on the aircraft carrier USS *Abraham Lincoln*. Stepping in front of a banner emblazoned with the words 'Mission Accomplished', Bush told cheering sailors that 'Major combat operations in Iraq have ended'. Some nine months later, the Washington headquarters for the seemingly moribund presidential campaign of Senator John F. Kerry received a phone call from Jim Rassman, a registered Republican, retired deputy sheriff and former Green Beret. Rassman told the receptionist that in 1969 Navy Lieutenant Kerry, himself wounded and under fire, had saved Rassman's life by pulling him from the Bay Hap River in Vietnam. A few days after the phone call Rassman and Kerry embraced onstage at a campaign rally. The event dramatised, if it did not cause, Kerry's rebound to victory in Iowa's presidential caucuses and the subsequent Democratic primary contests.

These two tableaux, both stage-managed for all they were worth, say something basic, and perhaps surprising, about American politics and society. Like many nations, the United States was forged in war; but very few advanced democracies share the American culture's ongoing warrior ethos. What might come as a surprise is that, even in a culture where the two major presidential candidates rely on such similar martial imagery, this ethos causes more polarity than unity.

In its election year of 2004, the United States was embroiled in the continuing trauma and controversy of no fewer than four wars, present and past. First, there was the 'war on terrorism'. This phrase provoked some semantic arguments which reflected, in turn, some strategic confusion; yet it would be foolish to deny that America was at war, since the war was declared by Osama bin Laden years before George W. Bush. Second, there was the unfinished war in Iraq: a central campaign in the war against terrorism, according to Bush and his supporters; a costly and even counterproductive diversion, according to many of his critics. Third, the war that ended with America's defeat in Vietnam haunted American politics three decades later. Fourth and finally, the residues of an American civil war that ended 140 years ago were discernable in the 'Red State/Blue State' divide on the electoral map, the clash of a conservative Texan and a Massachusetts liberal, as well as the religious, cultural and racial antagonisms roiling the surface of US society.

Terror recrimination

The solidarity and overwhelming support for Bush that followed the attacks of 11 September lasted longer than might have been expected. Early anger was stoked among Democrats by what they considered Bush's exploitation of that solidarity to enact his signature programme of tax cuts. Later, the diplomacy and conduct of the Iraq war became controversial. But serious recriminations about the administration's response to terrorism itself broke out only in the third week of March 2004, with a book and public testimony from Richard Clarke, a career public servant who was counter-terrorism coordinator for Bush's as well as Clinton's National Security Council (a position he still held on 11 September). Clarke's criticisms of the Bush White House had two strands. First, the administration did not respond to his own pleas to address the al-Qaeda threat more urgently in its first seven months in office. Second, its post-attack strategy went awry: the proper self-defensive war to depose bin Laden's Taliban protectors in Afghanistan was followed by the illogical and counter-strategic opening of a second front in Iraq. The predictable consequence, according to Clarke, was to divert resources and attention towards destroying an enemy that was vicious but well contained and, in any event, unconnected to al-Qaeda, meanwhile ensuring the recruitment of countless new jihadists to anti-American terrorism.

The White House and other Republican leaders worked furiously to undermine Clarke's credibility and reputation. This was an odd overreaction, given that the heart of Clarke's critique had almost nothing to do with disputed facts. It was really an argument about strategic philosophy. That there were plenty of warnings about al-Qaeda's general intentions was beyond serious dispute. But the Bush team nonetheless could have argued that a completely different strategic context made it reasonable to give priority to other issues. Hence, neither Bush nor Clinton really could have been expected to invade Afghanistan before the murder of some 3,000 Americans on 11 September 2001 made such a war politically conceivable. Clarke himself stopped short of saying that 11 September could have been prevented by any single initiative. What he did say, however, was that the Clinton administration had managed to thwart al-Qaeda's intentions to stage similar outrages on New Year's Eve 1999, largely because Clinton and his top aides were seized of the matter, responding to intelligence chatter by 'shaking the tree' of various agencies for enough attention and information to stop the terrorists. Regarding Iraq, Clarke complained that Bush had diverted money, special-operations forces, intelligence and general attention from destroying al-Qaeda abroad and defending against it at home into precisely the war that bin Laden wanted America to fight – one that confirmed the jihadists' inflammatory image of a Christian Crusader in the Arab Middle East.

Fair or unfair, these criticisms highlight something distinctive about Bush foreign policy that its architects and proponents themselves have been keen to underscore. Bush and his lieutenants had limited patience for

The Americas

containment, partial solutions and messy compromise. In summer 2001, receiving increasingly panicky intelligence briefings on al-Qaeda from Director of Central Intelligence George Tenet, President Bush said he was 'tired of swatting at flies' and wanted a plan to destroy the terrorist enemy. But the plan only reached his desk after the 11 September hijackings, and when it arrived it wasn't significantly different from what Clarke and his colleagues had ready as the new administration took office. Meanwhile, Bush's foreign-policy team was focused on the 'strategic' challenges of missile defence and a rising China. There was palpable disdain for the 'Clintonite' agenda of so-called 'transnational threats' – germs, global warming and stateless terrorists. 11 September did not fundamentally alter the Bush team's state-centric worldview, now focused on an 'axis' of evil states for whom terrorist networks like al-Qaeda represented another way of striking at the West in general, the US in particular.

This does not mean that Bush officials were oblivious to the social, political and religious pathologies that were fuelling radical Islamist hatreds. Nor did the decision to drive Saddam Hussein from power rely solely on alleged WMD programmes and disputed operational links between his regime and bin Laden's terrorist network. The rationale was, in a basic sense, offensive as well as defensive; it was an audacious effort to recast the playing field of pan-Islamic society by replacing a genocidal dictator with the Arab Middle East's first working democracy. To those who complained that evil could not always be subdued, and that democracy could rarely be implanted by military force, the White House could reply: what was the alternative to changing a poisonous Arab–Islamic status quo within a timeframe that might offer even the prospect of safety to Americans and Westerners?

It was hardly a stretch to call Saddam's regime evil, just as it was hard to believe that the Iraqi people would not recognise the good intentions of their American liberators. Yet at least a growing minority of Iraqis do not. America's conservative and neo-conservative leadership may be blinded to this reality by the conviction that to acknowledge any alternative judgements about good and evil is to tread into moral relativism and appeasement. In America's historical narrative, the lessons of Munich tend to resonate more than those of Vietnam. Related to this sometimes blinding moral clarity is the characteristically American insistence that where perpetrators of evil are also victims of injustice, the sequence of response must be to defeat the evil before addressing the injustice. Hence, the pleas of Bush's closest foreign ally, UK Prime Minister Tony Blair, to give the Israel–Palestine peace process as much attention as Iraq, were bound to be disappointed at least through the American election year. Bush recognised, and seemed sincerely to lament, the suffering and humiliation of Palestinians under Israeli occupation. Yet, so long as the body parts of innocent Jews were being blasted by suicide bombers along Israeli streets, 'moral clarity' appeared to trump America's strategic interest in pressing for a settlement. In an American body politic that identified intimately with Israeli society   in Omaha as much as in New York, among Democrats as well as Republicans – there would be few recriminations about the failure to lean on Jerusalem.

Mission in progress?

Iraq was another matter. Americans in general may have seemed remarkably unperturbed as the main casus belli – Iraq's refusal to give up nuclear, biological and chemical weapons programmes – was undermined post-war by some astonishing non-discoveries. Through summer and autumn, as coalition troops and the 'Iraq Survey Group' failed to find evidence of WMD, expert opinion came increasingly to the view that Saddam in the last years of his rule did not have either the weapons or active WMD programmes. American public opinion still generally favoured the war as the right thing to do. Yet at least one tracking poll shows that a sharp drop in Bush's public approval ratings coincided with the remarks of David Kay, who had just resigned as head of the Survey Group, and who told a congressional committee that he had come to the conclusion that, at the time of the US invasion, Iraq had no active programme to develop WMD.

In its defence, the Bush administration correctly noted that it had not been alone in claiming that Iraq was developing these weapons. The assessment was general: it included the conclusions of the UN Special Commission (UNSCOM), the Clinton administration, independent experts and the intelligence communities of nations that supported the war as well as those that opposed it. The assessment was based on the fact that the Iraqis had ambitious chemical, biological and nuclear programmes before the first Gulf War, that they clearly made an effort to continue them after the war and that they systematically lied about what was going on through the whole UNSCOM period (1991–98). The assessment also relied to a greater or lesser extent on the reasonable proposition that if they were lying so systematically they must have had something to lie about. Finally, there was a defensible inference that only active WMD programmes could explain Saddam's resistance to the UN Monitoring, Inspection and Verification Commission (UNMOVIC) and International Atomic Energy Agency (IAEA) inspections in late 2002 and early 2003 on pain of imminent coercive regime change.

Still, the missing WMD were a problem for the Bush administration that extended well beyond domestic politics. The credibility of future American appeals for preventive military action against WMD proliferators was likely to suffer. Though there had been general agreement that Iraq was violating its disarmament commitments, only the US, and perhaps the UK,

The Americas

considered the threat to be so urgent as to demand war before the summer. In the short period of the UNMOVIC and IAEA inspections, the inspectors issued reports that look, in retrospect, to have been more accurate than the intelligence agencies' assessments. Chief Inspector Hans Blix later would write that roughly one month before the war it started to dawn on him that Iraq might indeed be clean of WMD. But for top US officials, in the absence of full transparency on the part of the Iraqi leadership, the notion of disarmament by UN inspection was not going to be an option.

The US intelligence community also felt that its methodology had been overridden in the rush to war. The CIA's contribution to National Intelligence Estimates confirmed the judgement that Iraq possessed chemical and biological weapons, and was pursuing a nuclear capability. But its analysts were angry at what they considered to be disregard for their stipulations of uncertainty, and unprofessional 'cherry picking' of bits of intelligence that supported a preconceived case for war. They were particularly sceptical about the product of some human intelligence sources linked to Iraqi exiles, under the umbrella of Ahmed Chalabi's Iraqi National Congress, who were close to hardliners in the Bush White House and Pentagon, as well as conservative Washington think-tanks.

Bad blood between neo-conservatives and the US intelligence community has a 30-year history. Indeed, the intellectual embryo of neo-conservatism was arguably the 'Team B' of Cold War intellectuals appointed during the Ford administration to second-guess the CIA's allegedly complacent estimates of Soviet intentions and capabilities. As it turned out, for the 1970s Soviet threat as for twenty-first century Iraqi WMD, the CIA erred on the alarmist rather than the complacent side. Bad blood got worse in summer 2003, after retired US diplomat Joseph Wilson, who had been sent to Niger to check on a report of Iraq trying to purchase 'yellow-cake' uranium, wrote a *New York Times* op-ed complaining that the Bush administration had simply ignored his negative findings. To retaliate, a Bush administration official apparently leaked to a Washington newspaper columnist that Wilson's wife, Valerie Plame, was an undercover CIA operative. This leak – career-altering for Plame if not life-threatening to some of her foreign contacts – was also potentially a criminal act. Tenet, whose baggage included being a Clinton administration holdover as well as the 11 September and Iraqi WMD intelligence performances, was now squeezed between a resentful agency and a president who was known for a rigorous concept of loyalty running in both directions. Tenet requested a criminal investigation, which was continuing in April 2004.

Another species of intelligence failure writ large was revealed in the stunning inadequacy of foresight and planning for how to maintain security in Iraq after Saddam's fall. Again there were plenty of warnings, from outside experts and a State Department planning group, not to mention common sense. By winning the war quickly, the modest number of troops seemed to vindicate Defense Secretary Donald Rumsfeld's vision of transforming the US military into light, highly mobile and network-centric strike forces. Yet they were inadequate for keeping peace in a seething society that had had its despotic lid blown off – and were certainly inadequate for the arduous long-term task of state-building. Pentagon planners somehow expected that Saddam's regime could be surgically removed, while state institutions and Iraqi society would remain standing. What made this miscalculation particularly worrying was that, even assuming perfect planning, unlimited troops and abundant resources – and even given continued gratitude and progressive instincts in a majority of Iraq's population – there had always been salient Lebanon and Somalia scenarios. Islamic terrorists and Baathist insurgents were well aware that the 1983 suicide truck bombings of US marine barracks as well as French paratroopers in Beirut had convinced the Reagan administration promptly to withdraw. It was also not lost on them that US casualties in 1993 in an optional intervention in Somalia had hastened the American departure from that country, which remains a failed state.

The Bush administration, of course, had too much invested in Iraq to liquidate its position in the same way. And Bush's critics generally agreed with his supporters that premature withdrawal would constitute a triumph and red flag to jihadists around the globe, not to mention a tragedy for the Iraqi people. But the question of Americans' political burn point remained. Americans, to the dismay of their foreign partners, are not highly legalistic about the resort to war, nor are they intolerant of US military casualties, if they are convinced that it is the right thing to do, is in the national interest and will be successful. Saddam's cruelties, likely to be revisited in hideous detail when he went on trial, would lend credit to the argument that the war was a good deed. However, if it turned out to be only a good deed – if its strategic rationales became more and more suspect – then Americans could find themselves mired in what amounted to the most difficult and costly humanitarian intervention in history. There is no historical record to tell us how durable popular patience, under these circumstances, would remain. The closest parallels are the NATO interventions in Bosnia and Kosovo – but in those places the lion's share of post-war peacekeeping, generally welcomed by the Balkan peoples, was shouldered by America's allies. In Iraq, allies were in short supply.

Visible American success in Iraq was key to the war's strategic – as opposed to humanitarian – payoff. While it was hard to imagine that Iraq's people could find themselves worse off than they were under Saddam's police state, the US needed more than that: a stable and progressive democracy. Some progress was evident: rising salaries, especially among professionals; a vibrant press and open political scene; even hopes that the Shiite, Kurdish and Sunni communities were groping towards a viable constitutional arrangement. But the security situation, one year after the war, was grim. On 31 March 2004, Falluja, in the heart of the 'Sunni triangle', was the scene of the kind of horror that Americans do not want to contemplate. First, came the death-by-bombing of five US soldiers. Then, four civilian security contractors were shot, burned and mutilated Mogadishu-style by a mob of men and boys. The commanders of US troops deployed close by decided that prudence required their non-intervention in a grisly – and televised – ritual that included beating burnt corpses and stringing what remained of them from a nearby bridge.

With formal sovereignty devolving to an interim Iraqi government by 30 June, the US occupation authority was to be converted into the world's biggest American embassy. The US electoral calendar permitted no delay, but American troops would have to remain for years. In the best of cases, this would strain military morale and readiness. The worst case, suggested in the rage of Falluja, was that the new Iraq might collapse into state failure around them.

Vietnam flashback

There is no obvious precedent in recent American history for the polarising effects on the nation of George W. Bush. Richard Nixon had always aroused strong negative emotions, but mainly among liberal elites, who recalled his role in McCarthy-era demagoguery, and could not quite believe that he had returned from double defeat in the US presidential and then California gubernatorial campaigns. Clinton too was despised, this time by many conservatives, yet his overall public approval ratings remained high until he left office. Bush is different. To a good 40% of American voters he is a hero. Another 40% distrust or despise him, according to opinion polls. The level of anger towards the president became evident in the dynamics of the Democratic primary contests to challenge him in the November 2004 election. Howard Dean, a former governor of Vermont and family practice physician with a record of conservatism on fiscal issues and moderation on most others, became the early frontrunner with a rhetoric of straight talk and sharp disdain for Bush. He channelled the ire of a great many Democrats who were riled not only at Bush but also at a Democratic Party establishment that had allowed itself to be rolled by the Republicans on domestic issues and had, in many cases, at least nominally supported military action in Iraq. Most Democratic primary voters stand to the left of their party leadership on national security issues, especially in the first caucus state of Iowa, which retains some of the outlook of the pacifist religious communities that settled it in the nineteenth century.

It turned out, however, that Democratic primary voters did not care if candidates had been ambivalent about the war or even supported it. All they wanted was to get rid of Bush, and they were looking for the candidate that they considered most 'electable'. Howard Dean, by this standard, did not make the short list, which quickly came down to Senators John Edwards of North Carolina and John Kerry of Massachusetts. Edwards was a loquacious, telegenic millionaire trial lawyer with Clinton-esque political talents, an engaging, optimistic style and a compelling campaign narrative of 'two Americas' – one wealthy and indulged by the national leadership, one struggling through daily life. Despite his obvious talents, Edwards was seen as relatively inexperienced, having served only a single term in the Senate after his lucrative legal career.

What Edwards particularly lacked was military experience. So primary voters turned to the man who had started off as the perceived frontrunner, despite a reputation as a haughty and somewhat stilted legislator. Kerry's biography became his campaign platform, because he happened to be a highly decorated Vietnam war veteran – having earned, among other medals, a Silver Star for gallantry while commanding a US Navy patrol boat. His taunting challenge to President Bush was that he could tell him 'something about aircraft carriers for real'. Republicans endeavoured to tie Kerry's liberal Senate voting record to the fact that he had become famous immediately after his Navy service as a leader of 'Vietnam Veterans Against the War'. This was another example, they said, of his characteristic 'flip-flopping' and trying to have it both ways on the issues. Democrats countered that it was perfectly consistent to fight honourably in your country's war and still oppose it as a matter of policy when you came home. They counter-attacked by encouraging news organisations to revisit an old controversy about whether the young George W. Bush had actually completed his stint in the Texas Air National Guard – a form of service that in any case was widely recognised in the Vietnam era as a way of avoiding the wartime draft without the stigma that attached, at least in conservative circles, to conscientious-objector status or an extended vacation in Canada.

Civil disunion

That old arguments about the war in Vietnam could arouse such bitterness in 2004 was surreal. In part, the emphasis on Kerry's military service was meant to inoculate the candidate against the huge polling disadvantage that Democrats suffer against Republicans on national security issues. It didn't matter for Clinton, who also avoided the Vietnam draft but nonetheless soundly defeated Bush's father, a US Navy bomber pilot in the Second World War. But in the age of insecurity ushered in by 11 September, and against a Republican incumbent who repeatedly styled himself as a 'war president', the Democrats' structural disadvantage was expected to matter again.

In fact, the inoculation was meant to go further. The phrase 'Massachusetts liberal' was spoken of almost as a disqualification for the presidency. One could even dispense with the word 'liberal' – 'Massachusetts' said enough. Since the assassination of John F. Kennedy (another war hero from Massachusetts), no Democrat has reached the White House who did not grow up in the South. The American civil war ended in 1865, but its resentments and central issue – the status of black Americans – were unresolved 100 years later. In 1964, upon signing the civil rights act that did most to effect their full citizenship, President Lyndon B. Johnson, a Texas Democrat, lamented to an aide that he had probably 'lost the South' to his party for a generation. He was wrong only in not being sufficiently pessimistic. The subsequent realignment handing the once solidly Democratic South to the Republicans has been inexorable. The more recent development is that it has been matched by a solid Democratic grip on urban coastal states such as New York and California and, even more significantly, wealthy suburban states such as New Jersey. And the fiercest battle grounds of the antebellum struggle between 'Slave South' and 'Free North' – such as the Missouri territory – are among the states most up for grabs in 2004.

Race has not vanished as an issue, but it is no longer the most salient one. More important, but just as atavistic, are culture, religion and 'values'. Nearly 80 years after Clarence Darrow savaged creationism in the Scopes 'monkey' trial, the assumption that Darwinian evolution will be taught as established science can no longer be taken for granted in many American public school systems. Mel Gibson's controversial film, *The Passion of the Christ*, denounced as anti-Semitic in its interpretation and pornographic in its violence, was hugely successful in cinemas across the US. Tim LeHaye and Jerry B. Jenkins's 'Left Behind' novels – which interpret the Book of Revelation as prophesying a 'tribulation' during which the Antichrist establishes a worldwide government as head of the UN and must then be apocalyptically unseated by Jesus with the help of Jews converted to evangelical Christianity – have sold 40 million copies, outpacing John Grisham and rivalling J.K. Rowling. Matters of national security are another part of this cultural divide. Republicans derive huge political benefit from the heavy patriotism of southern and rural communities. This was exemplified in late March 2004, when Senator Zell Miller, an old-line southern Democrat who rivals most Republicans in his support for President Bush, fiercely denounced Clarke's criticisms of the Bush White House. 'It's obvious to me that this country is rapidly dividing itself into two camps – the wimps and the warriors', Miller said. 'The ones who want to argue and assess and appease, and the ones who want to carry this fight to our enemies and kill them before they kill us'.

Thus, when John Kerry made a point of campaigning with his 'band of brothers' – paunchy Vietnam veterans showing their late middle age – the subtext was not so much that he was a hero but that he was a 'real' American. The appeal certainly made sense insofar as the secular and socially liberal half of American society is every bit as determined to shape that society as the Religious Right. Abortion rights are, to most Americans, sacrosanct. When the US Supreme Court struck down a Texas law that made sodomy a criminal offence, conservative commentators lamented that it had logically paved the way for demands for gay marriage. They were right: the gay marriage movement was boosted by a Massachusetts Supreme Court ruling that equal rights protections in the state constitution demanded it, and by a San Francisco mayor who started handing out (largely symbolic) marriage licenses to same-sex couples. Bush asked Congress for an amendment to the US constitution banning the possibility, but he was very unlikely to get it; it was far more probable that individual states gradually would legitimise the practice, and that most Americans would come to accept it.

America was at a tipping point, but it was difficult to predict which way it would tip. In its increasingly strong hold on the judiciary, its occupancy of the White House and its reliable votes in both houses of Congress, a quite radical strain of US conservatism was arguably more powerful than at any time in modern US history. President Bush had successfully pushed through a series of very large tax cuts. The consequences for America's fiscal future were ominous, yet it was hard to see how even a President Kerry could reverse them in what was likely to remain a Republican House of Representatives and Senate. The powerful feeling of national insecurity was also likely to help the Republicans, though Richard Clarke's testimony and the unsettled situation of Iraq injected a degree of uncertainty into that assumption.

On most domestic issues, however, a significant majority of the American electorate told pollsters that they preferred Democratic to Republican positions. The passage of a hugely expensive prescription drug benefit for senior citizens had backfired politically on the president; even most elderly voters objected to its gimmicky cost estimates, and certainly to such provisions as the one prohibiting the federal government from bargaining with drug companies for lower prices. Bush was in some trouble with his conservative base, which liked his tax cuts but objected to the resulting federal budget deficit. Conservatives also objected to his move to provide new protections and opportunities for the millions of illegal immigrants in the US, most of them Hispanic. Here too was an uncertain tipping point. Both political parties could cite evidence that demographic trends would strengthen their position. For example, Republican strategists had fervent hopes that Mexican–American Catholics were natural conservatives. Democratic strategists could point to more immediate evidence that the Mexican influx was nudging once-safe Republican states such as New Mexico and Arizona towards the Democrats. The only safe conclusion was that here was yet another historical conflict – the Mexican–American War of 1846–1848 – with results yet to be determined.

The Americas

Brazil and Argentina: Tough on Trade

In 2003–04, Brazil and Argentina devoted intense attention to global and regional trade negotiations. The central event was the fifth ministerial meeting of the World Trade Organisation (WTO) in Cancún, Mexico, which reflected the disposition of both countries to act in a concerted way. The 12–14 September 2003 meeting, which included 148 countries, ended ahead of schedule without yielding an agreement, thus spreading pessimism about the future of global and regional trade negotiations. Nevertheless, both Brazil and Argentina left the meeting with a sense of victory. The two countries could not claim any important substantive accomplishment, such as reductions in heavy agricultural subsidies by the United States, European Union (EU) and Japan. Yet they could celebrate the establishment of a unified position against the US and EU's intentions to impose their views on the WTO members. American and European expectations of easy access to the markets of developing countries, at least through multilateral arrangements, were discouraged, and favourable conditions were created for the emergence of a durable consensus among developing countries with common interests in agriculture.

Led by Brazil, China and India, 22 developing countries also formed a surprisingly cohesive negotiating bloc – the 'G-20+' – to pressure for agricultural reform consistent with the liberalisation objectives of the 'Doha Development Agenda'. The group accounted for nearly 60% of the world's total population and 22% of the world's agricultural GDP. It included Argentina, Bolivia, Chile, Colombia, Costa Rica, Ecuador, Egypt, El Salvador, Guatemala, Indonesia, Mexico, Nigeria, Pakistan, Paraguay, Peru, Philippines, Senegal, South Africa, Thailand, Turkey and Venezuela. From a North–South global perspective, though, the Cancún meeting was a disaster with consequences that now threaten the WTO's basic objectives. Two years earlier, the fourth WTO Ministerial Conference in Doha, Qatar had produced an optimistic and ambitious agenda – to be implemented by January 2005 and to include agriculture, goods, services and trade rules – that paid special attention to the needs of developing countries. The Doha Declaration promised that 'particularly in the light of the global economic slowdown, to maintain the process of reform and liberalization of trade policies, thus ensuring that the system plays its full part in promoting recovery, growth and development' and pledged 'to reject the use of protectionism'. The interruption of the negotiations in Cancún has endangered the fulfilment of these promises.

When the Cancún meeting collapsed, US Trade Representative Robert Zoellick criticised the G-20+ and impugned the 'won't do' countries for the failure of the meeting, saying that their obstructionism perversely thwarted countries that actually would have cut agricultural subsidies and tariffs and thus triggered reform of farm policy in developed nations. Zoellick also specifically blamed Brazil, India and Egypt for having resorted to the 'rhetoric of resistance' to divert attention from their own high trade barriers. According to Zoellick, the United States' average bound agricultural tariff is 12%, India's is 112%, Egypt's 62% and Brazil's 37%. Finally, he announced that the United States would seek to promote free trade by stimulating bilateral and regional trade initiatives. Brazilian Foreign Relations Minister Celso Amorim countered that the G-20+ countries aligned together for essentially pragmatic reasons. Amorim stressed that the bulk of their suggestions were similar to positions previously defended by the US in the WTO Agriculture Committee. He underscored the relevance of the G-20+ in defending the Doha agenda and lamented that 'other participants' had chosen to blame the group 'for tactical reasons'. For him, the Cancún failure was caused by difficulties that had persisted since the preparatory phase in Geneva and by the 'arrogant way that developed countries addressed legitimate concerns of developing countries'. These centred on agriculture – the cotton trade in particular – and the so-called Singapore issues: investment; competition policy; trade facilitation; and transparency in governmental procurements. Argentine Foreign Trade Representative Alfredo Vicente Chiaradia echoed these sentiments. Battle lines, then, were drawn between the developed and developing worlds.

Genesis of failure

Disagreement over agriculture policies has long impaired the prospects for trade liberalisation between developed and developing countries. According to the WTO, agricultural subsidies extended to domestic producers by the EU, Japan and the United States in 1999 totalled $91 billion, $32bn and $74bn, respectively. These subsidies not only curb access to the markets of developed countries, they also exert downward pressure on world prices, harming the sectors in which developing countries have a comparative advantage.

A stalemate began to take shape as early as February 2003 over the negotiation modalities. In response to the Doha mandate and based on proposals submitted by WTO country members, Chairman of the WTO Committee on Agriculture Stuart Harbinson presented his proposal for the First Draft of Modalities. Harbinson proposed targets defined along the three pillars of agriculture negotiation: market access; export competition; and domestic support. But whereas the United States and the Cairns Group – constituted in 1986 and comprising 17 agricultural export countries that favour trade liberalisation – considered Harbinson's proposal too timid, the European Community and Japan considered it too ambitious and unbalanced. On 13 August 2003, the United States and the EU submitted a

The Americas

joint proposal, still in the form of a framework document, and not – as originally envisaged – a modalities document. As such, the proposal did not establish numerical targets, which attracted criticism from the developing countries. For these countries, the proposal was merely a manoeuvre to preserve American and European domestic agricultural policies (in particular, the 2002 US Farm Bill and the European Agenda 2000 and 2003 Common Agricultural Policy Reform).

Despite being relatively unified in their complaints against developed countries' subsidies, developing countries have rarely defended common positions in trade negotiations. In the run-up to Cancún, however, some of the most important developing countries presented a unified and consistent response. Replying to the US–EU proposal, on 20 August 2003, Brazil and Argentina joined 14 other developing countries and submitted their own joint framework proposal. With the subsequent enlistment of six other developing countries, the G-20+ thus coalesced. On 24 August, Chairman of the WTO General Council Carlos Pérez del Castillo released the Draft Cancún Ministerial Text, which provoked an almost immediate reaction by the G-20+. The group criticised the striking similarities between this text and the proposal that had been previously submitted by the US and the EU. This controversy carried over into Cancún. On 13 September, apparently ignoring the G-20+'s critical position, the meeting's chairman, Derbez Bautista, released a Revised Draft Cancún Ministerial Text. This revised draft, however, not only maintained all the general aspects that had upset the G-20+, but also included an extension of the 'peace clause' scheduled to end in 2003. The 'peace clause,' which had been agreed upon during the Uruguayan Round, had established a nine-year moratorium on disputes regarding certain agriculture subsidies. The G-20+ countries criticised the 'Revised Draft' for ignoring the Doha commitments and predicted delays in the Doha agenda should this draft be adopted. Aiming at neutralising the draft and realigning the negotiations to the Doha's commitments, the G-20+ offered a counterproposal, which followed the same general structure of the 'revised draft' (organised around market access, export competition and domestic support). This new proposal would not extend the 'peace clause', which would in theory facilitate the negotiation of agriculture reform.

Adding to the general rancour were comparably emotional and polarised disputes over cotton subsidies mainly between West African countries and the US. Benin, Burkina-Faso, Chad and Mali contended that a draft text proposed by the US disregarded their demands for reductions of American, EU and Chinese protective subsidies on cotton production. Moreover, they interpreted the draft as insinuating that they should simply stop producing cotton. Disagreement primarily between the EU and the African Caribbean Pacific group (ACP) over the Singapore issues – whose inclusion in the agenda had been proposed by Japan, North Korea and the EU – ultimately broke the momentum for consultation. The EU tried to push negotiations forward by offering to remove the two most sensitive issues investment and competition policy – from the agenda, but the offer came too late. Despite the controversial nature of the agricultural issues at stake and the complex negotiations over those proposals and counter-proposals, an agreement was slowly taking shape in Cancún. The abrupt termination of the meeting – proximately due to a stalemate over the Singapore issues – truncated this prospect.

Ramifications of Cancún

In the Western Hemisphere, fallout over the Cancún meeting began to surface almost immediately. During the October 2003 meeting of the Trade Negotiating Committee for the Free Trade Area for the Americas (FTAA) in Port-of-Spain, Trinidad and Tobago, representatives of 34 countries were unable to agree on a road map for the FTAA summit scheduled to take place in Miami in November 2003. The meeting stalled mainly because Brazil and the US – co-chairs of the FTAA negotiations – could not agree on the same issues that had caused the Cancún negotiations to collapse. The US would accede to negotiations on agriculture subsidies at the FTAA level, insisting such negotiations had to be held at the global level and must include European countries and Japan. Brazilian negotiators argued that Brazil could not reduce its domestic protection in the sectors of services, investment rules, government procurement and intellectual property without risking the loss of important bargaining chips at the WTO level. Backed by Argentina and the other two Southern Common Market (Mercosur) partners – and motivated by what it saw as its moral victory in Cancún – Brazil introduced a proposal aimed at scaling back the FTAA agreement in timing and scope, but designating the most controversial issues for negotiation in the WTO. Although the Brazilian proposal also suggested that Washington could hold bilateral negotiations with the Mercosur countries, the United States took issue with this triple-track approach and insisted on a comprehensive agreement covering everything from tariffs to investment rules. Counting on the support of countries of Central America and the Andean region as well as the Dominican Republic, Washington also insisted in keeping the December 2004 deadline for the FTAA. The meeting ended without an agreement on the road map for the FTAA, which was supposed to be approved at the Miami summit.

After the unproductive meeting in Port-of-Spain, FTAA co-chairs Brazil and the US agreed on a proposal for a 'flexible' approach to the negotiations, just a few days before the Miami summit. The FTAA would allow for two levels of commitments. At the first and most basic level, countries would sign up to a minimal, relatively uncontroversial range of provisions, yet to be established. At the second level, individual countries would be able to

The Americas

freely negotiate arrangements with any other country or group of countries. Due to the complexity of this proposal – soon tagged 'FTAA-lite' – the Miami meeting ended without achieving its promised results. While the proposal did not foreclose opportunities to continue negotiation, the second-level negotiations that it contemplates pose foreseeable problems. To wit, it is difficult to fine-tune compensations and tradeoffs between countries that accepted a whole package of conditions and those that accepted only some. Zoellick has suggested a remedy whereby benefits should be commensurate with obligations and 'crossed' bilateral compensations charged against those countries that choose only partially to sign up to the agreement. But the scheme looks unworkably intricate.

The next step towards the FTAA was to be mapped out in Puebla, Mexico, at a meeting of the FTAA Trade Negotiations Committee (TNC) in early February 2004. It was to consist in guidelines establishing a balanced set of rights and obligations to be observed by all country members during the negotiations. The TNC was also charged with establishing procedures to orient multilateral negotiations among FTAA members interested in promoting liberalisation beyond the initial level of general commitments. In the event, the Puebla meeting produced no results. Brazil and the Mercosur countries did not agree to negotiate the opening of their domestic markets if US agriculture subsidies were not on the table. Moreover, no deal could be established on how to commensurate the 'crossed' compensations proposed by the United States, then seconded by a group of 13 countries of the region (so as to constitute the 'G-14'). Thus, in a joint communiqué, the TNC announced that the delegations had not been able to finalise the guidelines for the FTAA negotiation groups. As a justification for their decision, the TNC co-chairs alleged that the Miami meeting had created an entirely new set of problems including the highly complex task of defining rules for multiple-level negotiations. Consequently, FTAA members decided to suspend the talks and reconvene again in March. The TNC later postponed that meeting in light of 'the complexity of the task' at hand.

After meetings in Washington on 24–25 March, Brazil and the United States agreed on a tentative three-step road map to advance the negotiations. In the first step, the 34 FTAA nations would meet again in Puebla on 22 April 2004 to seek a consensus on a set of 'common rules' for the negotiations. The second step would be defined by a new round (to be scheduled) to address individual country members' offers of market access in four sectors: agricultural products; non-agricultural products; services; and possibly investments. In the third step, the country members would negotiate bilateral and multilateral agreements to establish more ambitious rules. To make this arrangement possible, Brazil relaxed its demands for US commitments in reducing agricultural subsidies, while the US reduced its requirements of Brazil regarding foreign investments, government procurement and intellectual property rights. Nevertheless, the new arrangement is essentially procedural and merely postpones the substantive resolution of critical trade differences between the two countries, which are therefore bound to re-emerge.

Meantime, outflanking Mercosur resistance, the United States announced the launch of several bilateral free-trade agreements with other countries in the region. The most important was the US–Chile free-trade accord, which came into force on 1 January 2004. The US also announced that it was concluding free-trade agreements with four Central American countries (styled the Central America Free Trade Area, or CAFTA), as well as bilateral ones with Costa Rica, the Dominican Republic and Panama. Finally, the US stated that negotiations for bilateral trade agreements would get underway with four Andean countries, starting with Peru and Colombia. These announcements, of course, were more important from a political standpoint than a substantive economic one, as they reflect minimal changes compared to those that the FTAA would dictate. The basic differences over agriculture subsidies and the Singapore agenda, raised in Cancún, remained impediments to a large-scale global or regional accord.

The players' interests

The trade guidelines issued by the Bush administration in 2001 were not markedly different from those of previous US trade strategies: 'to pursue reinforcing trade initiatives globally, regionally and bilaterally'. However, because President Bush was able to secure congressional approval of the Trade Act of 2002, which renewed the president's trade negotiating authority, he was able to push an especially bold trade agenda in 2003. Hence, the Bush administration has been aggressive: encouraging the WTO negotiations; pushing the FTAA agenda; winning congressional approval for free-trade agreements with Chile and Singapore; initiating free-trade negotiations with 12 nations; announcing prospective free-trade arrangements with eight additional countries; and broadly promoting US trade interests in southeast Asia and the Middle East. It is clear that, by pushing multiple free trade initiatives, the United States intends to create 'competition for liberalisation' that ultimately would allow for the reduction of barriers abroad without much change in US domestic policies that are protective of critical sectors such as agriculture.

The growing trade deficits by the US global trade – its goods-and-services trade deficit constituted 4.6% of GDP in 2003, an increase of 0.6 percentage points from 2002 – have strongly motivated the promotion of aggressive trade policies capable of opening new markets for US exports. US global trade deficits from 2000 through 2003 with every major trading partner or trade bloc except Japan have increased considerably (see table on following page). This indicates that overall, despite some protectionist policies, the US should be considered an open economy in comparison with virtually all other regions of the world. This misunderstood reality goes a long way towards explaining American stubbornness vis-à-vis developing nations. For them, however, at the WTO level the US and other developed countries pose an acute and specific problem in that the exports of developing nations are predominantly agricultural products, which are exactly the ones protected by heavy subsidies in developed countries – including the US.

Although Brazil accounts for only about 1% of international trade, due to its wide range of exports (from agricultural products to passenger aircraft) and trading partners, it has played an increasingly salient role in trade disputes, especially in multilateral forums. Brazil's exports agenda is broad and diversified, as is its market distribution. The Brazilian approach to trade liberalisation was formulated well before the FTAA was launched, as a reaction to the Enterprise for the Americas Initiative (EAI) launched by US President George H.W. Bush in 1990. The EAI promoted trade and contemplated a hemisphere-wide free-trade zone. Hence, Brazilian officials calculated that the best way to avoid being forced to accept a regional trade agreement would be to negotiate Brazil's position as part of a group of countries rather than individually. Accordingly, Brazil has worked to strengthen Mercosur while becoming increasingly active in global and regional trade talks. In 2003, the election of Luiz Inácio 'Lula' da Silva as Brazil's president introduced a new variable in the trade negotiations. During the presidential race, he had underscored the importance of the Mercosur while criticising the FTAA. Stressing that Brazil would not join the FTAA if that meant 'to annex Brazil to the United States', Lula was particularly concerned that FTAA membership would impair his industrial

US Trade Balances with Selected Countries/Regions

$bn	2000	2001	2002	2003*
Canada	-51.9	-52.8	-48.2	-54.7
European Union	-55.0	-61.3	-82.1	-95.4
Japan	-81.6	-69.0	-70.0	-67.6
Mexico	-24.6	-30.0	-37.1	-40.7
China	-83.6	-83.1	-103.1	-128.1
Pacific Rim, except Japan and China	-50.0	-42.6	-41.9	-42.2
Latin America, except Mexico	-14.1	-9.2	-18.0	-27.1
Addendum: High income countries	-187.8	-183.7	-204.4	-222.7
Addendum: Low to middle income countries	-248.6	-228.5	-266.0	-328.6

* Annualised, based on January–October 2003 data.
Source: US Department of Commerce, Census Basis

policy, which is heavily based on distribution of incentives to national industries. A provision like the North American Free Trade Agreement's Chapter 11, which allows for the prosecution of governments for discriminatory treatment, would imperil such programmes.

Yet Lula's FTAA negotiation strategy has not been profoundly different from that of his predecessor, Fernando Henrique Cardoso. Both administrations have relied on Mercosur as the hard core of the strategy, underscoring Brazil's *demandeur* nature in the process. In addition, both administrations maintained simultaneous trade negotiations with the EU. To be sure, Lula has tried to raise Brazil's global position through the projection of his own – so far, positive – personal image. During the first year of his administration, Lula travelled overseas 18 times. Further, whereas Cardoso's tactical dispensation was to let the negotiations flow while reserving a final decision on whether to join fully until the last moment, Lula's approach has been to bargain hard at every step with an eye towards securing a 'balanced' arrangement. Since Cancún, though, the Brazilian negotiating strategy has faced increasing criticism at home. After the Port-of-Spain meeting, some members of Lula's cabinet – including the ministers of agriculture and industry – carpeted the Ministry of Foreign Affairs for not sharing information with other members of the Brazilian cabinet and for excessive stubbornness in the negotiations. By late February, following the Puebla deadlock, ten Brazilian associations interested in agribusiness presented a letter to Foreign Minister Amorim attacking Brazil's negotiation approach and demanding greater participation in formulating trade strategy. The letter also denigrated Brazil's proposal of an 'à la carte' FTAA, claiming that the proposed two levels of commitment were unrealistic, and recommended more flexibility in the rules of negotiation. As a consequence, Lula ordered the members of the trade negotiation team – led by Amorim – to 'fine tune' its positions. He also underscored Brazil's broad strategic commitment to the FTAA. But Amorim still defended a 'balanced and flexible' FTAA that would respect the differences between the participant countries.

A major reason that Argentina has been confident enough to maintain a stiff trade negotiation position – in spite of five years of negative indicators and a major currency crisis in 2001–02 – is that the period 2003–04 was relatively good for Argentina's economy. Economic growth was 8.4%, with a low 3.2% inflation rate, surpassing even the most optimistic predictions. Employment showed signs of improvement, and the fall in real wages appeared to have stopped, as the Argentine peso recovered about 25% of its original value against the US dollar. The balance of payments has been favourable, and global commodity prices have sustained it. Soybean prices soared during 2003 and Argentina, one of the world's leading producers, benefited from extraordinary international demand. Tax revenues were 43% higher than the previous year's figures. President Nestor Kirchner, who took office after winning a run-off election in May 2003, has pushed a programme of monetary and fiscal reforms, while the Argentine Congress passed important measures, including an anti-tax evasion package.

Argentina views foreign trade as both a partial way out of its chronic economic problems and a vehicle for asserting its status as a regional power. Its trade strategy was devised before the current administration took office, but Kirchner has emphatically underscored its guidelines, which basically align the Argentine approach with those of Brazil and Mercosur. The Argentine trade strategy is underpinned by both political and technical arguments. On the political side, Argentina's unrewarding adherence in the early 1990s to the 'Washington Consensus' economic agenda – which includes low trade barriers – made Argentine trade negotiators feel betrayed, when developed countries maintained protectionist policies. Their current refusal to reduce their tariffs and subsidies on agricultural goods – in which Argentina is highly competitive – has only reinforced this grievance. From a technical standpoint, on the basis of simulations and scenarios involving 16 products and ten countries and regions, the Argentine Ministry of Foreign Relations' Center for International Economics (CEI) concluded that the optimal trade architecture for Argentina would be secured by simultaneous trade arrangements including Mercosur, the FTAA, and the EU. Accordingly, Mercosur is considered an appropriate economic as well as political platform from which to angle for simultaneous trade arrangements with the US and the EU. Argentine negotiators have concluded they derive the greatest political leverage in negotiating as part of Mercosur. The CEI also concluded that the FTAA would be an important achievement (economically integrating an area with a total population of 800m and collective GDP of $12 trillion). Therefore, the agreement would impose high costs on those countries that opt not to join – though there would also be high short-term costs accruing to membership if integration proceeded too quickly. Consequently, the CEI concluded that Argentina should push ahead a 'realistic' FTAA.

Challenges ahead

Brazil and Argentina emerged from the WTO meeting in Cancún with a sense of success that motivated both countries to reconsider their importance on multilateral negotiations. The Cancún meeting appeared to have led them to the conclusion that their aggressive trade negotiation strategy had revitalised Mercosur as a negotiation platform and strengthened their position with respect to the FTAA. At the diplomatic level, the Argentina–Brazil bilateral relationship has been reinforced. In early October 2003, Kirchner and Lula met in Buenos Aires, where they pledged to maintain a unified position and launched the 'Buenos Aires

Consensus' which, in contrast to the 'Washington Consensus', focuses on development, job creation and social issues. The two presidents met again in Rio de Janeiro in March 2004 to define a common agenda aimed at convincing the IMF to reform its approach towards developing countries and to accord greater weight to their development needs. The alliance so far may have paid net dividends to Latin America's bargaining power. At the same time, broad frustration over Cancún and subsequent meetings reflects substantial risk in Brazilian and Argentine assertiveness. If they come to be durably perceived by developed countries as 'troublemakers' only interested in undermining regional negotiations and not interested in promoting a positive agenda, the entire region will ultimately suffer. But political realities in Argentina and Brazil cut against further North–South polarity.

The domestic criticisms of the Brazilian team – to the effect that hubris may have placed Brazilian aspirations for an FTAA of broad scope at risk relatively soon – are likely to make Brazil's approach more moderate and pragmatic in the future. Argentina faces comparable countervailing influences. While it has been able to resist capitulation to the US–EU agenda despite its economic difficulties and keep its free-trade agenda on track in strategic partnership with Brazil, the Argentine banking sector – still suffering from the credibility gap caused by the default on government bonds and the decline in depositor confidence in 2001–02 – is not a reliable source of credit for the private sector. Kirchner is counting on the International Monetary Fund (IMF) and the G-7 governments to inject fresh money to enable Argentina to deal acceptably with its $99.4bn in defaulted sovereign debt. In September 2003, the IMF agreed to lend Argentina $13.5bn, with tranches phased over three years, in exchange for Argentina's pledge to reform its economy and resume negotiations with private creditors. In March 2004, however, Kirchner announced that the country would repay bondholders only about $250 on each $1,000 in defaulted bonds, re-igniting international pressures that began in early 2002. Keeping the IMF on Argentina's side has become a more acute priority, and depends substantially on keeping the US on its side. The upshot is that Argentina's international financial needs may induce a more moderate approach to future trade negotiations. Such an adjustment would, in any case, chime with Argentina's long-term trade strategy, as the CEI holds that a successful WTO outcome is important based on its conclusion that only the WTO could ultimately eradicate agricultural subsidies.

Further progress on global negotiations cannot be made unless negotiations are re-launched on the basis of the Doha terms. Developing countries are aware that an effective WTO is critical to advancing their interests, and that bilateral and regional agreements probably could not comprehensively address trade diversion and discrimination, agricultural subsidies or dumping abuses. Developing countries therefore have a strong

The Americas

incentive to put together an agenda that offers potential benefits to Organisation for Economic Cooperation and Development countries as well as themselves. Brazil and Argentina, by their assertiveness on trade issues as well as more independent foreign policies on matters ranging from the Iraq intervention to the International Criminal Court to relations with Cuba, may now be satisfied that they have firmly registered their claim that 'automatic alignments' with Washington can no longer be assumed. This realisation, coupled with compromising factors in their respective domestic realms, is likely to make them marginally riper for free-trade advancement in 2004–05. That, however, may not be saying much. Substantial momentum would require a change of heart in Washington. Despite a congressional record as a free trader, Senator John Kerry – virtually certain to be the Democratic nominee for president – has shown himself to be as susceptible to protectionist impulses as Bush and has championed labour and environmental standards that could inhibit agreement.

New Complications in the Andes

In a somewhat disturbing turn of events, Colombia appears currently to have the most successful government in the northern Andes. But while the achievements of Alvaro Uribe Velez's hard-line policies have been remarkable, Bogota's relative superiority is merely indicative of the disarray of Colombia's Andean neighbours. Polarisation and political violence are on the rise in Venezuela as the opposition attempts to remove the increasingly authoritarian Hugo Chávez via referendum. Chávez has abandoned any efforts at civil relations with the United States and has instead strengthened ties with Cuba and called for resistance of US hegemony in Latin America. In September 2003, indigenous dissident groups forced Bolivian President Sánchez de Lozada to resign after a month of violent protests provoked by his free-market policies. Carlos Mesa, the new president, has inherited the predicament of how to implement reform without being overthrown. Ecuadorians have ousted every president who attempted economic reform in nearly a decade, and Lucio Gutiérrez may be the next. Peru's Alejandro Toledo is unpopular and weak, and presides over an administration ridden with scandals. Yet he must face the increased activity of Shining Path remnants who are now involved in the drug trade. Uribe's success at fighting terrorists and eradicating coca in Colombia has caused both violence and coca cultivation to spill over its borders, causing greater regional instability. Despite US pressure to step up eradication efforts, Ecuador, Bolivia and Peru have been frustrated in their attempts to confront the threat of destabilisation posed by coca farmers

Colombia's tough stance

In August 2002, Colombians overwhelmingly voted for candidate Alvaro Uribe, seeing him as the one candidate who might be able to restore a semblance of stability and security to war-ravaged Colombia. The leftist rebel Revolutionary Armed Forces of Colombia (FARC) continued its brutal campaign against the Colombian state, increasing attacks by 23% in 2003. But the Uribe government increasingly took the fight to the FARC, fighting almost twice as many battles (around 2,400) with illegal groups in 2003 than the year before. While the rise in attacks partly reflects the FARC's seemingly limitless drug-related revenues, it probably is also due to growing desperation in the face of greater counter-insurgency effectiveness. As the mid-point of his four-year term approached in April 2004, Uribe's accomplishments were impressive. Terrorist attacks decreased from 1,645 in 2002 to 850 in 2003. Some 6,967 suspected leftist rebels were arrested in 2003, an increase of 85% over the previous year. In 2003, over 3,000 leftist rebels and right-wing paramilitary troops disarmed and joined rehabilitation programmes. Desertions from the ranks of the illegal groups rose by 80% in 2003. These are operationally significant numbers. Colombia's general kidnapping and homicide rates, perennially some of the world's highest, dropped by 27% and 20%, respectively.

For the FARC, traditional rural insurgency has given way to an urban terrorist strategy. The FARC greeted Uribe's one-year anniversary in office with a series of car bombs throughout the country. On 17 August 2003, the group attempted to shoot down the president's helicopter when he was on a visit to a battle-weary region in the northern part of the country. On 15 November 2003, the FARC detonated bombs in two bars in an upscale district of Bogota, wounding 72 and killing one. US diplomats, contractors and journalists frequented both bars and there is a strong reason to believe that the attack was intended to kill Americans. In late November 2003, the FARC declared that all US troops were considered military targets. But the FARC was dealt a serious blow in early January 2004, when FARC Secretariat member Ricardo Palmera, known by his nom de guerre Simon Trinidad, was captured in Ecuador. Palmera, who is a Harvard-trained economist, was wanted on over 30 terrorism charges. The capture came only days after General Martin Orlando Carreno, the Colombian army commander, made a New Year's Day resolution to capture or kill at least one of the seven Secretariat members within a year or resign his command. Further, on 28 January, a joint operation among police in Colombia, Italy, Australia, France, Netherlands, Spain and Venezuela cracked a major drug

The Americas

smuggling ring run by an Italian crime organisation, the `Ndrangheta, which helped to finance Colombian terrorists. Over 150 people were arrested, including 29 in Colombia, and over five tonnes of cocaine were seized.

Notwithstanding this success, some of Uribe's security policies are controversial. As the terrorist and military campaigns have proceeded, the Uribe administration has worked towards reducing the FARC's military threat and recruiting power by way of demobilisation and amnesty agreements with the paramilitary groups. Following negotiations with the government on 15 July 2003, the Colombian Self-Defense Force (AUC) – composed of right-wing pro-government vigilantes – announced that it would lay down its arms before 2006. On 25 November, 855 AUC paramilitaries disarmed in the provincial city of Medellín. In a move that has drawn criticism for its disregard for justice, Uribe has offered the AUC immunity in return for disarmament. On 20 January 2004, former AUC leader Giovanni Marin addressed the Colombian Congress to urge protection for all paramilitaries who lay down their arms.

Uribe has stated that his inspiration for the disarmament/amnesty policy came from Northern Ireland's 1998 Good Friday peace agreement, under which terrorist prisoners from both sides of the long-running conflict there were released from prison in contemplation of continued cease-fires and eventual decommissioning of weapons. In Northern Ireland, however, the number of prisoners and other potential combatants numbered only in the hundreds, against over 35,000 paramilitaries in Colombia. Furthermore, the fact that the FARC appears to have received advice and assistance from hardcore members of the Irish Republican Army suggests that incentives will not tame everyone. One continuing concern is a potential deterioration in the security situation in areas that the paramilitaries abandon. For example, the Medellín suburbs were in paramilitary hands until the 25 November demobilisation. About 600 police officers were sent into the area, but the Colombian military is already stretched thin and the burden will only increase as more paramilitaries demobilise. Nevertheless, on balance, Uribe's ability to provide greater security for the population has resulted in high public-approval ratings, and reinforced a strong sense of law and order. A January 2004 Gallup poll reported that his popularity had risen from 70% to 80%, and that between 72% and 82% of Colombians approved of his policies on guerrillas, paramilitaries, drugs and corruption. Some 79% thought the government was respectful of human rights and 80% approved of the military's performance. An overwhelming 93% disapproved of the FARC and 82% disapproved of the AUC. Another January poll showed that 76% of Colombians favoured Uribe's re-election despite a constitutional ban on repeat presidential terms.

Beyond the domestic arena, the Uribe administration's relations with Washington remain strong. In September 2003, the US Congress approved another $393 million in new aid on top of the roughly $3 billion authorised in the previous four years. A minor dispute erupted in 2003 when Colombia hesitated to grant American soldiers stationed in Colombia immunity from being tried in the International Criminal Court. A small amount of American aid was temporarily held up until Colombia granted the exemption in September. US officials, having formally expanded American assistance efforts beyond counter-narcotics to counter-insurgency activities in recognition of the close organic connection between drugs and political violence, remain encouraged by the dramatic decrease in coca cultivation, especially in the southern region of Putumayo, where most of the US-led crop eradication programmes are focused. Nonetheless, a June 2003 US government report was generally critical of US drug policy in Colombia, citing poor oversight of programmes and poor training of Colombian pilots and maintenance of aircraft. In addition, the marked reduction in coca cultivation achieved over the past two years has not so far led to lower levels of cocaine entering the United States. In August 2003, US Secretary of Defense Donald Rumsfeld travelled to Bogota and presented evidence to Uribe showing more than a dozen instances of the Venezuelan Air Force entering Colombian airspace in order to provide cover for FARC forces retreating into Venezuela. For both Washington and Bogota, the Venezuelan military's now undeniable assistance to the FARC is moving from an irritant to a serious international issue. The Uribe administration's relations with Caracas remain frosty.

President Uribe's domestic political agenda suffered a major setback when all 15 of his proposals for structural reform of Colombia's political and economic practices were defeated in an October 2003 referendum that would have given the president more control over fiscal spending. Each one of the proposals received overwhelming support, but the referendum required a 25% voter turnout rate that did not materialise. Following the vote, it has been difficult for Uribe to argue to foreign donors – especially the United States, the World Bank and the IMF – that Colombia needs more foreign assistance when its electorate appears unwilling to support necessary changes. Losing the referendum has compelled Uribe to build a governing coalition with Congress to establish spending controls that are critical to Uribe's economic stabilisation strategy. In a critical test of Uribe's ability to raise more fiscal revenue, tax collection as a percentage of GDP rose from 10% to 13% in 2003. While this figure is encouraging, the fact remains that 740,000 Colombian citizens – out of an economically active population of 20m – pay income taxes.

Continued political decadence in Venezuela

Following the failure of the April 2002 coup attempt and the national strikes of late 2002 and early 2003, the opposition has tried three times to oust populist president Hugo Chávez. In late 2003, the opposition

The Americas

presented the National Electoral Council (CNE) with 3m signatures, which is 600,000 more than the 2.4m statutorily required to hold a recall referendum. But Chávez has co-opted the CNE. Though Organization of American States (OAS) and Carter Center monitors declared the signature-collection process legitimate, Chávez has insisted that there was fraud. Chávez stated in January 2004 that the CNE must persuade him 'signature by signature' that the petition was valid. In late February 2004, the CNE ruled that about 870,000 signatures were believed to be fraudulent; and announced that the individuals whose signatures are in dispute would be given the opportunity in the period 20–24 May to confirm their signatures. Some signatories have had their names posted on pro-Chávez websites, while the Venezuelan Workers Confederation has claimed that the government has fired thousands in retaliation for signing.

If the CNE rules that there are not enough valid signatures to warrant a referendum, there is a strong chance that mass anti-Chávez protests and violence would ensue. Polls conducted in late 2003 showed that 64% of Venezuelans would vote to remove the president, while only 26% would vote to retain him. Even if he does not constrain the CNE from authorising the referendum, he is likely to hedge against losing it by delaying the vote until after 19 August. In that case, under Venezuelan electoral rules Chávez would be replaced by his vice-president, who would serve through the end of his term until 2006, instead of a newly elected candidate.

Despite the high degree of the antipathy towards him, Chávez contends he would win a referendum. In an effort to secure his political base, he has embarked upon a concerted populist push. Chávez has bypassed institutions in order to implement his anti-neoliberal, distributive policies, prompting opposition fears that he is moving closer to a Castro-style command economy and authoritarian government. In December 2003, Chávez dismissed the board of directors of the Venezuelan Social Security Institute due to its delay in paying liabilities. He also began to advocate the government takeover of private banks as recourse for their failure to finance the agricultural sector. In January 2004, the president coerced the Central Bank of Venezuela into unconstitutionally releasing $1bn for agricultural projects. When analysts warned of the possible inflationary effects of such a move, Chávez declared that he was 'not interested in economic theories'. Chávez expedited the transfer of land titles to squatters, and the government is currently considering decriminalising theft of food and medicine when motivated by hunger or need. Chávez launched nationwide literacy and health campaigns with the controversial assistance of 12,000 Cubans. The purported results are that one million Venezuelans have become literate and that over 5,000 people have been sent to Cuba for free medical operations.

The intensified political polarisation that has occurred during the referendum process has made political violence an almost daily occurrence.

Combined with an economically fuelled rise in crime throughout the country, this trend has turned Venezuela into the second most dangerous country in the Western Hemisphere, surpassed only by Colombia. Dissident high-ranking military officers continue to protest in Altamira Plaza, which they have proclaimed a 'liberated territory' since October 2002. Meanwhile Defense Minister Garcia Carneiro has vowed to crush all rebellion attempts among officers. On 18 January 2004, 70 Chávez supporters with guns, rocks and bats broke up a demonstration by the opposition group Movement Toward Socialism and attacked a private television crew in the process. Pot-hanging protestors gathered throughout Caracas on 19 January to protest the sluggish pace of the referendum process. The opposition coalition Democratic Coordination planned a series of demonstrations beginning 23 January to demand a referendum, but Chávez warned that the military would shoot any officer who rebelled, seize private businesses that went on strike and close any television stations that promoted violence.

Gathering economic recovery from the strike and capital flight appeared to benefit Chávez in the short term. By December 2003, Venezuela's risk rating had fallen 700 points from its March level of 1,200, enabling the country to issue bonds less expensively. Official unemployment fell from 20% in early 2003 to a projected 14% at the close of January 2004, while 6.5% economic growth was expected in 2004. Yet Venezuela has the highest accumulated inflation in the region at 22.7%, and 70% of the population lives below the poverty line. Growing political violence and any intensification of instability could quickly reverse the post-strike gains. Most importantly, Chávez lacks a coherent economic plan. In this light, deteriorating standards of living and diminishing capacity to finance distributive policies are likely to erode his political base.

Chávez has increasingly alienated himself in the international arena and caused acute tension with the United States. Washington proclaimed it would guarantee the integrity of the Venezuelan referendum, but Chávez warned the US to stay out of Venezuela's domestic affairs and insisted that the US government's opposition to his government indicates the US, with the domestic opposition, intends to overthrow him. The US government, for its part, has said it has proof of Venezuelan assistance to the FARC. In addition, there have been accusations that Caracas has supported anti-government groups in Bolivia, Ecuador and Uruguay. Washington has long been critical of Chávez's close ties with Cuba, a concern exacerbated by the January 2004 announcement that Cuba and Venezuela had formed a strategic alliance aimed at helping the poor and defending against excessive US influence in Latin America. Chávez also announced that he would campaign internationally against neoliberalism and solicited the support of the Argentine and Brazilian presidents in his effort to block the US-supported hemispheric trade zone.

The Americas

Venezuela's future remains murky, with little hope for a peaceful end to domestic discord in the near term. Considering each side's determination to prevail and its distrust of the other, mutual acceptance of the legitimacy of a completed referendum process is highly unlikely. Most alarmingly, there is no assurance that the losers would form a loyal opposition. On one hand, if the opposition forced early elections and then fared poorly, it could resort to extra-judicial means of removing Chávez. On the other hand, if Chávez were democratically removed, the 30% of the population that remains fiercely loyal to him would probably attempt to undermine the new leadership. Venezuelan politics are increasingly perceived as a zero-sum game. It is doubtful that there will be a peaceful, electoral solution to the current crisis.

Bolivia's factional disarray

Over the past three years a series of violent protests have rocked Bolivia. In April 2000, violent protests in the city of Cochabamba over a plan to privatise the water utility led to cancellation of the government privatisation contract. In early 2003, the Bolivian government's attempt (under IMF pressure) to reduce its fiscal deficit from 8.6% to 5.5% by freezing public sector pay and implementing a 2.5% income tax sparked a protest in La Paz that was supported by police officers. The ensuring confrontation between the police and army left 27 dead and at least 100 wounded. Again, the government withdrew the fiscal measures, and President Gonzalo Sánchez de Lozada's cabinet resigned en masse to allow for restructuring. In September 2003, opposition to the Bolivian government's coca eradication and economic policies, particularly a proposed gas pipeline, provoked anti-government protests and violent clashes resulting in the deaths of roughly 80 protestors. The protests and instability continued for a month. On 17 October, 14 months into his presidency, Sánchez de Lozada resigned. In his letter to Congress, he characterised his resignation as 'a terrible precedent for democracy in Bolivia'. He later warned that civil war could arise between the more indigenous Andean region and the more prosperous Santa Cruz region of the country, home to those of Spanish descent.

The September episode represented the worst crisis in Bolivia's 21 years of continuous democracy. Bolivia's political ills are a reflection of a number of factors that are weakening the country's still fragile democratic institutions: social dissatisfaction with free-market economic policies; decreasing trust in the country's traditional political parties; and the recent emergence of radical indigenous groups. The political power of the coca-growers is a particularly disruptive problem. Coca-growers union leader Evo Morales was instrumental in the September 2003 protests. He barely lost to Sánchez de Lozada in the 2002 presidential elections (20.9% to

22.5%), won a congressional seat and, hyperbolically accusing Sánchez de Lozada of 'genocide', helped push him from office. Bolivia is the world's third largest producer of coca, and Washington has sent La Paz $1.3bn in anti-drug aid since 1993. Since 1997 the government has imposed a US-supported policy of 'forced eradication', which involves physically uprooting plants. In the first four years of the plan, Bolivia's illegal coca production dropped 90%. In the past few years, however, successful aerial fumigation efforts in Colombia have prompted increased Bolivian coca cultivation – the so-called 'balloon effect'. The Bolivian government has responded with increased eradication, which have outpaced programmes intended to financially assist farmers whose crops have been destroyed or earnings decreased owing to the switch to licit crops. After a January 2003 growers protest that led to a clash with security forces that left seven dead and 23 wounded, Sánchez de Lozada offered to conduct a study of the legal coca market and adjust the legal growing area accordingly. While Washington objected, Morales called for a complete halt to eradication measures. In early 2003, Sánchez de Lozada asked the Bush administration for an additional US$150m to fund alternative crop programmes but came away with less than 10% of that figure.

Bolivia's social, political and economic outlook is further complicated by the fact that 70% of its population is divided among three dozen indigenous groups. Almost all indigenous Bolivians live in poverty and 40% cannot meet their dietary needs. About 20% of indigenous children die before their first birthday. Bolivia's indigenous groups have, to be sure, become increasingly active in the orthodox political system. Political parties affiliated with indigenous peoples presently make up a quarter of the seats in Congress. Yet, paradoxically, greater enfranchisement has led to greater political disillusionment. Bolivia's top indigenous leaders may be members of Congress, but they also lead street protests against the government that are often violent.

Poverty is obviously a basic problem, but it is amplified by persistent, though perhaps understandable, political stubbornness and economic naïveté. Bolivia holds the second largest natural gas reserves in South America, with 1.5 trillion cubic metres of which only 5% will be demanded domestically over the next several decades. The IMF estimated that a proposed $6bn gas pipeline project could have added an average of 1% to Bolivia's annual GDP and would have generated $300m in annual revenues. This money could, among other things, help compensate farmers economically damaged by anti-coca policies – one of its original impetuses. But the pipeline proposal met stern resistance from indigenous groups. In the War of the Pacific (1879–83), Bolivia lost its sea coast and adjoining nitrate fields to Chile. Bolivian leaders raise this grievance perennially in the OAS. As a matter of historical pride, the indigenous groups objected to the pipeline's passing through Chilean territory and thereby extending the

The Americas

economic benefits of a Bolivian natural resource to Chile. Anti-American sentiment also fuelled criticism of the gas' final destination: California. The indigenous groups demanded that Bolivia 'industrialise' the gas instead of exporting it, though exactly how remains unclear. As one Bolivian political analyst put it, gas had 'become a catalyst for all of the grievances'. Ructions over the gas-pipeline project ended when the company decided to import gas from Indonesia. Having cut off free-trade talks with Chile and rejected its offers to find some middle ground, Bolivia had lost an economic opportunity.

Vice-President Carlos Mesa was sworn in as president in an emergency congressional session hours after Sánchez de Lozada resigned. Mesa is a political independent who has attempted to build a government without the traditional political parties that have become discredited over the past several years. His new cabinet consists mostly of little-known economists and intellectuals. While it has some legitimacy because of its fresh political blood, Mesa's cabinet might not hold enough political weight to move forward with necessary reforms. Initially Mesa said he would merely be a transitional president, but began 2004 by announcing his intention to serve out Sánchez de Lozada's term, which ends in 2007. He stated that he will attempt to repair Bolivia's primary problem: the breakdown of the relationship between the state and society. As of early 2004, his remedial moves had been largely cosmetic: attending a memorial service for some of the protestors killed during the riots; announcing plans for voluntary coca eradication and a survey of the legal coca market; and the creation of a new Ministry of Ethnic Affairs. In what many believed to be a thinly veiled threat, indigenous leader Felipe Quispe gave Mesa 90 days to institute policies to assist the native population.

Bolivia is currently experiencing a vicious cycle in which reform policies opposed by groups that are dissatisfied with the state of the economy and political system must be enacted if the system is to improve. If Evo Morales became the country's next elected president – a plausible scenario – prospects for reform would become even more uncertain. After years of effective Bolivian cooperation, US anti-drug efforts would be thrown into disarray. It is unclear whether a Morales government would take an unapologetically populist approach similar Chávez's, or more of a centrist, third-way path such as Luiz Inácio da Silva – known as 'Lula' – in Brazil or Ecuador's Gutiérrez. At the same time, a Morales victory would not necessarily lead to progress on the indigenous population's critical social problems: Bolivia's finances would be just as bankrupt and its institutions just as weak.

The United States may have contributed to Sánchez de Lozada's fall by not providing adequate aid to his government. In what was perhaps an attempt to amend for this oversight, on 16 January, Washington hosted a meeting to raise aid for Bolivia. On the same day, however, Quispe's 90-day deadline for reformed indigenous policies expired, and protests and roadblocks occurred throughout the country as Mesa returned from a visit to Guatemala and Mexico. Demonstrators in Cochabamba and La Paz demanded delivery of the $2.3m of earthquake assistance provided by international donors in 1998, which former president Hugo Banzer had reportedly used to buy a presidential plane. In La Paz there were clashes among university students, while relatives of those killed or injured in the September 2003 clashes demanded economic compensation outside the presidential palace. In the northern state of Beni, demonstrators asked for help with the aftermath of recent storms that affected 15,000 Bolivians. Bolivia's largest labour federation called for a nationwide strike.

By late 2003, months of instability were beginning to take their toll on Bolivia's economy. In October, Standard & Poor's lowered Bolivia's long-term standing credit rating from B to B-, six notches below investment grade, and changed the outlook on the rating from stable to negative. Faced with a budget gap of $100m, Mesa has asked for sacrifices from Bolivians by way of higher taxes. This strategy did not work for Sánchez de Lozada, and presently there is little indication that Mesa will have much more luck with it. Mesa is popular, with one poll placing his approval rating at 80%, yet it is unclear that he will be able to tackle the problem of how to implement reform in the face of the demands of radicalised groups. Continued pressure from them and paralysis from government will tend to weaken Bolivia's security, as a weak central government will be increasingly unable to confront armed non-state actors. In a potential indication of things to come, on 2 December 2003, Bolivian authorities arrested 16 Islamic terror suspects near Santa Cruz after being tipped off by French intelligence sources. In mid-December, several suspected terrorists from the National Liberation Army of Bolivia (ELN-B), an indigenous left-wing armed group backed by coca-growers, were arrested, though some were released due to Morales' threats to destabilise Mesa's government. And in late March 2004, in front of the Congress building in La Paz, a disgruntled former miner detonated dynamite strapped to his body, killing himself and two security officers. The man, Eustaquio Pichacuri, was one of thousands of unemployed mineworkers who have not received benefits promised by the government. Several days later, Mesa announced that monthly payments to retired workers would be capped to relieve pressure on the pension system and allow benefits to be more evenly distributed. Given that continued domestic instability could negatively affect US counter-narcotics programmes, American aid and diplomatic attention may be the most likely source of movement. Even so, Bolivia's political and economic impasse could proceed well into the future.

Ecuador's dampened expectations

Elected in 2002, Ecuadorian President Lucio Gutiérrez initially received strong support from Ecuador's impoverished majority, which identified with his rejection of the traditional political party system and free-market economic policies. The indigenous community, which makes up roughly 35% of the population, was particularly supportive and for the first time became part of a governing coalition. But while Gutiérrez was initially viewed as a populist leader, since taking office his policies have been anything but left-wing. In 2003 and 2004, Gutiérrez dropped his previously vocal opposition to the dollarisation of the country's economic system and aggressively implemented IMF-supported austerity packages. A good portion of Gutiérrez's newly discovered fiscal rectitude is pragmatic, as Ecuador's current financial troubles give him little wiggle room. As of early 2004, the budget deficit was 6% of GDP and repayment of external debt consumed 42% of the annual budget. Almost two-thirds of the population is unemployed or underemployed, giving Ecuador one of the highest unemployment rates in the hemisphere.

Gutiérrez's attempts at reigning in spending sparked numerous protests – especially among public sector union workers – and his popularity fell in 2003. In September, the Confederation of Indigenous Nationalities of Ecuador (CONAIE), the indigenous umbrella organisation, withdrew its support for Gutiérrez. The move resulted in the resignation of two indigenous cabinet members and the desertion of several congressional members of his governing coalition. These defections left Gutiérrez facing a formidable centre-left congressional opposition, while his own political movement held only six seats. Gutiérrez was forced to forge an alliance with the Social Christian Party, long associated with the economic elite that Gutiérrez attacked to win the election. Gutiérrez's tenuous position was bolstered by the creation of a new indigenous group (National Front of Independent Indigenous Peoples and Peasants, or FENACI) that supports the government.

The military remains more popular than almost all politicians, and it is plausible that they would intervene if the political climate continues to deteriorate. At the same time the indigenous-military coup that attempted to oust Jamil Mahuad in January 2000 was cut short due to US pressure, a fact that any potential coup plotters will take into account. A more likely scenario is a massive popular protest, as in Bolivia, that forces Gutiérrez to resign, or a constitutional impeachment or recall attempt. In late November 2003, Gutiérrez's government was directly imperilled by the disclosure that former governor César Fernández, charged with cocaine trafficking in October, contributed $30,000 to Gutiérrez's election campaign. Gutiérrez's claim that he'd never met Fernández was quickly disproved when a newspaper printed a picture of the two together. Five cabinet members resigned on 24 November. The Ecuadorian constitution requires the removal of any official elected with the help of drug money, and an investigation is underway. The scandal dropped the president's approval rating to 15% and could lead to his resignation. Even if he resists, other pressures could force him from office. On 2 December 2003, CONAIE leader Leonidas Iza announced that he would seek to revoke the president's mandate through a constitutional procedure establishing a referendum on the president's rule. CONAIE and other grass-roots organisations continue to reject government entreaties to negotiate. However Gutiérrez may benefit from fractures within his opposition. Due to the abstention of CONAIE, January protests failed to generate substantial popular momentum.

For almost a decade, any president who has attempted economic reform has been forcibly removed from office. Ecuador is trapped in a vicious cycle comparable to Bolivia's: popular dissatisfaction demands reform, but in the short term, reforms are likely to increase dissatisfaction. Like Bolivia, Ecuador is not without assets: it is Latin America's sixth-largest crude oil producer and fourth-largest exporter. Construction of a controversial oil pipeline was completed in August 2003, connecting oil fields in the Amazon region to the Pacific Ocean. Over 50% of Ecuador's economy depends on oil, and the pipeline was initially slated to boost annual GDP by 2.4%. On the day before its inaugural operation, though, dozens of local community members – furious at the neglect of their concerns – attempted to take over the pumping station. They were repelled by over 300 heavily armed police officers. While the protests have died down, due to production problems the government recently announced that the pipeline would only operate at half capacity for the foreseeable future.

On the security front, Colombia's civil war has continued to spill across Ecuador's northern border. There have been reports of increasing numbers of Colombian refugees entering Ecuador. Most of the refugee flows are due to the violence and displacement caused by terrorist organisations active in southern Colombia. In addition, after three years of US support, coca crop fumigation efforts are now fully operational and coca crops are being destroyed in southern Colombia faster than they are being replanted. But this is prompting insurgents to plant coca in other regions of Colombia and in Ecuador. While difficult to gauge the extent of this balloon effect, it is significant enough to have prompted a December 2003 presidential decree admitting that Ecuador has become a centre for drug trafficking and money laundering. In January 2004, the administration announced that it would launch Plan Ecuador to counter the repercussions of Plan Colombia, and in February Ecuador's National Council for the Control of Narcotics and Psychotropic Substances (CONSEP) issued a new national anti-drug plan. The government wants to rebuff allegations of any involvement in Colombia's drug trade and has not yet identified the specifics of Plan Ecuador beyond pressuring Colombia to tighten border security. Ties between the Gutiérrez administration and Washington remain strong. In November 2003, Minister of Foreign Relations Patricio Zuquilanda brokered an agreement allowing the US to construct three $250,000 'logistical sites' in Ecuador that will help channel aid to victims of natural

The Americas

disasters. To facilitate interdiction of suspicious boats in Ecuadorian waters, US Southern Command commander General James Hill continued to press for renegotiation of the 1999 treaty that established a US military base in the coastal city of Manta.

Marking the end of his first year in office, in his State of the Nation address on 17 January 2004, Gutiérrez reportedly promised, before God, to correct his mistakes. But with the drug-money allegations outstanding and minimal support in Congress, many observers are predicting that it is only a matter of time before Gutiérrez resigns or is forced from office. Gutiérrez has insisted that 'Ecuador will not see a repeat of the unrest in Bolivia'. Yet indigenous groups have removed two democratically elected presidents since 1996, and there is nothing to suggest that they would not do so, in one way or another, again.

Peru: the end of Toledo's honeymoon

Peruvian President Alejandro Toledo won the presidency with a loose political coalition, and enchanted the country with his rags to riches success story and the promise of hundreds of thousands of new jobs and public works projects. He entered office with 60% approval, but in the summer of 2003 that approval rating had sunk to 11% – defying the conventional wisdom that a president's popularity grows with the economy. 2003 was the second year in a row that Peru led Latin America in economic growth. Annual inflation, at 1.5%, was the lowest in decades. The problem was that economic growth had not translated into benefits for the poor. Unemployment rose in 2003 with the loss of 20,000 jobs. When his cabinet walked out amid paralysing general strikes, the president declared that Peru had 'reached the breaking point'. Toledo promised that in 2004 the people will see tangible gains from economic growth, but his record is not promising.

Economics are not Toledo's only problem. His government has been riddled with scandals. In February 2003, five congressional deputies left Toledo's Peru Posible (PP) party. After the desertion of his cabinet in June, the president fired his Cabinet Chief after she went public with accusations that a member of the PP was spreading rumours that she was a lesbian. His new Women's Minister stepped down after four days due to allegations of corruption. In January 2004, the Labor Minister resigned subsequent to charges of nepotism. Vice-President Raul Diez Canseco resigned as the minister of foreign trade and tourism due to charges of nepotism and corruption, and in late January stepped down from his position as vice-president. Toledo's former senior aide and lawyer is accused of conversing with and accepting money from the late Oscar Villanueva – the 'cashier' of indicted former intelligence chief Vladimir Montesinos, who was charged with, among other transgressions, selling arms to the FARC – with the promise of helping Villaneuva by bribing judges in the case against him.

More broadly, Toledo is considered weak and vacillating. In June 2002, the government abandoned privatisation plans due to mass protests, and in early 2003 Toledo gave in to demands of protesting transportation workers and coca farmers. This encouraged strikes and protests. Toledo, attempting to appease all sectors, has tended to make grand and often contradictory promises. He set ambitious eradication goals, yet promised coca growers that eradication would not be forced and that the government would allow more time for the transition to legal crops. He pledged to repress the revival of Shining Path terrorist activities, yet promised to cut military spending. Broken promises and lack of direction have made him so unpopular that in December 2003 sales of a Toledo piñata skyrocketed. Workers, coca growers and other disgruntled Peruvians are threatening to take to the streets again if Toledo fails to deliver on his promises.

Compounding Toledo's woes are ongoing and resurgent security problems. Despite pressure from the United States to step up eradication efforts due to increased coca cultivation in the period 2002–04, the Peruvian government has refrained from implementing eradication programmes in the areas where the leftist Shining Path insurgency has been active. A decade after the Shining Path was declared defeated – after 69,000 dead or missing and 20 years of violence – its remnants have risen again, forging an alliance with coca-paste traffickers to finance weapons and supplies and attract recruits. The Truth and Reconciliation Commission report, released in August 2003, blamed the Shining Path for the initiation of the conflict but held the government and military responsible for numerous human-rights abuses. Former president Alberto Fujimori was found to hold 'legal responsibility' for assassinations, abductions and massacres conducted by a government supported death squad. The Peruvian Roman Catholic Church was faulted for neglecting human rights. Potentially inflammatory trials of the Shining Path and Tupac Amaru Revolutionary Movement (MRTA) members were scheduled for March 2004. The government fears that the Shining Path could grow and carve out a 'liberated zone' as the FARC have done in Colombia. Farm labourers have reorganised into local self-defence groups and the military is rebuilding military bases abandoned after the Shining Path's defeat. Arming the self-defence groups poses risks: nearly all of their members are coca growers, who may tilt towards the terrorists if the government attempts eradication.

Despite strong macroeconomic performance, the Toledo administration is weak, discredited and may not be equipped to face the challenges of increased coca cultivation and terrorist activity. The political future of Peru remains unclear, as old presidential outcasts prove more popular than the current administration. While Fujimori remains exiled in Japan and has lower approval ratings than other opposition figures, he is more popular

The Americas

than the president, even though he has been banned from public positions for ten years, and claims there is a large popular movement to facilitate his return to power in 2006. In a radio speech on 3 January, he proclaimed 2004 the year of Fujimorismo and called on the people to stop politicians and political parties from ruining Peru. Alan Garcia of the American Revolutionary People's Alliance (APRA) in mid-2003 had an approval rating of 42%, despite the fact that his presidency in the 1980s brought hyperinflation and corruption that led to his exile. In November 2002 APRA won elections for regional presidents in 12 of the 25 regions, while the PP only gained one post. In December 2003, Garcia stated that early elections might be necessary if Toledo cannot end the current crisis. Others believe Toledo must serve the rest of his term for the sake of democratic stability.

Domestic instability, regional insecurity

Over the past couple of years, domestic instability has ominously risen in all of the Northern Andean countries. Most of their governments – with the notable exception of Venezuela – have been cooperative with US regional counter-narcotics and counter-insurgency efforts. But heightened domestic challenges are likely to preoccupy them over the next year, and may render such cooperation more difficult to extend for both political and practical reasons. At the same time, the regional political trend is towards a brand of populism that is challenging a US-determined agenda for South America, while the US has a standing security concern in stemming the drug trade and an intensifying one in denying transnational terrorists access to the continent.

Venezuela presents a special case. Chávez is overtly anti-American, and Washington has relatively little leverage over him: he appears unperturbed by the severe economic dislocations that his obstinacy has caused, and suspects the US of complicity in an abortive April 2002 coup attempt. Yet Venezuela's oil is a factor in US strategic planning, and the Chávez government's apparent willingness to provide tactical support to the FARC interferes with the US and Colombia's anti-drug and counter-insurgency policies. For both, regime-change is the preferred outcome in Venezuela. The preferred means is Venezuela's own peaceful constitutional procedures, but Chávez may impede them. Given the political polarity and existing level of violence in Venezuela, a military coup – even one discreetly backed by the US, followed quickly by a handover to civilian authorities and timely elections – would not hold strong prospects for Venezuela's stability, especially considering the failure of the April 2002 coup attempt.

These circumstances suggest that Washington's policy focus for South America – particularly the Northern Andes – is too narrow. While counter-narcotics and counter-insurgency have been effective in stemming coca production and strengthening the military – and by extension the state – in

Colombia, too little has been done to attenuate the regional balloon effect and local welfare problems produced by crop eradication and substitution schemes in Bolivia and Peru. Similar problems could soon exacerbate political tensions in Ecuador and Venezuela. The US therefore may see fit to become more attentive to the domestic difficulties of putatively sympathetic regimes. Doing so would require broadening the US agenda beyond counter-narcotics and counter-insurgency by trying to help them solve their problems through economic aid (both bilateral and multilateral) for more focused poverty eradication and economic reform, and diplomatic interventions aimed at better accommodations between national and local leaders. Venezuela's absence from the regional security dialogue facilitated by US Southern Command presents a conspicuous and acute challenge to US policymakers. Given the limited scope for direct US pressure on Venezuela, Washington could explore ways of enlisting Argentina and Brazil – for instance, through more open-minded engagement on free trade – to influence Chávez. President Bush did appeal to Argentine President Nestor Kirchner to urge Chávez to respect the referendum process, and though Kirchner stated he had discussed the matter with Chávez, more sustained and robust cooperation of this sort is necessary. The major regional powers have still not assumed sufficient responsibility for ameliorating the security and stability problems of the Northern Andes. A more broadly based US policy might increase their motivation.

The Americas

Europe/Russia

The Madrid bombings of 11 March 2004 – eleven bombs placed on commuter railway cars synchronised to detonate without warning during morning rush hour, killing 191 people – brought together a variety of European security concerns. This coalescence seemed likely to move European perceptions of the terrorist threat closer to those of the United States, whose debilitation presumptively remains al-Qaeda's ultimate objective. First, the attack confirmed that since 11 September – before which Europe appears to have been most useful to al-Qaeda and its affiliates as a recruiting, planning and staging venue – more rigorous homeland security in the US had increased Europe's attractiveness as a direct target. Second, the outfit responsible was the Moroccan Islamic Combat Group, and the individual suspects comprised largely Moroccans, some of them Spanish residents, under the leadership of a Tunisian, Sarhane Ben Abdelmajid Fakhet, who, along with three others, blew himself up during a police raid. The North African origin of the terrorists highlighted Europe's vulnerability to terrorist infiltration from the Mediterranean region, while the European residency of some demonstrated the growing susceptibility of European Muslims to radicalism premised on the policies of their hosts. Third, the attack was directed at a close US ally, one which had, in particular, lent substantial political and operational support to the US-led intervention in Iraq. This factor tended to confirm the view, expounded most emphatically by France, that regime change in Iraq would antagonise Islam in general and Muslim terrorists in particular.

While the Madrid attacks bolstered an energetic preventive approach to counter-terrorism that had taken hold after 11 September, convergent threat perceptions did not spell greater accord in US and European foreign policy. The Spanish electorate ousted the ruling Popular Party in the national elections three days after the Madrid attacks. The result reflected, in part, a collective judgement that intervention in Iraq needlessly inspired Islamic terrorists, and that Spain's support for the intervention made it a more inviting target and ignored the 90% majority of the Spanish people who opposed Spain's participation. The electorate was also reacting to outgoing Prime Minister José Maria Aznar's perceived cynicism in insisting that the Basque separatist group Euskadi ta Askatasuna (ETA) was the prime suspect in the bombings, even though mass-casualty attacks were roundly inconsistent with ETA's tactics and political agenda. Although incoming Socialist Prime Minister José Luis Rodriguez Zapatero

Map Europe/Russia

had campaigned on pledges to withdraw Spanish personnel from Iraq well before the Madrid bombings, they undoubtedly galvanised his broader vow to loosen Spain's alliance with the US. This reaction suggested that further terrorist attacks could weaken the support of other US allies. Such attacks in Europe seemed likely, as al-Qaeda and its affiliates appeared to be escalating up the chain of American allies from tentative to strong – Saudi Arabia, Turkey and then Spain. Logically, al-Qaeda would next hit the United Kingdom. Although popular opposition to the Iraq intervention there was not as overwhelming as it was in Spain, Prime Minister Tony Blair's government has made operational and diplomatic commitments more extensive than Spain's, and its human and economic losses have been more substantial. On balance, Blair is subject to political risk comparable to the risk that Aznar faced. Italian Prime Minister Silvio Berlusconi's government has also supported the US on Iraq, and could face similar domestic challenges.

In 2003 and early 2004, European disunity had marked European attitudes towards not only Iraq, but also European security policy, the European Union (EU) constitution and EU fiscal standards. But while the European project may have stalled in the areas of common foreign and security policy and refining and extending supranational power, there was no denying the transformative effect that EU and NATO enlargement were having on geopolitics in Eurasia. Enlargement had made Europe and Russia's respective 'near abroads' overlapping, and in so doing had prompted a sense of encroachment and a resurgence of Russian nationalism in Moscow. Accordingly, in late 2003 and early 2004, Russia behaved provocatively in Georgia, Moldova and Ukraine, and manifested mistrust of new EU and NATO members – particularly the formerly Soviet Baltic states. Furthermore, European criticism of what most EU member states see as Russia's politically intolerant policy in Chechnya is a durable bone of Russia–Europe contention. That said, Russia and the West remain dependent on each other in roughly equal measure. Russia needs Western trade to power its domestic modernisation programme, while the West needs Russia to support counter-proliferation efforts with respect to North Korea and Iran and to help reform the UN; Russia can't behave hegemonically towards the increasingly independent Commonwealth of Independent States and needs Western cooperation to maintain influence, while the West needs Russia's help to stabilise Central Asia. The net effect of these realities will be lower expectations as to Russia–West relations than the extravagantly high ones that emerged following 11 September, but this should spell merely more realistic engagement rather than renewed strategic rivalry.

If, among Europe's close neighbours, Russia reverted somewhat more to type, Turkey witnessed departures from the status quo. The ruling Justice and Democracy Party, which has strong Islamist leanings, consolidated its power, potentially raising challenges to Ataturk's secular creed – and implicitly to the military, which safeguards it – as well as putting at risk the vaunted Turkish model of a secular Muslim state. Turkey had also distanced the US – its most important ally – by failing to deliver permission for US forces to prepare a second front for the Iraq invasion in Turkey, and by courting Iran and Syria to hedge against attempts by Iraqi Kurds to establish an independent state. Yet that same government resolved to reinforce Turkey's European vocation – which had diminished in 2002 due to perceived coolness in Brussels – by pushing the Turkish Cypriot leadership towards a compromise with the Greek Cypriot government so that a united Cyprus could enter the EU in May 2004 free of an implicit Turkish threat to annex the northern 37% of the island on which 35,000 Turkish troops are deployed. A negotiating impasse impelled the UN to schedule for 24 April 2004 simultaneous referendums on the Turkish and Greek sides on the 'Annan Plan', which calls for two locally autonomous regions under a unified central government. Even if the referendums fail to yield an accord, Ankara's proactive and constructive participation in the negotiations may at least ensure that its prospects of EU membership will not be foreclosed. But in 2003 and early 2004, what kind of Europe Turkey might join became less clear.

Europe: Recovery and Reorientation

The dramatic divisions of 2002–03 remained apparent in Europe for much of 2003–04 as well. During the spring and summer months of 2003, the countries of Europe split over the US-led intervention in Iraq in the absence of express UN authorisation, both in war and in peace. As autumn approached, they split again over economic policies, and particularly over the requirement to avoid excessive fiscal deficits. In December, they failed to agree on a European constitution and opened a new controversy about the future budget of the European Union (EU). By the early months of 2004, it was therefore easy to be pessimistic about Europe's future. Nevertheless, the divisions were more apparent than real. Going into the March 2004 European Council summit, European governments began to take a more modest and conciliatory line on security, economics and institutional design. Specifically, they accepted the inevitability of enlargement at the European level and the necessity of accelerating market-structure reform within the various member states. The Islamist terrorist bombings of the commuter rail system in Madrid on 11 March 2004, in which 191 civilians were killed, added impetus to this pan-European reconciliation. Europe's policymakers have serious challenges to face and disagreements to overcome. Most important, they must forge agreement on a vision of Europe that is capable of engendering durable popular support. Against this daunting backdrop, it is easy to forget that the EU is the most advanced and successful supranational body in existence. From this broader perspective, it would be premature to write off the European project altogether.

Iraq

The conflict in Iraq split Europe along three dimensions: between Atlanticists and Europeans; between 'old' Europe and 'new' Europe; and between political elites and public opinion. The Atlantic–European dimension corresponded to a longstanding division over general support for US foreign policy between countries like the United Kingdom, which have traditionally closely supported the United States and the so-called Atlantic Community uniting North America and Europe, and those like France, which have typically been more independent. That the Iraq conflict reopened this split is hardly unexpected, but the intensity of feeling was more surprising. The division between 'old' Europe and 'new' is more recent. The phrasing comes from US Secretary of Defense Donald Rumsfeld's awkward public attempt on 22 January 2003 to distinguish between a conception of Europe that centres on France and Germany, and one where 'the centre of gravity is shifting to the east'. The remark triggered a diplomatic row that culminated in two controversial declarations of support for the Bush administration in Iraq – one by the more Atlanticist 'group of eight' on 30 January 2003 and the other by the 'new Europeans' of the 'Vilnius Ten' on 5 February 2003. French President Jacques Chirac responded with a stern admonition to the central and eastern European states about their lack of loyalty to Europe. Behind this to and fro of diplomatic insults, the importance of the growing divide between political elites and public opinion was perhaps under-appreciated. On 15 February 2003, peace protestors organised a worldwide demonstration against the threat of conflict. All five of the largest venues were in Europe, and three of them – London, Madrid and Rome – were the capitals of the United States' staunchest European allies. A second round of coordinated events took place on 15 March, shortly before the war started. A third wave crested between 20 and 24 March, just after the war began. While the protests themselves died down once the success of the ground campaign became apparent, the resentment that such protests represented remained potent, and grew in strength as it transpired that the occupation would be highly problematic.

Europe/Russia

War and reconstruction

Despite loud political pronouncements on all sides, Europe was largely absent from the war in Iraq owing to minimal material commitments. A number of countries participated in the 'coalition of the willing', including, for example, the Czech Republic, Denmark, Greece, Italy and Spain. But much of this participation was on a very small scale (a chemical decontamination team from the Czech Republic, a few naval units from Denmark) and some was largely symbolic (access to airspace and port facilities in Greece). Spain offered medical facilities in the event of a chemical or biological attack and Italy provided logistical support. The only exception was the United Kingdom, which contributed air and naval forces as well as more than 45,000 military personnel. British troops led in the recapture of the southern port city of Basra, where they remained to direct peacekeeping and reconstruction.

The material absence of Europe appeared to matter little to the United States, or at least not to the US military. However, it has had a lasting effect on the development of European public opinion. Those countries not materially implicated in the war were less politically responsible for securing the success of the peace. Italy and Spain have made significant contributions to the stabilisation of post-conflict Iraq. Italy sent almost 3,000 troops, in addition to a number of technical experts and political advisers. Spain provided 1,300 troops and Madrid hosted the major conference for donors to support the reconstruction of Iraq on 24 October 2003. Such contributions were symbolically important to the US and the image of the coalition's integrity, but constituted domestic political liabilities. When 12 Italian carabinieri, four Italian soldiers and an Italian civilian deployed in Iraq were killed in a terrorist strike in Nasiriya on 12 November 2003, opposition politicians in Italy used the attack as an argument for withdrawal. Soon after the terrorist attack in Madrid, the incoming socialist prime minister, José Luis Zapatero, made similar noises about the withdrawal of Spanish forces. The governments of both Italy and Spain remain engaged in the reconstruction of Iraq, but suggestions of bringing home the troops have a strong popular appeal nonetheless. Zapatero, in fact, has publicly pledged to withdraw Spanish forces from Iraq by July 2004.

Legitimacy

Europe's material opt-out from the Iraq war turns partly on the fact that virtually none of Europe's leaders had to stake their political credibility on the claim that Iraq represented an imminent threat due to its possession of weapons of mass destruction (WMD). The obvious exception is UK Prime Minister Tony Blair. Blair was a vocal and insistent proponent of the view that Hussein's Iraq was an immediate threat that necessitated an immediate response. He used this argument to bring the UK into the war and also to rally British public opinion behind the troops. Just days before the onset of war, only 39% of the British public supported intervention. Soon after the cessation of major hostilities on 1 May 2003, with Saddam Hussein's regime in ruins and evidence of mass atrocities coming to the surface, that figure was 61%. At that point, more than 75% of all French and Germans conceded that Iraqis were better off without Saddam Hussein.

Importantly, however, such concessions did not eliminate public concern altogether. Instead, attention shifted to the merits of the case for intervention itself. As coalition forces failed to turn up evidence of WMD, popular misgivings over the war returned. In the UK, these misgivings were further fuelled by the suicide on 19 July 2003 of David Kelly, a UK government weapons expert who had leaked information to the British Broadcasting Corporation (BBC) undermining the claim that Hussein's Iraq had WMD capable of quickly imperilling UK territory. The government launched an immediate inquiry chaired by Lord Brian Hutton. When Lord Hutton delivered his report on 28 January 2004, he largely exonerated the government of any wrongdoing while at the same time reserving criticism for the BBC for its poor handling of Kelly's leaked information. In the meantime, however, the search for WMD had been all but abandoned. Even US President George W. Bush appeared willing to concede that such weapons might not be found. The implication was that Kelly had some justification for undermining the government's position as to the imminence of Iraq's threat. Blair's credibility on the issue collapsed. In March 2004, most UK citizens believed that their government had been wrong to use force in Iraq despite the fact that 82% acknowledged that the Iraqi people were better off as a result.

Transatlantic dilemmas

Bush's retreat from the conviction that Iraq possessed WMD revealed more than just an intelligence failure in the case for war in Iraq. It also demonstrated the extent to which Blair had isolated himself through his decision to focus on maintaining the UK's 'special relationship' with the United States, and risked sacrificing much of his influence within Europe and over the European agenda within Britain. In particular, he lost his leading position with respect to European security cooperation. Yet Blair's dilemma was a real one. French President Jacques Chirac chose a different route, but he too has suffered politically, albeit in a different way. By courting conflict with the US, France has lost any influence it may have enjoyed over US foreign policy. While Chirac may have asserted leadership over European security cooperation, this was no guarantee either that France would lead within Europe generally or that Chirac would achieve his specific security objectives. A similar point could be made with reference to German Chancellor Gerhard Schröder, who also opposed

Europe/Russia

intervention. That major powers of France and Germany's calibre, acting together, could have so little practical effect only seemed to confirm the United States' unassailable primacy. In this light, it is far from clear that Blair made the wrong decision in terms of his country's strategic, as opposed to European, position.

The difficulty of asserting Franco-German leadership in security matters was apparent at the 29 April 2003 summit between France, Germany, Belgium and Luxembourg. The purpose of the summit was to develop proposals for an autonomous European command-and-control facility as well as to reinforce European capabilities for rapid reaction to military crises. Unfortunately, without the participation of the UK – which has Europe's most capable military – the summit was doomed to fail. Not only did the proposals sound unrealistic, but they also sparked the ire of the Bush administration. A US State Department spokesman dismissively characterised the summit's participants as Europe's 'chocolate makers'. More substantively, US Secretary of State Colin Powell pointed out that a European military command structure would duplicate NATO assets while at the same time competing for resources that should be dedicated to the common defence. Such charges rang particularly true given France and Germany's ongoing breach of European fiscal commitments, Belgium's immense outstanding public debt, and the small size of the Belgian and Luxembourg militaries. Belgian Prime Minister Guy Verhofstadt reported the summit's findings at the June 2003 Thessalonki European Council summit; they received only a mention in the conclusions of the European Council Presidency.

Inadvertently, the 'chocolate summit' revealed the continuing salience of European commitment to NATO. The timing could not have been worse for France and Germany. The EU had only just finalised its agreements with NATO for access to the alliance's infrastructure for joint operations that did not involve the US (so-called Berlin Plus operations, after the June 1996 Berlin summit where the procedures for cooperation were negotiated). Moreover, the first such operation came into force when the EU assumed responsibility for peacekeeping in the Former Yugoslav Republic of Macedonia on 31 March 2003. EU–NATO cooperation was not only possible in theory, it was working in practice. In that light, it was easy to understand why many EU members would resist reinventing the wheel.

Europe's dependence on NATO came hand-in-hand with the development of a new European security strategy by Javier Solana, the EU High Representative for the Common Foreign and Security Policy (CFSP). The original draft of the strategy was proposed at the Thessaloniki European Council summit in June 2003, and the final draft adopted at the Brussels European Council summit the following December. During the intervening period, the importance of European access to NATO assets increased. The June draft makes no reference to NATO and buries the notion of 'an effective multilateral system' within a section entitled 'strengthening the international order'. The December draft gives greater prominence to 'effective multilateralism' and makes it explicit that 'the EU–NATO arrangements, in particular Berlin Plus, enhance the operational capability of the EU and provide the framework for a strategic partnership between the two organisations in crisis management'. This continuing importance of NATO in the EU's security strategy reflects two underlying realities. First, the consensus in Europe is averse to risking the disempowerment of disbandment of NATO, and rejects the inevitability of a transatlantic dilemma like that faced by the UK, France and Germany over Iraq. Most European heads of state and government would prefer to choose for Europe and the United States rather than between Europe and the United States. Second, Europeans have few new resources to offer for their own defence and would prefer to use what is available more efficiently. Thus, the June draft asserts boldly the need for 'more resources for defence. If we are serious about new threats and about creating more flexible mobile forces we need to increase defense resources'. The December draft is more conditional: 'To transform our militaries into more flexible, mobile forces, and to enable them to address the new threats, more resources for defense and more effective use of resources are necessary'.

Political economy

Such countervailing realities were not limited to the realm of security. If anything, they were more prominent in reference to the single European currency, the euro. The irrevocable fixing of exchange rates in 1999 and the introduction of the euro in 2002 has revolutionised commerce, travel and investment in Europe. On balance, and for most of the 12 participating countries, the euro has provided easier trade, lower interest rates, increased exchange-rate stability and enhanced their capital liquidity. However, it has also brought with it a range of political controversies – all of which were both foreseeable and foreseen for many years before the single currency was introduced. The rules for fiscal stability have been tested. The euro has appreciated sharply against the dollar. And member states have failed to implement sweeping welfare-state reforms. Therefore, while the single currency has been a success, this success is mitigated.

The controversy over the rules for fiscal stability began in February 2002, when the European Commission recommended that the Council of Economics and Finance Ministers (ECOFIN Council) issue an early warning to Germany and Portugal for potentially failing to maintain their fiscal deficits below 3% of gross domestic product (GDP), in contravention of EU requirements. The ECOFIN Council demurred and instead accepted commitments from both countries that they would restore fiscal discipline. But this did not happen, with both countries exceeding the 3% reference value by autumn 2002. By then France too looked set to violate this fiscal norm. The ECOFIN Council had no choice but to initiate the 'excessive deficits procedure' for Portugal in November 2002, and for Germany the following January, when it also issued an 'early warning' to France.

The timing of these declarations is important insofar as they trigger a timetable for action set forth in the 1997 Stability and Growth Pact (and accompanying European Council legislation). The member states are supposed to achieve certain targets within certain intervals, and they are monitored by the European Commission. This is in effect what happened in the case of Portugal. However, the timetable was largely ignored by Germany and France. Worse, while the German government continued to signal its willingness to abide by European procedures, the French government refused. As a result, the ECOFIN Council made France subject to the excessive deficits procedure in June 2003, with the European Commission to review French compliance action the following October. Again the French government refused to abide by these procedures – this time, however, with the support of the Germans. Following that rebellion, the Commission not only gave both countries an unfavourable review but also recommended that the ECOFIN Council start the last phase of the procedure before sanctions become available. When the ECOFIN Council met to discuss the Commission's recommendations on 23 November 2003, the member states could not find a qualified majority in support of further action. The Stability and Growth Pact provided no guidance as to what to do in the absence of a qualified majority. The ECOFIN Council therefore chose to depart from the excessive deficits procedure and recommended that the fiscal rules be held in abeyance until France and Germany could make the necessary adjustments. France and Germany, then, were permitted to ignore the Stability and Growth Pact once it became inconvenient.

If the credibility of the pact has a price, it is not measured in dollars. The euro continued its long and rapid appreciation against the dollar. A euro was worth $1.06 when the excessive deficits procedure was initiated against Germany in January 2003, $1.16 when the procedure was initiated against France the following June, $1.17 soon before the ECOFIN Council met to discuss the Commission's recommendation that both France and Germany be made subject to sanction, and $1.23 in December 2003 after the ECOFIN Council recommended that the rules for fiscal stability be held in abeyance. Of course, much of the euro's strength is really the dollar's weakness. The rapid appreciation of the euro in 2003–04 had little to do with events in Europe and much to do with those in the US and Asia. As long as the United States continues to run substantial current account deficits and as long as so many Asian countries refuse to allow their currencies to appreciate against the dollar, the EU will bear the burdens of US adjustment in the form of a strong euro. The problem for European countries is twofold. First, a strong euro makes it difficult to export to US markets. European growth has been sluggish for the past two years, and exports to the United States are a necessary source of stimulus. The effects of a strengthening currency can be hedged, but not indefinitely. Therefore, both European manufacturers and European politicians began to complain about the strength of the euro by late 2003.

Such complaints only underscored the second part of the European exchange rate problem, which is that no one in the single currency is clearly responsible for setting exchange rates. The European Central Bank (ECB) is interested in exchange rates only insofar as they effect price stability. When the currency appreciates, the pressure on inflation goes down. Therefore, ECB president Jean-Claude Trichet could say little in response to the complaints of politicians and business leaders other than that exchange rates are not a problem for the single currency. In early January 2004, Schröder even took his case to Bush. But given that euro appreciation is part of the US economic adjustment process, Schröder's pleas fell on deaf ears. The euro eased a little against the dollar going into March 2003, but the vulnerability of European economies to unwarranted movements in euro-dollar exchange rates remains evident.

Welfare state reform – that is, the aggressive promotion of jobs, growth and competitiveness – is a theoretical solution to European economic vulnerability and fiscal instability, but it has proven nearly impossible to implement for over a decade. Few disagree that successful welfare state reform will substantially reduce the importance of movements in the euro-dollar exchange rates for the performance of Europe's economies. Yet no political leader in Europe has been successful in undertaking reforms on the scale that is required. This failure is not for want of trying. The March 2000 Lisbon strategy, for example, commits EU member states to creating the world's most competitive economy by 2010, and establishes an interactive method of coordination that allows for countries to learn from one another while at the same time ensuring that reforms undertaken in one do not have negative effects on another. Such efforts have been particularly manifest in Germany, where Schröder has challenged his own party to effect cuts in unemployment and pension benefits necessary to realise his own 'Agenda 2010'. The main barriers have involved collective wage bargaining and the reform of other labour market institutions.

The central problem is that structural reform, for all its institutional and intellectual backing, is politically difficult to carry through because of the short-term pain it imposes on voters. Time and again, European leaders have pressed ambitious reform agendas only to be punished by their electorates for failing to tackle major structural problems. Recent developments in Belgian politics are a case in point. In the national parliamentary elections of 18 May 2003, the ruling Flemish Liberals and Democrats (VLD) retained support while their green coalition partners fell out of the parliament altogether. Both groups were elected as reformists in

Europe/Russia

1999, but the VLD could survive only by maintaining the status quo. Moreover, that survival was only temporary. By March 2004, support for the VLD had collapsed as well. Although still the party of the prime minister, the VLD is expected to emerge as only the fourth-largest political movement in Flanders after the June 2004 regional elections – behind the Christian Democrats, the Socialists and the right-wing Flemish Bloc. Electoral losses at the sub-national level will hardly make the VLD unique in Europe. Such political misery loves company. Schröder's Social Democratic Party was decisively beaten in the Hamburg elections of 29 February 2004. Successive rounds of regional elections in France in March 2004 hugely weakened Chirac's Union for a Presidential Majority. Incumbents suffered consistent defeats in the 2003–04 period at the national as well as the regional level – as demonstrated in Greece on 7 March 2004 – continuing trends in operation since the 1990s. European electorates have become increasingly volatile and European leaders increasingly averse to taking risks. This explains why most European countries were willing to support US Iraq policy in word more than deed – and why many were not willing to support the US at all.

Constitutional crisis

The timidity of European leadership is not limited to transatlantic relations. Indeed, the crisis that surrounded European constitutional negotiations is best understood against this backdrop of electoral volatility. The major protagonists were a weak chancellor in Germany and a weak prime minister in Poland, supported by a weak president in France and a lame-duck prime minister in Spain. The European Convention closed its constitutional negotiations in time for the June 2003 Thessaloniki European Council summit. The draft constitutional treaty was itself ready for distribution by July. The incoming Italian presidency of the European Council expressed its determination to conclude a rapid intergovernmental conference, starting in October 2003 and ending by 13 December. Yet while the member states could readily agree on most of the provisions of the constitutional treaty, Germany and Poland could not agree on a new formula for qualified majority voting. The German government insisted on a dual majority system, which could take into account both the number of member states and their relative population size. The Polish government insisted on retaining the voting weights that had been agreed at the December 2000 European Council summit in Nice. Spain supported Poland, because both held disproportionate weight under the Nice rules. France supported Germany, although it was the French who had insisted on the Nice voting weights in the first place.

The impasse was obvious even before the European Council gathered in Brussels on 13 December. The Polish Prime Minister, Lezcek Miller, could not back down without giving the appearance of having sacrificed his country's national interest. Given Miller's domestic weakness, conceding was not a realistic political option. The German chancellor also could not relent. And neither Spain nor France was eager to encourage conciliation. The parties were thus compelled to allow the Brussels European Council summit to fail to reach an agreement so that each could emerge as a strong supporter of the national interest.

Budgetary wrangling

This agreement to disagree came at a cost. Any further constitutional negotiations would have to take place alongside consideration of European budgetary matters. The current budgetary authority of the EU expires at the end of 2006. Therefore, prudence would dictate that the Council of Ministers begin consideration of a new financial perspective for the 2007–13 period in 2004. It is here, however, that the problems of structural rigidity and electoral volatility intersect. And so it is here that Europe's leaders confront their greatest challenges – challenges that will have obvious repercussions for the CFSP as well. Six of the largest net contributor member states – Austria, France, Germany, the Netherlands, Sweden and the UK – launched the first salvo in these budgetary negotiations soon after the failed Brussels summit. In a joint letter to the European Commission, these six net contributors insisted that they would not support a level of EU expenditure in excess of 1% of gross national income (GNI) against a previously agreed ceiling of 1.24%. The Commission responded on 10 February 2004 with a draft financial perspective that is considerably more expensive – averaging 1.14% of GNI across the whole of the period from 2007 to 2013. Striking a balance between these positions will be difficult. The net contributors are unlikely to accept the Commission's proposals, while net recipients will be unwilling to accept the implications of any cuts. A standoff between the two groups will effectively replicate the coalitions that brought constitutional negotiations to a standstill, with France and Germany on one side, Spain and Poland on the other. This time, however, the stakes will be financial and not symbolic or political. As a result, room for manoeuvre will be even further reduced.

Any compromise is likely to draw down the EU's financial resources for foreign affairs. Most EU expenditure supports entitlement-style programmes for economic cohesion and agricultural subsidies. These programmes are as well budgeted at the European level, as most welfare-state programmes are within the member states. Given the expectations and dependencies that such outlays engender, they are extremely difficult to cut. Therefore, the Commission proposes to hold expenditure on cohesion and agriculture constant while allowing economic growth to generate funds for 'competitiveness', domestic security and foreign affairs. This way the share of EU resources dedicated to agriculture and cohesion will fall from 68% of the total budget in 2007 to 59% in 2013. The net contributors are likely to apply a different logic. Instead of allowing new resources to bolster new expenditures, they will insist that any growth dividend be used to reduce the burden of EU financial commitments overall. This will significantly restrict the EU's ability to develop new resource commitments. Of the three remaining discretionary categories, competitiveness and domestic security are likely to prove far more resilient than foreign affairs.

Fallout from Madrid (and Lisbon)

Such calculations are not, of course, impervious to developments in the outside world. The terrorist attack in Madrid inadvertently broke open the logjam in European constitutional negotiations. The right-wing Spanish government of José María Aznar mishandled the investigation of the bombing and was turned out in parliamentary elections only days later. The incoming left-wing prime minister, Zapatero, announced that he would accept a compromise proposal from Germany on dual majority voting. Zapatero's announcement isolated the Polish prime minister internationally at the same time that his public opinion rating was collapsing domestically. As a result, Miller chose to tender his resignation, setting the date for just after the completion of the accession process. European leaders suddenly expressed new optimism about the prospects for a constitutional treaty and set their sights on having negotiations completed by the June 2004 European Council summit.

Nevertheless, the increasingly salient threat of transnational terrorism overshadowed this change in the constitutional climate. The European Council summit held on 25–26 March 2004 focused considerable attention on developing an adequate security response. In a declaration on terrorism announced on 25 March, the heads of government agreed to redouble efforts to share information both bilaterally and through Europol, to tighten border controls and to strengthen cooperation with third countries. Most important, the European Council supported the appointment of a European counter-terrorism coordinator (former Dutch minister and liberal Euro-parliamentarian Gijs de Vries) to bring greater coherence to policies adopted with the CFSP.

In March, the European Council also announced a renewed commitment to the process of market structural reform under the Lisbon Strategy and to fiscal consolidation under the Stability and Growth Pact. This was predictable insofar as the spring European Council summits are organised specifically to address these economic issues. However, the tone set by the Presidency Conclusions was less strident and more realistic – probably as a result of the more sober atmosphere generated by the tragic events in Madrid. The Council acknowledged that it would have to prioritise efforts towards stimulating growth and creating jobs. By implication, the Council also admitted that member states could not make progress on all fronts at once. Looking to the future, the Council began preparations for a mid–term review of the Lisbon strategy to take place during the course of 2004–05. This review will most likely continue with a moderation of the Lisbon objectives.

The events in Madrid also underscored the significance of enlargement. Seven new countries joined NATO on 29 March 2004. Ten countries will accede to the EU on 1 May 2004. These countries all expressed their solidarity in responding to terrorist atrocities, and their willingness to pool resources for collective security. However, the problems of coordinating action across such a wide field of interests and vulnerabilities are daunting, both politically and economically. This coordination dilemma has long been recognised, but Madrid appeared to have at least tentatively increased the collective determination to solve it.

The European vision

As the EU and NATO expand, European leaders are likely to find it necessary to remind their respective publics why integration is important and where it is heading to attract their allegiance and support. The divisions of the past two years suggest that Europe is approaching the limits of an integration driven primarily by elites. Europe's politicians no longer have sufficient room to manoeuvre to bargain effectively even in small groups, let alone an EU of 25 or more. By the same token, the institutions of the EU – the European Council, the European Commission and the European Parliament – lack either the autonomy or the impetus to impel the process of integration on their own. The first big challenge will be the elections to the European Parliament, scheduled for June 2004. Should these elections yield a disappointing turnout – particularly in the accession countries, where voters will go to the European polls for the first time – the EU's popular democratic legitimacy will come into question. Poor turnout will also augur ill for future referenda to ratify the new constitutional treaty that is due to be agreed at the European Council summit later in the same month. A weak European Parliament also would be unable to lend either legitimacy or support to the incoming College of European Commissioners set to take over the Commission in October and November 2004.

Current realism by itself is not enough. European leaders must still address their vision for the future. Part of that vision is a Europe that speaks with one voice on foreign affairs. That too has been compromised by the strains of expansion and the growing pains of supranationalism. The result has been a cleavage by some EU members towards the US, a resort on the part of others to 'protest' stances that oppose US policy on

Europe/Russia

vague principles of balance or independence rather than specific and considered strategic policies. That is not to say that no signs of transatlantic convergence have appeared since the low point of the Iraq intervention in March 2003. De facto coordination on Iran's nuclear programme is in evidence, and an understood division of labour in Afghanistan may be conditioning greater US–Europe concord on the role of NATO. Furthermore, gradual American acknowledgment that it will need more UN and multilateral help than it had bargained for with respect to Iraq has helped restore some normality to transatlantic relations. But Europe is not likely to be fully cured of its relative paralysis in strategic affairs until it gets its own increasingly crowded house in order.

Russia and the West: The End of the Honeymoon

Two-and-a-half years after Russian President Vladimir Putin joined the US-led global war on terror in the wake of 11 September and flung open a window of opportunity for Russia's strategic alignment with the West, that window is rapidly closing. Russia's opposition to war in Iraq, more assertive policy towards the former Soviet states, negative rhetoric towards the European Union (EU) and NATO enlargements, and increasingly authoritarian trends in domestic politics indicate divergence between Russian and Western interests. Russia is emerging as an independent and unpredictable player in international affairs. This sobering development is prompting calls for a reassessment of US and European policies towards Russia. But despite the growing acrimony between Russia and the West, they remain interdependent in many areas of vital mutual interest. Russia needs Western support for Putin's ambitious domestic economic modernisation project, which is the main goal of his second term. The West still needs Russia to assist in the global campaign against terrorism. Moreover, stability in the increasingly volatile CIS (Commonwealth of Independent States), which now borders the EU and NATO, cannot be achieved without Russia's constructive engagement with the West. This interdependence provides a substantial constraint against the emergence of a new strategic rivalry.

Friction and mistrust

In stark contrast to the polite circumspection of Russia–West relations between 2001 and early 2003, confrontation ruled from mid-2003 through early 2004. In an unusually critical letter published on the front page of the Russian newspaper *Izvestia* on 26 January 2004, US Secretary of State Colin Powell questioned Russia's commitment to democracy and noted that political power in Russia was 'not yet fully tethered to the law'. In February 2004, the European Commission issued a strongly worded communication asserting that EU and Russia relations had 'come under increasing strain' on important issues from enlargement to energy and the environment, and questioning Russia's conviction to uphold core universal values and pursue democratic reforms. A number of European states and institutions, including the Organisation for Security and Cooperation in Europe (OSCE), renewed their criticisms of Russia's policy in Chechnya, which has become the largest source of asylum seekers in Europe. Critics also expressed concern over Moscow's handling of the December 2003 parliamentary and March 2004 presiential elections. Further questioned was Putin's selective application of the law in prosecuting Mikhail Khodorkovsky – the former chairman of Russian oil giant Yukos, Russia's richest man (with an estimated personal wealth of over $6 billion) and a political opponent of Putin's – for fraud, tax evasion and embezzlement. Russia and the OSCE also clashed over Russia's reluctance to implement its 1998 OSCE Istanbul summit obligation to withdraw troops from Georgia and Moldova, as well as Russia's unilateral push to mediate an ill-considered power-sharing agreement between Moldova and the breakaway republic of Transdniester, which was effectively vetoed by the OSCE and the EU.

In turn, Russia's resentment towards Western policies has been apparent. Russian political elites have criticised the EU for ignoring Russia's concerns over the economic costs that enlargement will impose on Russian businesses pursuing trade and investment in Central and Eastern Europe, and on Russians who now require visas to travel to new EU countries and special permission for travel to Russia's Koliningrad exclave bordering Lithuania and Poland. Moreover, the Duma adopted a resolution protesting NATO's inclusion of the three Baltic states and 'unfriendly' gestures such as the patrolling of Baltic airspace along Russia's borders by Belgian jets days after the enlargement had been finalised. Russia's leadership is increasingly suspicious of the US and European military presence in Central Asia and Georgia, and questions the credibility of US assurances that it does not intend to establish permanent military bases in these places. Russia has been highly critical of US and UK military action in Iraq and allied itself with France and Germany in the UN Security Council against the March 2003 intervention. Russia has also raised concerns that the American 'Greater Middle East Initiative', in attempting

Europe/Russia

to promote democracy aggressively, is likely to result in greater destabilisation in areas close to Russian borders from Central Asia to Iran. Putin angrily branded Western criticism of his Chechnya policy a 'double standard' that would ultimately weaken Russia by encouraging separatism. Russia has felt threatened by the US and European efforts to become more deeply involved in the political, security and economic affairs of its neighbours in the former Soviet Union, some of which – Ukraine, Belarus, Moldova and the three South Caucasus states – are now seen as a new 'near abroad' for the enlarged EU and NATO. Many Russian observers view Georgia's 'rose revolution' – in which unpopular President Eduard Shevardnadze was replaced by the young Western-educated, English-speaking Mikhail Saakashvilli – as a 'US-orchestrated plot' of regime change that could be a model for similar moves in Ukraine, Kyrgyzstan and other countries in which contentious elections are soon to occur. Finally, Western condemnation of Russia's 'undemocratic' elections is viewed as hypocritical in light of the US and NATO's strategic partnership with states like Uzbekistan, which are notorious for politically repressive policies.

This extensive menu of mutual concerns indicates not only a divergence of strategic interests, but a widening difference in worldview. Russia believes that its 'strategic concessions' to the West after 11 September in acquiescing to US military bases in Central Asia and supporting the intervention in Afghanistan have gone unreciprocated, and is focusing on internal modernisation and strengthening its influence in the CIS, where it still has leverage. The US and Europe, troubled by unfulfilled expectations attending Putin's pro-Western choice and by residual Cold War fears towards Russia's resurgence as an independent regional power, are reconsidering their tentative opting for cooperation over coexistence or containment. The possibility of reversing this tilt is reinforced by the EU and NATO enlargements, which have brought into these organisations countries with vivid national memories of Soviet domination. The Bush administration has been cautious, conscious of the need to maintain relative quiet on other diplomatic fronts while it deals with Iraq. If Democratic candidate John Kerry wins the US presidential election, however, US policy may shift towards a more critical stance on Russia, of which active resistance to Russia's assertive policies in the CIS could be a key component. At the annual Wehrkunde conference on European security in Munich in February 2004, when Russian Defence Minister Sergei Ivanov threatened to back out of an agreement to limit Russian armed forces on Russia's European front, US Senator John McCain responded that 'undemocratic behaviour and threats to the sovereignty and liberty of her neighbours ... will exclude [Russia] from the company of Western democracies'. William Safire, the influential conservative American columnist, commented that 'NATO must not lose its original purpose: to contain the Russian bear'.

Putin's consolidation of power

In Russia's 14 March 2004 presidential elections, Putin received over 71% of the vote. Notwithstanding international criticism of media manipulation and use of government resources to support his campaign, this outcome represents a powerful display of confidence. Furthermore, in the December 2003 parliamentary elections, the pro-Putin United Russia party got a decisive 37% of the votes, gaining a controlling majority in the lower house of the Russian parliament. The next highest tally was for the Communist Party, which traditionally receives over 20% of the vote, at only 13%. None of the 'liberal' parties (Yabloko and the Union of Rightist Forces) succeeded in crossing the 5% threshold and, for the first time since the collapse of the Soviet Union, none are represented in parliament. At the same time, a new nationalist party, Rodina (which means 'motherland'), created with help from the Kremlin, won about 9% of the vote, making it and the Liberal Democrats, at almost 12%, substantial voices in the legislature. This result was conditioned in part by the Russian people's resentment towards powerful oligarchs who have been implicated in dubious privatisation deals struck while Boris Yeltsin was president and on whose support 'liberal' parties customarily relied. But the rise of Russian nationalism in the face of Western policies perceived by Russians as inimical was also a factor. One of the Rodina leaders, Dmitry Rogozin, led Russian criticism of EU policies on Kaliningrad, and championed Russia's assertive support of Russian-speaking minorities in the Baltic states and CIS countries.

With the legitimacy of his power secured and full control over the parliament established, Putin turned to centres of power outside his immediate political control – in particular, the oligarchs. In October 2003, he had Khodorkovsky arrested. Although he was charged with white-collar crimes, many believe that Putin's real reason for targeting Khodorkovsky was his political ambition, expressed by criticising Putin and financing his opponents. But in March 2004, from jail, Khodorkovsky published a letter in the Russian newspaper *Vedomosty* stating that the presidential election results demonstrated the complete failure of 'liberalism' to take root in Russia and calling on his fellow oligarchs and liberal political parties to recognise criminal nature of privatisation in 1990s. He added that privatisation left much of the country's wealth in the hands of a few rich people who subsequently took their money abroad, that the money should be returned to Russia, and that Russia's modernisation should be undertaken on the basis of Russia's national interest and its own traditions rather than in emulation of the West. At the same time, he counselled Russians not to question legitimacy of Putin's power, recognising that he had brought stability, prosperity and dignity to the Russian people. The letter shocked Russian political elites and provoked active political debate. These statements, coming from one of the strongest critics of President Putin, coupled with the fact that less than 4% of the presidential vote went to the one liberal and pro-Western presidential candidate, Irina Khakamada, indicate that Russian society has overwhelmingly coalesced around Putin and his vision for Russia.

Political clans and regional governors also increasingly back Putin. In December 1999, when Yeltsin named Putin as his successor, Putin was relatively unknown and had to strike a balance among three powerful groupings in government and his administration. The first was Yeltsin's 'Family' and included Head of Presidential Administration Alexander Voloshin and Prime Minister Mikhail Kasyanov. This group was very powerful during Putin's first term, but even before the second-term elections Putin had removed both Voloshin and Kasyanov and marginalised other Yeltsin stalwarts. Simultaneously, he denounced Yeltsin's stewardship as having led to the destruction of the Russian state and economy. The second faction was the so-called St. Petersburg group: Putin's colleagues from his home town. Putin brought with him to the Kremlin many of these friends, who include new Head of Presidential Administration Dmitry Medvedev and head of Government Administration Dmitry Kozak, who is considered as one of the most influential moderates around Putin, as well as liberals put in charge of key economic posts such as Minister of the Economy German Gref, Minister of Finance Alexei Kudrin, Deputy Prime Minister Alexander Zhukov and Andrei Illarionov, Putin's economic advisor. The third powerful group comprises the 'siloviki' – a neologism derived from the Russian term for 'power'. These are Putin's former colleagues from the KGB and other military, intelligence and security organs, and they tend to value ideology and loyalty over rights and liberties. Putin has appointed a number of these people to key posts in government and as presidential representatives in the Federal Districts, which unite several regions into seven mega-provinces, and supported the election of several governors from the siloviki group. The siloviki, although not acting in close concert, generally favour a strong central state, crackdowns on oligarchs and more assertive policy in the CIS, and oppose foreign investment in strategic sectors such as oil and gas. Although many predicted that the siloviki would gain prominence in the second presidential administration and the new government, their power has not increased.

By appointing Mikhail Fradkov, a technocrat with no political power or ambition, as the new prime minister, Putin has signalled that he intends to exercise full control over the government. He already conducts an essentially presidential foreign policy, run out of his office, and has strong ties with Ivanov, who is often mooted as Putin's successor in 2008. The only delicate balance of power that Putin has to maintain is between economic liberals and conservative siloviki. But this balance has been appreciably stabilised through the allocation of domestic economic influence to the liberals, and foreign and security policy (including military reform) influence to the siloviki. A consensus is gathering that the political transition in Russia is now complete, and that the new system, despite its democratic deficit, is likely to be stable and sustainable and will dominate Russia beyond 2008. This reality is disappointing to Western capitals, which had high expectations about Russia's democratisation as recently as Putin's early period of office, but now see severe limits on the extent to which Russia's new system can be integrated with Western institutions. The widening gap between Russian and Western political priorities and values is emerging as a constant theme in Russia–West relations, and is likely to become increasingly problematic for future strategic relationships.

Russia's modernisation project

With power concentrated in one man's hands, subject to few checks and balances, the question arises of what Putin will do with this power. From the start of his presidency Putin has been determined to strengthen Russia and establish independence in foreign policy through economic modernisation and growth. The results have been impressive. Russia's economy has consistently grown over the four years of his presidency, with GDP increasing by 7.2% in 2003. In January 2004, Russia's budget surplus was $102.5bn (compared to $70bn in January 2003), and Moscow plans to increase that surplus to 1% of GDP. Russia's January 2004 trade surplus was $6.5bn, a 32% increase over the previous year. In 2003, foreign direct investment (FDI) rose by 12% and totalled $68bn. Moreover, for the first time FDI exceeded capital outflow, signalling increasing confidence among investors. Russian foreign debt decreased from 140% of GDP in 1998 to 35% of GDP in 2003.

While Putin's policy of lowering taxes and introducing greater political stability as well as extending guarantees to large foreign investors helped the economy, the main reason for high growth was higher oil prices. Not being part of OPEC, Russia has become the largest oil producer in the world. In 2003, Russia earned around $66bn from net oil export revenues alone and projected revenues of $63bn in 2004 – in constant 2000 dollars, the highest since 1990 and more than triple 1998 revenues. Energy accounted for roughly 50% of Russia's total export earnings and government revenues in 2003. Oil export revenues have also helped pay off Russia's large foreign debt – around $123bn in early 2003. This dependency on oil and gas makes the Russian economy highly vulnerable to external oil-price shocks. More broadly, Russia is developing into an 'oil economy' with few structural reforms or investment in non-oil sectors of the economy like technology or manufacturing. Typical oil economies, such as Saudi Arabia and Venezuela, do not offer durable models for development. Nevertheless, Russia does have a favourable environment for accelerating reforms while oil prices remain high, and Putin is inclined to take advantage of high prices to push through ambitious reforms in the government bureaucracy, social welfare and energy sectors. Putin wants to reduce poverty, such that less than 15% of Russians live below the poverty line by 2008, and to double Russia's GDP by 2010. He also wants to reassert government control over the energy sector by increasing taxes on oil exports and relying increasingly on state monopolies. The latter objective has worried Western investors that Russian state monopolies will be unreliable suppliers and will apply political pressure on importers.

Putin's reforms require closer cooperation with the West. After enlargement, the EU will account for over 50% of Russia's foreign trade turnover. Russia is also planning to begin exporting oil and gas from the Far East (Sakhalin) and eastern Siberia to Japan, China and South Korea, which are among the world's most dynamic energy markets, and wants to increase its oil exports to the United States, which began in 2002. Moreover, Russia needs US and European support for its goal of WTO membership, as well as for foreign investment, especially in the high-technology sector. Russia's economic priorities call for heavy doses of foreign trade and investment, which crucially underpin its foreign policy. Accordingly, despite Russia's broad cooling towards the West, Putin will seek to avoid any major confrontation with the US and Europe. By the same token, while concerns may grow over Russia's domestic developments, Western governments are unlikely to put serious pressure on Putin. Constraining factors include Russia's economic success and political consolidation, which have diminished Western leverage, and the West's interest in diversifying oil suppliers to diminish its dependency on Middle Eastern and Gulf sources.

An erratic set of relationships

Against this backdrop, Russian relationships with the West are likely to be erratic rather than broadly warm. For example, Russia's support for France and Germany's opposition to the war in Iraq underlined the fact that its seat on the UN Security Council can make it a key power-broker when UN approval for major action is required or desirable. That role, however, gives Moscow only episodic influence, and it remains an awkward ally for a Western European democracy. Once the UN standoff ended, no France–Germany–Russia axis emerged. Russia was left outside the European strategic power centre, which returned to being a partnership among the UK, France and Germany. On balance, Russia's joining the anti-intervention coalition was an act of opportunism that brought few strategic gains.

Europe's multilateral institutions tend to take a more critical line on Russia than some of their member states. Russia's efforts to ignore what

Putin has called 'Euro-bureaucracy' and to appeal directly to powerful EU member states first brought some benefits to Russia over the Kaliningrad transit agreement, but when Moscow applied the same tactic in other areas it became counterproductive and triggered a crisis in EU–Russia relations. In January 2004, the EU Council of Ministers called for more policy coherence towards Russia among EU member states, reacting to Italian Prime Minister Silvio Berlusconi's initiative to grant Russia more support on Chechnya, the Yukos affair and Putin's request for visa-free travel than the EU as a whole was prepared to undertake. Berlusconi's performance convinced Germany and France to join other member states in the search for a more consolidated EU policy towards Russia that would be less susceptible to Russian manipulation and divide-and-rule tactics. The EU took a strong and united position in opposition to Russia's refusal to extend the 1994 Russia–EU Partnership and Cooperation Agreement (PCA) to new EU members. This concerted opposition prompted Russia to back down. However, such unity is unlikely to be preserved on other divisive issues, including Russia's accession to the WTO. At the same time, a pro-European Russian position on divisive transatlantic issues in the future is not assured. Up against EU and NATO enlargement, Russia now feels increasingly isolated from Europe. Indeed, Moscow appears to regard the US under the Bush administration as a more predictable, pragmatic and beneficial partner.

Overall, however, common Western concerns cut against a major breach of the relationship between Russia and the West. First, the West needs Russia for the war on terror. Although Russia has not been an operationally crucial member of the global counter-terrorism coalition since the fall of the Taliban, its political support is important for sustaining momentum behind US-led counter-terrorism and non-proliferation policies. Moreover, Russia continues to play a useful role in dealing with proliferation threats from Iran and North Korea. Libya's decision to open its nuclear programme to international scrutiny exposed not only Pakistan's involvement but also Russia's role in the shadow commercial network for technology and materials required for nuclear weapons programmes. Accordingly, the US and Europe – which are increasingly coordinating non-proliferation policy – are keen to keep Russia on side. Second, Russia's membership in the 'quartet' that is overseeing the Middle East peace process makes its political backing on that issue important to the West – though stasis in Israeli–Palestinian relations may diminish this Western need. Third, the US and particularly Europe need Russia's support for UN reform. Conversely, Russia has a strong stake in securing a robust UN role in international affairs to ensure that the pre-emptive use of military force does not emerge as a new norm. Russia's position on the future of the UN, of course, is not in line with current reform trends. Russia stresses strong support for national sovereignty and shies away from legitimising the use of force for

Europe/Russia

humanitarian intervention – primarily with an eye towards restraining US power – whereas opinion prevalent in Western circles envisages an expanding UN role in conflict resolution and defending human rights. Russia's attitude could block reform that would make the UN better able to fulfil such a role and thus able to increase the United States' diminished post-Iraq inclinations to work through the UN. But, as Russia is a permanent member of the Security Council, the other permanent members cannot ignore its concerns.

NATO, the OSCE and the EU also have strong reasons to forge cooperation with Russia. For NATO, relations with Russia under NATO–Russia Council (NRC) constitute an important part of the Alliance's post-Cold War transformation goal of 'creating Europe whole and free' through a relationship of trust. NATO's taking in the three Baltic States in April 2004 strained this trust, reviving old perceptions in Russia of NATO as inherently threatening and to an extent institutionalising both the Baltics' fear of Russia's resurgence and Russia's refusal to normalise relations with them. As of April 2004, however, no major tensions had emerged in the NRC. The body met a number of times in 2003 at the levels of defence ministers, chiefs of general staff and ambassadors, yielding progress on the harmonisation of peacekeeping doctrines, interoperability and military-to-military cooperation. In general, serviceable NATO–Russia relations via the NRC are politically important for maintaining a stable regional atmosphere for NATO peacekeeping operations in Afghanistan and Kosovo. Likewise, cordiality between Russia and European members of the OSCE is key to its being an important player in addressing regional conflicts in Eurasia.

For the EU, good relations with Russia are becoming more crucial in the context of an enlargement that not only extends EU–Russia borders, but also should increase trade turnover. Any breakdown in EU–Russia trade relations would make it harder for the EU to absorb the new members economically and to diversify its energy supplies with Russian products. But Russia too has incentives to avoid a major falling out, as it would dampen Russia's WTO prospects. This consideration may moderate Russian inclinations to confront the EU on enlargement issues, especially given the EU's strong-willed and successful opposition to Russia's conditions for extending the PCA to new EU members. Russia's stake was essentially economic, while the EU's was more basic: namely, establishing its credibility in protecting the sovereignty and independence of the new members, including the Baltics. Equally, however, the friction over the PCA may be a durable source of tension and dysfunction. While the EU and Russia agreed at the May 2003 EU–Russia summit in St. Petersburg to introduce 'common spaces' between EU and Russia in economic relations, education, science and security, 'common spaces' have not been practically defined. Russia has been overtly reluctant to engage with Brussels on foreign-policy issues, as it is leery of the EU's growing interests in Russia's putative sphere of influence. The EU and Russia have made little progress in the area of military cooperation. On balance, Russia will remain an important partner for the EU and NATO, and an important member of the OSCE. The high expectations about the pace and depth of Russian cooperation that materialised soon after 11 September, however, have now shrunk to a more realistic level.

Overlapping 'near abroads'

The establishment of US and other NATO states' military bases in Uzbekistan and Kyrgyzstan were followed by NATO's engagement in the stabilisation mission in Afghanistan, necessitating its long-term presence in Central Asia. A US train-and-equip programme in Georgia has transformed the geopolitical landscape in the south Caucasus. NATO and EU enlargement into the Baltic states has ended the Cold War legacy in Europe by shifting the borders of Euro-Atlantic economic and security institutions to Russia's Western borders. As a result, Ukraine, Moldova and Belarus have emerged as Europe's new 'near abroad', prompting more active European engagement in economic as well as security issues in these states, including the unresolved conflict in Moldova. Many Russians perceive these developments as constituting an encirclement that aims to exploit Russia's weakness, when Moscow should be rewarded for the support and geopolitical concessions it offered after 11 September. Moreover, this strategic encirclement – termed 'the end of Eurasia' by Russian scholar Dmitri Trenin – has not been accompanied by more vigorous efforts to integrate Russia into Western institutions or to assist it in addressing its own security concerns. This has left Moscow feeling isolated and insecure in a region where it has traditionally had special interests and influence. Russia clearly is not content to accept these changes as the new strategic reality. Even the most liberal pro-Western politicians, such as the Union of Rightist Forces party luminary Anatoly Chubais, have called for Russia to begin establishing a 'liberal empire' in the CIS through the expansion of Russia's business into CIS states to regain benign political influence. Nationalist politicians such as Dmitry Rogozin from the Rodina party have counselled a more assertive protection of the rights of Russian-speaking minorities in the CIS as a means of re-establishing Russia's regional power.

In October 2003, the Russian military elaborated a new doctrine contemplating pre-emptive military action to redress cross-border threats emanating from neighbouring regions. Among the external threats enumerated are: deployment of foreign troops on territories of neighbouring states without Russia's consent and without UN sanction; military deployments that could change the existing military balance in countries along Russia's borders and those of Russia's CIS allies; and

Europe/Russia

expansions of military alliances at the expense of Russia's and its allies' security. The military doctrine concludes that in the evolved strategic environment Russia can no longer ensure its security by political means – e.g., cooperation with international institutions or partnerships with Western countries. Beyond this declaratory policy, Russia moved to consolidate its military presence in the CIS by transforming the Collective Security Treaty into the CIS Collective Security Treaty Organisation and taking steps to make Russia's military assets in Tajikistan – principally, the Russian army's 201st Motorised Division – an official and permanent military base. President Putin has officially opened a new Russian military base in Kant, Kyrgyzstan, just a few kilometres from a US-led coalition base in Manas, raising immediate concerns about logistical matters such as air traffic management between the two facilities. Russia's presence in Kant remains symbolic, with few aircraft performing operational flights. However, the lack of cooperation and even communication between Russian and Western forces in Central Asia has raised tensions while failing to address regional security concerns, as the March 2004 terrorist attacks in Uzbekistan demonstrate. Russia also conducted a number of large-scale military exercises in 2003–04, including several in the Caspian region as well as an inaugural anti-terrorism exercise in Central Asia under the auspices of the Shanghai Cooperation Organisation, which includes China, Russia and the four Central Asian states, Kazakhstan, Uzbekistan, Tajikistan and Kyrgyzstan. Russia has hardened its position on its withdrawal of military bases from Georgia, often in reaction to increased pressure from the US and OSCE, claiming that Russia has already fulfilled its obligations under the 1998 Istanbul agreement.

Furthermore, Moscow opposed the EU's proposals to undertake a mission in the former Soviet republic of Moldova to broker a resolution of a dispute between Moldova and the breakaway republic of Transdniester – a secessionist region of Moldova populated primarily by ethnic Russians which hosts a Russian military base. In November 2003, Putin pre-emptively dispatched Dmitry Kozak (then the deputy head of Putin's administration) to negotiate a unilateral settlement whereby Russia's political influence and military presence would be preserved. The EU and the OSCE prevailed on Moldovan President Vladimir Voronin not to sign the deal. Russia's attempt to co-opt the Moldovan leadership failed for two main reasons. First, it was undertaken without the consultation of other interested parties – including Ukraine, the OSCE and the EU. Second, the deal that Moscow struck granted veto powers over Moldova's domestic and foreign policy decisions to a Transdniestrian leadership that has been involved in transnational criminal activities such as arms and human trafficking into Europe, which made the deal substantively unacceptable to the OSCE and the EU. But Kozak cast their opposition as simply anti-Russian power politics, which resonated with Russia's political elites.

As a result, Russia has taken a broadly less tolerant position with respect to the involvement of outside actors in resolution of conflicts in the CIS.

In the south Caucasus too, Russia has continued to play at best a passive role in UN efforts to resolve conflict in Georgia's breakaway region of Abkhazia. Moscow has applied no pressure on the Abkhaz leadership to rejoin the Geneva peace process sponsored by the UN Secretary-General's 'Group of Friends of Georgia', which includes Russia, Germany, the UK, France and the US. In fact, Russia has acknowledged that it issued Russian passports to 50,000 Abkhaz residents, which constitutes more than a quarter of Abkhazia's current population. Especially given Russia's intensifying commitment to protecting the rights of ethnic Russians and Russian citizens abroad, this action cast doubt on Russia's credibility as an impartial mediator in the Georgian–Abkhaz conflict. Russia has also insisted that the withdrawal of Russian military bases in Georgia be negotiated bilaterally between Moscow and Tbilisi, despite Russia's conflicting obligation under the agreement on modifying the Conventional Armed Forces in Europe Treaty signed in 1998 at the OSCE Istanbul summit. Although Russia provocatively assembled the leaders of the separatist regions of Georgia during the November 2003 'rose revolution', Saakashvilli's visit to Russia in February 2004 and Russia's neutrality during the crisis between Tbilisi and the Adjarian leadership the following March improved Georgian–Russian relations. Against the background of Russia's renewed resentment against external 'interference' in settling frozen conflicts in CIS, including those involving Abkhazia, Nagorno-Karabakh and Transdniester, prospects for settlement of those conflicts in the near future are dim.

In addition to existing regional conflicts, a new source of instability has emerged in Russian–Ukrainian relations. In October 2003, without notifying Ukraine, Russia began to build a dike connecting its coast with the island of Tuzla in the Kerch Strait, near Ukraine's Crimean Peninsula. Ukraine issued a protest asserting Ukraine's non-negotiable sovereignty over the island. Russia did not respond to Ukraine's requests for an explanation for nearly two weeks after construction began, and then claimed that it did not recognise Ukraine's sovereignty over the island. Russia's gambit provoked a crisis, as Ukraine deployed 50 troops to Tuzla to protect its border and threatened to abandon free-trade arrangements with Russia should the dike cross Ukraine's border. Putin did not order construction halted for almost a month, with the dike only 100 metres from Ukrainian territory. Major damage had been done to Ukrainian–Russian relations, prompting Ukraine's leadership to seek greater security guarantees through closer cooperation with NATO and by reaffirming its intent to join the Alliance despite Russia's opposition.

The Tuzla episode illustrated that Russia's increasingly unilateralist policy in the CIS is counterproductive and is likely to weaken rather than

Europe/Russia

strengthen its role in the region. A contradictory policy under which Russia continues to expand cooperation with NATO and the EU, but considers similar moves by CIS states like Ukraine and Georgia as threatening to Russia's interests and security, is diplomatically unsustainable. A more sensible and moderate approach would be for Moscow to acknowledge more openly that NATO and EU enlargement have prompted a major change in the strategic environment around the CIS that makes it impossible for the US and Europe to avoid involvement with the countries with which Russia shares a common border. Conceding at least some of their interests would make Russia's assertion of its own competing interests more credible. Moreover, Russia's zero-sum mentality in regard to the CIS is unrealistic. Given its preoccupation with domestic reforms, Russia is not in a position to consolidate the CIS, reclaim a monopoly on the regional security agenda and promote regional economic development. Thus, Moscow should further recognise that Russia and the West have common concerns about the stability of the CIS. Russian military doctrine states that local conflicts along its borders as well as potential failed states threaten Russia's security. The EU, the OSCE and NATO share this worry.

Given the new strategic reality of 'overlapping near abroads', Eurasia is the key arena in which tensions between Russia and the West will be played out. Russia must either cooperate with new regional actors or find itself further marginalised from key political, economic and security processes in CIS states, which also seek stabilisation and domestic modernisation. The West, in turn, has to acknowledge to Moscow that the CIS region cannot be stabilised without Russia's constructive contributions – and indeed, in some areas, its leadership. The West, therefore, would be best served by accepting Russia's assertion of its legitimate interests in the region – that is, those that are conducive to further democratisation, economic development and regional stability. In the security sphere, the ultimate objective for both Russia and the West in Eurasia should be to create viable states with effective security sectors that can ultimately maintain their own security on the basis of international norms and normal relations with all neighbours. This, however, can only be achieved once regional conflicts are resolved.

Dampening the pendulum

Since the end of the Cold War, Russia's relations with the West have followed an unhealthy 'pendulum' pattern. Fulsome expectations after the demise of the Soviet Union about Russia's fast integration into the West were followed by a backlash and a cold peace over the first round of NATO enlargement and NATO's Kosovo campaign. In 2003, comparably soaring hopes over a new 'strategic bargain' following Russia's post-11 September support for the global war on terror gave way to mutual resentment over the bumpier relationship that actually materialised. Lower hopes have the most profound implications for post-Soviet states in Eurasia, where the Cold War legacies are dying hard. Yet, in 2004, neither Russia nor the West could afford to implement new containment policies. Russia's economic modernisation project requires closer integration with Western institutions, which powerfully inhibits Russia's strategic adventurism in Eurasia. At the same time, the current phase of global instability makes it costly for the US and Europe to lose Russia as a counter-terrorism and counter-proliferation partner. Finally, Eurasia has been at least partially transformed. Despite domestic weakness and regime instability, the CIS states have become better prepared to pursue cooperation with both Russia and the West without compromising their independence.

It would be preferable for Russia and the West to abandon the dizzying cycle of high and dashed expectations and focus on practical areas of cooperation where interests coincide. Grand strategic partnerships and geopolitical designs should yield to a new pragmatic agenda. Although less visionary, this more incremental approach would stand a better chance of establishing a firm basis for a stable relationship. While domestic political trends in Russia may cause legitimate concern in the West, the fact remains that the Russian people gave Putin a powerful democratic mandate for reform. If his reforms are successful, diverging values in the short term should not be an obstacle to promoting greater convergence over time. In Russian–Western relations, strategic patience should replace strategic opportunism. The honeymoon is over. The task is not to seek an amicable divorce, but rather to preserve an awkward partnership.

Europe/Russia

Turkey in Flux

The landslide victory for Turkey's ruling Justice and Development Party (JDP) in the 28 March 2004 local elections crowned a remarkable 12 months for the party and its chairman, Prime Minister Tayyip Erdogan. Barred by the Turkish constitution from holding public office as the result of a 1998 conviction for inciting religious hatred, Erdogan had been unable to stand in the November 2002 general elections, which had seen the moderately Islamist JDP sweep to power with 34.3% of the popular vote and 363 seats in the 550-seat unicameral parliament. It was not until 14 March 2003, after the new government headed by JDP Deputy Chairman Abdullah Gul had amended the constitution and held a by-election, that Erdogan was finally able to enter parliament and take over as prime minister.

Erdogan's appointment as prime minister coincided with crises in Turkey's relations with both the US and the EU. On 1 March 2003, the Turkish parliament had failed to endorse a government motion to allow US troops to transit the country in the run-up to the war against Iraq, infuriating Washington and sending US–Turkish relations into a tailspin. On 11 March 2003, another crisis had broken in The Hague when UN-brokered efforts to reunify the divided island of Cyprus collapsed due to the intransigence of Turkish Cypriot leader Rauf Denktash. This development left the way open for the Greek Cypriots to enter the EU on their own on 1 May 2004 – a result which would not only indefinitely postpone Ankara's own hopes of accession, but could also derail its internal democratisation process, which had been primarily driven by the prospect of eventual EU membership.

But, by the end of Erdogan's first 12 months in office, fears about his and the JDP's stewardship of the nation subsided. In 2003, the economy had recorded its second year of robust growth, while parliament had passed a battery of democratic reforms. In the 28 March 2004 local elections, the JDP won 41.7% of the popular vote. The main parliamentary opposition, the Republican People's Party (RPP), finished second with 18.3%. These results gave the JDP control of 58 of Turkey's 81 provinces. The JDP's huge margin of victory appeared to guarantee a long period of relative political stability. Even if they lacked some of their former warmth, relations with Washington had recovered to the point where US officials were again citing Turkey as a model for other Muslim countries. Perhaps most remarkably, in an astonishing about-face, Turkey had forced Denktash back to the negotiating table in what appeared to be the best chance in a generation for a settlement of the Cyprus problem. Even the string of terrorist bombings in Istanbul in November 2003 only temporarily deflated a buoyant public mood. By early 2004, Erdogan was repeatedly assuring the Turkish people that the country had now completed all of the criteria for EU membership, and that only religious prejudice could prevent Turkey from being given a date for the beginning of formal accession negotiations at the EU summit in the Netherlands in December 2004.

Beneath the surface, however, many problems and challenges remained. Economic recovery had yet to become rooted in structural change, while the implementation of democratic reforms was proceeding slowly. The government did not appear to have thought through the full repercussions of a solution to the Cyprus problem or, indeed, of Turkey's receiving a definite accession date from the EU. The situation in Iraq, not least the political status of its Kurdish population, still had the potential to trigger another round of regional instability. Perhaps most critically, the role of Islam in public life in Turkey was not only unresolved, it had yet to be fully addressed.

A tentative challenge to Kemalism

Through 2003 and into early 2004, the JDP passed a series of democratic reform packages ostensibly to try to bring Turkey into line with the Copenhagen political criteria for EU accession. They included: strengthening laws against torture and human-rights abuses; narrowing the scope of anti-terrorism legislation and abolishing capital punishment even in war time; embedding decisions of the European Court of Human Rights (ECHR) in Turkish law; putting the country's State Security Courts, which have traditionally been the main legal mechanism for suppressing free speech, on an equal footing with other courts; further easing restrictions on the use of the Kurdish language, including allowing parents to give their children Kurdish names and creating the legal framework for broadcasting in Kurdish; and lifting obstacles to the establishment and operation of foundations and associations by non-Muslim minorities. Some of the reforms were passed out of genuine conviction, others merely from a desire to comply with the Copenhagen criteria. The JDP also had its own political motives for attempting to fulfil EU edicts on civilian control of the military. The JDP has always seen the staunchly secularist Turkish military as its main opponent. Most of the JDP's leading members of government are former members of the Islamist Welfare Party, which was forced from power by a military-engineered civilian coup in 1997. Knowledge that the military's political influence would be severely curtailed by EU membership is undoubtedly one of the reasons for the JDP's drive for accession.

In 2003, the JDP government passed a series of measures to curb the political influence of the military and bring it under de facto as well as de jure civilian control, including: making military spending subject to civilian scrutiny; forbidding the prosecution of civilians in military courts during peacetime; reducing military service from 18 to 15 months (thus also trimming the overall size of the armed forces and the officer corps); and, most significantly, restricting the military's ability to exercise leverage through the National Security Council (NSC). In theory, the NSC is merely an advisory body which brings together high-ranking members of the armed forces and civilian government to discuss security issues. In practice, its monthly meetings have been used as a platform at which the Turkish General Staff (TGS) has set parameters for government policy. The NSC Undersecretariat, which has always been headed and largely staffed by members of the armed forces, has often effectively served as an alternative policymaking unit, gathering information and preparing detailed briefing documents for presentation at NSC meetings. However, under amendments introduced in July 2003, the requirement that the NSC Secretary-General be a military officer was abolished and the period between regular NSC meetings increased from one to two months. In December 2003, parliament voted to remove the secrecy surrounding the

Europe/Russia

operations of the Undersecretariat by lifting the ban on the publication of NSC regulations, appointments and personnel.

Implementation of democratic reforms, however, has lagged well behind their enactment. In March 2004, human-rights abuses, though reduced, remained widespread and there were still restrictions on the expression of a Kurdish identity. The predominantly Kurdish People's Democratic Party (HADEP) was banned by the Turkish Constitutional Court in March 2003, and a case was immediately brought for the closure of its successor, the Kurdish Democratic People's Party (DEHAP), on charges of advocating separatism. A verdict was expected in late in 2004. In March 2004, four former MPs from one of HADEP's predecessors, the Democracy Party (DEP) which had also been outlawed by the Constitutional Court, remained behind bars, even though the ECHR had ruled that their 1994 conviction for alleged links to the violent Kurdistan Workers' Party (PKK) was unsound. They included Leyla Zana, a three-time nominee for the Nobel Peace Price and the recipient in 1995 of the European Parliament's Sakharov Prize. Although a ban on teaching Kurdish had been lifted in 2002, not until 13 March 2004 was a small language school in the southeastern town of Urfa able to offer the first Kurdish courses. Dozens of applications by other schools remained mired in government bureaucracy or were simply rejected, mostly on what appeared to be spurious pretexts. Nor had there yet been any broadcasting in Kurdish, mainly because broadcasting in languages other than Turkish was only permitted for stations with nationwide coverage. This suggested that, if and when Kurdish broadcasting did start, it would likely be limited to a few hours a day on the tightly controlled state television and radio.

In response to foreign criticism of this record, the government blamed an independent judiciary and conservative elements in the state bureaucracy. But it also appeared to lack the conviction to ensure implementation. There is little doubt that the JDP was wary of antagonising the Turkish establishment. But this does not explain the contrast between JDP officials' silence in the face of continued restrictions on the public expression of a Kurdish identity and their frequent vociferous protestations about limitations on the public expression of an Islamic identity, such as the ban on women wearing headscarves in state institutions, including schools and universities. Throughout 2003 and early 2004, the headscarf issue remained one of the main battlegrounds in a coded duel of symbols and gestures between the government and the secular establishment, particularly the TGS. The Turkish military sees itself as having a sacred duty to protect the secular legacy of the republic's founder Mustafa Kemal Ataturk as embodied in the state ideology of Kemalism. To the military, the wearing of a headscarf on state premises is not just illegal but an act of sacrilegious insurrection – and the JDP's support for it proof that, despite its protestations to the contrary, the party harbours a secret radical Islamist agenda.

On 23 April 2003 the TGS boycotted a reception held by Parliamentary Speaker Bulent Arinc of the JDP when it learned that it would be co-hosted by his headscarved wife. On 29 October 2003, JDP MPs staged their own boycott of a reception hosted by Turkish President Ahmet Necdet Sezer when he refused to extend invitations to their headscarved wives. JDP leaders, including Erdogan and Gul, adopted a policy of taking their headscarved wives with them when they travelled abroad on official trips, but pointedly leaving them at home when they attended official functions inside Turkey. There were more subtle skirmishes in other areas. Chief of Staff General Hilmi Ozkok adopted a strategy distinguished by nuance and restraint rather than direct confrontation. Sometimes the military communicated its views in private meetings with ministers. At other times, a leading member of the TGS would comment on a specific issue at a high-profile function attended by the media. For example, in October 2003, the government announced a package of educational reforms that included plans to increase enrolment at Turkey's imam training schools. A few days later, General Ilker Basbug, the Deputy Chief of Staff, publicly questioned the motives behind the schools' planned expansion, noting that they already produced 25,000 graduates annually for the less than 1,000 positions that fell vacant each year. The reforms were subsequently quietly shelved.

Ozkok's strategy was more the product of pragmatism than a radical reappraisal of the role and responsibilities of the Turkish military. There is no indication that he is any less committed to secularism or Kemalism than his predecessors. But in recent years the TGS has exerted political leverage primarily through its public prestige rather than the implicit threat of putting troops on the streets. Although it distrusts the EU, the TGS is anxious for Turkey to begin accession negotiations, not least because it believes that membership will increases levels of development and wealth in Turkey, which will eventually reduce the electoral appeal of Islamist parties. It is also aware that the overwhelming majority of the Turkish people support EU membership and that any overt military meddling in politics could jeopardise Turkey's prospects for accession, which in turn would erode the military's domestic prestige. As a result, throughout 2003 and into 2004, the military had little choice but to adopt a relatively low profile and assess which issues were sufficiently important to justify pressure on the government. However, such restraint often stoked frustration in the TGS at what many saw as a long-term campaign of attrition by the JDP against the secular state. They believed that the government was occasionally testing the military's resolve on issues such as the headscarf ban before backing down, while discreetly chipping away at Ataturk's secular legacy through massive tax hikes on alcohol and closing state canteens during Ramadan, removing all 12 female members of the board of state-owned television and increasing religious programming, and gradually filling the government bureaucracy with JDP supporters.

Europe/Russia

At the end of 2003, tensions within the military boiled over into the public arena. On 29 December 2003, a leading JDP MP, Fehmi Husrev Kutlu, angrily complained that the portraits in parliament of Ataturk in military uniform made him feel as if he was imprisoned in a barracks. On 30 December 2003, General Aytac Yalman, commander of the Turkish Land Forces, issued a furious public condemnation of Kutlu's statement. In an unprecedented break with the military hierarchy, Yalman had acted independently, publicly attacking Kutlu without first clearing what he was going to say with Ozkok. Unwilling to punish this act of virtual insubordination for fear of weakening the TGS' public prestige, Ozkok issued his own statement on 31 December 2003 supporting Yalman and condemning Kutlu. By March 2004, the tensions between Ozkok and Yalman appeared to have dissipated. On 3 March 2004, Ozkok delivered his most explicit warning to the JDP government when he dispatched Yalman to head a high-echelon TGS delegation to attend a conference organised by a Kemalist NGO to mark the eightieth anniversary of Ataturk's abolition of the Ottoman Caliphate. Surrounded by television cameras, the TGS delegation occupied the entire front row in the auditorium and vigorously applauded as a succession of speakers warned of the dangers facing secularism and affirmed their determination to defend it at whatever cost.

While there is little doubt that the JDP does have an Islamist agenda, it is probably much less extreme than the TGS fears. That said, in substance it is likely still sufficient to breach the military's definition of secularism. Opinion polls conducted in January 2004 suggested that only 15% of JDP supporters favoured the introduction of full sharia Islamic law, while 61% opposed it and 24% were undecided or did not answer. However, on issues such as basing certain elements of civil law on the sharia, including rights of inheritance and issues related to family life, support rose to 50–60%. Virtually all of those questioned favoured the lifting of the headscarf ban. But the JDP leadership is aware that the party needs time to establish itself in the state bureaucracy and, through familiarisation, become accepted by moderate Turkish secularists. In early 2004, sources close to the JDP leadership privately predicted that the party would probably need to win a second term with an even larger majority before it could tackle sensitive issues such as the role of religion in public life. In the short term, the JDP had two priorities: securing a date for the beginning of EU accession negotiations and ensuring sustained economic growth.

Moving beyond feel-good economics

In early 2004, many of Turkey's macroeconomic indicators appeared encouraging, even impressive. Turkish Gross National Product (GNP) grew by 5.9% in 2003, following 7.8% growth in 2002. Industrial output rose by 21.2%, while exports during the year stood at US$46.7 billion, up

30% on 2002. Shares on the Istanbul Stock Market posted an average real return of 51.7%, while annual consumer inflation fell from 29.7% in 2002 to 18.4% in 2003, slipping still further to 11.8% at the end of March 2004. The JDP could probably take a large share of the credit for the fall in inflation and the bullish stock market. These were mainly attributable to a combination of public expectations that Turkey's first single-party government in a decade would ensure relative political stability and the JDP's adherence to the strict fiscal discipline of an economic austerity programme agreed with the IMF by the previous administration in the wake of the currency collapse of February 2001. But several of the factors underlying the improved statistics were likely to be temporary; and others had the potential to inflict long-term damage which would outweigh their short-term benefits.

The increases in the GNP growth rate, industrial output and exports were all primarily driven by a rebound from the 2001 recession, when the economy shrank by 9.5%, and by an overvalued Turkish lira. Turkish industry is heavily dependent on imports of raw materials and semi-finished goods. The real appreciation in the value of the lira from late 2002 onwards was exacerbated in late 2003 and early 2004 by the international weakness of the dollar, in which a large proportion of Turkish foreign trade is denominated. As a result, Turkish imports rose by 33.3% in 2003 to $68.7bn. Cheap imported inputs fuelled an increase in industrial output. However, most of the extra production was for inventories, which had been allowed to decline in 2001, and consumer demand swelled by purchases postponed during the recession two years earlier. By March 2004, Turkish exporters were complaining that they were unable to compete, with many reporting that they were selling at cost or even a loss just to maintain market share. A 41.1% increase in the foreign trade deficit to $21.8bn in 2003 had fuelled a widening of the current account deficit from $1.5bn in 2002 to $6.8bn in 2003 – a level which was sustainable in the short term but not in the long term, and which would persist or increase unless there were an adjustment in the value of the lira.

There were also concerns about the long-term impact of the JDP's taxation policy and its attitude towards the graft and nepotism that had become endemic under previous administrations. In its 2002 election campaign, the JDP had pledged that, once in power, it would limit immunity to allow the investigation and prosecution of MPs involved in corruption. In 2003, the JDP initiated investigations into corruption claims involving 25 former ministers in previous administrations, but reneged on its promise to limit parliamentary immunity. In February 2003, the JDP introduced a tax amnesty under which companies and individuals who had falsified their tax returns were promised immunity from prosecution provided that they declared and paid their previously hidden earnings. Over 2.5 million applied for this forgiveness. The short-term result was a

Europe/Russia

sudden inflow of tax revenue, although arguably at the cost of setting a precedent which would serve as disincentive to pay future taxes on time. Perhaps more worryingly, one of the beneficiaries was Finance Minister Kemal Unakitan, whose ministry had drafted the amnesty and who, before entering parliament in November 2002, had been facing prosecution on multiple charges of falsifying tax returns by issuing false invoices. In March 2004, Ihsan Gida Pazalarma, a food distribution company co-owned by Erdogan, admitted that it had falsified its tax returns in 1998, 1999, 2000 and 2001.

Arguably the most worrying economic development in 2003 was demographic. In March 2004, the State Institute of Statistics announced that the unemployment rate in December 2003 was 10.3%, down from 11.0% a year earlier. Yet a closer inspection of the figures revealed that, while the working-age population had increased by nearly 900,000, the number of those available for work had contracted by 1.1m as around 2m people, mostly women, simply withdrew from the workforce. In 2003, despite 5% economic growth, the number of employed fell by 850,000. The problem was particularly acute in the impoverished east and southeast of Turkey, where decades of government neglect, a high birth rate and the ravages of the still simmering war against the PKK had produced unemployment rates often twice the national average and created a fertile recruiting ground for radical groups of all political persuasions.

Islamist terrorist attacks in Istanbul

On 15 November 2003, two pickup trucks driven by Islamist suicide bombers exploded within 15 minutes of each other outside two Istanbul synagogues. Five days later, on 20 November, Istanbul was hit by two more suicide truck bombs that blew up outside the British Consulate General and the Turkish headquarters of the London-based HSBC bank. A total of 63 people were killed in the four blasts. Three British diplomats, including Consul-General Roger Short, and six Turkish Jews lost their lives. The rest of the dead, and the vast majority of the more than 750 injured, were Turkish Muslims. In December 2003, a series of police raids in Istanbul and the central Anatolian city of Konya resulted in the arrest of 20 suspected Islamist militants and the seizure of 500 kilograms of explosives, which the Turkish authorities claimed had been prepared for use in more suicide bombings in Istanbul.

By mid-March 2004, the Turkish authorities had charged 69 people – all Turkish nationals – in connection with the Istanbul bombings, mostly with membership of an illegal organisation rather than direct involvement in the attacks. But several of the ringleaders remained at large and were believed to have fled abroad. Police sources reported that interrogations of the suspects in custody had indicated that the bombings had been carried

out by an ad-hoc 10-man cell with links to al-Qaeda, which they claimed
had financed the operation. But the Istanbul bombings were as much the
product of conditions inside Turkey as they were imports. During the late
1980s and early 1990s, the Turkish authorities actively tolerated the spread
of radical Islam in the predominantly Kurdish southeast of Turkey in
the hope that religion would serve as a bulwark against the ostensibly
Marxist, and thus atheistic, PKK. The result was the creation of a large pool
of radicalised, poorly educated young men with little prospect of finding
employment. Some joined violent indigenous Islamist groups. Many more
went abroad to fight for Islamist causes in the Balkans and the Caucasus,
with most spending some time in military and terrorist training camps
in Pakistan and Afghanistan. Little attempt was made to monitor their
activities when they eventually returned to Turkey. Almost all of the
young men suspected of planning and carrying out the 2003 bombings in
Istanbul were originally from southeast Turkey and acquired the technical
and organisational skills used to carry out the attacks in camps in Pakistan
and Afghanistan.

Taken collectively, the November 2003 Istanbul bombings represented
the worst act of terrorism in modern Turkish history. Even the relatively
unsophisticated, small-scale attack on a Masonic lodge in the Istanbul
suburb of Yakacik on 9 March 2004 – two people including one of the
assailants were killed, and another six injured, as terrorists sprayed
restaurant diners with machine-gun fire before attempting to detonate 14
homemade bombs – served as a reminder of the continued threat of
Islamist violence. One of the assailants and several of the support players
subsequently arrested apparently had previously fought alongside Islamist
militants in Chechnya. This not only prompted the country's security and
intelligence services finally to begin targeting the pool of Islamist militants
who had trickled back into the country after receiving terrorist training
abroad, but also appeared to soften public hostility to the US war on
terrorism. According to a survey by the Pew Research Center published in
March 2004, the proportion of Turks who supported Washington's global
anti-terrorism campaign rose from 22% in May 2003 to 37% in March 2004.
Significantly, the only other countries covered by the survey where support
for the US campaign had increased were Morocco and Russia, both of
which had also suffered major terrorist attacks since March 2003.

Turkey and America: no longer lovers but still good friends
On 1 March 2003, after the Turkish parliament refused to endorse a motion
allowing 62,000 US troops to transit the country prior to launching a second
front against Iraq, US–Turkish relations plummeted to their lowest level in
decades. The decision not only contradicted an earlier parliamentary
motion of 6 February 2003 to allow US personnel to upgrade facilities in

Turkey in preparation for the arrival of US troops, but infuriated US war-planners who had already begun shipping materiel to Turkey and calculated that the inability to open a second front would cost the US 1,000 additional casualties. The Turkish parliamentary decision also came as a major blow to the TGS. Traditionally, the alliance between Washington and Ankara had been based on a military-to-military relationship that stretched back to the Korean War. For the TGS, the US was more than just a strategic ally. It was the main foreign supplier both of military hardware and the training concepts and modules used in Turkish academies. The majority of high-ranking Turkish officers both spoke English and had attended training courses in the US. During the 1990s, the US had been much more tolerant of the measures employed by the TGS in its counter-insurgency against the PKK than had Turkey's other Western allies, several of which had embargoed sales of arms to the country. The TGS had not merely presumed that the motion would pass, but had planned to send Turkish troops into northern Iraq with the US, calculating that Turkish forces on the ground with operational leeway from Washington would blunt any ambitions Iraqi Kurds might have to establish an autonomous region or independent state, which the TGS feared would fuel secessionist sentiments among Turkey's 12m Kurds. But the failure of the 1 March parliamentary motion removed virtually all of Turkey's emotional and military leverage with the US. The TGS was forced to watch with dismay as US Special Forces airlifted into northern Iraq fought alongside Kurdish peshmerga.

The relatively swift conclusion of the US-led military campaign in Iraq, and lower than expected coalition casualties, enabled Turkey and the US to begin to rebuild bridges during the second quarter of 2003. However, relations nose-dived again – and this time it was the TGS which was infuriated – when, on 4 July, US troops detained 11 members of the Turkish Special Forces in the northern Iraqi city of Sulaymaniya. Privately, US military sources were adamant that they had incontrovertible evidence that the Turkish soldiers were plotting to assassinate a local Iraqi Kurdish official. Both publicly and privately the TGS was equally insistent that its soldiers were innocent and were manning a liaison office established to coordinate intelligence on the activities of the PKK. Perhaps more damagingly for the proudest institution in an acutely proud nation, the Turkish soldiers had been bundled into US helicopters with sacks over their heads and interrogated for two days on a US military base before being released. For the TGS, the incident was a national humiliation, creating what Chief of Staff General Ozkok described as 'the greatest ever crisis of confidence' between the TGS and the US military. In mid-July 2003, Washington accepted a proposal from the TGS to establish a joint commission composed of US and Turkish officers to investigate the incident. The commission was unable to bridge the gap between the contrasting versions of what the Turkish Special Forces had been doing in

Sulaymaniya, and the two sides agreed merely to express their shared 'regret' at what had happened. But the fact that the commission had met at all was seen as a mutual acknowledgement of the need to repair relations.

Mutual grumbling gradually subsided through summer 2003 and the frequency of both formal and informal communications – including that between the two militaries – increased. Relations received a major boost when, on 7 October, the Turkish parliament approved a motion to allow the dispatch of Turkish troops to support US peacekeeping operations in Iraq. Even though Turkey was forced to withdraw the offer on 7 November following opposition from the Iraqi Governing Council (IGC), particularly the Iraqi Kurds, it had still demonstrated that the two countries were prepared not just to talk together but cooperate in the political and military arena. Nevertheless, bilateral relations have been circumspect. By the time of Erdogan's official visit to Washington in January 2004, US officials were once again citing Turkey as a model for other Muslim countries and proof that that Islam and parliamentary democracy were not mutually exclusive. For the US, however, the 1 March 2003 parliamentary vote had shown that it could no longer assume that it could rely on Turkey. On the Turkish side, the cooling in transatlantic ties had coincided with the coming to power of a party which, regardless of what it said in public, remained deeply suspicious of the US. For the JDP a good working relationship with Washington was an economic, financial, political and military necessity. But privately, most JDP officials remained viscerally anti-American, their doubts fuelled by the perceived hunger for oil and anti-Islamic prejudice that they believed underlay the US global campaign against terrorism in general and its invasion of Iraq in particular. While the TGS had tended to see the US as a friend as well as an ally, an emotional bond, already strained on 1 March 2003, had snapped with the detention of the Turkish Special Forces in July 2003. However, the TGS too was prepared to be pragmatic. During the second half of 2003, wounded pride gradually gave way to growing alarm about Turkey's lack of influence in northern Iraq, particularly when the US declined to browbeat the IGC into accepting Turkish peacekeeping troops. Turkey was not without its own sources of leverage, given the continued viability of its secular creed and its civilised relations with Israel. The alliance was intact, but it had lost its former assurance.

Towards a new regional alliance?

During the late 1990s, a series of military training agreements and the award of a string of Turkish defence procurement contracts to Israeli firms seemed to herald a new strategic alliance in the eastern Mediterranean. Israeli and Turkish officers, particularly members of the air forces, trained at each other's facilities, the navies held joint search and rescue exercises,

Europe/Russia

and intelligence agencies exchanged information on the activities of Islamist and Kurdish militants. But hopes – not least in Washington – that the 'mil–mil' relationship between Israel and Turkey could be underpinned by closer economic and political ties were constrained by limited scope for economic cooperation and widespread anti-Israeli sentiments among the Turkish public. Plans for Turkey to sell water to Israel – one area in which there was considerable potential for strategic economic cooperation – foundered on a protracted wrangle over price. It was not until 4 March 2004, after years of negotiation, that Turkey finally signed a 20-year contract to export 50m cubic metres of water from the Manavgat River to Israel starting from 2006. But Turkish public anger at the Israeli response to the second Palestinian intifada effectively blocked any closer cooperation in the political arena.

The JDP victory in the 2002 elections dealt a further blow to hopes of deepening the relationship. Although JDP officials were careful publicly to repeat their commitment to maintaining ties, privately they were often virulently hostile towards Israel. The majority of the party's grassroots support was not just anti-Israeli but anti-Semitic. By late 2003, relations between Turkey and Israel appeared if not moribund then indefinitely stalled. At the same time, the TGS was becoming increasingly alarmed by the possibility of an autonomous or independent political entity emerging in northern Iraq – which Turkey has made clear to the US it will not tolerate – and a potential rapprochement between Israel and the Iraqi Kurds. The partial deterioration of Turkey–US relations made Turkey sceptical that the US would be willing to stifle the Iraqi Kurds' political aspirations, despite Washington's repeated assurances that it would protect Iraq's territorial integrity. Reinforcing this scepticism, the TGS had become increasingly frustrated by the US's failure to move against an estimated 4,500 PKK militants, armed but effectively inactive, holed up in camps in mountains on the Iraqi side of its border with Turkey, and considered American excuses, premised on terrain difficulties and US military overstretch, to be dubious. Turkey's initial recourse in 2003 was to strengthen the Turkish-speaking Turkoman minority in northern Iraq as a counterweight to the Iraqi Kurds. But the Turkomans were vastly outnumbered in Kurdish areas, and lacked military resources to confront the peshmerga. Hopes of compensating for these deficiencies with Turkish troops on the ground had been dashed by the parliamentary motion in March 2003 and the IGC's rejection of Turkish peacekeepers in October 2003. Although Ankara enjoyed considerable influence with the main Turkoman organisation, the Iraqi Turkoman Front (ITF), it was wary of overtly manipulating – much less arming – the ITF for fear of antagonising the US.

JDP officials had long advocated forging closer links with Turkey's Muslim neighbours for ideological reasons. Syria and Iran, two of Turkey's former bêtes noirs, both had substantial Kurdish minorities of their own and shared Turkey's concerns about the possible emergence of an independent Kurdish state in northern Iraq. Accordingly, in 2003, though for pragmatic rather than ideological reasons, the TGS too began to consider closer cooperation with Syria and Iran. On 6 May 2003, US Deputy Defense Secretary Paul Wolfowitz had publicly urged the JDP government to follow Washington's line in its relations with Iran and Syria. Yet ties between Ankara, Tehran and Damascus continued to improve. On 29 July 2003, Syrian Prime Minister Mohammed Mustafa Miro arrived in Turkey to discuss ways of deepening bilateral relations. In the wake of the November 2003 Istanbul bombings, Syrian security forces cooperated closely with their Turkish counterparts in locating and extraditing Turks in Syria who were believed to have been involved in the attacks. Even though the Syrians failed to arrest all of the suspects wanted by Turkey, privately Turkish officials admitted that this was the result of a delay in providing Damascus with a list of names rather than any lack of effort on the part of the Syrians. On 6 January 2004, President Bashar Assad paid the first ever official visit to Turkey by a Syrian head of state. Contrary to some reports in the Western media, which suggested that the trip prefaced Ankara brokering peace negotiations between Syria and Israel, the agenda of Assad's meetings with Turkish officials, including the TGS, focused almost exclusively on two issues: strengthening bilateral economic ties and political cooperation to prevent the emergence of an independent Kurdish state in northern Iraq.

On 10 January 2004, Foreign Minister Gul flew to Tehran, ostensibly to offer his condolences to his Iranian opposite number, Kamal Kharrazi, for the devastating Bam earthquake in December 2003, but in reality to discuss ways in which the two countries, together with Syria, could stifle Iraqi Kurdish secessionist aspirations. Turkish officials continued to hold meetings with their Syrian and Iranian counterparts through early 2004. By mid-March 2004, the three countries had yet to draw up a detailed plan of action. However, clashes in Iran on 9 March 2004 between police and Kurdish demonstrators celebrating the signing of the interim Iraqi constitution followed, on 12 March, by riots involving local Kurds in northeastern Syria that left up to 30 dead, can have done little to allay fears in Tehran and Damascus as well as Ankara of a contagious Kurdish nationalism. The resilience of this prospect is likely to keep motivations towards closer relations among the three capitals alive.

Brussels via Nicosia?

After the breakdown of the March 2003 negotiations in The Hague to reunify the divided island of Cyprus, both the UN and the EU laid the blame for the failure on Turkish Cypriot leader Rauf Denktash, whom they accused of being unconstructive and even obstructionist. On 11 March 2003,

European Commission spokesperson Jean-Christophe Filori announced that Turkey had been warned that, unless a solution could be found by 1 May 2004 – when the Greek Cypriots were due to enter the EU in the name of the whole island – Turkey's own hopes for accession could suffer. Yet in the months that followed Ankara appeared untroubled, even complacent. Denktash refused to return to the negotiating table and described the UN blueprint for reunification drawn up by UN Secretary General Kofi Annan, commonly referred to as the Annan Plan, as 'dead and buried'. Privately both the Turkish Foreign Ministry and the TGS attempted to persuade Denktash to resume talks without accepting the Annan Plan in its entirety. They argued, with considerable justification, that the Greek Cypriots were as unhappy with Annan Plan as was Denktash, albeit for diametrically opposed reasons. The Annan Plan proposed eroding the 29-year division of the island on ethnic grounds by allowing restricted freedom of movement and settlement and creating two locally autonomous regions under a unified central government. For Denktash, who would have preferred a confederation of two states, the proposals went too far. For the Greek Cypriots, who ultimately wanted complete freedom of movement and settlement within a single state, they did not go far enough. If Denktash returned to the negotiating table, Ankara calculated, the Greek Cypriots would leave and international opprobrium would fall on them rather than Denktash or Turkey.

Denktash remained unmoved. On 23 April 2003, the Turkish Cypriot authorities eased restrictions on the movement of Greek and Turkish Cypriots across the UN-monitored green line that had divided the island since 1974. Denktash was apparently projecting that by allowing Greek Cypriots to enter the north of the island, albeit only for a few hours (they were not allowed to stay overnight), they would be forced into a de facto acknowledgment of the jurisdiction of the Turkish Republic of Northern Cyprus (TRNC), which had only been recognised by Turkey. It is also likely that he expected some clashes to occur, which he then could have used to demonstrate that Greek and Turkish Cypriots could not live together. Remarkably, given the long history of animosity between the two communities and the tens of thousands who crossed the green line over the following months, there were no serious incidents. But neither, during summer 2003, was there any sense of urgency in Ankara. On 8 August 2003, Turkey signed a free-trade agreement with the TRNC – something which would have been unnecessary had Ankara expected an imminent solution and also violated the terms of the 1995 free-trade agreement Turkey had signed with the EU.

Apparently many in Ankara simply refused to believe that the EU would allow the Greek Cypriots to join on 1 May 2004 if a settlement had not been reached by that date, despite its earlier pledge to do so. It transpired that whatever the merits of this judgement, it was beside the point. The annual

European Commission progress report on Turkish candidacy, published on 5 November 2003, again warned that a failure to solve the Cyprus problem would pose a serious obstacle to Turkey's own accession. In the TRNC, opinion polls suggested that parties that favoured a solution based on the Annan Plan would win the forthcoming parliamentary elections on 14 December and could even prevent Denktash, president of the TRNC, from serving as the Turkish Cypriot representative if negotiations were resumed. Turkey finally realised that time was running out. In cooperation with the TGS, the Turkish Ministry of Foreign Affairs (MFA) began to draw up a 'road map' of proposals and responses it hoped would enable Denktash to return to the negotiating table and secure a settlement that would be, if not perfect, then at least acceptable; and, more importantly, would clear the way for Turkish accession to the EU. The first public sign of an imminent change in Ankara's policy on Cyprus came on 2 December 2003 when, after over four years of stubborn refusal, Turkey announced that it would abide by a July 1998 ECHR ruling to pay €1.1m in compensation to Titina Loizidou, a Greek Cypriot woman who had lost property in the north following the 1974 Turkish invasion.

The 14 December 2003 elections in northern Cyprus ended in a dead heat, with proponents and opponents of the Annan Plan each winning 25 seats in the 50-seat unicameral assembly. But, as the head of the largest single party, the pro-settlement Republican Turkish Party (RTP), Mehmet Ali Talat became prime minister of a coalition government. On 8 January 2004, the 'road-map' drawn up by the MFA and TGS was approved at a high-level summit in Ankara attended by Erdogan, Ozkok and President Sezer. After Denktash had been presented with a copy of the road map and told he was expected to follow it to the letter, Turkey informed the UN and US that the Turkish Cypriots were ready to return to the negotiating table. On 13 February 2004, after three days of talks between Denktash and Greek Cypriot President Tassos Papadopoulos at the UN in New York, Annan announced that negotiations would resume on the basis of the Annan Plan in the Cypriot capital of Nicosia on 19 February. If the two sides could not reach an agreement by 23 March, then the negotiations would be joined by representatives of Greece and Turkey. If any issues still remained unresolved by 29 March 2004, Annan would 'fill in the blanks' and the resulting document would be put to referenda in the two communities on 20 April 2004. If both communities approved the document, a reunited Cyprus would enter the EU on 1 May 2004. If not, the Greek Cypriots would accede in the name of the whole island and Turkey, through 35,000 troops in the north, would be engaged in the military occupation of not merely a foreign country but also an EU member state.

As soon as negotiations resumed on 19 February 2004, it became clear that neither Denktash nor Papadopoulos was prepared to make the concessions necessary for an agreement. Denktash publicly declared that he

Europe/Russia

still opposed the Annan Plan and had only agreed to resume negotiations under intense pressure from Ankara. On 19 March 2004, as the first phase of the renewed conclusions ended without any progress, Denktash declared that he would boycott the four-way discussions due to begin in Switzerland on 23 March 2004. Opinion polls suggested that, although the Turkish Cypriots were evenly divided, the majority of Greek Cypriots would reject the plan when it was put to referendums on 20 April 2004. Talat and Papadopoulos met, without Denktash, on 22 March 2004. Four way talks between the Greek Cypriots, Turkish Cypriots, Greece and Turkey began in Bürgenstock, Switzerland, on 24 March. Kofi Annan presented the fourth version of the Annan Plan to the two Cypriot sides on 29 March. The fourth version of the Annan Plan contained several changes. They include: transfer of 65 villages to Greek Cypriot control and the reduction of the territory to be administered by the Turkish Cypriots from 36.4% to 28.6 % of the island; a reduction in the number of the number of Greek Cypriot refugees allowed to return to northern Cyprus from 21% to 18% of the Turkish Cypriot population; phased reduction in the number of Turkish troops on the island from the roughly 35,000 deployed at present to 6,000 by 2011 and 3,000 by 2013, with Greece permitted to station an equal number of troops on the island. Talks continued for two more days, through 31 March, but did not yield agreement. The referendums on Cyprus, to be held simultaneously in the two communities, were rescheduled for 24 April 2004. A poll of viewers conducted by a Turkish Cypriot television station, Kibris Genc TV, on 2 April 2004, suggested that 51.1% of Turkish Cypriots would approve the Annan Plan in the 24 April referendum, while 48.7% would vote against it. Talat said he would campaign for its approval, while Denktash was virtually certain to press for its rejection.

Raising the stakes on an uncertain future

By focusing so persistently on Turkey's receiving a date for the beginning of accession negotiations, and insisting that only religious prejudice can prevent it, the JDP government has not only raised the stakes ahead of the EU summit in December 2004 but stoked what is already a highly emotive issue. For most Turks, EU membership is as much about the psychological reassurance accruing to acceptance into an elite of nations as it is about economic benefits or concepts of shared values. A failure to give a date – or at least provide an unequivocal indication that one is imminent – would be regarded as a gross insult, with a potentially devastating impact on the future of Turkey's relations with the EU and also on Turkey's domestic political and economic stability. Not only would it trigger a furious nationalist backlash inside the country – particularly given Ankara's dilution of its longstanding policy on Turkish Cypriot sovereign protection, which is a national issue – but it could stall, or even reverse, the democratisation process and lift restraints on both Islamists in the JDP and their secular rivals, both of whom are currently constrained for fear of jeopardising Turkey's prospects for accession.

From a different perspective, in March 2004 there was also a tendency in Turkey to see receiving a date for the start of accession talks as an end in itself rather than the beginning of a long and tortuous process. There was a real danger that, if Turkey were given the green light in December 2004, the democratisation process might lose momentum anyway because a strategic objective had virtually been achieved. Particularly in light of its resounding victory in the March 2004 local elections, the JDP would find it increasingly difficult to convince an impatient grassroots that it still needed time to tackle sensitive issues such as the headscarf ban. Although a full-blooded coup could be triggered by something as radical as the overnight abolition of secularism – which in any case is so unlikely as to be theoretical – the TGS still retains considerable public prestige and political influence and is likely to continue to resist even the partial erosion of Ataturk's legacy. Even if accession negotiations were to begin, full membership would be unlikely any time soon. Turkey is far from ready to accede, and the EU simply is far from ready to absorb it. Indeed, given the time it is likely to take to absorb ten new members from May 2004, Brussels is not likely to be ready to do so for the foreseeable future.

Yet, although Turkish officials often declare that they accept that the accession process could continue for 10–15 years, it is difficult imagine Turkey sitting back and waiting patiently. If Turkey is accorded a date certain in December 2004, the initial public euphoria is likely to be relatively short-lived and gradually replaced by nagging doubts about whether the EU will finally accept Turkey or just let the accession negotiation process drag on indefinitely. Unless Turkey can somehow be offered a series of intermediary targets that mark palpable progress towards its ultimate goal, resentment is likely to grow at the failure to receive anything in return for what are widely seen in Turkey as sacrifices that the country has made to appease the EU. Nowhere is the bitterness likely to be more acute than over Cyprus. If the Annan Plan is rejected at the April 2004 referenda, the Greek Cypriots will enter the EU. But, despite assumptions in Ankara to the contrary, the international community would be very hard-pressed to recognise the TRNC, much less allow northern Cyprus to be annexed by Turkey. If, on the other hand, a reunited Cyprus enters the EU on 1 May 2004, sovereign links between the TRNC and Turkey will be severed, and 15,000 to 30,000 Turks who have settled in northern Cyprus will have to return to the Turkish mainland where, to opponents of the JDP government, they will become living symbols of national betrayal.

As of April 2004, Turkey enjoyed greater domestic stability than it did a year previously, and was not as lonely strategically as it was immediately after the March 2003 parliamentary debacle. For Turkey to maintain its

Europe/Russia

European vocation comfortably, however, both a date certain and a settlement on Cyprus are needed. Were both forthcoming, Turkey's bilateral relationship with the US would stand to regain more of its former strength. Washington is a strong supporter of Turkey's EU membership for the strategic purpose of bolstering Turkey as Islam's exemplar of Western-oriented secular democracy. But the dampening of Turkey's EU prospects, combined with residual Turkey–US coolness over Iraq and Ankara's worries about Kurdish nationalism, would probably reinforce Ankara's nascent enthusiasm for stronger relationships with Muslim neighbours. While the TGS' entrenched secularism and the ongoing practical importance of the Turkey–US relationship would limit the depth of these relationships, they would further flatten Turkey's trajectory as a strategic partner of the West.

Europe's Southern Exposure

It has become common in strategic circles on both sides of the Atlantic to speak of an arc of crisis stretching from the Maghreb to Pakistan, with the whole now fashionably described as the 'Greater Middle East'. The terminology indicates a very real concern on the part of European and American policymakers regarding new (and some old) security risks emanating from the 'South'. For Europe, events in 2003–04, including terrorist bombings in Istanbul and Madrid, underscore the importance of the Mediterranean as an area of strategic concern, with a bearing on internal as well as regional security. Southern Mediterranean societies and policies are evolving rapidly, and the region as a whole might better be described as an arc of change rather than one of crisis. Looking ahead, Europe's southern exposure is set to play a more central role in European Union (EU) and transatlantic security debates.

A changing proliferation landscape

Europe has diverse stakes in developments across the Mediterranean. In 'hard' security terms, Europe, especially southern Europe, is exposed to the proliferation of weapons of mass destruction (WMD) and the means of delivering them at trans-Mediterranean ranges. Algeria, Libya, Egypt, Syria and more distant arsenals in the Gulf are all part of this equation. These risks are variable, however, as Libya's early 2004 decision to divest itself of its chemical, biological, nuclear and missile programmes suggests.

Yet, for all of the prominence of proliferation risks in American strategic thinking since the first Gulf War, Europe is even more exposed to such risks. Indeed, the only instance of a missile strike on Western territory from the 'South' was Libya's ill-aimed Scud attack on the Loran station on the Italian island of Lampedusa in 1986.

Europe has traditionally displayed a relatively relaxed attitude towards proliferation trends across the Mediterranean, but this approach may be reaching its limits. The European strategy document drafted by EU High Representative Javier Solana in late 2003 clearly identifies proliferation risks as a high-priority concern for Europe's evolving security and defence policy. Europe has put non-proliferation squarely on the agenda in its relations with Iran. European negotiators played the lead role in Iran's 2003 decision to accept more intrusive International Atomic Energy Agency (IAEA) inspection of its nuclear facilities – though the agreement is viewed with considerable scepticism in Washington. In the same time frame, European policymakers have also sent strong signals to Syria, which concluded negotiations on an association agreement with the EU in December 2003 regarding the importance of proliferation issues in determining the pace and extent of Syria's relations with the EU.

The vulnerability of European population centres also affects the calculus of security cooperation with Washington, in light of North African and Middle Eastern instability, and the possibility of US intervention in those regions. As Europe becomes more exposed to the retaliatory consequences of American – and its own – strategic decisions across the greater Middle East, coalition arrangements will inevitably become more complex and politicised. Even for centre-right European governments that may be open to security cooperation with the US in Mediterranean and Middle Eastern contingencies, the looming vulnerability of bases and population centres on their own territory must be part of the equation. For governments less sympathetic with American policy, a sense of declining sanctuary will only strengthen the logic of an arms length approach. Turkey, as part of the European security system, but adjacent to the Middle East, is clearly the most exposed, and among the most concerned about proliferation risks. Existing ballistic missile arsenals in Iran and Syria are capable of reaching urban targets in central and eastern Turkey, and the defence of Incirlik Air Base, Adana and Iskenderun have figured in theatre missile defence planning for the last decade. This sensitivity was clearly reflected in Ankara's demand that NATO early warning and WMD response assets be deployed in Turkey in the run up to the 2003 intervention in Iraq. Similarly, cooperation on WMD-related intelligence continues to be part of Turkey's strategic relationship with Israel. While that relationship could expand further via Turkish participation in Israel's *Arrow* programme for missile defence, it is also constrained by limited potential for economic cooperation; broad anti-

Europe/Russia

Israeli sentiments among the Turkish public; and Turkey's warming towards Syria and Iran.

The most dramatic and transforming development in this area has been the abrupt reversal in Libya's decades-old pattern of confrontation with the West, including the pursuit of chemical, biological, nuclear and missile programmes. Given Libyan President Muammar Gaddafi's repeated threats to employ unconventional weapons against European countries intervening in North Africa or elsewhere in the Middle East, his decision in late 2003 to open Libya's full range of WMD-related programmes to international inspection, and to cooperate with American, British and UN agencies in dismantling the country's unconventional arsenal, is a watershed for regional security. In reality, of course, Libya's search for an opening in relations with the West has been underway for several years. 'Track-two' dialogues have been in place with European and American institutions in the wake of the Lockerbie verdicts, and in 2003, Libyan and American negotiators finally reached agreement on compensation for the Pan Am 103 victims. Starting early in the Bush administration, quiet US and UK pledges to end UN sanctions if Tripoli changed its tune on Pan Am 103 and American indications that US sanctions could be dropped if Libya forswore support for terrorism and WMD programmes also helped. The resolution of the Lockerbie dispute awaits a May 2004 deadline for payment of the final tranche of compensation tied, in Libya's view, to the lifting of American economic sanctions. In the meantime, the dismantling of Libya's nuclear and other WMD programmes has been proceeding rapidly, and has been accompanied by increasingly active political engagement, including a path-breaking visit to Tripoli by an American congressional delegation in January 2004 and UK Prime Minister Tony Blair's March 2004 meeting with Colonel Gaddafi in Tripoli.

The change in Libyan policy may have been reinforced by the regime-change demonstration effect of the American-led intervention in Iraq, and the declining utility of proliferation and support for terrorism as policy instruments in relations with the West. But it probably owes more to the longer standing desire of the Libyan regime to end its economic and political isolation, and in particular, to open the way for much needed investment in Libya's energy sector. To the extent that Libya's international reintegration proceeds apace, it will offer new challenges and opportunities for the region, and in a transatlantic frame. Neighbours, including Egypt, will have to adjust to the return of a potentially significant security and energy partner for Europe, and a country capable of vying with Maghrebi neighbours for regional influence. The EU will have to decide on the scope and pace of relations with Tripoli in a Euro-Mediterranean framework. Over the next year or two, NATO may well decide to bring Libya into a reinvigorated programme of Mediterranean dialogue – a development unthinkable just a year ago. Broadly, the Libyan experience is likely to increase the scrutiny of, and pressure on, other Mediterranean proliferators, including Syria with its active chemical and missile programmes, and perhaps Algeria. Even Egypt may not remain immune.

Conventional scenarios

Given a military balance in the Mediterranean that overwhelmingly favours the North over the South, Europe has few points of concern in conventional terms. Most flashpoints for military conflict in the Mediterranean are South–South. But a small number of conventional contingencies could involve Europe directly, and a larger number could affect European and transatlantic interests. In the western Mediterranean, the Perejil crisis of July 2002, though quickly resolved, suggests that the continuing possibility of a clash between Spain and Morocco over the Spanish enclaves of Ceuta and Melilla is not entirely remote. Despite the many factors arguing for restraint on the Moroccan side, the question of the enclaves remains a flashpoint for nationalist and sovereignty-conscious sentiment.

European security interests may also be indirectly affected by South–South frictions in the Maghreb. The failure of the UN's and bilateral efforts to resolve the dispute over sovereignty in the Western Sahara poses a continuing risk of conflict between Morocco, bent on the consolidation of its de facto control over the region, and Algeria, whose on-again, off-again support for the Polisario Front is seen as provocative by Rabat. More remote scenarios with the potential for military confrontation include renewed border frictions between Libya (whose dependence on cross-border transit may decline as wider international links are re-established) and Tunisia, or Egypt. Egypt itself may regard the changing character of the civil war in Sudan, and the prospect of further instability, as threatening to its own regional interests, including predictable management of Nile river waters and the containment of refugee flows. Threats to either of these interests could well encourage an Egyptian intervention across the border, although most likely in a multilateral context.

In the eastern Mediterranean, the conventional risks affecting European security centre on Turkey's Middle Eastern borders, and the balance with Iran, Iraq and especially Syria. The end of Saddam Hussein's regime has removed, at least for a time, the possibility of a conventional clash between Turkey and Iraq (always remote in any case), while raising the prospect of more active Turkish intervention against Kurdish elements in northern Iraq. On multiple occasions in 2003 and 2004, and most recently with Turkish Prime Minister Tayyip Erdogan's January 2004 visit to Washington, Turkish policymakers and key members of the Turkish General Staff have made it clear that Turkey will not tolerate arrangements in northern Iraq leading to the establishment of an independent Kurdish state. Against a background of Turkish military operations across the border dating to 1994,

Europe/Russia

and with a substantial political and security presence still in place, Ankara could chose to move against remnants of the Kurdistan Workers' Party (PKK) – now known as the Kurdistan Freedom and Democracy Congress (KADEK) – as well as Ansar al-Islam and other groups with anti-Turkish agendas in northern Iraq.

The prospect of a Greek–Turkish conflict over Cyprus or interests in the Aegean Sea – a looming possibility in the mid-1990s – has declined enormously in recent years. Notwithstanding continued friction over Cyprus, détente between Athens and Ankara has been one of the most positive and transforming developments in the Mediterranean security environment over the last decade, particularly when viewed from an EU or NATO perspective. With the Republic of Cyprus set to join the EU in May 2004, and with Turkey determined to improve its own prospects for the opening of accession talks, the pressure for a Cyprus settlement on the basis of the 'Annan Plan' is likely to reach a critical point in 2004. Any agreement will need to address the future of the 30,000 Turkish troops remaining in Northern Cyprus. With Turkish military and conservative opposition to a Cyprus settlement waning, and with substantial incentives for resolution on both sides of the island, the 2004–05 period could see the disappearance of one of the Mediterranean's most durable and paralysing disputes.

A more proximate rationale for the employment of European military power in the Mediterranean region may be the need to evacuate Western citizens from countries plagued by political violence and instability. Algeria continues to be the leading cause for concern along these lines. Insurgency, counter-insurgency, terrorism and private vendettas have claimed upward of 100,000 lives in Algeria since the early 1990s. As the prospect of an Islamist takeover has waned, and as the regime has continued to muddle through and even reinforce its ties to the West in the wake of 11 September, political violence in Algeria has received declining attention in Europe and the US. But the violence has continued, imposing human, political and material costs. The tempo of political violence in Algeria – and European attention to the problem – could well increase in anticipation of presidential elections scheduled for April 2004, and President Abdelaziz Bouteflika's uncertain future. Continued instability in the country can be expected to reinforce the regime's interest in closer political and security ties with the West, which the US and France have been keen to deepen since 11 September. But an unstable Algeria will still prove a difficult security partner, despite a common interest in containing Islamist networks in Europe and across the Mediterranean. Overall, the potential for European military involvement in Algeria has clearly declined from a high-point in the mid-1990s. But extremist movements with an Algerian connection are now a significant part of the internal security equation within the EU itself, as demonstrated by the arrests of over 50 predominantly Algerian terrorist suspects across five European countries in early 2003.

Migration, terrorism and trans-regional challenges

Arguably, the leading source of exposure in Europe's relations with the southern Mediterranean is in Europe itself. Extreme scenarios of economic migration from South to North, anticipated by many European analysts in the 1980s and 1990s, have not materialised. Despite turmoil in Algeria and elsewhere, the last decade has not witnessed uncontrollable, large-scale refugee flows. That said, Europe, including countries of southern Europe more used to being sources of migration, has experienced economic and political migration on a significant scale. Spain, Italy and Greece now contend with the arrival – and very often the drowning – of boat people from North Africa, the Middle East and beyond. The result has been almost daily media coverage of incidents involving migrants in the Strait of Gibraltar, southern Italy and the Aegean. Such incidents interact with broader anxieties regarding the economic and cultural implications of migration from the South to put the movement of people across the Mediterranean, including the organised trafficking in persons, firmly on the European political and security agenda. With the progressive extension of the Schengen agreement, the political and material burden of securing Europe's borders against illegal migration has shifted dramatically to the south and east – a development likely to be reinforced by the substantial enlargement of the EU in 2004. As a result, enhanced cooperation on surveillance and interdiction across southern Europe is now central to strategic discussions, and new multilateral arrangements, from Portugal to Turkey.

The 11 September attacks gave new weight to long-established European concerns about spillovers of extremism, political violence and terrorism from the South. Algeria is arguably the most important link in this regard, with a variety of extremist groups, including the Armed Islamic Group (GIA) and the Salafist Group for Preaching and Combat (GSPC) using Europe as a rear area for recruitment, fundraising, planning and arms purchases. Indeed, North Africans have figured prominently in a range of terrorist schemes uncovered over the past few years, and have made up the bulk of persons arrested and prosecuted in Europe for ties to internationally oriented terrorist networks since 11 September. Recent terrorist incidents across the Mediterranean, most prominently the deadly bomb attacks in Morocco in May 2003, in Istanbul in November 2003, and in Madrid on 11 March 2004 have dramatically strengthened the European perception of risk emanating from the South, and underscore the more specific risk of spillovers inside Europe. Algerian groups, already a source of concern, have been joined by an increasingly active network of Moroccans, many with experience in Afghanistan, and most often with experience of living in European societies. A network composed mainly of Moroccans, probably led by Tunisian Sarhane Ben Abdelmajid Fakhet, with at least loose ties to al-Qaeda, has been implicated in the Madrid attacks.

One important consequence of the Madrid bombings has been a marked acceleration of EU efforts at intelligence sharing, police cooperation and coordination of counter-terrorism policy. The EU plans to appoint a European counter-terrorism coordinator, and this opens the possibility of a more substantive Washington–Brussels line of communication on terrorism risks and responses.

The European experience with North African networks also encourages a view of Islamic terrorism that departs significantly from prevailing images in the US, where al-Qaeda is often portrayed as a coherent, even hierarchical group. European analysts, and an increasing number of American observers, tend to see Moroccan, Tunisian and Algerian networks as harbingers of a much looser, ad hoc constellation of extremists, with a variety of motives and modes of action, in which the al-Qaeda link may or may not be significant. Most troubling from the perspective of European security interests, groups such as the GSPC, the Moroccan Islamic Combat Group and Ansar al-Islam appear to be acquiring a more diverse base of operations in Europe, and may be looking beyond their original 'diaspora' aims in Algeria and Iraq, recruiting and training cadres for terrorist operations in Europe, the US and the Middle East as a whole. GSPC has also been implicated in the kidnapping of Europeans in Niger and Mali, and has reportedly established training camps in west Africa. Ansar al-Islam has been linked to the November 2003 Istanbul bombings, as well as to planning for chemical attacks in western Europe.

Against this background, and with roughly 15 million Muslims resident in Europe, some 5m in France alone, the wider question of relations with Muslim communities at a political and cultural level is inescapable. In the wake of 11 September – and 11 March – European politicians and policymakers are as sensitive as their counterparts in the US to the necessity of avoiding 'civilisation' frictions in pursuit of counter-terrorism objectives. But in Europe's secular societies, overt religiosity, political activism and political violence are easily seen as a continuum with strong internal security implications. In 2003–04 the debate over French legislation (enacted in February 2004) banning Islamic headscarves, among other items, from schools, while giving official recognition to a broader range of religious practices, will be a flashpoint for political and security concerns, as well as concerns about identity. To date, and despite broad sympathy for the Palestinians, Chechens and even admiration in some quarters for Osama bin Laden, Muslim communities in France and elsewhere have not become politicised in the sense that many have feared. But the worry that younger, alienated immigrants might drift toward radicalism in larger numbers remains. The fact that many of the perpetrators in recent acts of Islamic terrorism, including the 11 September and 11 March attacks, share the experience of working or studying in Europe reinforces this concern.

The November 2003 suicide bombings in Istanbul illustrate another point of exposure to terrorism emanating from Europe's southern periphery. It is arguable that those responsible for the Istanbul bombings conceived of the attacks as a strike against European interests: in the narrow sense, as attacks against a British bank, the British consulate and the non-Muslim 'other' in the form of two prominent synagogues; or in the wider sense of an attack on Turkey as aspirant to EU membership, the Western model of choice for a secular Muslim country and a key Western partner. In European security terms, the Istanbul attacks are significant at several levels. First, the attacks came at a sensitive time in Turkey's economic recovery, and at a time of flux in Ankara's relations with Washington and Europe. Despite genuine expressions of solidarity from all sides, it appears that a significant part of Turkish public opinion has interpreted the bombings as the inevitable product of Western, and especially American, policies in the Middle East. Further attacks hold the potential of upsetting Turkey's European trajectory by undermining political cohesion inside the country, and by encouraging an already ambivalent Europe to worry about the security consequences of embracing Turkey as a full member of the EU. Second, there has long been a close connection between the extreme fringes of political Islam in Turkey and radical groups based in Europe. With almost 2m Turkish immigrants in Germany alone (perhaps a third of whom are Kurds), radical Islamist and Kurdish groups have generally had greater freedom of action to organise and fundraise outside Turkey over the past several decades. These networks are capable of operating alongside indigenous movements such as Turkish Hizbullah – allowed to operate with the blessing of the Turkish security forces as a counter to the PKK in the 1990s – in efforts to destabilise the Turkish state and to carry out attacks elsewhere in Europe, or on the European periphery.

Third, the Istanbul bombings and the increasing activism of North African and Middle Eastern terror networks in Europe suggests the potential for further attacks on soft, symbolic targets in southern Europe and the Balkans – areas close to the Middle East, with porous borders, but part of the West. The 2004 Olympics in Athens should be a serious point of concern. After years of perceived neglect, Greek authorities acted swiftly in 2003 to arrest and prosecute the nucleus of the leftist terror organisation known as 17 November, and this has no doubt removed a significant source of risk to the games. Extensive and well-coordinated Greek efforts to enhance counter-terrorism-related intelligence and intervention now confront a more potent risk in the form of transnationally oriented Islamic terrorists with a demonstrated interest in symbolic attacks and mass lethality – a larger and very different threat from 17 November's targeted assassination of individuals. In light of events in both the western and eastern Mediterranean, it is not surprising that Mediterranean diplomatic forums, including the recently revived 'Five plus Five' grouping (France,

Europe/Russia

Italy, Malta, Portugal and Spain, with the five states of the Arab Maghreb Union – Algeria, Tunisia, Libya, Mauritania and Morocco), which met in Tunisia in December 2003, are now firmly focused on the challenge of militant Islam and trans-regional terrorism.

Wider geopolitical stakes

Beyond these direct and indirect sources of risk, a wider set of European security interests are engaged around the Mediterranean, and these are set to acquire greater prominence in strategic plans and policies over the next few years. Energy security, the Middle East peace process and the evolution of transatlantic relations and institutions are key elements to watch.

Europe, especially southern Europe, is heavily and increasingly dependent on imports of natural gas from North Africa. Indeed, the security of supply from Algeria has been one of the leading sources of European concern regarding the continued violence and insurgency in the country. To date, energy-related facilities have been spared serious attack, and gas exports, including those shipped via the trans-Maghreb pipeline stretching from Algeria through Morocco to Spain, have continued without significant interruption. From Gibraltar to Turkey's eastern borders, a wide range of energy transportation projects are underway, linking energy and economic security interests on a South–South as well as a North–South basis. An increasingly dense web of infrastructure for the supply of oil and, above all, gas, is making the Mediterranean and southern Europe a critical entrepot for Europe's energy needs, and a critical engine of development for states across the greater Middle East. The reintegration of Libya will accelerate this trend.

With the prospective opening of the Baku–Tbilisi–Ceyhan pipeline, and the likelihood of ever larger amounts of oil flowing through existing pipelines from Iraq to the Mediterranean, Turkey will be at the centre of this phenomenon. Greece and Italy will also play a larger part in these expanding trans-regional networks. Partly as a result of this vital energy trade, the security of sea lanes, especially at Gibraltar, the Sicily–Malta–Tunisia gap, the Bosporus exits and Suez, is set to receive greater attention from security planners in government and the private sector – reminiscent of the 'chokepoint' worries of the Cold War, but with non-state actors as the adversaries. In 2002, for instance, Moroccan authorities arrested a group of Saudis plotting to attack shipping in the Strait of Gibraltar. The sheer scale of tanker shipping in the Mediterranean, including that of highly explosive liquid natural gas, highlights the potential risks to population centres, the environment and economies posed by maritime terrorism in the region.

The grim state of the Middle East peace process, and the possibility of rising tensions in Israeli–Palestinian and regional relations, form a critical part of the political and security backdrop in the Mediterranean, and affect European interests. In the 1970s and 1980s, much of the terrorism associated with Palestinian groups was conducted in Europe – an experience that continues to influence European counter-terrorism thinking. With Israeli–Palestinian problems likely to persist, and with the emergence of new terrorist networks in Europe and on Europe's periphery, there is some potential for a renewed campaign against European and Western targets in Europe, with a strong Palestinian dimension. Even short of this, many would argue that continued Israeli–Palestinian conflict fuels a wide range of terrorist and proliferation risks affecting Europe's security. It is also a 'permanently operating factor' shaping North–South relations in the Mediterranean, and sets clear limits to what is possible in the various Mediterranean dialogues conducted by the EU, NATO, the Organisation for Security and Cooperation in Europe and within regional groupings. As all of these institutions look to enhance their Mediterranean initiatives over the coming years, they will face similar constraints – southern Mediterranean scepticism, reinforced by policy differences over the Israeli–Palestinian crisis, Iraq, and trade and immigration disputes. Above all, a more concerted approach on North–South relations will be difficult to construct as Europe and the US view the southern Mediterranean as a source of risk, and Arab partners fear Western intervention in the south.

Finally, the transatlantic dimension will be critical – and problematic. The Mediterranean region is, in many aspects, Europe's 'near abroad'. For all of the American criticism of Europe's failure to develop a coherent strategy and capability for defence, the Mediterranean periphery – North Africa and the Levant – is a place where European states can project political, economic and military power to effect. As Washington presses for a more explicit NATO role in security across the Greater Middle East, the Mediterranean will be at the core of European interests, and the place where transatlantic roles and capabilities are more evenly matched. The result could be deepening friction, or an agreed division of labour, between European allies focused on Mediterranean risks and US policymakers looking to stretch security institutions towards more distant problems in the Gulf, Central and even southeast Asia.

Middle East/Gulf

In his State of the Union address on 28 January 2004, US President George W. Bush urged the rapid democratisation of the Middle East. Substantive details of Bush's plan were leaked to the London-based newspaper *al-Hayat* two weeks later, as a document branded 'the Greater Middle East Initiative' (GMEI). They amounted to a reform package intentionally recalling the 1975 Helsinki Accords (which challenged the Soviet bloc to respect individual freedoms and human rights) and particularly focused on replacing autocracy with participatory democracy. The initiative seemed to fit into Bush's larger vision, dubbed the 'forward strategy of freedom', which has been advanced as the core of the administration's Middle East foreign policy. Superficially, the initiative is innocuous and salutary, targeting three 'deficits' identified in the UN Arab Human Development Report – freedom, knowledge and female empowerment – as the bases for its own proposals, and couching outside involvement in the non-threatening language of development assistance. A more nuanced reading of the document, however, illuminates a bottom-up approach that would largely bypass states in favour of local stakeholders. For this reason, regional powers, including Egypt and Saudi Arabia, were indignant. Egyptian President Hosni Mubarak complained that 'we hear about these initiatives as if the region and its states do not exist, as if they had no sovereignty over their land'.

To control the damage, the Bush administration dispatched Under Secretary of State Marc Grossman to Morocco, Jordan, Egypt, Bahrain and Turkey to assure his counterparts that the purpose of the GMEI was to complement existing reform efforts, rather than impose an American plan on regional states. The Arab League was expected to formalise these objections at its upcoming conference in Tunis on 29–30 March. But the Tunisian government's cancellation of the summit – on grounds that members had evinced an insufficiently robust commitment to reform – constituted a reprieve for Washington. The US stood a chance of diplomatically salvaging the GMEI by recasting it as a prescription for support rather than an outside imposition. In any case, there were some authoritarian regimes that the US would not want to alienate in the near future. These included the secular, anti-Islamist governments of Egypt and Jordan – both of which have made peace with Israel – and the relatively cooperative Yemeni regime. Another would be the government of Algerian President Abdelaziz Bouteflika, who is credited with taming an Islamic insurgency unleashed in 1992 when an Islamist victory in democratic

Map Middle East/Gulf

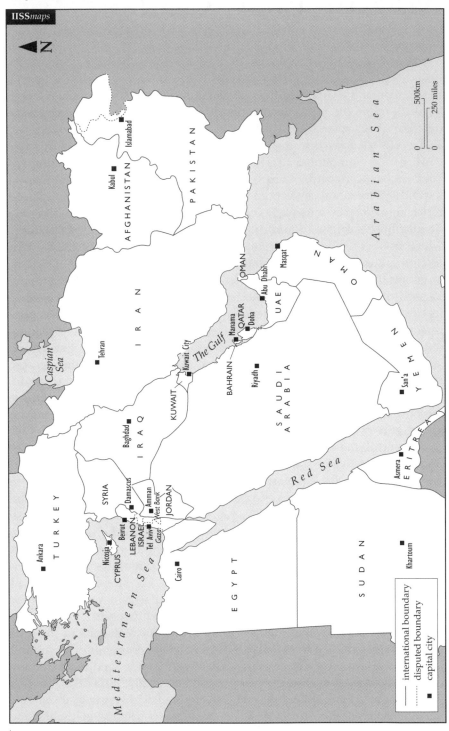

elections was invalidated, has been a strong US counter-terrorism partner, and on 8 April was re-elected with 83% of the vote in an election deemed generally fair by international observers.

The values embodied in the initiative, however, are not likely to change. It enshrines the idea that US security concerns are best served not by cultivating relationships with autocrats but by directly addressing the root causes of terrorism. Moreover, the GMEI implicitly rejected the idea that resolution of the Palestinian issue is a prerequisite for progress elsewhere. But the conventional wisdom, espoused by the authoritarian leaders themselves, is that until the Palestinians have attained a just settlement, illiberal states will continue to be justified as necessary to maintaining order and insulating policy from the passions of the 'Arab street'. Several prominent European leaders sympathise with this view and oppose the GMEI. Washington's decision to downplay conflict resolution between the Israelis and Palestinians was consistent with the Bush administration's general aversion to strategic micromanagement, but squared less easily with the administration's express advocacy of a two-state solution. However, it did seem to reflect realistically low expectations for the 'road map' for peace that was rolled out in May 2003 and has since met with frustration due to persistent Palestinian terrorism and the inflexibility of both the Israeli and Palestinian leaderships. Marginalising the conflict implied recognition that Palestinian terrorism and Israel's determination to diminish its citizens' vulnerability – by building a security barrier and withdrawing from Gaza and parts of the West Bank – had conclusively interred the Oslo process. Yet there was a danger that the subordination of the Israeli–Palestinian problem could lead to missed opportunities and increasing discomfort among allies.

The ouster of Saddam Hussein had severely limited the options of Syrian President Bashar al-Assad. Deprived of cheap oil, a market for its exports and a regional partner in opposing US interests and Israel, Syria was suddenly bereft of key economic and diplomatic options. The occupation also planted on its doorstep 130,000 troops from a superpower angered by Syria's steady and calculated assistance to Saddam and to Palestinian terrorist groups. Furthermore, the Alawite Bashar appeared unsettled by the ouster of an Iraqi Baathist regime that had been, as Syria's Baathist rule remains, based on the dominance of a minority group. Starkly illuminating the leadership's anxiety, the state television station broadcast a four-hour special on Islamic architecture while satellite channels replayed footage of a statue of Saddam being ripped down by American tanks in central Baghdad. After flirting with more disruptive strategies, Bashar appeared to conclude that enlisting affirmative American help via a constructive role as a peacemaker rather than being a regional provocateur was in Syria's interest. In late November 2003, Bashar made an offer – presented in an interview published by the *New York Times* – to reopen dialogue with Israel on the Golan Heights. This outstanding territorial issue has given Syria a pretext for occupying Lebanon, provoking Israel and supporting Palestinian terrorism. As of April 2004, however, neither the US nor Israel appeared seriously interested in Syria's overture. The prospect of US sanctions under the Syrian Accountability and Lebanese Sovereignty Restoration Act of 2003, signed into law in December 2003, and Syria's own military weakness made it controllable. Furthermore, Israeli Prime Minister Ariel Sharon's preoccupations with managing Israel's prospective withdrawal from Gaza and fending off right-wing domestic pressure made it difficult for the Israeli government to contemplate negotiations with Syria. But securing Israel an Arab interlocutor could encourage positive Palestinian movement and improve Israeli and American standing in the region while engaging Damascus could further constrain Syria. Only a proactive American approach to conflict resolution could move Israel to sit down with Syria.

Jordan took political risks in supporting intervention in Iraq and has well established credentials as a strong counter-terrorism partner. (In April 2004, for instance, it sentenced eight terrorists to death for killing US diplomat Lawrence Foley in Amman in October 2002.) But Jordan faced continuing anger from Islamists over both Iraq and Palestine, and the Muslim Brotherhood – whose political wing, the Islamic Action Front, ended a six-year boycott of elections in May 2003 – constitutes credible political opposition there. Furthermore, in a secret meeting with Israeli Prime Minister Ariel Sharon in March 2004, Jordan's King Abdullah II registered acute worries that the construction of the security barrier, Israeli disengagement from the territories and the political vacuum would prompt Palestinians to flee to Jordan for work and safety and disrupt its demographic, political and economic balance. With anti-American unrest growing in Iraq and likely to antagonise Muslims in the region for some time, deeper US engagement in the Israeli–Palestinian conflict was one of few avenues for easing pressure on an important ally. Other allies may not feel the same degree of stress. There remains strong support for the US among the smaller Gulf states, which have welcomed US strategic protection by hosting American military forces and shown the greatest enthusiasm among Arab countries to democratise. Saddam's removal may have engendered greater stability in US–Saudi relations and opened space for political reform by facilitating the withdrawal of the US military presence from Saudi Arabia, and al-Qaeda-backed terrorist attacks in Riyadh in May and November 2003 have stiffened the Saudi regime's counter-terrorism posture. But the warmth of US relations with any Arab ally will be limited by American acquiescence to Palestinian strife. Indeed, linkages could develop between some Arab states' democratisation – the GMEI's core goal – and deeper US engagement in an Israeli–Palestinian peace process.

IISS*maps*

Strategic Geography **2003/4**

———	international boundaries	▣	capital cities
– – –	province or state boundaries	●	cities/towns/villages
- - - -	disputed and other boundaries	💥 ✷	attack(s)/incident(s) and skirmishes
═══	roads	◠◡	rivers
LOFA	province or state	⬭	lakes
⬗	built-up areas	▲	mountain peaks (height in metres)

Global trends UN peacekeeping deployments

United Nations Mission in Sierra Leone (UNAMSIL)

[2] Under UNSCR 1270 (1999) of 22.11.99; revised under UNSCR 1289 (2000) of 07.02.00 and UNSCR 1346 (2001) of 30.03.01

HQ Freetown

[i] 11,274 troops, 256 military observers, 142 civilian police personnel (as of 29.02.04)

[contributors] Bng, Bol, Can, Chn, Cro, Cz, Da, Egy, Gam, Ger, Gha, Gui, Indo, Jor, Ken, Kgz, Mal, Mali, Nep, NZ, Nga, Pak, RF, Slvk, Swe, Tz, Th, Ukr, UK, Ury & Zam

[$] 01.07.03–30.06.04: $543.49m

United Nations Mission in Liberia (UNMIL)

[2] Under UNSCR 1509 (2003) of 19 September 2003

HQ Monrovia

[i] 11,453 total uniformed personnel, including 10,903 troops and 108 military observers; 442 civilian police supported by 198 international civilian personnel and 10 local staff (as of 31.01.04)

[contributors] Bng, Ben, Bol, Bra, Chn, Cro, Den, Ecu, Eth, Fin, Fr, Gam, Gha, GuB, Indo, Irl, Jor, Ken, Mlw, Mali, Mol, Nba, Nep, Neth, Ngr, Nga, Nor, Pak, Par, Peru, Phi, Pol, RoK, Rom, Sen, RSA, Swe, Tog, Tur, UK, US, Zam & Zw

[$] (proposed) 01.08.03–30.06.04: $564.61m

UN Operation in Côte d'Ivoire (UNOCI)

[2] Under UNSCR 1528 of 27 February 2004

HQ Abidjan

[i] (total authorised) 6,240 military personnel including 200 military observers; as well as 350 civilian police, 435 international civilians, 529 local civilians and 119 UN volunteers

[contributors] (initial) Bng, Ben, Fr, Gha, Mor, Ngr, Pak, Sen, Tog, Ukr

[$] projected budget: $303m for 6 months

[2] date established

HQ headquarters

[i] strength

[contributors] contributors of military personnel

[$] approved budget (gross)

[$] appropriation for year 2003

United Nations Mission for the Referendum in Western Sahara (MINURSO)

[2] Under UNSCR 690 (1991) of 29 April 1991

HQ Laayoune, Western Sahara

[i] 205 military observers, 26 troops, supported by some 139 international civilian personnel and 110 local staff (as of 31.01.04)

[contributors] Arg, Ast, Bng, Chn, Cro, Egy, EIS, Fr, Gha, Gre, Gui, Hon, Hun, Irl, It, Ken, Mal, Mgl, Nga, Pak, Pol, RoK, RF, Ska & Ury

[$] 01.07.03–30.06.04: $43.40m

United Nations Mission in the Democratic Republic of the Congo (MONUC)

[2] Under UNSCR 1291 (2000) of 24 February 2000

HQ Kinshasa, DRC. Liaison offices in Addis Ababa (Eth), Bujumbura (Bur), Harare (Zw), Kampala (Uga), Kigali (Rwa), Lusaka (Zam), Windhoek (Nba)

[i] Military personnel: 10,866 including 10,209 troops and 542 military observers; 115 civilian police personnel; 629 international civilian personnel and 919 local civilian personnel (as of 31.03.04)

[contributors] Ag, Bng, Belg, Ben, Bol, BiH, BF, Crn, Can, Chl, Chn, Cz, Da, Egy, Fr, Gha, Ind, Indo, Irl, Jor, Ken, Mlw, Mal, Mali, Mgl, Mor, Moz, Nep, Ngr, Nga, Nor, Pak, Par, Peru, Pol, Rom, RF, Sen, FRY, RSA, Sp, Ska, Swe, Swit, Tun, Ukr, UK, Ury and Zam

[$] 01.07.03–30.06.04: $608.23m

UN Mission in Kosovo (UNMIK)

[2] Under UNSCR1244 of 10 June 1999

HQ Pristina

[i] 39 military observers; 3,600 civilian police (as of 31.12.03)

[contributors] Belg, Can, Cz, Den, Fr, Ger, Hun, It, Luxembourg, Neth, Nor, Pol, Por, Sp, Tur, UK, US, Arg, Ast, Az, Bulg, Fin, Geo, Lith, Mor, Rom, RF, Slvk, Slvn, Swe, Swit & Ukr

KOSOVO

GEORGIA

CYPRUS

LEBANON

Golan Heights, SYRIA

ISRAEL

WESTERN SAHARA

SIERRA LEONE

LIBERIA

CÔTE D'IVOIRE

ERITREA and ETHIOPIA

DEMOCRATIC REPUBLIC OF CONGO

Top ten military and civilian police contributors to UN operations, 31 December 2003

Pakistan
Bangladesh
Nigeria
India
Ghana
Nepal
Uruguay
Jordan
Kenya
South Africa

0 1000 2000 3000 4000 5000 6000 7000

United Nations Observer Mission in Georgia (UNOMIG)

Under UNSCR 858 of 24 August 1993. The latest SCR related to UNOMIG (UNSCR 1524 (2004)) concerned the extension of its mandate until 31 July 2004

HQ Sukhumi

127 military personnel, 116 military observers, 10 civilian police, 102 international civilian personnel and 179 local civilian staff (as of 31.01.04)

Alb, Aut, Bng, Ca, Da, Eg, Fr, Ger, Gr, Hun, Indo, Jor, Pak, Pol, RoK, RF, Swe, Swit, Tur, Ukr, UK, US & Ury

S 01.07.03–30.06.04: $32.10m

UN Peacekeeping Force in Cyprus (UNFICYP)

Under UNSCR 186, 4 March 1964

HQ Nicosia

1,262 troops and 47 civilian police; supported by 47 international civilian personnel and 106 local civilian staff (as of 31.01.04)

Arg (and troops from other South American countries), Ast, Can, Fin, Hun, Irl, RoK, Slvk, UK

S 01.07.03–30.06.04: $45.77m, incl. $14.57m from Cyprus and $6.5m from Greece in voluntary contributions

United Nations Military Observer Group in India and Pakistan (UNMOGIP)

Deployed in January 1949

HQ Rawalpindi (November–April); Srinagar (May–October)

44 military observers, supported by 23 international civilian personnel and 44 local civilian staff (as of 31.01.04)

Belg, Chl, Cro, Den, Fin, It, RoK, Swe & Ury

S $ 9.2m

Kashmir, INDIA and PAKISTAN

UN Interim Force in Lebanon (UNIFIL)

Under UNSCRs 425 and 426 of 19 March 1976. Extended by UNSCR 1525 (2004) until 31.07.04

HQ Naqoura

1,991 troops, assisted by some 50 UNTSO military observers and supported by 120 international civilian personnel and 296 local civilian staff (as of 31.01.04)

Fr, Gha, Ind, Irl, It, Pol & Ukr

S 01.07.03–30.06.04: $94.06m

UN Disengagement Observer Force (UNDOF)

31 May 1974

HQ Camp Faouar, Golan Heights

1,037 troops, assisted by some 80 military observers of UNTSO's Observer Group Golan; supported by 38 international civilian personnel and 93 local civilian staff (as of 31.01.04)

Ast, Can, Japan, Pol & Slvk

S 01.07.03–30.06.04: $41.81m

United Nations Mission in Ethiopia and Eritrea (UNMEE)

Under UNSCR 1320 (2000) of 15 September 2000, adjusted by UNSCR 1430 (2002) of 14 August 2002

HQ Offices in Asmara, Eritrea and Addis Ababa, Ethiopia

4,013 military personnel, including 3,809 troops and 204 military observers, UNMEE also includes 250 international civilians and 244 local civilians (as of 31.01.04)

Alg, Aus, Ast, Bng, Ben, BiH, Bulg, Chn, Cro, Cz, Den, Fin, Fr, Gam, Gha, Gre, Ind, It, Jor, Ken, Mal, Nba, Nep, Nga, Nor, Par, Peru, Pol, Rom, RF, Slvk, RSA, Sp, Swe, Swit, Tz, Tun, Ukr, UK, US, Ury & Zam

S 01.07.03–30.06.04: $196.89m

EAST TIMOR

UN Truce Supervision Organisation (UNTSO)

May 1948

HQ Government House, Jerusalem

154 military observers, supported by 99 international civilian personnel and 110 local civilian staff (as of 31.01.04)

Arg, Aus, Ast, Belg, Can, Chl, Chn, Den, Est, Fin, Fr, Irl, It, Nep, Neth, NZ, Nor, RF, Slvk, Slvn, Swe, Swit & US

S $27.69m (year 2004)

UN Mission of Support in East Timor (UNMISET)

Under UNSCR 1410 (2002)

HQ Dili, East Timor

78 military observers, 1,666 troops and 319 civilian police supported by 381 international and 678 local civilians (as of 31.01.04)

Aus, Ast, Bng, Bol, Bra, Cro, Da, Fiji, Irl, Jap, Jor, Ken, Mal, Moz, Nep, NZ, Pak, Phi, Por, RoK, RF, FRY, Sgp, Slvk, Swe, Th, Tur & Ury

S 01.07.03–30.06.04: $193.34m

Military personnel and civilian police serving in peacekeeping operations	45,732
Countries contributing military personnel and civilian police	94
International civilian personnel	3,269
Local civilian personnel	6,369

Information effective as at 31 December 2003

Global trends Cross-border terrorism, 2003–04

2003–04 has, so far, seen attacks around the world that appear intended to hit Western interests – especially those of nations supporting the intervention in Iraq. However, the attacks had been confined to soft targets in countries with security capabilities or inclinations that were not judged to match those of Western countries post 11-September.

The bombings in Madrid continue the soft-target strategy, but marked the first move onto Western territory since the attacks on New York and Washington. Security analysts believe that operational planning is being actively pursued by terrorist groups and that, although the US must be assumed to be the subject of such planning, until

There have been a series of terrorist incidents in Iraq with many fatalities resulting. Individuals from outside Iraq have been implicated in some of these attacks, which have often been of significant scale and impact. More can be seen in the maps dealing with Iraq.

11 March 2004: 191 die in bombing of commuter trains. According to press reports, Madrid hospitals treated over 1,800 people after the attacks. Claim made by the 'Abu Hafs al-Masri Brigade', followed by declaration of 'truce' after incoming Socialist leader stated intention to withdraw Spanish troops from Iraq. Suspicion later fell on the Moroccan Islamic Combat Group.

3 April 2004: Seven suspects in the Madrid bombings commit suicide by blowing up their flat.

2 April 2004: Bomb found on railway line near Toledo.

16 May 2003: 43 (mainly Moroccans) die when five suicide bombers detonate explosions within 30 minutes, targeting a Jewish community centre, Spanish restaurant and social club, an international hotel and the Belgian consulate.

30 April 2003: Suicide bomb attack by a Briton kills three, injures 60. Another Briton's bomb-belt fails – he is later found dead.

August 2003: Press sources report Saudi seizure of vehicle carrying surface-to-air missiles. On 13 August British Airways suspended flights to Saudi Arabia for a short time.

9 November 2003: Suicide car-bomb and gun attack on the al-Muhaya residential compound (housing mainly expatriate Arab labour), killed 18 and injures 120.

13 May 2003: Estimated 25 die when suicide bombers attack Al-Hamra, Vinell Corp and al-Jadawal housing complexes, as well as the office of the Saudi Maintenance Company, a US-Saudi joint venture.

an attack on the US is feasible, Europe will likely remain al-Qaeda's most prominent target.

The continuing appearance of messages allegedly made by senior al-Qaeda figures, such as bin Laden's second-in-command Ayman al-Zawahiri, serve as notice that, although the network may have been operationally hobbled, and may have had to resort to 'subcontracting' many attacks, it remains a singularly valuable rallying point for those groups or individuals that are sympathetic with its violent pan-Islamic agenda. The recorded messages from al-Zawahiri and others, by threatening attacks, may also achieve the subsidiary objective of disrupting daily activity in the West.

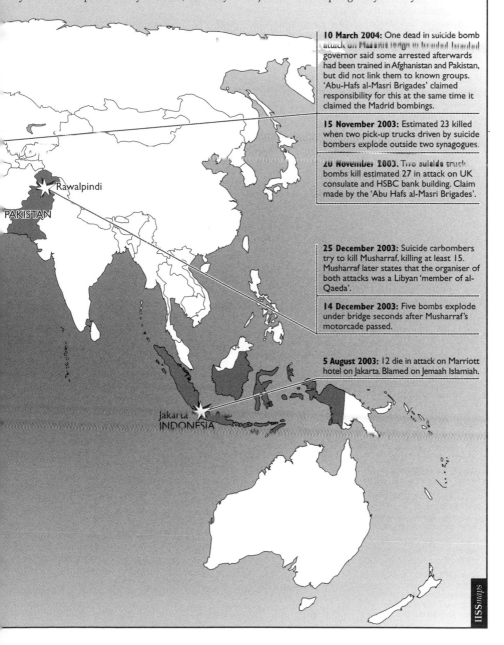

10 March 2004: One dead in suicide bomb attack on Madrid train in Istanbul. Istanbul governor said some arrested afterwards had been trained in Afghanistan and Pakistan, but did not link them to known groups. 'Abu-Hafs al-Masri Brigades' claimed responsibility for this at the same time it claimed the Madrid bombings.

15 November 2003: Estimated 23 killed when two pick-up trucks driven by suicide bombers explode outside two synagogues.

20 November 2003: Two suicide truck bombs kill estimated 27 in attack on UK consulate and HSBC bank building. Claim made by the 'Abu Hafs al-Masri Brigades'.

25 December 2003: Suicide carbombers try to kill Musharraf, killing at least 15. Musharraf later states that the organiser of both attacks was a Libyan 'member of al-Qaeda'.

14 December 2003: Five bombs explode under bridge seconds after Musharraf's motorcade passed.

5 August 2003: 12 die in attack on Marriott hotel on Jakarta. Blamed on Jemaah Islamiah.

Rawalpindi

PAKISTAN

Jakarta

INDONESIA

IISSmaps

Global trends Interdicting illicit cargoes

The Proliferation Security Initiative (PSI), unveiled by President Bush in Krakow on 31 May 2003, is a multilateral strategy to interdict shipments of WMD material and contraband that originate from states of 'proliferation concern'. According to John Bolton, US Under Secretary of State for Arms Contro and International Security, Washington's long-term objective with the PSI is to 'create a web of counterproliferation partnerships that will impede trade in WMD, delivery systems and related materials

Although the US views the PSI as 'not so much an organization as an activity', the plenary meetings held under the PSI sought initially to arrive at a set of 'interdiction principles'; these were released on 4 September after the Paris meeting. However, interdictions took place before the announcement of the PSI. For this reason, the PSI has been seen by some analysts as reflecting a 'bottom-up' strategy, 'designed to complement and enhance existing export control regulations and inspection processes'. The US stresses that 'all interdiction activities conducted by PSI partners will be consistent with relevant national and international authorities.' As of February 2004, land, sea and air interdiction exercises were proceeding apace.

NORWAY

UNITED KINGDOM

DENMARK

POLAND

London
9/10.10.03

GERMANY

Paris
3/4.09.03

NETHERLANDS

PORTUGAL

FRANCE

CANADA

Madrid
12.06.03

SPAIN

ITALY

Mediterranean Sea

Ionian Sea

TURKEY

UNITED
STATES

Washington DC
16/17.12.03

Red
Sea

1 July 2003: Spain holds ship carrying cargo of light armaments reportedly heading from South Korea to Senegal. Seoul protests Madrid's action.

Liberia

ATLANTIC
OCEAN

19 February 2004: *Exercise Air Brake* – Italian-led air interdiction exercise.

25–27 November 2003: *Basilic '03* – maritime interdiction exercise in the Mediterranean; French-led.

14–17 October 2003: *Sanso '03* – maritime interdiction exercise in the Mediterranean; Spanish-led.

June 2002: French commandos storm suspected drug smuggling freighter, the *Winner*, 1,100km southwest of the Canaries. US, Spain and Greece also involved.

Early 2004: A key development was an agreement between the US and Liberia providing 'authority on a bilateral basis to board sea vessels suspected of carrying illicit shipments of [WMD], their delivery systems or related materials.'

Planned PSI exercises (at October 2003)
Early 2004   Polish-led ground interdiction exercise

Spring 2004   German-led maritime interdiction
exercise in the Mediterranean

Spring 2004   French-led air interdiction exercise

March 2004   German-led interdiction exercise at
an airport

~~? October 2003 | US-led command post exercise~~

May 2003: US government reports that Germany seized
30 tonnes of sodium cyanide bound for North Korea.

22 June 2003: Greek forces board non-registered freighter,
the *Baltic Sky*, carrying nearly 700 tonnes of explosives.
Reported intended destination – Sudan.

April 2003: Paris orders French ship to unload suspicious
cargo in Egypt. Originating in Germany, cargo contains
22 tonnes of aluminium tubes, (alleged to be centrifuge
components).

January 2002: Israeli forces board vessel, the *Karine-A*,
transporting arms, reportedly from Iran to the Palestinian
territories.

**PSI participants committed to a number of
interdiction principles – a selection follows:**

• to undertake effective measures, either alone or in
concert with other states, for interdicting the transfer
or transport of WMD, their delivery systems, and
related materials.

• to board and search any suspect vessels flying their
flags in their internal waters, territorial seas, or areas
beyond the territorial seas of any other state.

• to obtain consent under the appropriate circumstances
to the boarding and searching of their own flag vessels
by other states, and to the seizure of such WMD-related
cargoes.

• to stop and/or search suspect vessels in their internal
waters, territorial seas, or contiguous zones, and enforce
conditions on suspect vessels entering or leaving their
ports, internal waters, or territorial seas.

• to require suspect aircraft that are transiting their
airspace to land for inspection and seize any such
cargoes, and deny aircraft transit rights through their
airspace.

Early June 2003: Japanese
officials inspect North Korean
ferry, the *Mangyongbyon-92*,
reportedly suspected of
engaging in hard-currency
smuggling.

August 2003: Taiwanese
customs seizes reported 158
barrels of dual-use chemicals
from North Korean vessel,
the *Be Gae Hong*, in a
Taiwanese port.

11–17 January 2003: *Sea
Saber* – US-led maritime
interdiction exercise in the
Arabian Sea.

December 2002: Spanish
frigate briefly seizes North
Korean vessel, the *Sosan*,
carrying *Scud* missiles to
Yemen. The vessel and its
cargo were later released.

January 2003: *Pacific Protector*
– maritime interdiction
exercise in the Coral Sea;
Australian-led.

April 2003: Australia seizes
North Korean ship, the *Pong
Su*, carrying $50m of heroin
to Australia. Reported that
an official from North Korea's
ruling Workers' Party was
onboard.

North
Korea

JAPAN

Taiwan

Arabian
Sea

Yemen

SINGAPORE

Coral
Sea

AUSTRALIA

Brisbane
9/10.07.03

SPAIN — countries that have been
participants since the first
PSI meeting in Madrid

TURKEY — countries that have
become involved in
varying capacities since
the Madrid meeting

[O] location of PSI meetings

May [X] selected PSI exercises *

May [⚓] interdictions (not
necessarily PSI related)

* Australia, Denmark, France, Germany, Italy,
Japan, the Netherlands, Singapore, Spain, Turkey, UK
and US participated (not all operationally)

IISS*maps*

Global trends Opium cultivation

In the late-1990s, the UN estimated that 'some 180 million people worldwide – 4.2 per cent of people aged 15 years and above – were consuming drugs […] this figure includes 144 million consuming cannabis, 29 million people consuming amphetamine-type stimulants, 14 million people taking cocaine and 13 million people abusing opiates, 9 million of whom were addicted to heroin.' National governments, and the wider international community – for instance through multilateral institutions – are continuing their attempts to contain and roll back the spread and consumption of illicit narcotics. The scale of the problem, and its impact on diverse societies, is great and growing. But anti-narcotics success in some areas has been met with greater difficulty in others, particularly where it is difficult to persuade local communities of the benefits of not cultivating a crop that will, more often than not, generate greater returns than food crops, or where the control of central government is weak. Although there are myriad illicit narcotics that are the concern of law and order agencies, these pages concentrate on production and trafficking in opium poppy.

According to the UN Office for Drugs and Crime (UNODC), the majority of illicit opium and heroin comes from a certain few countries. In 2003, UNODC listed Afghanistan as providing three quarters of global production, with Myanmar, Laos and Colombia following. The substantial post-2000 increase in Afghan production (charted in last year's *Strategic Survey*) led, according to UNODC, to world-total illicit poppy cultivation reaching 180,000 hectares in 2002 (as opposed to 222,000ha in 2000 and 144,000ha in 2001). But the long-term trend is seen as favourable, with an overall 25% decline in area since 1998, when the total was 238,000ha.

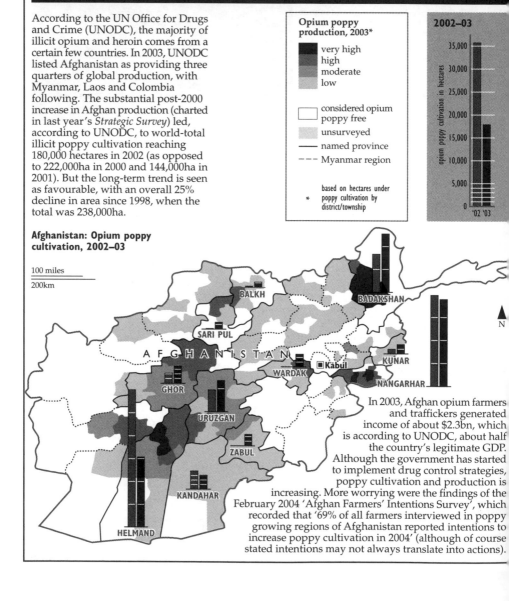

Afghanistan: Opium poppy cultivation, 2002–03

In 2003, Afghan opium farmers and traffickers generated income of about $2.3bn, which is according to UNODC, about half the country's legitimate GDP. Although the government has started to implement drug control strategies, poppy cultivation and production is increasing. More worrying were the findings of the February 2004 'Afghan Farmers' Intentions Survey', which recorded that '69% of all farmers interviewed in poppy growing regions of Afghanistan reported intentions to increase poppy cultivation in 2004' (although of course stated intentions may not always translate into actions).

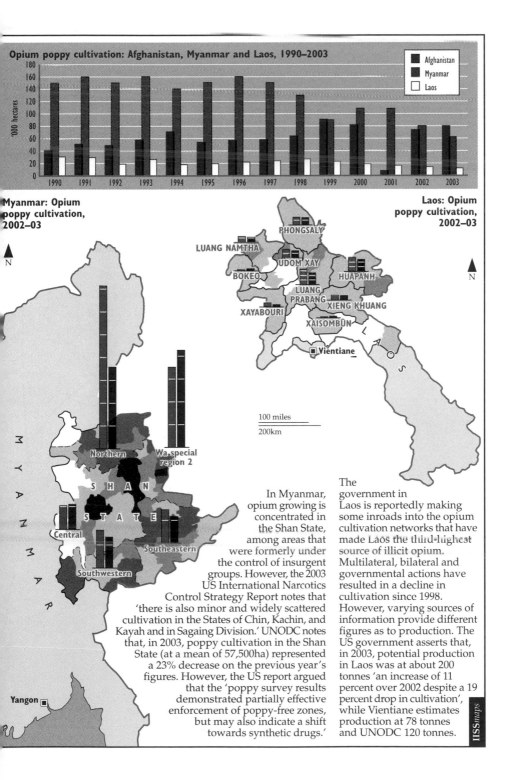

Opium poppy cultivation: Afghanistan, Myanmar and Laos, 1990–2003

Legend:
- Afghanistan
- Myanmar
- Laos

y-axis: '000 hectares (0, 20, 40, 60, 80, 100, 120, 140, 160, 180)
x-axis: 1990 1991 1992 1993 1994 1995 1996 1997 1998 1999 2000 2001 2002 2003

Myanmar: Opium poppy cultivation, 2002–03

N

Laos: Opium poppy cultivation, 2002–03

N

PHONGSALY
LUANG NAMTHA
UDOM XAY
BOKEO
HUAPANH
LUANG PRABANG
XAYABOURI
XIENG KHUANG
XAISOMBÛN

■ Vientiane

MYANMAR

Northern

Wa special region 2

S H A N

S T A T E

Central

Southeastern

Southwestern

Yangon ■

100 miles
200km

In Myanmar, opium growing is concentrated in the Shan State, among areas that were formerly under the control of insurgent groups. However, the 2003 US International Narcotics Control Strategy Report notes that 'there is also minor and widely scattered cultivation in the States of Chin, Kachin, and Kayah and in Sagaing Division.' UNODC notes that, in 2003, poppy cultivation in the Shan State (at a mean of 57,500ha) represented a 23% decrease on the previous year's figures. However, the US report argued that the 'poppy survey results demonstrated partially effective enforcement of poppy-free zones, but may also indicate a shift towards synthetic drugs.'

The government in Laos is reportedly making some inroads into the opium cultivation networks that have made Laos the third-highest source of illicit opium. Multilateral, bilateral and governmental actions have resulted in a decline in cultivation since 1998. However, varying sources of information provide different figures as to production. The US government asserts that, in 2003, potential production in Laos was at about 200 tonnes 'an increase of 11 percent over 2002 despite a 19 percent drop in cultivation', while Vientiane estimates production at 78 tonnes and UNODC 120 tonnes.

IISS*maps*

Global trends Opium trafficking

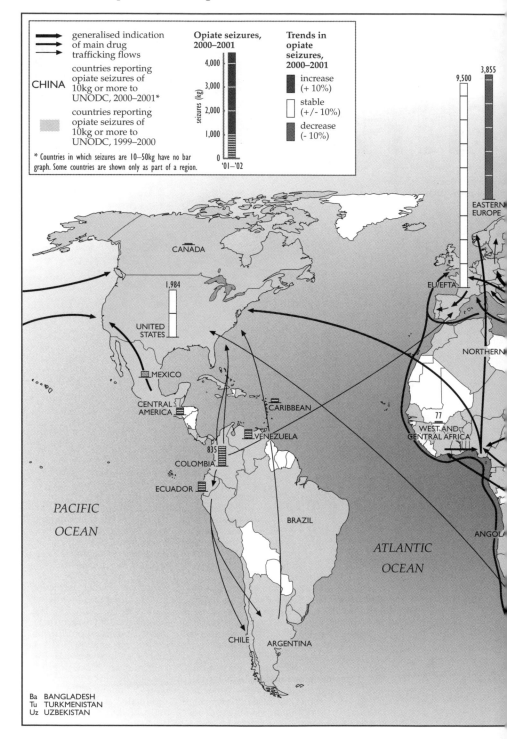

generalised indication of main drug trafficking flows

CHINA countries reporting opiate seizures of 10kg or more to UNODC, 2000–2001*

countries reporting opiate seizures of 10kg or more to UNODC, 1999–2000

* Countries in which seizures are 10–50kg have no bar graph. Some countries are shown only as part of a region.

Opiate seizures, 2000–2001

seizures (kg)

4,000
3,000
2,000
1,000
0

'01–'02

Trends in opiate seizures, 2000–2001

increase (+ 10%)

stable (+/- 10%)

decrease (- 10%)

Ba BANGLADESH
Tu TURKMENISTAN
Uz UZBEKISTAN

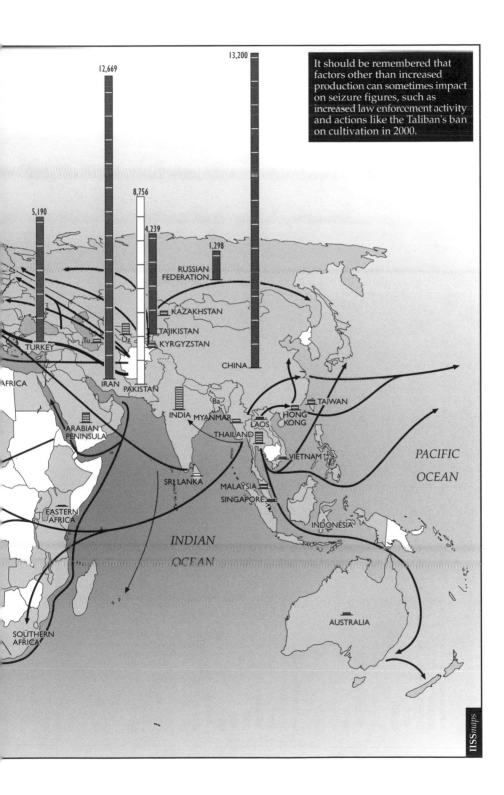

12,669

13,200

It should be remembered that factors other than increased production can sometimes impact on seizure figures, such as increased law enforcement activity and actions like the Taliban's ban on cultivation in 2000.

8,756

4,239

5,190

1,298

RUSSIAN
FEDERATION

KAZAKHSTAN

TAJIKISTAN

TURKEY

Tu

Uz

KYRGYZSTAN

AFRICA

CHINA

IRAN

PAKISTAN

TAIWAN

ARABIAN
PENINSULA

INDIA

MYANMAR

Ba

HONG
KONG

LAOS

THAILAND

VIETNAM

PACIFIC

OCEAN

EASTERN
AFRICA

SRI LANKA

MALAYSIA

SINGAPORE

INDONESIA

INDIAN

OCEAN

AUSTRALIA

SOUTHERN
AFRICA

IISS*maps*

Global trends Regional arms transfers and deliveries

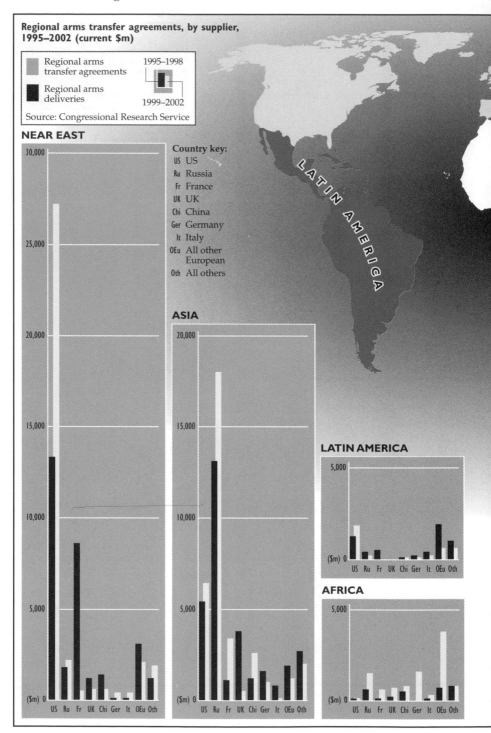

Regional arms transfer agreements, by supplier, 1995–2002 (current $m)

Regional arms transfer agreements — 1995–1998

Regional arms deliveries — 1999–2002

Source: Congressional Research Service

NEAR EAST

Country key:
US US
Ru Russia
Fr France
UK UK
Chi China
Ger Germany
It Italy
OEu All other European
Oth All others

ASIA

LATIN AMERICA

AFRICA

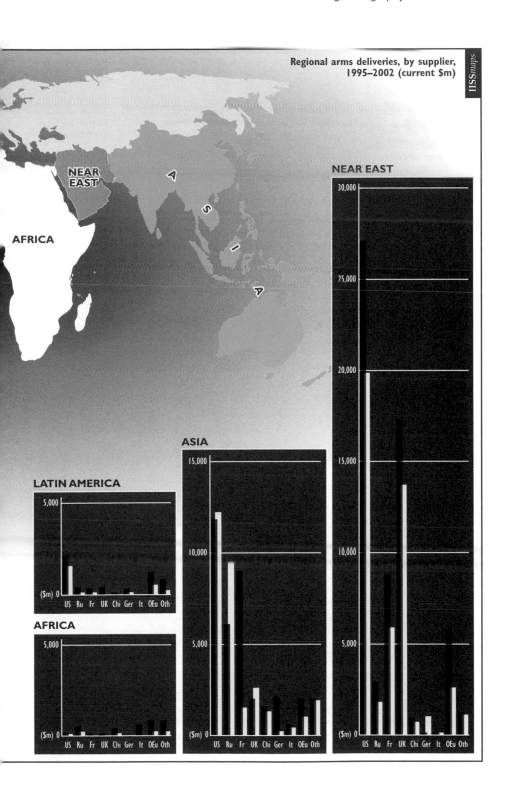

Regional arms deliveries, by supplier, 1995–2002 (current $m)

IISS*maps*

NEAR EAST

AFRICA

ASIA

NEAR EAST

ASIA

LATIN AMERICA

AFRICA

Global trends Weapons delivered in the Near East and Asia–Pacific

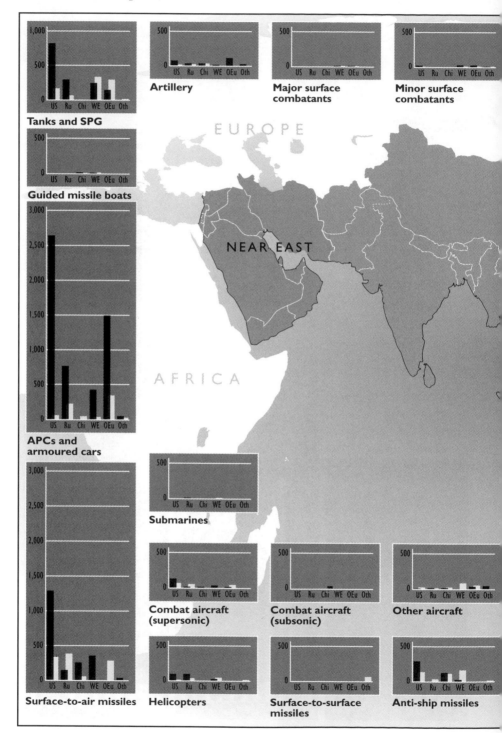

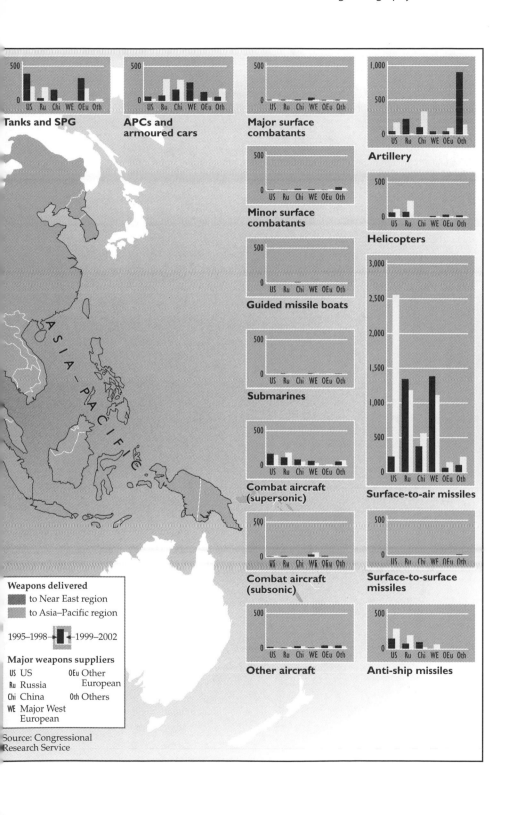

Tanks and SPG

APCs and
armoured cars

Major surface
combatants

Artillery

Minor surface
combatants

Helicopters

Guided missile boats

Submarines

Surface-to-air missiles

Combat aircraft
(supersonic)

Combat aircraft
(subsonic)

Surface-to-surface
missiles

Other aircraft

Anti-ship missiles

Weapons delivered
to Near East region
to Asia–Pacific region

1995–1998 ← → 1999–2002

Major weapons suppliers
US US   OEu Other
Ru Russia   European
Chi China   Oth Others
WE Major West
     European

Source: Congressional
Research Service

Middle East/Gulf Iraq: successful invasion

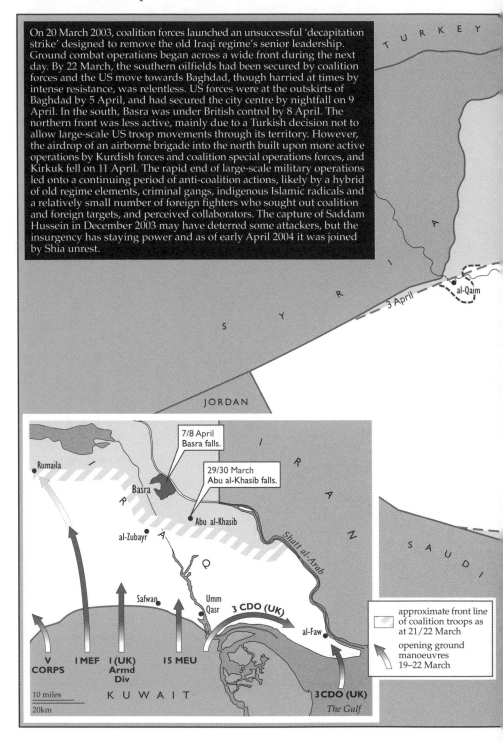

On 20 March 2003, coalition forces launched an unsuccessful 'decapitation strike' designed to remove the old Iraqi regime's senior leadership. Ground combat operations began across a wide front during the next day. By 22 March, the southern oilfields had been secured by coalition forces and the US move towards Baghdad, though harried at times by intense resistance, was relentless. US forces were at the outskirts of Baghdad by 5 April, and had secured the city centre by nightfall on 9 April. In the south, Basra was under British control by 8 April. The northern front was less active, mainly due to a Turkish decision not to allow large-scale US troop movements through its territory. However, the airdrop of an airborne brigade into the north built upon more active operations by Kurdish forces and coalition special operations forces, and Kirkuk fell on 11 April. The rapid end of large-scale military operations led onto a continuing period of anti-coalition actions, likely by a hybrid of old regime elements, criminal gangs, indigenous Islamic radicals and a relatively small number of foreign fighters who sought out coalition and foreign targets, and perceived collaborators. The capture of Saddam Hussein in December 2003 may have deterred some attackers, but the insurgency has staying power and as of early April 2004 it was joined by Shia unrest.

TURKEY

SYRIA

al-Qaim

3 April

JORDAN

IRAQ

7/8 April
Basra falls.

29/30 March
Abu al-Khasib falls.

Rumaila

Basra

Abu al-Khasib

al-Zubayr

Shatt al-Arab

SAUDI

Safwan

Umm
Qasr

3 CDO (UK)

al-Faw

V
CORPS

I MEF

I (UK)
Armd
Div

15 MEU

3 CDO (UK)

approximate front line
of coalition troops as
at 21/22 March

opening ground
manoeuvres
19–22 March

10 miles

20km

KUWAIT

The Gulf

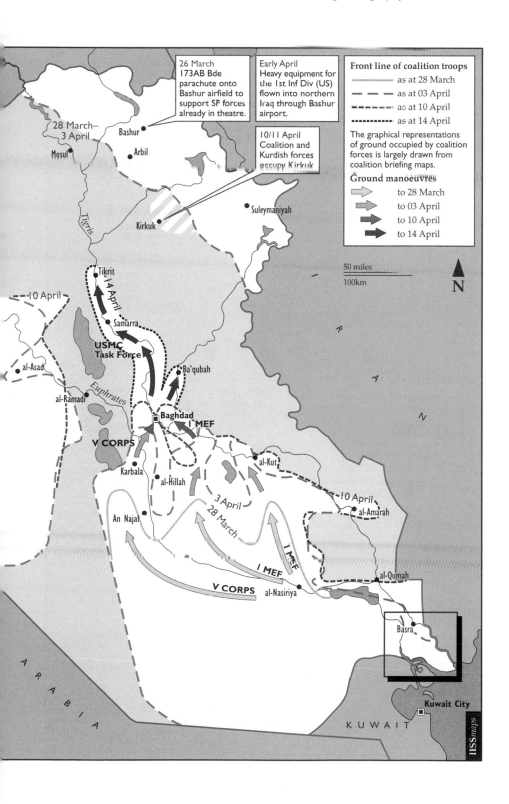

26 March
173AB Bde parachute onto Bashur airfield to support SF forces already in theatre.

Early April
Heavy equipment for the 1st Inf Div (US) flown into northern Iraq through Bashur airport.

10/11 April
Coalition and Kurdish forces occupy Kirkuk

Front line of coalition troops
- ············· as at 28 March
- — — — as at 03 April
- ▬▬▬▬ as at 10 April
- ▪▪▪▪▪▪▪ as at 14 April

The graphical representations of ground occupied by coalition forces is largely drawn from coalition briefing maps.

Ground manoeuvres
- ⇨ to 28 March
- ⇨ to 03 April
- ➡ to 10 April
- ➡ to 14 April

50 miles
100km

N

28 March–3 April

Mosul

Bashur

Arbil

Tigris

Suleymaniyah

Kirkuk

Tikrit

14 April

Samarra

USMC Task Force

10 April

al-Asad

Ba'qubah

al-Ramadi

Euphrates

Baghdad   I MEF

V CORPS

Karbala

al-Hillah

al-Kut

3 April

28 March

10 April

al-Amarah

An Najaf

I MEF

I MEF

V CORPS   al-Nasiriya

al-Qurnah

Basra

ARABIA

Kuwait City

K U W A I T

IISSmaps

Middle East/Gulf Iraq: complex aftermath

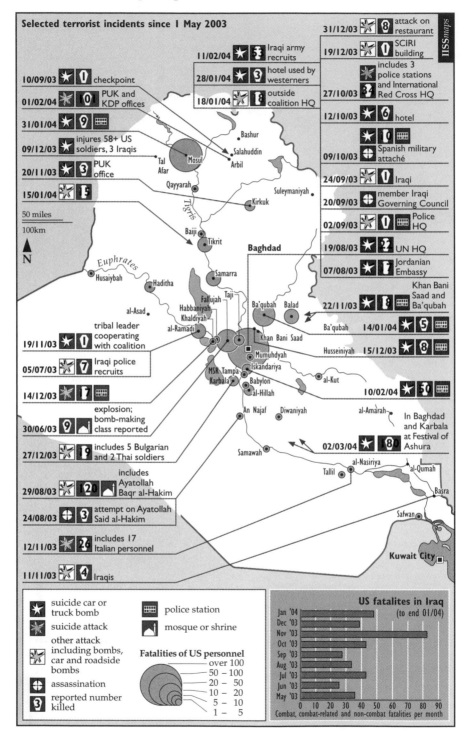

Selected terrorist incidents since 1 May 2003

IISS*maps*

31/12/03 — 8 attack on restaurant

19/12/03 — 0 SCIRI building

11/02/04 — 3 Iraqi army recruits

28/01/04 — 3 hotel used by westerners

18/01/04 — 8 outside coalition HQ

27/10/03 — 34 includes 3 police stations and International Red Cross HQ

12/10/03 — 6 hotel

10/09/03 — 1 checkpoint

01/02/04 — 0 PUK and KDP offices

31/01/04 — 9

09/12/03 — injures 58+ US soldiers, 3 Iraqis

20/11/03 — 3 PUK office

15/01/04 — 1

09/10/03 — 0 / Spanish military attaché

24/09/03 — 0 Iraqi

20/09/03 — member Iraqi Governing Council

02/09/03 — 0 Police HQ

19/08/03 — 2 UN HQ

07/08/03 — 1 Jordanian Embassy

Bashur
Salahuddin
Tal Afar Mosul Arbil
Qayyarah Suleymaniyah
Kirkuk
50 miles
100km
N
Baiji
Tikrit
Samarra
Baghdad
Euphrates
Husaiybah Haditha
Fallujah Taji
Habbaniyah Ba'qubah Balad
al-Asad Khaldiyah
al-Ramadi Khan Bani Saad

Khan Bani Saad and Ba'qubah
22/11/03 — 8

Ba'qubah 14/01/04 — 5

Husseiniyah 15/12/03 — 8

19/11/03 — 0 tribal leader cooperating with coalition

05/07/03 — 7 Iraqi police recruits

14/12/03 — 1

30/06/03 — 9 explosion; bomb-making class reported

27/12/03 — 19 includes 5 Bulgarian and 2 Thai soldiers

29/08/03 — 120 includes Ayatollah Baqr al-Hakim

24/08/03 — 3 attempt on Ayatollah Said al-Hakim

12/11/03 — 26 includes 17 Italian personnel

11/11/03 — 4 Iraqis

Mumuhdyah
Iskandariya
MSR Tampa
Karbala Babylon
al-Hillah
An Najaf Diwaniyah al-Amarah
al-Kut

10/02/04 — 50

02/03/04 — 180 In Baghdad and Karbala at Festival of Ashura

Samawah
al-Nasiriya al-Qumah
Tallil Basra
Safwan

Kuwait City

Legend

⭐ suicide car or truck bomb

☷ police station

✳ suicide attack

🕌 mosque or shrine

✳ other attack including bombs, car and roadside bombs

⊕ assassination

Fatalities of US personnel
— over 100
— 50 – 100
— 20 – 50
— 10 – 20
— 5 – 10
— 1 – 5

3 reported number killed

US fatalities in Iraq

(to end 01/04)

Jan '04
Dec '03
Nov '03
Oct '03
Sep '03
Aug '03
Jul '03
Jun '03
May '03

0 10 20 30 40 50 60 70 80 90
Combat, combat-related and non-combat fatalities per month

Following the announcement of the end of major combat operations in May 2003, Iraq has, for administrative purposes, been divided into six zones – including Baghdad. Early-to-mid 2004 is seeing the US conduct one of the largest rotations of ground forces since World War II, designed to replace its ground forces in Iraq, some of whom had remained in-country since the war. It is projected that the 2003 responsibilities undertaken by four divisions will pass to three divisions, with a larger National Guard and reserve component. Press accounts indicated in early 2004 that numbers were projected to fall from nearly 130,000 to around 110,000, although actual figures will likely be determined by the security situation in Iraq.

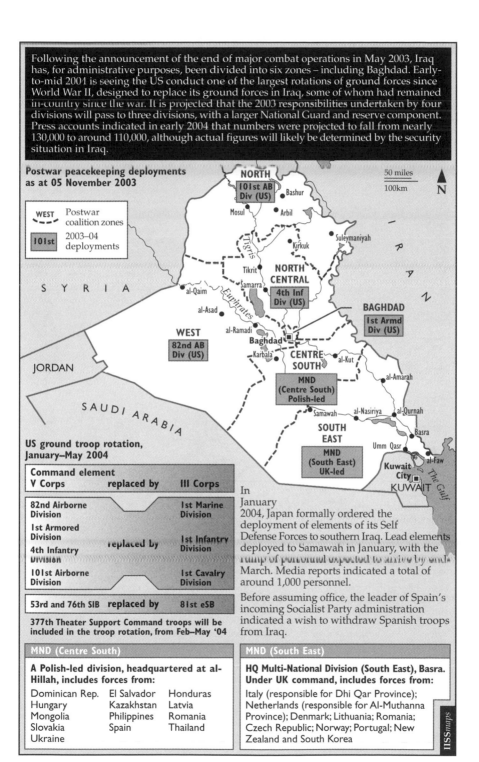

Postwar peacekeeping deployments as at 05 November 2003

WEST	Postwar coalition zones
101st	2003–04 deployments

NORTH
101st AB Div (US) • Bashur
Mosul • • Arbil
• Suleymaniyah
• Kirkuk
Tikrit • NORTH CENTRAL
Samarra • 4th Inf Div (US)
al-Qaim •
al-Asad •
al-Ramadi • WEST 82nd AB Div (US)
Baghdad • BAGHDAD 1st Armd Div (US)
Karbala • CENTRE SOUTH • al-Kut
MND (Centre South) Polish-led • al-Amarah
Samawah • al-Nasiriya • al-Qurnah
SOUTH EAST • Basra
MND (South East) UK-led Umm Qasr
Kuwait City • al-Faw
KUWAIT

SYRIA
JORDAN
SAUDI ARABIA
IRAN
The Gulf

Tigris Euphrates

50 miles
100km
N

US ground troop rotation, January–May 2004

Command element V Corps	replaced by	III Corps
82nd Airborne Division		1st Marine Division
1st Armored Division	replaced by	1st Infantry Division
4th Infantry Division		
101st Airborne Division		1st Cavalry Division
53rd and 76th SIB	replaced by	81st eSB

377th Theater Support Command troops will be included in the troop rotation, from Feb–May '04

In January 2004, Japan formally ordered the deployment of elements of its Self Defense Forces to southern Iraq. Lead elements deployed to Samawah in January, with the rump of personnel expected to arrive by end-March. Media reports indicated a total of around 1,000 personnel.

Before assuming office, the leader of Spain's incoming Socialist Party administration indicated a wish to withdraw Spanish troops from Iraq.

MND (Centre South)

A Polish-led division, headquartered at al-Hillah, includes forces from:

Dominican Rep.	El Salvador	Honduras
Hungary	Kazakhstan	Latvia
Mongolia	Philippines	Romania
Slovakia	Spain	Thailand
Ukraine		

MND (South East)

HQ Multi-National Division (South East), Basra. Under UK command, includes forces from:

Italy (responsible for Dhi Qar Province); Netherlands (responsible for Al-Muthanna Province); Denmark; Lithuania; Romania; Czech Republic; Norway; Portugal; New Zealand and South Korea

IISS*maps*

Middle East/Gulf Israel–Palestine: construction continues

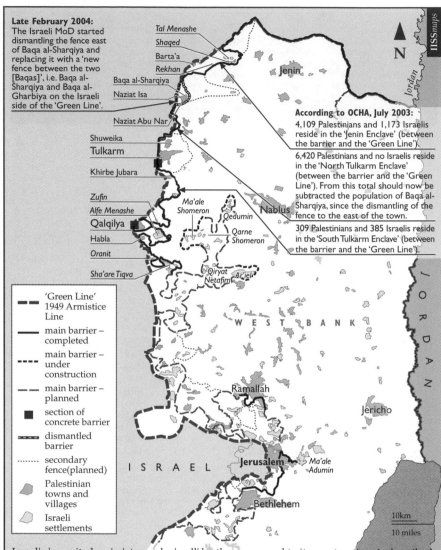

Late February 2004:
The Israeli MoD started dismantling the fence east of Baqa al-Sharqiya and replacing it with a 'new fence between the two [Baqas]', i.e. Baqa al-Sharqiya and Baqa al-Gharbiya on the Israeli side of the 'Green Line'.

Tal Menashe
Shaqed
Barta'a
Rekhan
Baqa al-Sharqiya
Naziat Isa
Naziat Abu Nar
Shuweika
Tulkarm
Khirbe Jubara
Zufin
Alfe Menashe
Qalqilya
Habla
Oranit
Sha'are Tiqva

Ma'ale Shomeron
Qedumin
Qarne Shomeron
Qiryat Netafim
Ariel

Jenin
Nablus

N

According to OCHA, July 2003:
4,109 Palestinians and 1,173 Israelis reside in the 'Jenin Enclave' (between the barrier and the 'Green Line').

6,420 Palestinians and no Israelis reside in the 'North Tulkarm Enclave' (between the barrier and the 'Green Line'). From this total should now be subtracted the population of Baqa al-Sharqiya, since the dismantling of the fence to the east of the town.

309 Palestinians and 385 Israelis reside in the 'South Tulkarm Enclave' (between the barrier and the 'Green Line').

W E S T   B A N K

Ramallah

Jericho

ISRAEL   Jerusalem   Ma'ale Adumin

Bethlehem

J O R D A N

10km
10 miles

Legend:
- – – 'Green Line' 1949 Armistice Line
- —— main barrier – completed
- - - - main barrier – under construction
- – – main barrier – planned
- ■ section of concrete barrier
- - - - dismantled barrier
- .... secondary fence (planned)
- Palestinian towns and villages
- Israeli settlements

Israel's 'security barrier', termed a 'wall' by those opposed to its construction, is described by the Israeli government as 'solely a defensive measure, intended to protect Israelis from suicide bombings and other terrorist attacks. It is not a political act. It is not intended to be a border or prejudice any future negotiations with the Palestinians.' But it is seen by the Palestinian authorities as a means of 'entrenching the occupation and the de facto annexation of large areas of Palestinian land. ... It will render the two-State solution to the Israeli–Palestinian conflict practically impossible', and was so described in a February 2004 presentation to the International Court of Justice. The barrier is composed mainly of wire fencing, in conjunction with sensors and patrols, and in certain places is made up of concrete walls. The IDF states that there will be 41 agricultural gates, 9 crossing points and 4 goods checkpoints to facilitate Palestinian movement, but the UN notes that access problems still exist, and that 'it seems inevitable that more people, unable to reach their land to harvest crops, graze animals or earn a living, will face economic hardship.' Meanwhile, Israeli authorities say that construction is justified by a reduction in terrorist attacks inside Israel.
Sources: IISS (*Survival*); B'Tselem; OCHA; IDF; NAD (PLO)

Europe/Russia Russia's eastern energy resources

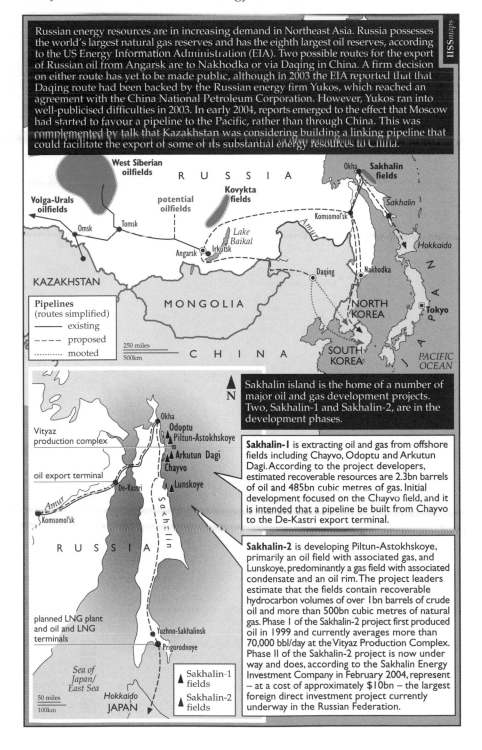

Russian energy resources are in increasing demand in Northeast Asia. Russia possesses the world's largest natural gas reserves and has the eighth largest oil reserves, according to the US Energy Information Administration (EIA). Two possible routes for the export of Russian oil from Angarsk are to Nakhodka or via Daqing in China. A firm decision on either route has yet to be made public, although in 2003 the EIA reported that that Daqing route had been backed by the Russian energy firm Yukos, which reached an agreement with the China National Petroleum Corporation. However, Yukos ran into well-publicised difficulties in 2003. In early 2004, reports emerged to the effect that Moscow had started to favour a pipeline to the Pacific, rather than through China. This was complemented by talk that Kazakhstan was considering building a linking pipeline that could facilitate the export of some of its substantial energy resources to China.

IISS*maps*

West Siberian oilfields

R U S S I A

Okha **Sakhalin fields**

Volga-Urals oilfields

potential oilfields

Kovykta fields

Sakhalin

Omsk Tomsk

Komsomol'sk

Lake Baikal

Hokkaido

Amur

Angarsk Irkutsk

KAZAKHSTAN

Daqing Nakhodka

J A P A N

Pipelines (routes simplified)
—— existing
- - - proposed
········· mooted

M O N G O L I A

250 miles
500km

C H I N A

NORTH KOREA Tokyo

SOUTH KOREA

PACIFIC OCEAN

▲ N

Sakhalin island is the home of a number of major oil and gas development projects. Two, Sakhalin-1 and Sakhalin-2, are in the development phases.

Vityaz production complex

Okha
Odoptu
▲ **Piltun-Astokhskoye**
▲ **Arkutun Dagi**
Chayvo

oil export terminal

De-Kastri ▲ **Lunskoye**

Amur

Komsomol'sk

R U S S I A

S a k h a l i n

Sakhalin-1 is extracting oil and gas from offshore fields including Chayvo, Odoptu and Arkutun Dagi. According to the project developers, estimated recoverable resources are 2.3bn barrels of oil and 485bn cubic metres of gas. Initial development focused on the Chayvo field, and it is intended that a pipeline be built from Chayvo to the De-Kastri export terminal.

Sakhalin-2 is developing Piltun-Astokhskoye, primarily an oil field with associated gas, and Lunskoye, predominantly a gas field with associated condensate and an oil rim. The project leaders estimate that the fields contain recoverable hydrocarbon volumes of over 1bn barrels of crude oil and more than 500bn cubic metres of natural gas. Phase 1 of the Sakhalin-2 project first produced oil in 1999 and currently averages more than 70,000 bbl/day at the Vityaz Production Complex. Phase II of the Sakhalin-2 project is now under way and does, according to the Sakhalin Energy Investment Company in February 2004, represent – at a cost of approximately $10bn – the largest foreign direct investment project currently underway in the Russian Federation.

planned LNG plant and oil and LNG terminals

Yuzhno-Sakhalinsk
Prigorodnoye

Sea of Japan/ East Sea

50 miles
100km

Hokkaido

JAPAN ▶

▲ Sakhalin-1 fields
▲ Sakhalin-2 fields

Europe/Russia Satellite navigation

The EU's *Galileo* satellite navigation programme, due to become operational between 2005–08, will be the third such deployment, after the US Global Positioning System (GPS) and the Russian Global Navigation Satellite System (GLONASS). *Galileo* forms the third leg of a Global Navigation Satellite System (GNSS). The European Space Agency (ESA) states that all three systems will be fully interoperable, so that a position can be determined 'with any receiver picking up signals from any combination of satellites belonging to any of the three systems.' Prior to *Galileo*, the EU was – at end 2003 – in the transmission testing stage for its European Geostationary Navigation Overlay Service (EGNOS), designed to augment GPS and GLONASS. In March 2004, a contract was signed for the launch of 'two experimental *Galileo* vehicles by two *Soyuz* launch vehicles'. The first will be from Baikonur by end 2005.

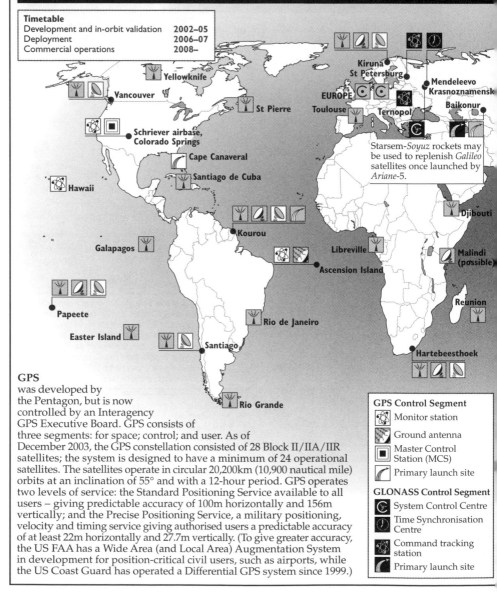

Timetable	
Development and in-orbit validation	2002–05
Deployment	2006–07
Commercial operations	2008–

Starsem-*Soyuz* rockets may be used to replenish *Galileo* satellites once launched by *Ariane*-5.

GPS
was developed by the Pentagon, but is now controlled by an Interagency GPS Executive Board. GPS consists of three segments: for space; control; and user. As of December 2003, the GPS constellation consisted of 28 Block II/IIA/IIR satellites; the system is designed to have a minimum of 24 operational satellites. The satellites operate in circular 20,200km (10,900 nautical mile) orbits at an inclination of 55° and with a 12-hour period. GPS operates two levels of service: the Standard Positioning Service available to all users – giving predictable accuracy of 100m horizontally and 156m vertically; and the Precise Positioning Service, a military positioning, velocity and timing service giving authorised users a predictable accuracy of at least 22m horizontally and 27.7m vertically. (To give greater accuracy, the US FAA has a Wide Area (and Local Area) Augmentation System in development for position-critical civil users, such as airports, while the US Coast Guard has operated a Differential GPS system since 1999.)

GPS Control Segment
Monitor station
Ground antenna
Master Control Station (MCS)
Primary launch site

GLONASS Control Segment
System Control Centre
Time Synchronisation Centre
Command tracking station
Primary launch site

Galileo is envisaged as an independent European global satellite navigation system that will be interoperable with GPS and GLONASS. Total project costs are currently estimated at €3.2–3.4 billion. ESA argue that '*Galileo* will provide the first satellite positioning and navigation system specifically for civil purposes'. *Galileo* will comprise a constellation of '30 satellites (27 operational and three spare), positioned in three circular Medium Earth Orbit planes 23,616km above the Earth, and at [an orbital plane inclination] of 56° with reference to the equatorial plane'. Programme material states that '*Galileo* will deliver real-time positioning accuracy down to the metre range…. It will guarantee the availability of the service under all but the most extreme circumstances and will inform users within seconds of a failure of any satellite'. In September 2003, the EU announced that China was investing some €200m in the project.

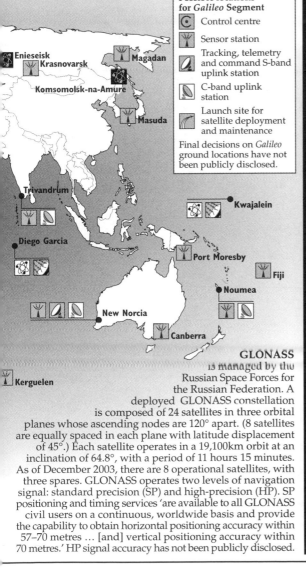

Possible locations for *Galileo* Segment

- Ⓒ Control centre
- Sensor station
- Tracking, telemetry and command S-band uplink station
- C-band uplink station
- Launch site for satellite deployment and maintenance

Final decisions on *Galileo* ground locations have not been publicly disclosed.

Map labels: Enieseisk, Krasnovarsk, Magadan, Komsomolsk-na-Amure, Masuda, Trivandrum, Kwajalein, Diego Garcia, Port Moresby, Fiji, Noumea, New Norcia, Canberra, Kerguelen

GLONASS is managed by the Russian Space Forces for the Russian Federation. A deployed GLONASS constellation is composed of 24 satellites in three orbital planes whose ascending nodes are 120° apart. (8 satellites are equally spaced in each plane with latitude displacement of 45°.) Each satellite operates in a 19,100km orbit at an inclination of 64.8°, with a period of 11 hours 15 minutes. As of December 2003, there are 8 operational satellites, with three spares. GLONASS operates two levels of navigation signal: standard precision (SP) and high-precision (HP). SP positioning and timing services 'are available to all GLONASS civil users on a continuous, worldwide basis and provide the capability to obtain horizontal positioning accuracy within 57–70 metres … [and] vertical positioning accuracy within 70 metres.' HP signal accuracy has not been publicly disclosed.

Galileo **levels of service**

The *Open service*, for mass-market applications, will provide signals for timing and positioning free of charge. It 'will not provide integrity information computed by the system, and the quality of the signals will only be determined by algorithm at the user level…. '

The *Safety of Life Service* 'will be used for most transport applications where lives could be endangered if the performance of the navigation system is degraded without real-time notice.' The main difference from the Open Service is the 'worldwide high integrity level for safety-critical applications'.

The *Commercial Service* 'is aimed at market applications requiring higher performance than offered by the Open Service. It will provide added value services on payment of a fee'. Two signals will be added to the Open Service, which are protected by commercial encryption, with access controlled at the receiver level.

The *Public Regulated Service* 'will be used by groups such as police, fire, ambulance, military and customs. … PRS is required to be operational at all times and in all circumstances [and] is separate from the other services, so that they can be denied without affecting PRS operations'. Civil bodies will control access to the encrypted PRS.

A *Search and Rescue Service*, which is intended to improve international SAR coverage, for instance by the near real-time reception of distress messages, precise satellite location, and multiple satellite detection to overcome any topographical obstructions.

The Americas Colombia's continuing conflicts

The security situation in Colombia remains precarious. President Uribe's security strategy led in 2002 to the end of the *despeje*, controlled by FARC guerrillas, and recent operational successes by government forces in combating them. Conflict with the FARC and ELN continues, as does the government's policy of applying strong military and political pressure, but a positive development has been the negotiations, since 2003, between the government and the paramilitary AUC (aimed at disarmament before 2006). Terrorist attacks dropped to 850 in 2003, from 1,645 in 2002. Also in 2003, over 3,000 leftist rebels and right-wing paramilitaries disarmed and joined rehabilitation programmes, while desertions from illegal groups rose 80%.

Colombia's continuing security problems (compounded by poor weather in late 2003) have led, according to the WFP, to Colombia having the largest IDP population in the western hemisphere, estimated to be over 2 million (80% of these are believed to lack proper access to food supplies). The WFP currently feeds 350,000 IDPs, largely in northern Colombia, and the problem has also impacted on neighbouring states.

As well as having security problems, Colombia is a major producer of cocaine. But figures released by both the Colombian government, the US and UNODC point to substantial reductions in cultivation. Washington's figures state that net coca cultivation dropped to 113,850 hectares in 2003 from 144,450ha in 2002. But this still yields about 450 tonnes of pure cocaine.

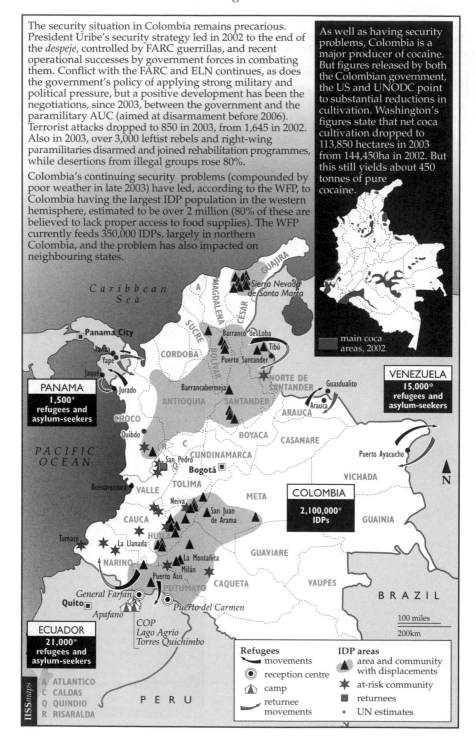

main coca areas, 2002

PANAMA
1,500*
refugees and asylum-seekers

VENEZUELA
15,000*
refugees and asylum-seekers

COLOMBIA
2,100,000*
IDPs

ECUADOR
21,000*
refugees and asylum-seekers

A ATLANTICO
C CALDAS
Q QUINDIO
R RISARALDA

Refugees
movements
reception centre
camp
returnee movements

IDP areas
area and community with displacements
at-risk community
returnees
* UN estimates

The Americas Haiti: slowly stabilising

Haiti has, since its creation, suffered economic, political and institutional weakness. It was reported that the spark for recent violence was an assault on students by pro-Aristide militants, although election results from 2000 were disputed, and political antagonism heightened in late-2003, with opposition groups boycotting government. Armed incidents between rebels and pro-Aristide militia increased in early-2004, with some former gang leaders switching allegiance to anti-government forces. Under international pressure, Aristide resigned and left the country on 29 February. There is now an interim President and Prime Minister, pending parliamentary and presidential elections scheduled for 2005.

Humanitarian issues were of concern to the international community. Although much food remained in storage in Haiti, the humanitarian crisis brought on by conflict was compounded by the interruption of the transportation routes used to move supplies, and the suspension of work by many NGOs active in the country. On 9 March, the UN appealed for $35m in a 'flash appeal'. It estimated that 3m people (37% of the population) had been affected by the crisis – the majority living in Port-au-Prince, Gonaïves, Cap-Haitien, Saint-Marc, Port-de-Paix and Hinche. As of 23 March, with the UN interim force in place, the UN reported that the situation was slowly stabilising, though it remained volatile in the north of the country.

As of 23 March: Former prisoners remain in control of Fort Liberté.

Late March: French troops begin deploying to Cap-Haitien.

22 February: Looters ransack WFP warehouse containing 800 tonnes of food aid in Cap-Haitien.

22 February: Rebels capture Cap-Haitien.

25 February: Rebels capture Tortue Island.

24 February: Rebels capture Port-de-Paix.

5/6 February: Rebels (the Freedom and National Reconstruction Front according to OCHA) seize Gonaïves.

11 February: Reported that government forces regained control of Saint-Marc and Dondon.

29 February: Initial deployment of multinational force to Port-au-Prince.

On 23 February, the US deployed a small team to protect the US embassy and staff in Port-au-Prince. With the situation deteriorating, and after the resignation and departure of then-President Aristide, a larger US force was deployed on 29 February as the lead element in an international force under UN authorisation (Resolution 1529). The UNSC determined that the interim force should be deployed for no longer than three months. Press reports indicate that Brazil will send troops to assist the interim force in the future, and that it is willing to head the UN's multinational follow-on force – after the 90-day interim period expires.

N

Île de la Tortue

Port-de-Paix

Cap-Haitien

Bassin-Bleu
Anse-Rouge
Gros-Morne
Limbé
Trou-du-Nord
Fort-Liberté
Milot
Plaisance
Dondon
Grande Rivière du Nord
Ouanaminthe
Gonaïves
Ennery
Saint Michael de l'Attalaye

Maissade
Hinche

Saint-Marc
Petite-Rivière de l'Artibonite

25 miles

50km

ZONE NORD
France 825

ZONE SUD
US 1,940
Canada 500
Chile 330

Île de Gonâve

Mirebalais

H A I T I

ZONE UN zones at 23 March 2004

CHILE country and
330 approximate number of military personnel assigned to UN-authorised interim force (1 April 2004)

Miragoàne
Petit-Goàve
Grand-Goàve

Croix des Bouquets

24 February: Dominican Republic send extra 1,200 troops to border with Haiti.

As at 27 February 2004

⊙ rebel held towns

✳ armed confrontation

Les Cayes

Jacmel

Caribbean Sea

DOMINICAN REPUBLIC

December 2003: Over 10,000 refugees reportedly cross Dominican border. Dominican authorities later reinforce the border.

IISS*maps*

Asia Selected US military deployments

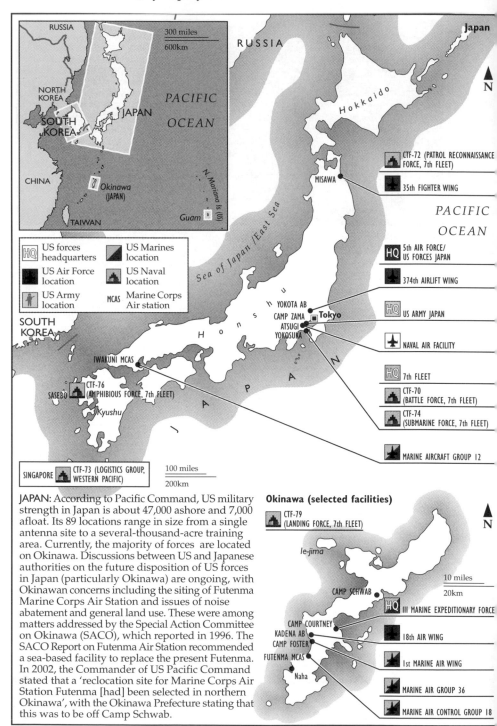

JAPAN: According to Pacific Command, US military strength in Japan is about 47,000 ashore and 7,000 afloat. Its 89 locations range in size from a single antenna site to a several-thousand-acre training area. Currently, the majority of forces are located on Okinawa. Discussions between US and Japanese authorities on the future disposition of US forces in Japan (particularly Okinawa) are ongoing, with Okinawan concerns including the siting of Futenma Marine Corps Air Station and issues of noise abatement and general land use. These were among matters addressed by the Special Action Committee on Okinawa (SACO), which reported in 1996. The SACO Report on Futenma Air Station recommended a sea-based facility to replace the present Futenma. In 2002, the Commander of US Pacific Command stated that a 'reclocation site for Marine Corps Air Station Futenma [had] been selected in northern Okinawa', with the Okinawa Prefecture stating that this was to be off Camp Schwab.

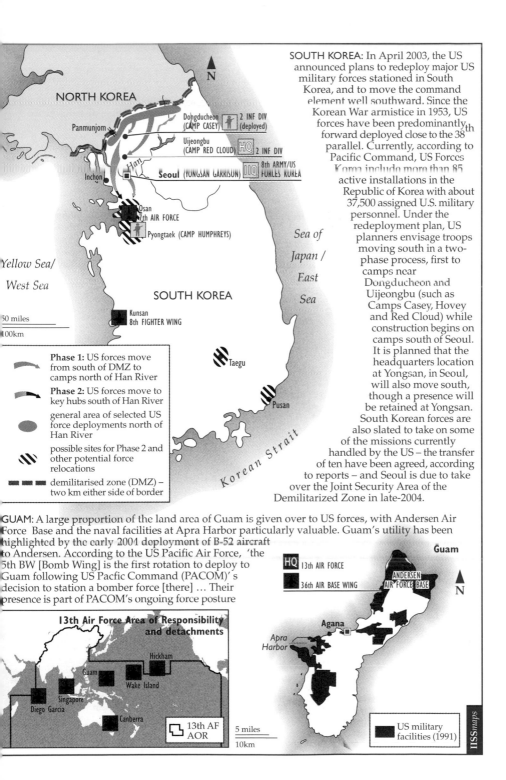

NORTH KOREA

Panmunjom

Dongducheon (CAMP CASEY) | 2 INF DIV (deployed)

Uijeongbu (CAMP RED CLOUD) | HQ | 2 INF DIV

Inchon

Seoul (YONGSAN GARRISON) | HQ | 8th ARMY/US FORCES KOREA

Han

Osan 7th AIR FORCE

Pyongtaek (CAMP HUMPHREYS)

Yellow Sea/ West Sea

SOUTH KOREA

Sea of Japan / East Sea

50 miles
100km

Kunsan 8th FIGHTER WING

Taegu

Pusan

Korean Strait

Phase 1: US forces move from south of DMZ to camps north of Han River

Phase 2: US forces move to key hubs south of Han River

general area of selected US force deployments north of Han River

possible sites for Phase 2 and other potential force relocations

demilitarised zone (DMZ) – two km either side of border

SOUTH KOREA: In April 2003, the US announced plans to redeploy major US military forces stationed in South Korea, and to move the command element well southward. Since the Korean War armistice in 1953, US forces have been predominantly forward deployed close to the 38th parallel. Currently, according to Pacific Command, US Forces Korea include more than 85 active installations in the Republic of Korea with about 37,500 assigned U.S. military personnel. Under the redeployment plan, US planners envisage troops moving south in a two-phase process, first to camps near Dongducheon and Uijeongbu (such as Camps Casey, Hovey and Red Cloud) while construction begins on camps south of Seoul. It is planned that the headquarters location at Yongsan, in Seoul, will also move south, though a presence will be retained at Yongsan. South Korean forces are also slated to take on some of the missions currently handled by the US – the transfer of ten have been agreed, according to reports – and Seoul is due to take over the Joint Security Area of the Demilitarized Zone in late-2004.

GUAM: A large proportion of the land area of Guam is given over to US forces, with Andersen Air Force Base and the naval facilities at Apra Harbor particularly valuable. Guam's utility has been highlighted by the early 2004 deployment of B-52 aircraft to Andersen. According to the US Pacific Air Force, 'the 5th BW [Bomb Wing] is the first rotation to deploy to Guam following US Pacic Command (PACOM)'s decision to station a bomber force [there] … Their presence is part of PACOM's ongoing force posture

Guam

HQ | 13th AIR FORCE

36th AIR BASE WING

ANDERSEN AIR FORCE BASE

Agana

Apra Harbor

13th Air Force Area of Responsibility and detachments

Hickham

Guam

Wake Island

Singapore

Diego Garcia

Canberra

13th AF AOR

5 miles
10km

US military facilities (1991)

IISSmaps

Africa West Africa's interlinked conflicts

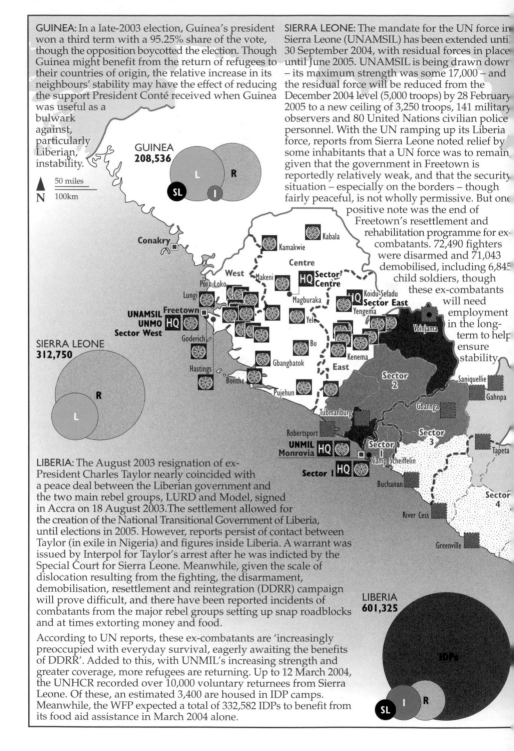

GUINEA: In a late-2003 election, Guinea's president won a third term with a 95.25% share of the vote, though the opposition boycotted the election. Though Guinea might benefit from the return of refugees to their countries of origin, the relative increase in its neighbours' stability may have the effect of reducing the support President Conté received when Guinea was useful as a bulwark against, particularly Liberian, instability.

GUINEA
208,536

50 miles
100km
N

SIERRA LEONE
312,750

SIERRA LEONE: The mandate for the UN force in Sierra Leone (UNAMSIL) has been extended until 30 September 2004, with residual forces in place until June 2005. UNAMSIL is being drawn down – its maximum strength was some 17,000 – and the residual force will be reduced from the December 2004 level (5,000 troops) by 28 February 2005 to a new ceiling of 3,250 troops, 141 military observers and 80 United Nations civilian police personnel. With the UN ramping up its Liberia force, reports from Sierra Leone noted relief by some inhabitants that a UN force was to remain, given that the government in Freetown is reportedly relatively weak, and that the security situation – especially on the borders – though fairly peaceful, is not wholly permissive. But one positive note was the end of Freetown's resettlement and rehabilitation programme for ex-combatants. 72,490 fighters were disarmed and 71,043 demobilised, including 6,845 child soldiers, though these ex-combatants will need employment in the long-term to help ensure stability.

Kabala
Conakry
Kamakwie
Centre
West Makeni HQ Sector Centre
Port Loko
Lungi Magburaka Koidu-Sefadu HQ Sector East
UNAMSIL Freetown Yengema
UNMO HQ Yele Voinjama
Sector West
Goderich Bo
Hastings Kenema
Gbangbatok East
Bonthe Sector 2 Saniquellie
Pujehun Gahnpa
Tubmanburg
Robertsport Sector 3
UNMIL HQ Tapeta
Monrovia Sector 1
Camp Scheiffelin
Sector 1 HQ
Buchanan Sector 4
River Cess
Greenville

LIBERIA: The August 2003 resignation of ex-President Charles Taylor nearly coincided with a peace deal between the Liberian government and the two main rebel groups, LURD and Model, signed in Accra on 18 August 2003. The settlement allowed for the creation of the National Transitional Government of Liberia, until elections in 2005. However, reports persist of contact between Taylor (in exile in Nigeria) and figures inside Liberia. A warrant was issued by Interpol for Taylor's arrest after he was indicted by the Special Court for Sierra Leone. Meanwhile, given the scale of dislocation resulting from the fighting, the disarmament, demobilisation, resettlement and reintegration (DDRR) campaign will prove difficult, and there have been reported incidents of combatants from the major rebel groups setting up snap roadblocks and at times extorting money and food.

According to UN reports, these ex-combatants are 'increasingly preoccupied with everyday survival, eagerly awaiting the benefits of DDRR'. Added to this, with UNMIL's increasing strength and greater coverage, more refugees are returning. Up to 12 March 2004, the UNHCR recorded over 10,000 voluntary returnees from Sierra Leone. Of these, an estimated 3,400 are housed in IDP camps. Meanwhile, the WFP expected a total of 332,582 IDPs to benefit from its food aid assistance in March 2004 alone.

LIBERIA
601,325

IDPs
SL I R

IISS*maps*

COTE D'IVOIRE: The signing of the Linas-Marcoussis peace deal in 2003 has not resulted in the degree of progress hoped for, despite the efforts of the French and regional governments. The peace deal was to inaugurate a power-sharing administration and legislative reforms, leading to elections in 2005. But as of end-March 2004, violence in Abidjan led to a number of deaths, after a march in defiance of a government ban on demonstrations. This led to the rebels (the Forces Nouvelles) and the main opposition party again pulling out of the power-sharing government. However, the news of the UN peacekeeping deployment has raised hopes that security may be improved in the long term.

In late-March 2004, the first elements of a planned UN force began arriving in Côte d'Ivoire. Authorised under UNSCR 1528 (2004), the UN Operation in Côte d'Ivoire (UNOCI), took on the forces and responsibility of the existing MINUCI and ECOWAS forces on 4 April 2004. UNOCI will, at maximum, comprise 6,240 personnel, with 200 military observers, 120 staff officers and 350 police officers. The force will initially be led by Senegalese Maj Gen Fall (who was leading the ECOWAS force) and is slated to initially include troops from Bangladesh, Benin, France, Ghana, Morocco, Niger, Pakistan, Senegal, Togo and Ukraine. France's *Operation Licorne* troops will continue to operate independently, with UN authorisation continued under UNSCR 1527 (2004).

CÔTE D'IVOIRE
662,215

Korhogo

IDPs

SL L R

Forces Nouvelles (rebel forces)

Zone of confidence

Bondoukou

GHANA

Bouaké

ML Man

Zone of confidence

Bouaflé
Tiébissou
Priko

Daloa

Duékoué

Yamoussoukro

ECOWAS Tactical HQ Zambakro

Tchien

MINUCI (UNOCI) HQ
ECOWAS HQ
FRENCH HQ

1 April 2004: First small party of UN peacekeepers deploy.

Abidjan

Grand Cess

Harper

ML San-Pédro

Refugees from
SL Sierra Leone
L Liberia
I Côte d'Ivoire
returnees
IDPs
601 total number of refugees and IDPs by country

HQ UN headquarters
UN presence
planned deployment
ML military liason
French forces
ECOWAS location

Liberia's refugees and IDPs by county of origin, December 2003
40,001 – 200,000
10,001 – 40,000
4,001 – 10,000
1,000 – 4,000
--- UN sector
Deployments as of January 2004

Refugees and IDPs
500,000
250,000
100,000
50,000
10,000

Given porous borders and the changing security situation, refugees and IDPs are increasingly returning spontaneously, although there continue to be planned returns, such as those by Sierra Leonean refugees in Liberia, arranged by UNHCR. Numbers may fluctuate according to source and date. The data here is from the UN's OCHA, and is dated late March 2004.

Africa Ethiopia/Eritrea: border dispute persists

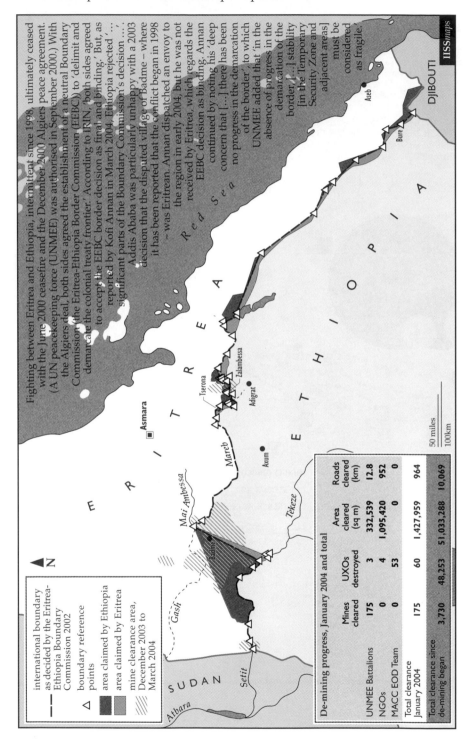

Fighting between Eritrea and Ethiopia, intermittent since 1998, ultimately ceased with the June 2000 ceasefire and the December 2000 Algiers peace agreement. (A UN peacekeeping force (UNMEE) was authorised in September 2000.) With the Algiers deal, both sides agreed the establishment of a neutral Boundary Commission, the Eritrea-Ethiopia Border Commission (EEBC) to 'delimit and demarcate the colonial treaty frontier.' According to IRIN, 'both sides agreed to accept the EEBC border decision as final and binding.' But, as reported by Kofi Annan in March 2004, Ethiopia rejected '… significant parts of the Boundary Commission's decision …'. Addis Ababa was particularly unhappy with a 2003 decision that the disputed village of Badme – where it has been reported that the conflict began in 1998 – was Eritrean. Annan dispatched an envoy to the region in early 2004, but he was not received by Eritrea, which regards the EEBC decision as binding. Annan continued by noting his 'deep concern that […] there has been no progress in the demarcation of the border', to which UNMEE added that 'in the absence of progress in the demarcation of the border […] stability [in the Temporary Security Zone and adjacent areas] must be considered as fragile.'

IISS*maps*

De-mining progress, January 2004 and total

	Mines cleared	UXOs destroyed	Area cleared (sq m)	Roads cleared (km)
UNMEE Battalions	175	3	332,539	12.8
NGOs	0	4	1,095,420	952
MACC EOD Team	0	53	0	0
Total clearance January 2004	175	60	1,427,959	964
Total clearance since de-mining began	3,730	48,253	51,033,288	10,069

N

international boundary
as decided by the Eritrea-
Ethiopia Boundary
Commission 2002

boundary reference
points

area claimed by Ethiopia

area claimed by Eritrea

mine clearance area,
December 2003 to
March 2004

Africa Sudan: destruction in Darfur

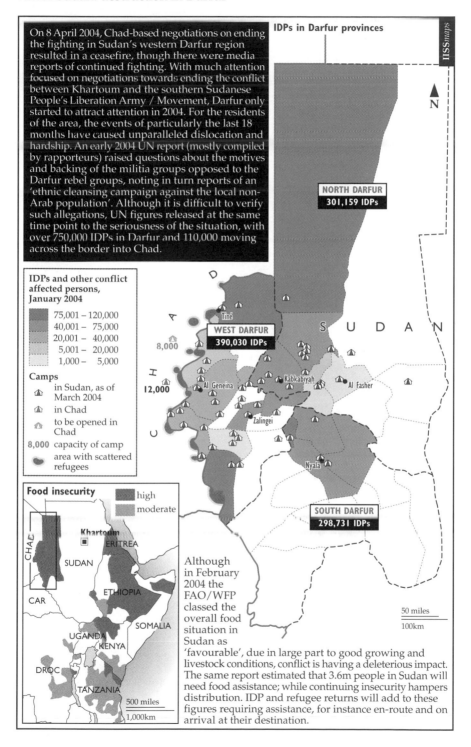

On 8 April 2004, Chad-based negotiations on ending the fighting in Sudan's western Darfur region resulted in a ceasefire, though there were media reports of continued fighting. With much attention focused on negotiations towards ending the conflict between Khartoum and the southern Sudanese People's Liberation Army / Movement, Darfur only started to attract attention in 2004. For the residents of the area, the events of particularly the last 18 months have caused unparalleled dislocation and hardship. An early 2004 UN report (mostly compiled by rapporteurs) raised questions about the motives and backing of the militia groups opposed to the Darfur rebel groups, noting in turn reports of an 'ethnic cleansing campaign against the local non-Arab population'. Although it is difficult to verify such allegations, UN figures released at the same time point to the seriousness of the situation, with over 750,000 IDPs in Darfur and 110,000 moving across the border into Chad.

IDPs in Darfur provinces

IISS*maps*

N

NORTH DARFUR
301,159 IDPs

S U D A N

IDPs and other conflict affected persons, January 2004

- 75,001 – 120,000
- 40,001 – 75,000
- 20,001 – 40,000
- 5,001 – 20,000
- 1,000 – 5,000

Camps

- in Sudan, as of March 2004
- in Chad
- to be opened in Chad
- **8,000** capacity of camp
- area with scattered refugees

Tiné

WEST DARFUR
390,030 IDPs

8,000

12,000

Al Geneina

Kabkabiyah

Al Fasher

Zalingei

Nyala

SOUTH DARFUR
298,731 IDPs

Food insecurity   high
                       moderate

Khartoum
CHAD
ERITREA
SUDAN
CAR
ETHIOPIA
SOMALIA
UGANDA
KENYA
DROC
TANZANIA

500 miles
1,000km

50 miles
100km

Although in February 2004 the FAO/WFP classed the overall food situation in Sudan as 'favourable', due in large part to good growing and livestock conditions, conflict is having a deleterious impact. The same report estimated that 3.6m people in Sudan will need food assistance; while continuing insecurity hampers distribution. IDP and refugee returns will add to these figures requiring assistance, for instance en-route and on arrival at their destination.

Africa Using the Nile

The Nile Basin Initiative (NBI) was established in February 1999 'to achieve sustainable socio-economic development through the equitable utilization of, and benefit from, the common Nile Basin water resources'. In March 2004, ministers from ten African states that share the waters of the Nile basin met in Nairobi under the auspices of the NBI to, according to IRIN, 'to flesh out a treaty regulating the use of the [Nile's] waters.'

Demand for Nile water is rising from power and agriculture, as well as the rising populations in the countries of the Nile basin. Presently, Nile water-usage is largely governed by a 1929 treaty between Egypt and Britain which, according to IRIN, 'forbids any southern country to take any action potentially capable of bringing about a reduction of the volume of Nile water reaching Egypt.' Countries in the south of the basin are now proposing power and irrigation schemes that would lower the volume reaching Egypt.

NBI member states are trying to realise NBI objectives through two key mechanisms:

● Shared Vision Programs such as the Nile Basin Regional Power Trade Program

● Subsidiary Action Programs for the Eastern Nile and for the Nile Equatorial Lakes.

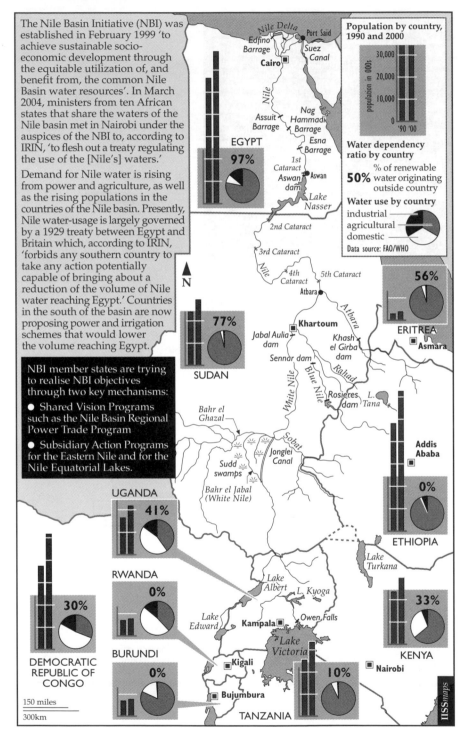

Population by country, 1990 and 2000

Water dependency ratio by country

50% % of renewable water originating outside country

Water use by country
industrial
agricultural
domestic

Data source: FAO/WHO

Such considerations may eventually shift Washington's priorities towards the Israeli–Palestinian conflict. As of April 2004, however, the US had its hands full in Iraq. Against hopes of improving security to ease the scheduled handover of sovereignty to the Iraqis on 30 June 2004, US retaliation for the ambush and brutal killing of four American security contractors in the conservative town of Falluja, west of Baghdad, on 30 March triggered a Shi'ite then a Sunni uprising against the US-led occupation. By 13 April, over 600 Iraqis and about 70 Americans had been killed over the course of less than two weeks, and a number of foreign nationals had been kidnapped and held hostage. Ceasefires were brokered in Falluja by 11 April. US military commanders were reporting a new and broad-based Shi'ite armed movement in addition to the existing Sunni insurgency that had begun in spring 2003. They also noted tactical cooperation between Shi'ites and Sunnis – which contradicted coalition assumptions that the traditional enmity between the two sects would guarantee that they would remain divided and easier to manage – though there was no evidence of command-level collaboration.

The initial US response was to try to kill or capture Moktada al-Sadr, the vitriolically anti-American Shi'ite cleric whose militia had spearheaded the revolt. But some may have doubted the wisdom of this approach, as it hearkened back to an unsuccessful strategy in Somalia in 1993–94, when a vindictive and distracting US hunt for warlord Mohamed Farah Aideed rallied Somalis against US and other peacekeepers. While the option of punishing Sadr was not discarded, by the second week of fighting the US adopted a more consultative approach and enlisted other Shi'ite clerical leaders – including Grand Ayatollah Ali al-Sistani, Grand Ayatollah Sayed al-Hakim and Muhammad Ridha, Sistani's son – in an attempt to calm the uprising without resort to maximal force. This salutary development preserved at least the possibility that the US would be able to keep the Shi'ite leadership on side, which is a minimal prerequisite to a successful state-building effort. Broadly, however, the US faced intensifying counterinsurgency challenges in Iraq. US officials were disinclined to postpone the 30 June deadline for the formal handover of sovereignty to the Iraqis – a position fortified by ever louder calls from Arab quarters for the US to quit Iraq. US generals were contemplating sending more troops to Iraq and voicing the need for fledgling Iraqi security forces – however unprepared they were – to assist in pacifying the country. Among several vexing questions was to what extent Hizbullah and Iran – whose conservative Shi'ite establishment had manipulatively enervated the reformist movement in February 2004 elections – may have been supporting the Shi'ite revolt in Iraq. In April 2003, a US military victory in Iraq was imminent. By April 2004, it had come and gone, and an American political triumph in Iraq and major peace dividends in the region seemed neither close nor assured.

Middle East

The Iraq War's Messy Aftermath

The ramifications of the invasion of Iraq in March 2003, its occupation by coalition forces and the potential for its successful reconstruction as a stable and democratic state go well beyond the country itself. For the United States, the aftermath of the invasion has important consequences for the projection of American power. If the US is seen to fail in Iraq, America's foreign policy will have to be rethought. The long-term instability of Iraq would act as potent symbol, highlighting the limited power of the US to intervene successfully against rogue states. In any case, the Bush doctrine and regime change in Iraq is set to have major political and legal repercussions with respect to standards of international intervention and, more broadly, sovereignty in the developing world. The future of Iraq also has important regional implications. Since Saddam Hussein's rise to power in the late 1970s, the country has been a fount of regional instability. If the domestic situation does not stabilise, violence and political unrest could spread over Iraq's long and porous borders. But if US plans succeed, Iraq, as a westward-leaning beacon of democracy and free markets, is likely to inspire a measure of political and economic reform that could both ameliorate the region's endemic problems and improve the chances of a better accommodation between the Arab world and the West.

America's challenge

For Iraqi society, the US-led invasion of March 2003 was in many ways welcome, but it also unleashed a series of unpredictable socio-political dynamics. Both the coalition occupiers and those Iraqis seeking to build a new state are struggling with Saddam Hussein's legacy. By the late 1980s, the Baathist regime had atomised Iraqi society, using military and economic power to break all organisations that it did not control. The eight-year war with Iran, the 1990–91 Gulf War and the imposition of draconian sanctions in its aftermath greatly undermined the coherence and efficiency of Iraqi state institutions. Thus, the task undertaken by the Bush administration when it decided to embark on regime change in Baghdad was enormous on the political level. Once the initial military opposition had been overcome and Baghdad seized by the coalition, plans to take state institutions more or less intact and use them to rule Iraq proved to be misguided. After 12 years of sanctions, the fabric of Iraqi government had been stretched very thin, and 2003 saw the institutions of the Iraqi state face a third war in 20 years. These realities, combined with the three weeks of looting and the general lawlessness that greeted liberation in April, drove large numbers of civil servants simply to go home and stay there.

The US-run Coalition Provisional Authority (CPA), instead of finding a coherent state, found a governmental shell that will take many years and a great deal of money to rebuild. The crucial question faced by the Iraqi population, the region and the international community is whether a stable and reasonably democratic state can be built in the aftermath of war and tyranny.

Military interventions into failed or rogue states with the overt aim of reforming their political systems have become increasingly common in the post-Cold War era. To date, however, they have been largely unsuccessful. The Cambodia mission, the first large-scale UN attempt at root-and-branch political reform, resulted in a comparatively stable polity but failed to deliver meaningful change in state-society relations. Intervention in Somalia resulted in the ignominious exit of US troops and the collapse of the UN mission. Direct military intervention in Haiti to facilitate regime change did virtually nothing, in the longterm, to alter the invidious underlying political dynamics of that country. In the cases of Bosnia, Afghanistan and especially Kosovo, mixed results and ongoing problems of intervention suggest that it is too early to pass judgement on the lasting effectiveness of these missions. In Iraq, the removal of Saddam Hussein has proved to be the beginning rather than the culmination of a protracted and uncertain process of occupation and state-building. The lawlessness and looting that greeted the liberation of Baghdad on 9 April 2003 was replaced by widespread criminality, violence and instability. A year later, US troops and newly constituted Iraqi forces faced an insurgency that had become a solid obstacle to rebuilding the country and moving it towards democracy and stability. The lack of popular support for a sustained US presence in Iraq is substantially a product of the disorder that the insurgency has been able to visit on the country since the taking of Baghdad.

Insurgency

CPA Administrator Paul Bremer's decision to embark on root-and-branch de-Baathification on 16 May 2003 and to dissolve the Iraqi army a week later, in conjunction with a spate of assassinations by radical Shi'ite groups, no doubt provided impetus to the coalescence of the insurgency. The occupation tactics adopted by US troops – a combination of heavily armed motorised patrols and large fortified bases – framed a target by making the foreign military presence detached and largely remote from the Iraqi population. Furthermore, as the daily toll of US casualties mounted, American forces were increasingly perceived as weak and their presence in and commitment to the country as temporary. Thus encouraged, Baath Party loyalists apparently began to reorganise in the spring of 2003 and, with the help of the remnants of Saddam's security services, who sensed an opportunity to take advantage of US force vulnerability, began launching hit-and-run attacks with increasing frequency and skill. In August 2003, the insurgency escalated into an all-out campaign of sabotage and terror. On 7 August, a car bomb blew up outside the Jordanian embassy in Baghdad, killing 17 people and injuring 50. In mid-August, Iraq's main oil pipeline, the economic lifeline of the country, was blown up two days after its post-war return to service. On 19 August, a lorry packed with 450kg of explosives was detonated below the office window of Sergio Vieira de Mello, the UN Secretary-General's Special Representative, killing him and 21 others. De Mello was the man in whom the UN had invested its hopes for the regeneration of Iraq. Over the next two weeks, a massive explosion outside the Imam Ali Mosque in Najaf (one of the holiest shrines of Shia Islam) killed about 100 innocent civilians, including Ayatollah Mohammed Bakr al Hakim. Al Hakim was the leader of the Supreme Council for the Islamic Revolution in Iraq – one of several organisations claiming to represent Iraqi Shi'ites and a group that both the UK and US had been assiduously courting to form the cornerstone of a new political order in post-Saddam Iraq.

As US troops took a less public role and began to be redeployed to more secure bases, the insurgents sought out more accessible targets. The embryonic institutions and personnel of the new Iraqi state provided them. A rocket attack occurred in late October on a hotel in Baghdad, and coordinated and nearly simultaneous suicide attacks on the Red Cross and two police stations followed the next day. There were subsequent car bombings of police stations in Khalidyah in western Iraq, Mosul in the north, and Iskandariya and Hillah south of Baghdad. A devastating car-bomb assault on an army-recruiting centre in Baghdad killed 53 people in February 2004. In addition, by targeting Shi'ites, the insurgency has tried to stoke sectarian resentment and encourage a civil war between Iraq's distinct religious and ethnic communities, which serves the overall objective of making Iraq ungovernable by either the US or a new Iraqi government. This approach was apparent on 29 August 2003 with the car bomb at the Imam Ali mosque in Najaf, as well as the simultaneous 2 March 2004 strikes on the Shi'ite festival of Ashura in Baghdad and Karbala, which killed over 180. The inference that such attacks were intended to trigger civil war was further strengthened by the February 2004 discovery in Baghdad of a 17-page letter apparently written by Abu Musab al Zarqawi, a Jordanian who US intelligence officials believe is the principal point of contact between Ansar al-Islam and al-Qaeda. The letter argued that the only way for al-Qaeda to continue its jihad against the infidels in Iraq was by provoking the Shi'ites into a sectarian war which 'will awaken the sleepy Sunnis who are fearful of destruction and death at the hands of the Shia'. In February 2004, the tactic of fomenting sectarian divisions was extended to the Kurdish areas of Iraq, when two suicide bombers killed 101 people in Irbil at the offices of the Kurdish Democratic Party (KDP) and

Patriotic Union of Kurdistan (PUK). On 4 April, there were disturbing indications that Shi'ites could rebel without Sunni provocations, as the coalition's closing of an anti-American newspaper and arrest of an aide to firebrand cleric Moktada al-Sadr prompted Shi'ite militiamen loyal to him to kill seven American soldiers in Sadr City in a coordinated operation.

The summer of 2003 witnessed 10–15 attacks per day. Over the course of the autumn, the insurgency gained momentum, and attacks rose to 20–35 daily and became better organised and more sophisticated – as demonstrated by the October attacks on the Red Cross and the police stations in Baghdad. Although the quantitative and qualitative upsurge seemed to coincide with the infiltration of foreign jihadists into Iraq – as of November 2003, US forces had detained about 250 foreigners, 19 of whom are reported to be probable al-Qaeda members – the precise composition of the insurgency remained unclear. While nearly 300 American and several British soldiers were killed in hostile circumstances during the eight months following the formal end to the main military campaign on 1 May – compared to only 114 US dead before that date – most of the insurgency's victims have been Iraqis. Non-American foreigners, as in the attack on the UN on 19 August, have also been hit. Although most attacks have occurred inside the 'Sunni triangle' of Baghdad, Tikrit and al-Ramadi, many have also occurred outside that region, in Kurd and Shi'ite areas. These target choices and locations are consistent with both insurgent and al-Qaeda objectives. The attacks against Iraqis are intended to intimidate the local population and discourage cooperation with the US and its partners, and, by their indiscriminate character, to lay the blame on the occupation for the loss of Iraqis, reinforcing resentment among indigenous survivors. The UN is part of the foreign occupation. Jordan and Turkey, whose embassy was also attacked, are Muslim nations that have actively supported US military operations. While the coordinated onslaught on the Red Cross and the police stations occurred on the first day of Ramadan, suggesting a distinctly jihadist cast, the timing could also have been intended to evoke the Tet Offensive in Vietnam – a tactical victory for the US but a strategic defeat.

On balance, the efficiency of the attacks, their regularity and the speed with which they were organised in the aftermath of Saddam's fall point to predominantly Iraqi involvement. The shadowy organisation behind these sectarian attacks is likely to be a hybrid, with elements of the old regime acting in alliance with 'industrial scale' criminal gangs operating in the urban centres of Basra, Baghdad and Mosul; indigenous Islamic radicals; and a relatively small number of foreign fighters. It appears that mid-ranking members of the old regime have been able to deploy their training and weapons stockpiles, gain ideological purchase and resonance with a new brand of Islamic nationalism, and to mobilise Sunni fears of Shi'ite and Kurdish domination and a growing resentment at foreign occupation. It is unlikely that there has been a 'hidden hand' centrally coordinating and funding the insurgency. Against hope that Saddam Hussein's being apprehended would deflate the insurgency – inspirationally if not operationally – the long-awaited capture of a confused and dishevelled Saddam in a dirty bunker near Tikrit by US Special Forces on 13 December 2003 did not produce a decline in insurgent terrorist activity. Only in spring 2004 did evidence begin to emerge that a national organisation was starting to coordinate the actions of disparate insurgent groups.

The continuing cohesion of the Baathist security networks that guaranteed Saddam's survival in power for so long suggest that the insurgency has some staying power. In addition to the 'Sunni triangle' – essentially, a homogeneous block of insurgency supporters, offering material and ideological comfort to the fighters – there is a more expansive 'shadow state' still in place in northwest Iraq, consisting of flexible networks of patronage and coercion that were used to shape Iraqi society according to Saddam's fiat. That said, only a small minority of Iraqis supports the insurgency, many more having been alienated by its use of indiscriminate violence. Nevertheless, the carnage has been a major setback for state-building and stability and, in causing ethnic and religious groups to close ranks, increased sectarianism and inhibited the blossoming of a democratic, pluralistic ethos.

Counter-insurgency

The lack of solid intelligence on the US side means that American forces have only a partial understanding of who is attacking them, their coalition partners and their Iraqi allies, who is organising the insurgency and the nature of its relations with the wider community. *Operation Peninsula Strike*, *Operation Sidewinder* and *Operation Soda Mountain* – a series of large-scale swoops through northwest Iraq by US troops – resulted in the capture of large amounts of munitions, but the deployment of large numbers of troops, mass arrests and widespread house searches has also perversely inspired insurgent violence. Without accurate, time-sensitive intelligence wedded to local knowledge, such raids will only slowly locate remaining key players of Saddam's ruling elite. But in the process they will also alienate large sections of the population in the targeted areas. Blanket arrests, detention in harsh conditions and non-transparent methods of interrogation and trial are bound to fuel resentment and swell the ranks of the violently disaffected.

While foreign jihadists appear to be a comparatively minor source of anti-coalition violence in Iraq, Iraqi Islamists – both Sunni and Shi'ite – are major sources. They also provide a sobering insight into the mobilising dynamics of future Iraqi politics. An early indication can be seen in the town of Falluja, 56km west of Baghdad. Notwithstanding US Deputy Secretary of Defense Paul Wolfowitz's assertions to the contrary, Iraqis did not regard Falluja, prior to the war, as a 'hotbed of Baathist activity'.

To the contrary, Falluja had a reputation in Iraq as a deeply conservative and pious town, famed for the number of its mosques and its close adherence to Sunni Islam. In the immediate aftermath of regime change, Iraqi troops and Baath Party leaders left the town. Imams from the local mosques stepped into the socio-political vacuum, bringing an end to the looting, even managing to return some of the stolen property. Heavy-handed searches by US troops in hunting for leading members of the old regime have more to do with Falluja's becoming a centre of violent opposition to US occupation than does Baath loyalism. Resentment escalated when two local imams were arrested, and reached a climax when US troops broke up a demonstration with gunfire resulting in 17 Iraqi fatalities and 70 wounded. On 31 March 2004, insurgents ambushed vehicles carrying four American civilian security contractors in Falluja, shooting them dead and then burning them. A mob then dragged their charred remains through the streets for hours, beating and mutilating their bodies and hanging two of them from a bridge. The scene uncomfortably recalled the similar 1993 episode when Somalis dragged slain US soldiers through the streets of Mogadishu, which contributed to Washington's truncation of the US-led humanitarian intervention in Somalia. Moreover, the episode triggered a wider Shi'ite uprising against the US occupation, which in turn enouraged Sunni unrest.

Disarmament is a delicate problem in Iraq, as it was in Somalia. It is noteworthy that – as brutal as Saddam's regime was – it never sought to disarm the Iraqi population. The killing of six British soldiers in June 2003 in the southern town of Majar al Kabir, probably carried out by Shi'ites, was preceded by a British Army operation aimed at recovering weapons by searching houses. The combination of the CPA's inability to guarantee personal safety and its inconsistent and biased application of disarmament edicts – for instance, allowing Kurdish militias to retain their arms while demanding that certain Shi'ite ones relinquish them – has also encouraged groups who feel deprived of a means of defending themselves to look to militias. Increasingly organised along sectarian lines, they have increased their power and visibility on the streets of Iraq's major towns.

US policy drift

Against a backdrop of increased insecurity, US plans for rebuilding the political and administrative structures in Iraq appeared to become increasingly reactive, proceeding through four distinct phases. Initially, Jay Garner, an ex-US Army general, headed a team mainly of retired diplomats, senior military figures and ex-CIA staffers who were charged with rebuilding the Iraqi state in the immediate aftermath of the liberation of Baghdad. General Garner almost immediately paid the price for a broad US lack of pre-war planning and post-war progress, and was replaced by

Bremer in May 2003. As a former Foreign Service Officer politically close to the Pentagon, Bremer was meant to tamp down disagreements between Department of Defense neo-conservatives in charge of post-war construction and their colleagues at the State Department. With Bush's strong backing, Bremer was successful at the bureaucratic level in coordinating the CPA's disparate factions and providing the US effort with strategic leadership.

One of Bremer's first policy decisions upon arriving in Baghdad was to delay delegating power to a leadership council mainly composed of the formerly exiled parties. Prior to Bremer's arrival, movement towards creating a democratic body had been hasty but also shambolic. The first two meetings, at Ur near Nasiriyah on 15 March 2003 and then in Baghdad on 28 April 2003, were designed to draw together Iraqis in some form of representative assembly. The first meeting was notable mainly for the significant number of Iraqis who chose not to attend and the large protest demonstration outside. These factors respectively highlighted the small number of delegates (80) and drew into question the veracity of their claims to be representative. Although the turnout in Baghdad was larger at 300, it did not reach the 2,000–3,000 hoped for and predicted. The fact that over half the attendees were recently returned exiles pointed to a larger problem – namely, indigenous Iraqis' lack of confidence in the US occupation. The evolving dynamic was one whereby many Iraqis, aware of the unpopularity of the US presence in their country and believing it to be temporary, avoided involvement in the political process until the situation became clearer and the risks of association lower.

The third phase began with the creation of the Iraqi Governing Council (IGC) in July 2003. Although the IGC was picked by Bremer after extended negotiations among the CPA, the UN and seven dominant formerly exiled parties, the CPA touted the IGC as 'the most representative body in Iraq's history' on account of the purportedly 'balanced' composition of its membership. The politicians were chosen to reflect the ethnic makeup of Iraq, with 13 members being Shi'ites, five Sunnis, and a Turkoman and a Christian thrown in for good measure. But the contrived and skewed reality of the arrangement was fairly transparent. For example, the Iraqi Communist Party's Hamid Majid Mousa and the avowedly secular Ahmed Chalabi were included within the 'Shia bloc' of 13.

By mid-November 2003 the shortcomings of the IGC had become apparent to decision-makers in both Washington and London. More broadly, the two main coalition partners faced multiple pressures to reduce their exposure in Iraq. The insurgency was maintaining a high level of lethality and effectiveness. The failure to find weapons of mass destruction had called the intervention's legitimacy more acutely into question. Washington was beginning to realise that both materially and politically it would be better to involve its European allies and the UN more deeply in state-building in Iraq, and both of those camps were pressing for a quicker transfer of sovereignty to the Iraqi people. The occupation also provided a potent global recruitment pretext for al-Qaeda, had galvanised the transnational Islamic terrorist movement and probably increased terrorist activity worldwide. With a US presidential election only a year away and the Bush administration growing correspondingly more averse to political risk, the US government was impelled to change its Iraq policy a third time. Washington sought to reduce significantly the length and nature of its political commitment to Iraq, and Bremer was tasked with handing sovereignty back to the Iraqis by 30 June 2004. On 15 November 2003, the IGC endorsed an American plan calling for the drafting of a 'fundamental law' – in effect, a provisional constitution – by the end of February 2004. This would then be followed by the creation of a transitional assembly of between 200 and 500 delegates. The assembly was to select a cabinet and leader for Iraq and guide the country to democratic elections.

Problematically, the proposed assembly that was to play such a pivotal role in Iraq's future would not be directly elected. Instead, a system of indirect polls and caucuses were to be held, with town and city leaders 'electing' delegates to the assembly in a series of countrywide town hall meetings. Many Iraqis were sceptical and suspicious of this attenuation of representative government. Most importantly, the senior Shi'ite cleric Marja Ayatollah Ali al-Sistani publicly opposed the caucusing approach, restating his long held position that a constitutional assembly must be elected by universal suffrage. Sistani's position had been clearly articulated weeks before Bremer's November meeting with the principals in Washington, where the American plan was hatched. The fact that his opposition and its ramifications were then, in effect, ignored, reflects the CPA's chronic inability to comprehend fully the dynamics of Iraqi politics. While Sistani maintained his opposition to the caucus dispensation, he was not without some pragmatic instincts. The drafting of the interim Iraqi constitution – also known as the Transitional Administrative Law (TAL) – as contemplated by the American plan proceeded. After many weeks of sometimes bitter debate, the document was agreed in the early hours of 2 March 2004. It is temporary, intended to guide the new government through the end of 2005, when a permanent constitution and an elected government are scheduled to replace it. In spite of its temporary role and predominantly aspirational as opposed to mandatory language, the TAL has been the focus of intense political debate and acrimony. The most controversial issues that it raised involves what roles Islam and the Kurds are to play in the new state.

A viable framework for government?
The TAL has set a timetable for progress towards democracy, stating that

Middle East

national elections must be held no later than the end of January 2005. This would result in a 275-seat national assembly that would in turn choose a president and two deputies. These three officials would be responsible for picking a prime minister, who would be the chief executive of the national government. In the meantime, it remains unclear who will run Iraq until the election, and how thereafter the country will be constituted.

The two main Kurdish parties, the PUK and the KDP, have effectively run two independent fiefdoms in the north of Iraq since 1991. How, and indeed if, these two areas are to be reintegrated into post-Saddam Iraq is one of the most difficult issues the country will have to face over the next few years. The fact that the KDP and PUK both have independent and well-armed militias has given them considerable leverage in the negotiating process. US officials had to persuade the KDP and PUK to postpone their central demand that they be given a fixed percentage of oil revenue and be allowed to increase the geographic area of rule to include the large cities of northern Iraq not yet under their control. Theoretical agreement about the political position of the north has also been secured, as the constitution recognises that Iraq will not only be democratic but also federal, which allows for the devolution of substantial power to the regions. But the negotiations postponed, until the end of the transitional period in 2005, a decision about what type of federal system will be used and the degree of autonomy that the two Kurdish organisations will be allowed to retain.

The associated problem of the continued existence and role of private militias was also averted in order to secure an accord. The TAL does ban militias that are not directly controlled by the federal government, but with the proviso that their members will be integrated into the government's security services or helped in making the transition to civilian life. As this process would necessarily take time to start and implement, militias will remain intact in the short term.

Competing visions among governing council members about how a new Iraq would take shape came into play on the issue of religion. The liberal ambitions of some IGC members resulted in a TAL provision protecting the freedom of worship for all Iraq's citizens. However, arguments about the role that Islam will play in the political – in particular, the legislative – life of the country were divisive. The debate centred on whether Islam should be the only or a main source for future legislation. In January 2004, the IGC voted to allow Islamic law to override civil law in matters of divorce and inheritance. But Bremer refused to recognise the January decision and forced a compromise in the wording of the constitution.

Still trouble ahead
The signing of the provisional Iraqi constitution, although largely symbolic, is a step towards rebuilding the state and institutionalising the rule of law.

However, the most important task has yet to begin in earnest. The 25 ministers appointed by the IGC to rebuild the institutions of the state and make their influence felt across Iraq face a daunting task. The Iraqi population needs to see state institutions making a direct and positive impact on their everyday lives. This has yet to happen in a systematic way. Instead, the country is facing a security vacuum that has given rise to a series of politically motivated militias and terrorists who appear to strike with impunity.

Against this background, US plans to hand power back to Iraqis on 30 June appeared three months beforehand to be risky at the very least. The lack of communication among the American civil servants and military personnel, their IGC allies and the wider population of Iraq has undermined the CPA's attempts at state-building. Intelligence gathering has proved difficult because the majority of Iraqis feel alienated from the CPA – a factor that the dearth of Arabic speakers or Iraq experts on the CPA's staff has exacerbated. Thus, the CPA has relatively little knowledge about the country they are trying to control. The small group of Iraqi exiles the CPA brought back to Baghdad were meant to compensate for this ignorance by becoming the main channel of communications between the wider Iraqi population and US officials and their main source of information about Iraqi society and politics. Most importantly, they were supposed to become the core of a new political elite. But the Iraqi exiles have not been able to fulfil any of these roles robustly or convincingly. Instead, the exiled politicians are very unpopular. In spite of setting up numerous party offices around Baghdad, printing an abundance of newspapers and liberally spending money to burnish their appeal, they have not managed to penetrate Iraqi society, mobilise support or engender allegiance. This means that the IGC – the preferred and expected core of a new post-CPA government – is detached from the very people it is meant to represent.

The gap between the political structures left by the departing CPA and the population itself does not bode well for the vanquishing of the insurgency or the growth of democracy. For state-building to stand any chance of success, and for a stable and democratic government to emerge from the chaos of Baathist rule and regime change, large numbers of troops, foreign aid and international oversight will probably have to remain in the country for years to come. State-building measures may be even harder to bring to bear after the US no longer has direct administrative control of the country. As of early April 2004, a Shi'ite uprising was imperilling American plans for a 30 June handover. The United States' coalition partners expressed increasing anxiety about the security of their personnel. At the same time, US forces faced the vexing task of energising counterinsurgency efforts against Shi'ites as well as Sunnis – without further alienating the Shi'ite majority whose cooperation Washington has counted on and requires to make state-building work.

Middle East

The Israeli–Palestinian Conflict: Fin de Siècle?

Although this was not a year of stasis in the conflict between Palestinians and Israelis, it ended much as it began. Israeli military forces control much of the West Bank and Gaza, Yasser Arafat and Ariel Sharon dominate the political domain, violence continues – at a somewhat lower level – while the economies of the antagonists suffer. Yet two significant developments did occur, both the results of developments that had long been in gestation. The Likud party awoke to the demographic nightmare of a Jewish minority in an Israeli-controlled territory stretching from the Mediterranean Sea to the Jordan River. And the disintegration of Palestinian politics began to accelerate rapidly. The former spurred the Israeli quest for unilateral disengagement; the latter prevented a coherent Palestinian response to the challenge.

Trench warfare

The previous stage in the al-Aqsa uprising that began in 2000 ended with completion of major Israeli military operations in the West Bank and Gaza. *Operation Defensive Shield* in April 2002 and *Operation Determined Path* in May of that year effectively buried the Oslo arrangements, as Israeli forces reoccupied Area A (designated for Palestinian control under Oslo) in the face of largely desultory Palestinian resistance. The stimulus for the campaign was a significant spike in Israeli civilian casualties earlier in the year, inflicted by terrorists crossing into Israel from Palestinian towns close to the Green Line. As of April 2004, Israeli formations were deployed in most of the same places, although their posture in Gaza is more of a crouch than it is in the West Bank. The only change has been in the command structure, which has been streamlined in the West Bank as a cost-saving measure. In that theatre of operations, Israel still maintains two divisions; a third is deployed to Gaza. In the West Bank, the military footprint is designed for sustainability. Troops ring the cities and towns, maintaining a manageable presence – from an Israel Defense Force (IDF) perspective – and enter urban areas only for the purpose of raids based on specific intelligence gathered through surveillance, eavesdropping or information provided by the vast network of informants cultivated by the Internal Security Agency (Shin Bet) and shared with the IDF.

Israel's approach has been augmented during the past year by an intensified commitment to targeted killings; that is the assassination of commanders – or would-be commanders – of the various groups that have executed attacks against Israeli civilians. During this period, Palestinian tactics have changed little. Suicide bombers remain the weapon of choice. The supply of bombers, which began to include females during this period, is sufficient for an intensive campaign, munitions are ample and the political effect can occasionally be powerful – as in the August 2003 Jerusalem bus bombing that killed 23 and, in effect, ended the brief and forlorn tenure of Mahmoud Abbas as Palestinian prime minister. Other tactics used by militants, though with relatively little impact, have included the infiltration of IDF posts and subsequent shooting of soldiers as well as the use of stand-off weapons such as mortars or crude rockets. In an isolated incident, two British nationals entered Israel and exploded a bomb in a beachfront Tel Aviv café around the corner from the US embassy. This was probably not a trend-setting event, but there remains an outside chance that the popularisation of the Palestinian cause in Europe through the combination of jihadist propaganda and resurgent anti-Semitism may make this attack a precedent for others.

Overall, the number of deaths on both sides has declined since the intensive phase of Israel's operations in the West Bank and Gaza petered out towards the end of June 2003. The reasons are many: the security barrier that Israel began erecting in early 2003 – especially in the northwest West Bank – makes it harder for suicide bombers to penetrate Netanya and Tel Aviv; increased penetration of militant groups has led to more frequent interdiction of bombers; and the broad Palestinian offensive is probably more difficult to sustain after three-and-a-half years of combat. With fewer attacks come fewer Israeli counter-attacks. As in previous years, however, Palestinian fatalities routinely exceeded Israeli deaths by factors anywhere between two and ten. In terms of political significance, the precise casualty count has not necessarily driven specific outcomes, at least on the Palestinian side; the prominence of targeted individuals ensures substantial political effect regardless of the small number of fatalities caused by such strikes.

Confrontation over prosperity

Death or mutilation by Palestinian suicide bombs or Israeli rifle fire are the worst kinds of suffering experienced by the two sides, but not the only kind. Economic hardship compounds the misery. Unemployment in Palestine hovers between 42% and 53%, depending on how the labour force is defined. National product is down by 60%, a problem made worse by burgeoning population growth that steadily reduces the per-capita share of national income. Credit is non-existent. Economists estimate that even under optimistic assumptions regarding foreign investment, employment in Palestine will not reach pre-intifada levels until 2010 at the earliest. The decline in income, combined with the effect of curfews and closures,

Middle East

has contributed to an increase in acute malnutrition, which affected 7.8% of West Bank and Gazan children in 2002, the last year for which reliable data are available; for chronic and acute nutrition combined, the figure approaches 20%. A substantial segment of Palestine's public-use infrastructure has been destroyed, damaged or weakened through lack of maintenance and repair. One-third of Palestinians remain 'off the grid', using generators for power and, in consequence, damaging the environment and increasing the incidence of respiratory disease. The burning of uncollected trash makes the pollution problem worse. Public health also suffers from the diminishing availability of clean water, the deterioration of centralised health-care delivery and funding for the health ministry, and, of course, from the severe stress induced by violence and frequent maltreatment by the IDF, on one hand, and the breakdown of civic order in the Palestinians' own communities, on the other.

The participation of Palestinian security services in the intifada – and Israel's robust targeting practices during the early phases of the uprising – led to the destruction of the law enforcement and judicial infrastructure. Courthouses, police stations and jails are no longer available to support the administration of justice – which was never a strong point of the Palestinian Authority (PA) even during the heyday of Oslo. Armed gangs dispense justice and engage in running gunfights among themselves. Against this wretched background, women are increasingly confined to their homes, and excluded from whatever economic opportunities would otherwise be available to them. Despite relatively high school enrolments, the education of Palestinian children has declined as access to schools has become interrupted due to insecurity and prevailing tensions have made students lose focus and concentration. Thus, the past year has seen greater damage to Palestine's economic prospects, public health, social cohesion and development of human capital than any other year of the intifada.

Neither has the violence had a salubrious effect on Israel. Unemployment has been a flat 10–11% over the past year. Average income has fallen to 7,000 shekels per month, or about $1,550. The number of citizens below the poverty line is now 1.3 million, about one-fifth of the population. The number of homeless individuals is greater than ever, perhaps 3,000. The cost of military operations in the West Bank and Gaza constitute about one-fifth of a defence budget that consumes 10% of GDP. The indirect costs of large-scale mobilisation of reservists add to the economic penalties of occupation under wartime conditions. Although the violence of the intifada was not the sole reason for Israel's three-year recession – umbilical links to a collapsing high technology market were an important contributor – it discouraged trade, investment and tourism in a way that made a bad situation worse. The Bank of Israel estimated the cost of the intifada in 2002 at between 3.0 and 3.8% of GDP. The economy has now officially emerged from recession, according to the Bank of Israel, with growth rates of around 0.8–2.4% projected for 2004. This modest, jobless recovery, however, is due as much to Finance Minister Binyamin Netanyahu's slashing of social services and nationalisation of debt-ridden pension funds as to the resurgence of high-tech industries. In other words, while the macroeconomic situation will improve, the effects of poverty will be felt ever more keenly by Israel's growing number of have-nots. Two metrics of the anxieties of existing in a 'Still Life with Bomb,' as the title of a recent book characterises contemporary Israeli life, are emigration and immigration rates. The number of Israelis living abroad has increased from 550,000 to 760,000 since the uprising began, while the number of Jews who settled in Israel in 2003 is about one-third below the previous year.

Politics, of a kind

The logic of the emerging road map in spring 2003 created strong European and American pressures on Arafat to appoint a prime minister. The hope, if not conviction, was that a prime minister would provide an untainted interlocutor for Americans and Israelis and so create manoeuvring room for diplomatic progress. Other benefits were presumed to ensue from this. Arafat – 'the abominable no-man' – who is seen to have done so much to plunge his people into their present parlous state, would be marginalised. With his influence, patronage and status diminished, the chief impediment to a negotiated settlement with Israel would be overcome. An effective prime minister backed by the Palestinian parliament and propped up by powerful outside sponsors like the US would be in a position to consolidate and streamline the security services, subordinate them to a constitutional authority and use them to choke off the intifada. In other words, such a prime minister would launch the implementation of the road map. Moreover, an acceptable prime minister would begin to push aside Arafat's cronies – the so-called outsiders who accompanied Arafat from Tunis – in favour of younger 'insiders' who are said to possess modern sensibilities more in line with democracy, transparency and accountability than the autocratic and corrupt Arafat. This 'new guard' would presumably have the vision and credibility to reach a territorial agreement with Israel and meet the security responsibilities that such a settlement would entail.

The man designated for the job was Mahmoud Abbas, also known by his 'kunya', or honorific name, Abu Mazen. Abbas had worked at Arafat's side since the founding of Fatah, the dominant Palestinian party and cornerstone of the nationalist resistance. He seemed to be a logical choice: a staunch nationalist, close associate of Arafat, long-time fixture of peace process diplomacy and a man who abjured violence, believing that terrorism inevitably played into Israel's hands, making Palestinian political gains all the more elusive. That he had no domestic constituency and was seen by many as an apparatchik at best and Israeli stooge at worst was

Middle East

overlooked in view of the foregoing qualities. When the US and Europe finally girded themselves for the battle of Palestinian political reform in April 2003, they succeeded in getting Arafat's grudging agreement to Abbas's accession to the prime minister's office. The ten tense days of wrangling that resulted in Arafat's concessions regarding Abbas, his portfolio and the composition of the cabinet were seen as a tough but worthwhile prelude to rationalised government and an empowered prime minister. In reality, these ten days allowed Arafat's wrestling act to reinforce the popular view of him as the defender of Palestinian prerogatives in the face of pro-Israeli foreigners, and to plant a perception of Abu Mazen as the willing instrument of Palestine's adversaries. It was a brilliant performance and it had its intended effect. Abbas was hamstrung from his first day in office.

The Bush administration looked for ways to buttress Abbas's position and endow him with greater stature and credibility. With a furtive look back to Clintonian symbolism and pageantry without Clintonian commitment, the Bush administration arranged back-to-back summit meetings to showcase Abbas as a world leader embraced by fellow Arab statesmen: President Hosni Mubarak of Egypt, Crown Prince Abdullah of Saudi Arabia, King Abdullah II of Jordan and King Hamad of Bahrain. Two meetings were required because Mubarak wouldn't appear alongside Sharon on Egyptian soil at Sharm al-Sheikh; the need to have Sharon and Abbas side-by-side therefore required a separate venue, which King Abdullah II agreed to provide at Aqaba. In the event, Abbas's acknowledgement that the violence had to stop was salutary. But his appearance on a sun-drenched beach in Egypt, flanked by Mubarak and Bush, inspired mockery and outrage in the Palestinian street and imparted additional momentum to his slide in public esteem. Arafat, who had been emphatically excluded from the US-engineered jamborees in Egypt and Jordan, spoke from his dilapidated headquarters cum jail cell in Ramallah, redeeming his failures through proud isolation.

The premature conclusion of Abbas's term as prime minister was heralded by the 19 August 2003 detonation of a five-kilogram explosive device packed with ball bearings on the No. 2 bus in Jerusalem, which killed 23 people. In the first instance, the attack signalled the end of a truce, or 'hudna', that Abbas had painstakingly worked out with Fatah, Islamic Jihad and Hamas. (The Nablus and Jenin factions of al-Aqsa Martyrs Brigade had not agreed to the truce.) The signatories to the truce had already declared that subsequent Israeli raids in search of weapons or fugitives were considered breaches of the truce, so it was only a matter of time before they struck. In the wake of the attack, however, Abbas pleaded with the parliament to support his bid for control over the Palestinian security forces – still under Arafat's authority – so that his government might at least try to take steps that would forestall Israeli retaliation by demonstrating Palestinian commitment to the road map. His plea was unavailing, however, and Arafat himself was not going to bail him out. Shortly thereafter Israel, announced its policy of liquidating leaders of key militant groups, particularly Hamas. On 6 September 2003, a 250kg bomb dropped by an Israeli F-16, intended to kill the Hamas leader Sheikh Ahmed Yassin, instead killed a number of women and children. Undercut by his president and the legislature, confronted by a serious escalation by Israel, Abbas had no choice to resign, which he did on the same day as the Israeli attack.

After a turbulent interval, Arafat appointed another colleague of longstanding, Ahmad Qurei, also known as Abu Ala. Like Abbas, Qurei had been deeply involved in the Oslo process, was adept at working with Israel and was deeply experienced in the complexities of life in Arafat's court. He also enjoyed a web of political connections owing to his tenure as speaker of the Palestinian parliament. His appointment was greeted with cautious optimism by the US, for which Qurei's emotional stability, compared with Abbas's depressive nature, and his inclination to co-opt rather than confront Arafat, were significant assets. In combination with other presumably dependable Palestinian players – Muhammad Dahlan, the security chieftain whose Gazan hometown of Khan Yunis is popularly known as Dahlanistan and Salam Fayyad, the IMF official turned finance minister – Qurei was thought to have a reasonable shot at implementing the road map and nudging forward reform measures. Changes underway in Israel, however, were about to alter the terms of the conflict substantially.

Sharon giveth, Sharon taketh away

At a conference in Herzliya on 18 December 2003, Sharon gave a speech that was by turns hailed as an audacious breakthrough, dismissed as cynical manipulation and condemned as a blatant land grab. Indeed, his remarks contained elements that could be interpreted as trailblazing, patronising or exploitative. Ambiguities notwithstanding, the thrust of the speech made clear that the Sharon government would wait perhaps six months for a responsible Palestinian counterpart to begin negotiating provisional borders on the basis of the road map. If this did not materialise, Israel would resort to 'unilateral disengagement'. As a practical matter, this would entail the withdrawal of Israeli forces behind defendable lines and the completion of the security barrier already under construction. Palestine, he acknowledged – or, rather, warned – would get far less land under this arrangement than under a negotiated settlement, although he was careful to say that at such time as Palestine was prepared to resume a negotiating process, it could push for better territorial terms. In this context, Sharon emphasised that he wished for a viable and territorially contiguous Palestinian state. Nevertheless, the sovereign Palestinian entity that would emerge from Sharon's unilateral disengagement plan would resemble the state he had long insisted he could accept: very small, occupying about half the West Bank plus all of Gaza. Given that the so-called Clinton parameters established at Taba in January 2001 envisioned a Palestinian state on slightly more than 95% of the West Bank and the 'Geneva Accord' negotiated by progressively oriented Israeli and Palestinian outcasts in 2003 endorsed a Palestine on about 98% of the West Bank, Sharon's conception clearly would not fly with either Palestinians or Americans.

How much Sharon's preferred outcome matters is open to debate. Against the background of his February 2004 follow-on proposals, which contemplate the withdrawal of 17 of 20 settlements from Gaza and from three to six deep in the West Bank, it appears that he has unleashed a process over which he himself can have only limited control. Israeli attitudes on territorial compromise have long been flexible. About 70% of Israelis would accept withdrawal if it led to a reduction in violence. More important, a large number of Likud party Knesset members were openly sceptical about the continued feasibility of Israeli rule over Palestinians, even in the short term. Thus, as of April 2004, Israel was clearly looking for a way out of a tragic impasse. Sharon, therefore, might well be banking cynically on Palestinian disarray to guarantee his preferred outcome – a caged and shrunken Palestine – but the process could well unfold in a way that results in a more sweeping Israeli withdrawal from the West Bank and the concomitant dismantling of all but the large settlement blocs that hug the Samarian highlands and encompass Jerusalem. Certainly, if he is indicted, like his son Gilad, for accepting bribes from David Appel, a Likud party stalwart and real estate magnate, Sharon may not be in as position to influence the direction of the policies that he has recently launched. Furthermore, Sharon himself has a history of shifting his own strategic perspective. In the wake of the Camp David agreement of 1979, Sharon – the architect of the settlements in Sinai – dismantled them. In early 2003, he equated the importance of Netzarim – the largest Gaza settlement, now slated for evacuation – to Tel Aviv. Clashing with the Likud Central Committee, he has accepted the concept of a Palestinian state, which he once reviled.

Moreover, Sharon's proposal has energised a dormant regional diplomatic dynamic. Mubarak and Bush scheduled a meeting in early April to discuss an Egyptian plan for mobilising a more effective Palestinian government still subordinate to Arafat but empowered to act against militants. Although scepticism is warranted regarding the feasibility of this idea, Egypt's re-entry into the fray is likely to prove constructive. At the heart of the proposal is the consolidation of the multiple Palestinian security services under unified command. It also entails an Egyptian role in securing Gaza in the wake of an Israeli withdrawal. This role would not involve substituting an Egyptian occupation for the receding Israeli one, but would help the PA maintain control in Gaza by tamping down internecine tension within the PA – earlier this year, for example, Dahlan's agents sacked the office of an Arafat-appointed police chief and beat him severely – and by ensuring that Hamas did not use Gaza as a platform to carry out attacks against Israelis, as Hizbullah continued to do long after Israeli forces departed from southern Lebanon.

Washington: nowhere to hide

The developments of late 2003 and early 2004 ensnared the White House in Arab–Israeli diplomacy that it was hoping to avoid. Sharon's withdrawal plan presented a distracted, even beleaguered administration, with the proverbial curate's egg – good in parts. The dismantling of settlements could scarcely be criticised, but the abandonment of the road map implied by unilateral withdrawal was a departure for which Washington had no considered response. Indeed, Bush's chief Middle East advisor, Elliott Abrams, had said that there will not be a Palestinian state because the conditions essential to statehood were unachievable in the foreseeable future. For those holding this view, the relatively sudden withdrawal of Israeli authority from Gaza and chunks of the West Bank presented an unwelcome challenge. High expectations on all sides accompanied these plans. In early April, three high-ranking US officials – Abrams, Deputy National Security Adviser Stephen Hadley and Assistant Secretary of State William Burns – went to Israel to discuss the withdrawal plan with each side. On 31 March 2004, Qurei offered tempered support for the plan, conditioned on its being only a first step in a comprehensive Israeli withdrawal and political process, but broadly condemned suicide attacks as providing a pretext for Israeli retaliation – a departure from the usual terse and perfunctory criticisms. Symbolically, Israel eliminated two rudimentary settlements. On 2 April, a newspaper published an interview with Sharon in which he stated that he had ordered all development work on Gaza settlements to halt. Three days later, though, he manifested his anxiety about losing right-wing support when he said in a newspaper interview that he would not feel bound by a three-year old promise to Bush not to harm Arafat.

Sharon was scheduled to alight in Washington on 14 April, just as Mubarak headed back to Cairo. For Sharon, a meeting with the president that generated American approval of his audacious proposal and the promise of substantial economic and diplomatic rewards would keep him from toppling into a political abyss at home. It would also enhance his leverage to impose his proposal on disenchanted Likudniks and coalition partners on his right flank, including the National Religious Party and Yisrael Beiteinu, and thus avoid the need for elections or a national unity government that includes Labor. Whether a wounded Sharon under the

Middle East

threat of indictment can give the White House the detailed plan it seeks and the confidence that he can deliver in a way that doesn't cause an upsurge in violence or diplomatic complications for the US is highly uncertain. Equally unclear is whether Bush, in an increasingly fraught election year and coping with a faltering foreign policy and growing difficulties in Iraq, can give Sharon what he needs: American blessing for de facto annexation of the large settlement blocs along the northern West Bank ridgeline and clustered around Jerusalem; compensation for relocation of Gazan settlers to these blocs; and a 'free pass' from obligations to negotiate until Palestinian violence ends. Although a trial balloon along these lines was rejected by the Bush administration in March 2003, some variation on them will likely re-emerge. In any case, Washington would appear to have little choice but to tackle the substantive issues at the worst possible time from a domestic political standpoint.

Bigger fences, better neighbours

Among the complicating factors in the withdrawal process will be the location of the security barrier, of which a third is now complete. A combination of high walls and concentric chain link fencing studded with sensors of various kinds runs between Umm al Fahm, Tulkarm and Qalqilya in the northern West Bank and around some of the settlement blocs encasing Jerusalem. Some Israelis have thought about such a barrier since Yitzhak Rabin mused in 1994 about taking Gaza out of Tel Aviv in the wake of a young girl's murder. By 2002, over 80% of Israelis favoured the creation of a security barrier, a viewpoint that was reinforced by a newspaper story describing the unimpeded journey taken by Israeli reporters from Tulkarm to Netanya – the route of a number of suicide bombers. Not all Israelis see the barrier as a security tool. If the barrier is successfully hijacked by the right, it will be configured to include most of the West Bank settlements; some Israelis are lobbying for a so-called encirclement fence, which would seal off Palestinian areas from the Jordan valley and enable the eastern segment of the fence to capture Kiryat Arba, a settler community slightly southeast of Hebron. Despite Israeli claims that the barrier would not represent the final border between Israel and Palestine, the fact is that these maximal barrier configurations would yield a politically and economically unviable Palestinian state, with little hope of salvation at the hands of a more conciliatory future Israeli government.

There are, however, other conceptions in play. Among these are fence lines proposed by the IDF, which would swallow around 15% of the West Bank, and the 'Clinton Parameter' barrier, which would carve out about 5%. If a fence were to conform to the boundaries postulated by the Geneva Accord document – admittedly an unlikely scenario – it would pretty much coincide with the Green Line, except in the Jerusalem area.

The key criterion will be what proportion of the two contending populations, the settlers and Palestinians, will be caught on the wrong side of the barrier. The 'Clinton Parameter' barrier provides the fairest outcome: 74% of the settlers would wind up on the Israeli side along with 0.4% of Palestinian West Bankers, about 7,000 people. If Israel did opt for this fence configuration, it would still have to be constructed to permit the easiest possible transit for Palestinians on the Israeli side, consistent with the security needs that dictated the existence of the fence to begin with.

Wildcards

Sharon has made withdrawal from Gaza and four settlements in the West Bank subject to a Likud party referendum to be held upon his return from Washington in mid-April. During this same timeframe, Israeli Attorney-General Menachem Mazuz, a new Sharon appointee, will decide whether to accept the recommendation of the state prosecutor and charge Sharon for bribery. If the referendum fails, the withdrawal plan will probably be dead; if Sharon is indicted as well, it will certainly be dead. This scenario would mean continued occupation and escalating violence. In the alternative, a referendum that approved withdrawal would probably ensure the plan's viability even if Sharon were forced to resign by an indictment. His likely successors, Netanyahu or Ehud Olmert, the deputy prime minister, would both be inclined to push it forward. The idea, in fact, originated with Olmert. But Netanyahu, who is described by Israeli commentators as the man who can sell ice to Eskimos, would probably win over Likud malcontents more effectively than Olmert, and thereby preserve a more convincing semblance of party unity. Either would be prepared to enter a unity government with Labor and eject the National Union and National Religious parties from the current coalition. This would bring Shimon Peres back to the foreign ministry, his portfolio in Sharon's first term, 2000–01. If these events transpire, Israeli settlements in Gaza and the north central West Bank could be resonant with the sound of Arabic and scent of cardamom by the close of 2004. If not, the anguish will persist.

Not all the wildcards are east of the Israeli side of the Green Line. If internecine fighting within Fatah and between Hamas and the PA breaks out or intensifies, there may be no way to prevent attacks against Israeli forces – particularly in Gaza – or against civilians within Israel. Under these conditions, Israel would probably choose to abandon its withdrawal plans, rather than leave under fire. Images of Hamas gloating over a perceived triumph recall too vividly Hizbullah's claiming victory over Israel after its withdrawal from south Lebanon in 2000 – and ever since. From Israel's perspective, this would invite further attack. Although the Palestinian areas have not descended into anarchy, civic order is under severe threat. In Nablus, there have been 30 documented political or mixed-motive murders in the past year and a botched attempt on the mayor's life. (The mayor later resigned, after taking a full-page advertisement in the newspaper *al-Ayyam* condemning the growing disorder in Palestine under Arafat.) Khalid al Zaben, director of Arafat's media office and an associate since the 1960s, was gunned down in Gaza City on 2 March 2004. Against this background, the Palestinian street is unenchanted by its leaders. Arafat's own performance ratings, as measured by the premier Palestinian pollster Khalil Shikaki, are hovering around 25%, while attitudes towards Sheikh Yassin and his successor Abd al Aziz al-Rantisi appear equally jaded. In certain key areas, however, Hamas is doing well. Although the US vetoed a UN resolution moved by Algeria and Libya condemning Israel's targeted killing of Sheikh Yassin on 22 March 2004, the act elicited vehement popular and official protest from Europe and throughout the Muslim world, and may have galvanised Hamas's local support. The funeral marches in Gaza following Yassin's death were a deliberate and impressive show of force by Hamas. Although the organisation qua political party seems to get even less respect than Fatah according to Shikaki's March 2004 survey, the fact that one out of six Palestinians receives some sort of social service from Hamas gives it an edge. The disintegration of the PA's sources of such assistance, which were never very efficient, imparted this momentum to Hamas. Disarray in the PA and the impending Israeli withdrawal could open the door for Hamas's primacy and, consequently, continuing instability. In this context, if Israeli security services consider Yassin's killing to have established a compelling precedent, it may be a risky one for Israel to follow.

Some of the wildcards lie outside both Israel and Palestinian territories. An event or sequence of events that distracted or politically wounded the White House during a supercharged election season – a lucky mortar strike that killed scores of American soldiers in Iraq, a terrorist attack at home – could remove the vital American 'steering' needed to transform unilateral withdrawal into an end to the uprising and the beginning of a renewed bilateral peace process.

End of an era

This was the year that the Likud party, the institutional keepers of the flame, surrendered the dream of 'Eretz Yisrael ha-Shlema' – Greater Israel. The lamps that the faithful kept burning since the miracle of 1967 have guttered. At the same time, Palestinian institutions, under attack from outside and corroded from within, appear scarcely capable of responding to this momentous shift in Israel's worldview. Nearly four years of brutal violence and episodic sieges may not have reduced Palestinian society to a state of nature, but such an outcome is no longer difficult to imagine. The United States, just when its energy and compassion are most needed to keep the parties from the abyss, is engaged in a self-centred war against terror and a state-building project that has exhausted its diplomatic interests and capacities. These are savage and constraining ironies of Likud's belated awakening. Overcoming them will require extraordinary restraint on the part of the Palestinians and extraordinary commitment on the part of the US.

Iran: Domestic Retrogression and International Scrutiny

Middle East

As the new Persian year of 1382 started on 21 March 2003, two overwhelming factors influenced virtually every aspect of decision-making in Tehran. The bruising political battles at home had over the previous year acquired a 'civilisational' dimension in becoming a growing clash of values and political outlook between the country's two main political factions. The reformist movement's disenchantment with the conservative establishment had increasingly manifested itself in their more daring, and sometimes rather far-fetched, demands for faster introduction of reforms in the economy and an overhaul of the constitution and the national institutions of power whereby the locus of decision-making would be transferred from the clerical establishment to elected officials. The former consists principally in the 12-man Council of Guardians (CG), which is entrusted by the constitution with vetting candidates for political office and every piece of legislation for its compatibility with Islamic law and values and with the Iranian constitution itself. The reformists' political power lies in their popular support, and is exercised through the Majlis (national parliament), the various ministries and the executive branch – subject, however, to the CG's veto and the countervailing power of its elected and other official allies. In 2002, the CG had already refused to approve several pieces of important legislation passed by the Majlis, including two proposed by reformist President Mohammed Khatami designed to increase the authority of the president. This domestic political wrangling was overshadowed by concerns about Iraq and the launch of the US-led *Operation Iraqi Freedom* in March 2003.

The Iraq war proved to be a mixed blessing for Tehran. The US-led coalition's ouster of Saddam Hussein removed a deep and painful thorn from Iran's side, and liberated Iranian Shi'ites' religious brethren – the 65% Shi'ite majority that Saddam had brutally repressed. Tehran was nonetheless uncomfortable with the United States installed as a powerful occupying force in both Afghanistan and Iraq, on its eastern and western flanks. Moreover, the liberation of the Iraqi Shi'ites stood to further deepen the political and doctrinal cleavages in Iran's Islamic political system, which hinges on the Velayat-e Faqih, or absolute clerical rule. In that system, political influence and power are derived from the clerical establishment in Iran. Any law or governing standard must be 'Islamic', and that determination falls to Supreme Leader Ayatollah Ali Khamenei and the CG, which he hand-picks. In Iraq, a new and powerful source of Shi'ite religious authority beyond Tehran's control could arise and test the already vulnerable doctrinal basis of a regime founded on a fairly narrow interpretation of Shia thought. In particular, Iraqi Shi'ites' traditional opposition to the mixing of religion and politics was by February 2004 providing considerable intellectual support for those in Iranian politics who questioned the prudence of paramount religiously based political authority in Iran. More broadly, the rise of the Iraqi Shi'ites is likely to challenge Iran's international primacy, and give the non-Iranian Shi'ites – from Lebanon and Yemen, to Azerbaijan and India – a greater say in Shia affairs.

Demise of Iran's reformists

One of the clerical members of the CG, Ayatollah Momen, effectively flattened the reformists' political prospects by announcing in September 2003 that none of about 2,500 reformist signatories of a letter to Ayatollah Khamenei complaining about the regime's repressive tendencies would be allowed to enter the race for the seventh Majlis elections in February 2004. The CG confirmed the ruling in January 2004. The CG probably would not have behaved so inimically towards a movement that the US favoured over the religious establishment had the US state-building effort in Iraq not become so fraught. Yet, while the US presence in Iraq emboldened the reformists, it also stigmatised them. In the event, the CG's provocative action divided the reformist movement. Some members boycotted the elections in protest while others participated in spite of the hopelessly truncated list of reformist candidates. In the event, the conservatives secured a substantial majority of over 160 out of 290 seats in the seventh Majlis, as against a minority of less than 60 in the sixth Majlis. Voter turnout was only 50%, compared with 67% in the 2000 polls.

The conservatives' engineered victory will reverberate in political circles for some time to come. That Khamenei warmly endorsed the outcome as a victory for Islam, while Khatami acquiesced in it, denoted a significant retrogression in the overall balance of power in Iran in favour of the conservatives. Khatami announced on 17 March that he was withdrawing the proposed legislation increasing the presidential powers relative to those of unelected institutions of the republic. His stated reasons were defensive, as he voiced fears that the incoming conservative parliament would use the presentation of the bill perversely as a pretext for further diminishing presidential powers. The president, he said deflatedly, 'is no longer the second figure after the supreme leader charged with upholding the constitution and defending the rights of the people'. Rather, he was merely 'an official in charge of logistic affairs of the system'.

It is possible, as Ray Takeyh has suggested, that 'the success of the conservatives' strategy contains the seeds of their own destruction' – that their manipulation and oppression will give rise to a broader and angrier movement that will not stay within the boundaries of conventional politics and orderly government all the way to counter-revolution. Given that the Iranian right is itself divided between ideologues (under Khamanei) and pragmatists (led by powerful former president Akbar Hashemi Rafsanjani), sharing mainly an opposition to democratic pluralism, the conservatives are indeed vulnerable. Iran's dependency on oil (which accounts for over 85% of its hard currency), lack of global economic integration, and endemic corruption and unemployment, coupled with its population's youthfulness (70% are under 30) and high rates of urbanisation (70%) and literacy (above 80%), indicate a very weak popular base for the conservatives. It is also significant that in the 2001 presidential elections, 70% of the Revolutionary Guards voted for the reformist Khatami. But the conservatives' control strategy of short-term economic growth plus public apathy may at least buy them some time, and they are likely to calculate that a proactive and at times provocative foreign policy will extend their tenure by casting the United States – the 'Great Satan' – as a threatening foe that requires solidarity behind the pious elite.

Iran and the US

The dwindling of the reformists' political fortunes, then, only strained Iran's already fraught relations with the United States. Tehran's destabilising involvement in the Israeli–Palestinian conflict – crowned by its thwarted attempt to supply arms to Fatah via the ship Karine-A in December 2001 – had extinguished any American inclinations towards a rapprochement. Beyond that, US concern about Iran's nuclear programme moved President George W. Bush to include Iran in the 'axis of evil' in his January 2002 State of the Union address and some in Washington to contemplate regime change in Iran. Regime change in Iraq, however, was the immediate priority. The US-led intervention, like the Afghan campaign, offered an opportunity for US–Iranian cooperation. The US was moving to topple a regime that threatened Iranian security; Iran had extra-territorial interests in the targeted country; Washington sought Iran's political acquiescence and limited operational cooperation; while Tehran feared further encirclement. Numerous meetings between American and Iranian diplomats in Europe and New York under UN auspices paid dividends during and immediately after the war in the absence of confrontation in circumstances where the proximity US and UK forces to Iranian forces might have led to clashes. The White House took this for a positive development and approved the State Department's recommendation to add the People's Mujaheddin (MEK), a large and heavily armed insurgent army dedicated to overthrowing the clerical regime in Tehran, to its list of terrorist organisations. This initiative was followed by coalition bombing of the MEK's Iraqi cantonments and a demand that MEK fighters surrender their heavy weapons. But cooperation foundered on intelligence suggesting Iranian collusion with senior al-Qaeda terrorists and suspicions that Iran was encouraging armed Shia resistance to coalition forces in southern Iraq.

On 3 June 2003, Washington suspended contacts with Iran amid a debate over what policy the US should adopt. The precipitating event was the bombing of Western residential and business targets in Riyadh on 12 May that claimed 34 victims, including Americans, Saudis, Jordanians, Filipinos and others. In the weeks following the attack, the Bush administration reported 'very troubling intercepts' in which al-Qaeda figures in Iran allegedly discussed the bombing in a way that suggested their own complicity and a planning link to Iran. Secretary of Defense Donald Rumsfeld remarked that there was 'no question' about it. For others in the administration, particularly at the State Department, evidence of Iranian collaboration with al-Qaeda was ambiguous and the al-Qaeda operatives were probably exploiting the anarchic situation on Iran's Afghan border. But reports of the al-Qaeda elite – Saad bin Laden (Osama's son and heir apparent), Suleiman Abu Ghaith and Saif bin Adl – in Iranian safehouses created the countervailing impression that the situation was far more serious. Whatever the real story, this was the spark that ignited latent perceptions of an Iranian leadership ready to proffer superficial cooperation while working assiduously with America's most dangerous adversaries to undermine US interests. That the Riyadh bombing occurred only about a week after the US had informed Iran, in a secret meeting in Geneva, of its decision to dismantle the MEK only reinforced the sense of double-dealing.

In summer 2003, the Bush administration finally began the serious debate about its Iran policy that had been postponed for so long. Not all suggestions were feasible. The Pentagon, reportedly with the support of Vice-President Dick Cheney, advocated actions that would lead to the overthrow of the clerical regime in a popular revolt. A more vigorous approach endorsed the adoption of the MEK as a kind of Northern Alliance or Kurdish militia that could be used to seize Iranian territory during or even before an uprising (a stratagem complicated by the MEK's recent terrorist designation). Even more robust was the suggestion that the US strike Iran's nuclear facilities. The State Department waged a rearguard battle, questioning the Pentagon's bold assumptions about popular unrest in Iran and the likelihood that US political intervention would be welcomed. This argument gained saliency as the Iraq occupation became increasingly plagued by a mainly indigenous insurgency. None of these discussions moved the administration closer to a coherent policy, but they did generate further momentum. On 18 June 2003, Bush declared that the US 'will not tolerate the construction of a nuclear weapon' in Iran. Yet this 'carefully worded escalation', as the West Wing described the announcement, carried no hint of what the US could do to stop it, apart from appealing to the solidarity of the 'international community'. Notwithstanding the appetite in some parts of the administration for dramatic actions, a more moderate and diplomatic US approach ensued, in part because the troublesome occupation of Iraq limited Washington's freedom of action.

Iran's nuclear and missile programmes

Since the introduction of the Clinton doctrine of 'dual containment' of Iran and Iraq in 1993, the United States and the EU have had their differences over Western policy options towards these oil-rich neighbours. Although past and present hostilities barred 'dual containment' from encouraging the emergence of any strategic or tactical partnership between Tehran and Baghdad, both countries were from the mid-1990s heavily engaged in courting European countries (including Russia) as a means of weakening containment. They also banked on winning European support through successfully exploiting potential transatlantic rifts over President Bill Clinton's Middle East policy. The 'axis of evil' designation was widely read as placing both Tehran and Baghdad (as well as Pyongyang) on notice that the US would not tolerate what it considered rogue behaviour – particularly involving weapons of mass destruction (WMD) and support for terrorism. Many, if not most, European capitals considered the speech gratuitously provocative. Yet this disagreement did not enable either Iran or Iraq to enlist the EU as a protective shield against the United States. The Iraq intervention, however, was perceived as sufficiently unilateral to convince European powers that Washington was prepared to engage in costly and sustained military interventions if it felt that they would constitute effective preventive security measures. Recognition of the United States' ability and willingness to act without the consent of the UN encouraged a degree of convergence between Tehran and the EU.

In the charged diplomatic atmosphere following the failure of UN debates on Iraq, both Iran and the EU had much to gain from demonstrating that the EU's 'constructive engagement' of Tehran could produce tangible results. Tehran was motivated to deflect overly aggressive American attention, while the EU could claim to be taking direct and effective action

Middle East

to bring Iran into line without resort to the threat or use of force. The focus of European diplomacy was Iran's nuclear programme, which both Washington and European capitals saw as an Iranian bid to obtain a nuclear weapons breakout option. The EU troika (Germany, France and the United Kingdom) was able in October 2003 to convince Iran to give a full account of its nuclear programme before the 31 October deadline set by the International Atomic Energy Agency (IAEA) board to suspend its uranium enrichment and reprocessing activities, and to bring all of its nuclear activities under stronger IAEA inspections. Both Brussels and Tehran portrayed this development as a victory for dialogue over coercion. But the onus was on Tehran and the EU to convince a sceptical United States that the agreement reached in Tehran on 21 October between the troika's foreign ministers and the Iranian government, through the office of its National Security Council, was comprehensive and robust enough not to require referral to the UN Security Council for further actions, including potential economic and political sanctions. The latter option had been the United States' preferred mode of dealing with Iran since 2002, when revelations about Iran's clandestine nuclear activities began to surface. Questions about the Iranian–European deal rose immediately before the March 2004 IAEA Board of Governors' meeting, when the IAEA reported that Iran had failed to fully report its past enrichment programme and was continuing to build centrifuge machines, despite its October 2003 commitments. Faced with the prospect that the US and Europe might join forces to report Iranian non-compliance to the Security Council, Tehran again made tactical concessions, agreeing to expand the suspension to include construction of additional centrifuge machines, while the IAEA Board responded to Washington's unhappiness by giving Iran another 'last chance'. As of March 2004, many observers believed that additional revelations of Iran's nuclear activities could still emerge, making it undeniable that Iran's nuclear programme was intended to give Iran a nuclear weapons option.

While Brussels and Washington may have approached Iran differently, Tehran was left in no doubt that, in the aftermath of the Iraq war and the North Korean nuclear stand-off, capitals on both sides of the Atlantic took Iran's nuclear programme extremely seriously and were dismayed by the direction of its activities. Unlike the case of Iraq, which split the Western alliance over the assessment of the threat, there was no fundamental disagreement within the transatlantic community that Iran was within a few years of achieving a nuclear weapons option. Even Moscow, the supplier of Iran's nuclear power plant, entered the fray by expressing concern about the nature of the ongoing nuclear research in Iran. Moscow publicly urged Tehran to sign the IAEA's Additional Protocol, requiring more intrusive inspections. In a blunt warning, Russia also stated that it too would not tolerate a nuclear-capable Iran in west Asia, on Russia's own doorstep. At the same time, Moscow joined the European powers in opposing Washington's efforts to report Iran's nuclear activities to the UN Security Council.

The nuclear programme itself has become much more open since 2002, when a string of revelations by an Iranian opposition group forced the Iranian authorities to acknowledge that they had in fact sought enrichment and reprocessing facilities. They announced in early 2003 that Iran's nuclear programme aimed 'to complete the circle [cycle] of fuel for plants for peaceful purposes' Gholam-Reza Aqazadeh, the head of the country's atomic energy programme, declared on 10 February 2003 that the agency had begun work on a large-scale uranium enrichment plant near the city of Kashan (known as the Natanz site), stating that 'very extensive research [had] already started'. The feed material for this centrifuge plant would come from the brand new Uranium Conversion Facility built in the industrial city of Isfahan. The Isfahan plant was to be complemented by another facility for fabricating fuel for nuclear power reactors. These announcements further heightened international concerns about Iran's nuclear ambitions, particularly as only a day earlier Tehran had said that it had successfully enriched uranium and was planning to process spent fuel from its operating nuclear facilities. Khatami himself appeared on national television on the anniversary of Iran's Islamic revolution in February to congratulate his countrymen on their nuclear achievements, enumerating their research successes, and then underlining Aqazadeh's statements. Such political reinforcement suggested a significant degree of bipartisan support among reformists and conservatives for the continuation of Iran's nuclear programme.

The IAEA immediately followed up on these official Iranian statements. Of greatest concern to the IAEA were the sites being developed in the cities of Natanz and Arak, of whose existence the agency had first discovered through the declarations of the Iranian opposition group and intelligence sources and not the Iranian authorities themselves. Iran's late notification of the two sites to the IAEA, though technically legal under the NPT, reached the Vienna-based organisation only in September 2002 – a month after an opposition group had blown the whistle by publishing details of the Natanz and Arak facilities. The revelations showed that the underground site near Natanz would house Iran's main gas centrifuge plant for enriching uranium, while the Arak facility would produce heavy water, an ingredient used for plutonium production in certain types of reactors. The IAEA's February 2003 inspection of Natanz revealed that Iran not only had been able to develop and advance the Pakistani-supplied technology to assemble a 'cascade' of 160 centrifuge machines, but had assembled sufficient quantity of parts for installing a further 1,000–5,000 centrifuge machines between 2003 and 2005. Natanz, Iran has told the IAEA, is designed to produce low-enriched uranium for Iran's planned expansion of nuclear power plants, and is therefore not designed to generate weapons-grade highly-enriched uranium. The scientific community, however, is concerned that the Natanz plant could be reconfigured in a short period of time to produce highly enriched or weapons-grade uranium. From the US and European perspective, of course, Iran's intention to process and complete the nuclear fuel cycle would only have one purpose: to develop nuclear weapons. Once the facilities were operational, Iran could legally withdraw from the NPT (giving three months' notice) and convert the facilities to produce highly enriched uranium for nuclear weapons.

In early November 2003, Iran announced that it was suspending the development of the *Shihab*-4 – a ballistic missile that, unlike the more established *Shihab*-3, had not yet reached the production stage but was estimated to have sufficient design range to strike targets in Europe. The announcement, which came soon after Tehran said that it would suspend its uranium-enrichment activities, probably marked a response to mounting international concerns about Iran's missile and nuclear programmes. If the gesture was intended as a tactical measure to placate European and American critics of Iran's nuclear programme, however, it did not appear to form part of any overall slowdown in Iran's missile development efforts.

Overall, during 2003 Tehran openly upgraded its domestic missile capabilities. The CIA estimates that Iran, as of late 2003, possessed 'a few hundred' short-range ballistic missiles, including the 150 kilometre-range *Tondar*-69/CSS-8, the 300km-range *Shihab*-1/*Scud*-B, and the 500km-range *Shihab*-2/*Scud*-C. In addition, Iran has tested the *Fateh*-110, a solid-fuelled ballistic missile with a range sometimes reported as 300–400km. But the development of the *Shihab*-3 has caused most concern among Western defence planners. The *Shihab*-3 is based on the North Korean *No-dong* missile. It is a single-stage, liquid-fuelled, road-mobile system that has evolved from *Scud* technology. Early estimates gave it a nominal range of 1,300km – enough to reach Israel, other US partners in the Middle East and parts of Europe – with a nuclear payload. However, recent Iranian statements have set its range at 1,700km, while Israel has warned that the range might be extended to 2,500km. It is not clear whether the claimed longer ranges would be achieved partly by reducing the payload, which has been estimated at 750–1,000kg. Still, the various claims of an ever-increasing range, taken with the assessments contained in a CIA report to Congress released on 10 November, strongly suggest that *Shihab*-3 upgrades are indeed underway. If so, this will further diminish the significance of Iran's decision to suspend development of the *Shihab*-4 – as will Iran's continuing interest in developing a 'space-launch vehicle' that might have military applications. It is true that the *Shihab*-3 programme has only featured about nine tests, of which just four have been reasonably successful. But in July 2003, Khamenei announced that the *Shihab*-3 had been 'inaugurated' into Iran's military forces.

From the progress of Iran's ballistic missile programme, outside parties are likely to infer that despite international pressure Iran has left the door open for following through on nuclear weapons development as well. It is true that even if Iran's nuclear programme made significant progress, its ability to deliver a nuclear-armed ballistic missile would still face some short-term constraints. First-generation nuclear warheads may exceed the weight and diameter constraints of the *Shihab*-3 and, at the very least, limit options for extending the range of Iran's ballistic missiles by reducing payloads. Still, Iran's past relationship with Pakistan may have provided Tehran with access to nuclear-weapon design information that could be applied to Iran's *No-dong*-based missiles.

Within Iran, however, the advisability of Iran's developing a nuclear weapons option is a live, and often testy, debate. While the conservative religious establishment is the more retrograde grouping in terms of overall diplomatic relations between Islam and the West, it also contains more doubters on the nuclear issue than does the reformist movement. Five main arguments on nuclear capability circulate in Iran. The first is rooted in the rights and responsibilities of states that have signed the NPT. Some contend that Iran, a signatory, has never violated the terms of the NPT but nonetheless should take maximum legitimate advantage of the opportunities that the NPT offers member-states to acquire nuclear technology and know-how for peaceful purposes. Others argue that the costs associated with nuclear research are so great that Iran should not even enter this field. In addition, there are environmental issues to consider, and the fact that by building nuclear facilities Iran will create more strategic targets for its adversaries to strike at. Second, proponents of a nuclear option argue that for Iran to be taken seriously as a dominant regional actor it must be seen to be having an extensive nuclear research and development programme, even though in practice it may not translate its research into actual weapons. North Korea, Pakistan and India are cited as countries that have become immune from American aggression thanks to their nuclear-weapons capabilities. Opponents of this view argue that the Soviet and North Korean examples show not only that the positive technological spin-offs from nuclear research are minimal, but that any advances in this field will inevitably occur at the expense of another, probably vital, civilian sector; thus, Iran would not be able to recoup the costs of nuclear research.

The third set of contentions flows from geopolitical insecurity. Substantial camps among both conservatives and reformists believe that Iran's neighbourhood is insecure and interstate relations endemically uncertain. With Israel and Pakistan in possession of nuclear weapons, they say, it would make strategic sense for Iran to at least develop the option, if not actually declare itself as a nuclear-weapon state. But others argue that with the Iraqi threat now practically removed Iran no longer has any

Middle East

natural enemies and faces no existential threat, and point out that its borders have been breached only once over the last 200 years (in the 1980–88 Iran–Iraq war). Accordingly, there is scant security justification for Iran's possession of nuclear weapons, which could provoke a regional nuclear arms race – the dangers of which the pro-nuclear camp acknowledges. The fourth argument downplays the regional aspects of Iran's security in favour of its global dimension. It runs that without nuclear weapons, Iran will remain vulnerable to threats from the United States. The other side claims that there is no evidence to suggest that Iran will be more secure as a consequence of nuclearisation, that the United States will change its policies towards the Iran on that account, or that the regional countries themselves will submit to Iran's will. Some advisors to Khatami have suggested that Iran's deployment of nuclear weapons will adversely affect its relations with all of its neighbours, including Russia. They also fear that nuclear weapons deployment could encourage the militarisation of the polity and reckless adventurism in Iran's foreign relations.

The final argument relates to national resources. Proponents of total freedom of action for Iran in all fields of nuclear research and technological development assert that completing the nuclear fuel cycle will allow the construction of several nuclear power stations without substantial dependence on outside suppliers, securing for future generations a practically endless supply of energy. Opponents of this view point to the immense start-up costs of such a huge programme, as well as its prohibitive maintenance and periodical modernisation expenses. Given that Iran is endowed with some of the largest oil and gas deposits in the world, it is also hard to convince the international community that Iran's interest in nuclear technology turns on an urgent need for energy supplies – however long term they may be.

The debate over the national nuclear programme does not seem to have reached a conclusive point in Iran, and the outcome will depend as much on the balance of power between the various factions, as it will on how the West reacts to Iran's nuclear ambitions. The IAEA Board of Governors' resolution of 13 March 2004 criticised Iran because its October 2003 declarations 'did not amount to the complete and final picture of Iran's past and present nuclear programme considered essential by the board's November 2003 resolution'. The IAEA expressed particular concern regarding Iran's advanced centrifuge design, its laser enrichment capabilities and its hot cells facility at its heavy-water research reactor. The Iranian expression of outrage at the resolution at all levels of its leadership and the calls from the leadership of the Islamic Revolutionary Guards Corps for Iran to withdraw from the NPT altogether were soon tempered with a more conciliatory line that Iran remained committed to the agreements reached with the EU troika, which had in effect become the reluctant guardians of Iran's relationship with the IAEA.

The resolution also praised Iran for its cooperation and openness. The positive tone made it difficult for the US to pull Iran in front of the Security Council for nuclear indiscretions. Furthermore, the US needs Iranian acquiescence for its presence and activities in Iraq and Afghanistan, and must increasingly call on the EU and European powers for diplomatic and military support in those countries. Finally, Iran is confidently believed to be several years away from a nuclear-weapons capability. Thus, Washington is unlikely to escalate Iran's nuclear aspirations to a crisis point in the short to medium term. For the moment, the United States' only realistic option seems to be to ensure that the EU and the IAEA continue to prise open Iran's nuclear secrets by pressing Tehran to comply with its NPT obligations without delay. The US will probably be content with its own rhetorical condemnation of Tehran – and its role as 'bad cop' in a de facto transatlantic 'good cop/bad cop' approach to managing Iran. If Iran is again found to be in breach of NPT obligations, however, or if it resumes its enrichment programme at some point, US pressure would increase.

Pressure from all quarters

If the Iraq war divided the Western alliance, then concerns over Iran (links with terror groups, a clandestine nuclear programme, opposition to the Israel–Palestine 'road map', interference in Iraq and Afghanistan, stalled reforms at home and human-rights issues) helped bring the two sides closer together. Tehran, to be sure, did not substantially interfere with the stabilisation of Afghanistan and Iraq in the aftermath of the respective US-led interventions, assisted the West and its regional allies in targeting al-Qaeda in their broader war on terror, and even toned down its hostility to the 'road map'. Nevertheless, the WMD issue, the country's continuing close links with the Lebanese Hizbullah and Syria, and its refusal to declare the full extent of its nuclear programme have ensured sustained collective transatlantic pressure on Iran. Tehran expects American suspicion and coolness, and is disposed to endure it. But European mistrust, against a backdrop of 'constructive engagement', is more discomfiting.

In the course of 2003, Tehran became acutely concerned about overt European worries about its domestic policies as well as references at virtually any bilateral meeting to the Iranian 'files' routinely mentioned by the United States. In fact, some Iranian officials began to express doubts about the efficacy of an 'EU-first' Iranian foreign policy. To these largely conservative-leaning policy advisors, the European posture increasingly resembled the American one. They made the case that if Europe is merely to mimic the US vis-à-vis Iran, and is not able to offer a distinctly favourable alternative to America's hostile line, then Tehran should cut out the European middle-man and try and deal directly with the United States in addressing matters of bilateral concern. But the balance of official Iranian

Middle East

opinion still perceives palpably greater sympathy among European governments. Thus, Europe has remained at the top of Iran's diplomatic priority list and is likely to stay there.

Russia, the only eastern European country with close links to Iran, plays an important part in Iran's interaction with the US and its allies. For Tehran, Russia is a source of nuclear material, know-how and technology, military hardware and training, and diplomatic support. Russia, for its part, regards its nuclear partnership with Iran as a valuable source of hard currency. The nuclear relationship also affords Russia considerable leverage in its relations with Iran, as well as with the United States, and this unique position has enabled it to exact valuable strategic rent from each country. Furthermore, Tehran and Moscow share similar geopolitical and security outlooks across west and central Asia. Both fear the spread of Salafi Islamic fundamentalism, al-Qaeda (Sunni) terrorism, and creeping American influence and military presence in and around the potentially hydrocarbon-rich Caspian Sea. But due to lack of trust, neither party is closely coordinating its regional policies with the other. Over oil and gas rights in the Caspian, for example, Tehran and Moscow are hopelessly divided and therefore unable to impose a solution on the other three littoral states – Azerbaijan, Kazakhstan, Turkmenistan – which in turn leaves the door open for the United States to chart closer links with all of these three former Soviet Muslim republics.

Meanwhile, the Iranian clerics' consolidation of power – however dubious its legitimacy may be – will probably make Iranian policy more coherent. Whereas before the March 2004 elections they executed a policy of episodic cooperation to keep Washington focused on them as interlocutors, rather than on the attraction of a notional partnership with anti-clerical reformers, the reformers no longer appear to be viable players – at least in terms of direct diplomacy. At the same time, the US has managed to marshal broader international pressure on Iran over Tehran's nuclear programme than it was able to prior to 2003. The upshot is a stronger possibility of a US–Iran deal whereby American security guarantees and economic incentives are exchanged for Iran's nuclear forbearance. Movement in this direction would be premised on transatlantic cooperation with respect to Iran – a highly positive development in the wake of severe divisions over Iraq. But it would not obviate the need for a more comprehensive and nuanced US policy on Iran, which still poses the threat of terrorist sponsorship in the Middle East and other challenges to the US. Such a policy is likely to emerge, especially if the situation in Iraq improves, allowing minds in Washington to focus on other problems. If Bush is re-elected, a hardline policy centred on further isolation could emerge. If not, a new Democratic administration could opt for a strategy of economic and political re-engagement to afford reform-minded Iranians more exposure to the global economy and corresponding pressures towards political liberalisation, and to deprive Iranian conservatives of a distracting enemy. The latter course would guarantee further European cooperation. In either case, the objective will be a change of regime.

Asia and Australia

Within each major Asian region, salient security concerns produced broadly shared priorities in 2003–04. In northeast Asia, controlling North Korea was key. Pyongyang's threat to move forward with its nuclear-weapons programme, though always a potential crisis, in 2003 and early 2004 had the paradoxically salutary effect of bringing the US, Europe and Asian powers closer together. Beijing hosted multilateral talks involving the US, North Korea, South Korea, Russia, Japan and China itself. Although only slow and grudging progress was made, dialogue remained open and held out qualified hope for a diplomatic solution. More broadly, against the domestic backdrop of a relatively smooth leadership transition, China's activism in pursuing more extensive economic and diplomatic relationships with the US, Europe and southeast Asian states bespoke both patience and conviction in its drive towards greater regional primacy, as well as a strong hedging instinct vis-à-vis the US. Japan, for its part, strengthened its alliance with the US and continued the trend of relative extroversion in foreign and security policy on both the regional and the global level, expanding its maritime defence operations and its missile defence collaboration with the US as well as supporting the US-led state-building effort in Iraq with funding and a substantial (and unprecedented) non-combat military deployment.

In southeast Asia and Australia, countering transnational Islamic terrorism topped the regional 'to do' list. Although there were elections scheduled for 2004 or early 2005 in Indonesia, Malaysia, the Philippines and Thailand, no upsets appeared probable except perhaps in the May 2004 poll in the Philippines. Existing security relationships thus seemed likely to remain largely intact. That said, they were less than robust, as meaningful cooperation has been difficult to forge. Indonesia manifested limitations, born of domestic Islamist political influences, in its willingness to confront Jemaah Islamiah (JI) – arguably al-Qaeda's best organised and most potent regional affiliate. Jakarta's broader insistence on non-interference dampened potential for coordinating counter-terrorism efforts, despite pressure and material encouragement from Australia and the US. Thailand, though more alert after several attacks in its largely Muslim southern provinces in January 2004, awakened tardily to the terrorist threat, and the Philippines faces resilient terrorist impulses in both the Abu Sayyaf Group and the Moro Islamic Liberation Front as well as JI. Australia's proximity to Indonesia, its close strategic alignment with the US, its loss of over 80 citizens in the October 2002 Bali bombing and its

Map Asia and Australia

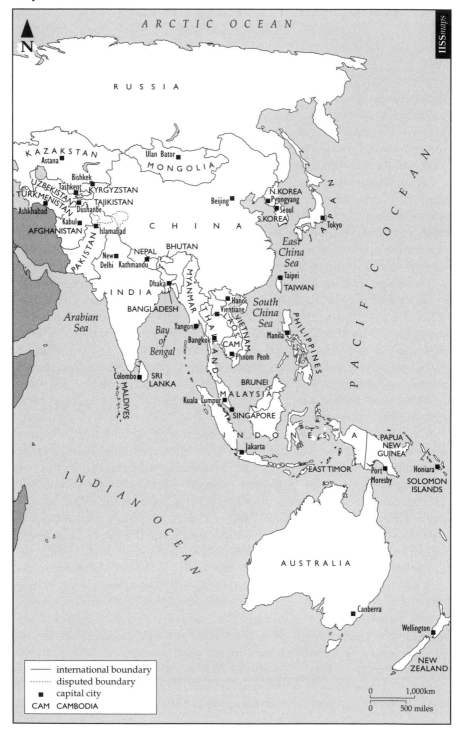

express inclusion on various al-Qaeda target lists reinforced a strong homeland defence posture, with an emphasis on maritime security and forward measures. These included, at the institutional level, the establishment of the Indonesia Centre for Law Enforcement Cooperation, which will be funded largely by Australia.

Both major players on the South Asian subcontinent were inclined to move beyond crisis stability towards bilateral accommodation on Kashmir, but the India–Pakistan peace process is fragile. As of April 2004, the ceasefire was holding, Pakistani President Pervez Musharraf was hardening his stance on terrorism and Delhi had acknowledged Islamabad's stake in the resolution of the Kashmir conflict. But no durable agreement can crystallise quickly, so diplomatic and political stamina will be required. To build staying power, the wider military and political leaderships of each country would have to wholeheartedly buy into the process and Musharraf would have to make good on pledges to dismantle terrorist infrastructure as well as to stop infiltration. Nuclear instability also remains a serious problem, as the conventional imbalance in India's favour has discouraged Pakistan from adopting a no-first-use policy and India from undertaking any serious refinement of its nuclear doctrine beyond 'minimum deterrence'. Proliferation concerns centring on Pakistan were also amplified by revelations that A.Q. Khan, formerly Pakistan's top government nuclear scientist, had sold nuclear weapons know-how and technology to Iran, Libya and probably North Korea.

In Central Asia, the US, Russia, Europe and the Central Asian states themselves shared an interest in regional security, particularly against terrorist infiltration. In Afghanistan, US and coalition forces continued to engage in low-intensity conflict with Taliban and al-Qaeda loyalists, while Pakistani forces (with US logistical and intelligence support) attempted to close in on the al-Qaeda leadership believed to be hiding in Pakistan's tribal areas near the Afghan border. The military priorities of the US-led coalition, however, sometimes worked at cross-purposes with multilateral peace-building initiatives, effectively empowering warlords by using them for intelligence purposes and acquiescing in their coercive control tactics with respect to fellow Afghan Muslims. Thus, key post-war reconstruction programmes have been frustrated and warlords have filled the resulting political, economic and security vacuums. The prospects of installing an Afghan government with genuine democratic legitimacy and effective authority over a substantial portion of the country in the elections scheduled for June 2004 remain slim. While regional security in the short term turned appreciably on stable US military and political relationships with regional allies like Uzbekistan, the status quo was subject to increasing domestic pressure on the US government to use its leverage to promote democratisation and better human-rights practices in those states and Russian anxieties about permanent US outposts in a putative sphere of

Russian influence. As of April 2004, however, US–Russian tensions in the region appeared manageable.

Across Asia's landscape, then, potential crises and key relationships were being better handled in 2003–04 than they were in 2001, when the collision between a US spy plane and a Chinese fighter imperilled US–China relations; 2002, when India and Pakistan nearly went to war; and early 2003, when the US, Europe and Asia were divided on how to deal with North Korea. Intra-regional economic and political links also thickened – particularly those between China and southeast Asia. China concluded a free trade agreement and a 'Strategic Partnership for Peace and Security' with the Association of Southeast Asian Nations (ASEAN) and acceded to ASEAN's Treaty of Amity and Cooperation. Localised conflicts like Nepal's were relatively quiescent. The ceasefire between the Sri Lankan government and the Liberation Tigers of Tamil Eelam endured for a second year and the new government planned to restart negotiations suspended in April 2003 – though attacks in early April 2004 by a 6,000-strong Tamil Tiger breakaway faction led by 'Colonel Karuna' on the mainstream group complicated the situation. There was also scope for disruption in more strategically important areas. A positive result in the India–Pakistan peace process rests heavily on the willingness of the two individual leaders to take political risks, and Pakistani President Pervez Musharraf has been threatened repeatedly by assassination attempts. Taiwan's leadership became more vigorous in asserting the island's identity separate from China; further provocation from Taipei could quickly trigger a crisis. Although Japan's deepening joint development with the US of a theatre missile defence is primarily a response to the North Korean threat, China fears that the system could be extended to Taiwan; from this perspective, US–Japan collaboration could potentially reorient the regional balance of power and, in the worst case, move China to confront both Japan and the US. Finally, Afghanistan's viability as a state, in the face of warlordism and the threat of al-Qaeda and Taliban remnants, could not be taken for granted.

North Korea: A Mouse That Roared?

North Korea spent most of 2003 hurling nuclear threats at the United States and its allies Japan and South Korea, insisting that it was developing nuclear weapons and that it had a right to use them in any way it wished. While there is no clear evidence on how far along this road North Korea might be, it would be imprudent to assume that North Korean leader Kim

Jong Il, for all his braggadocio, is not telling the truth. The dangers inherent in leaving nuclear weapons in the hands of the unpredictable regime in North Korea can hardly be exaggerated.* It would have a deleterious effect on the stability and security of East Asia, possibly triggering an arms race if South Korea, Japan or Taiwan decides that developing their own nuclear capability is the better part of valour. Although it is clear that any attack by North Korea upon one of its neighbours would spell the end of both the existing regime and the country, it is plausible that a desperate North Korean regime might be willing to commit suicide if it felt that its existence was threatened anyway, taking hundreds of thousands of lives with it. Equally dangerous would be the willingness of the North Korean regime to peddle know-how, weapons or both to the highest bidder, whether a rogue regime or an al-Qaeda-like terrorist organisation.

Teasing Kim Jong Il's true intentions out of the miasma that envelops North Korea's words and deeds has always been difficult. The North Korean leader may indeed believe that the only way to ensure his regime's security is to possess the frightful power of nuclear weapons. But he is probably also playing a more subtle game. The country desperately needs massive food, material and financial aid from abroad if it is ever to even begin a slow climb out of the pit of economic disaster it has dug for itself. Many observers believe that the regime is trumpeting threats, as it has before, in order to offer generously to remove them in exchange for a security agreement and recognition by the United States and economic aid from the US and regional powers. North Korea has made just enough concessions to keep this perception credible, and South Korea, China and Russia all appeared to feel that North Korea can be enticed to accept such carrots to give up its nuclear weapons programme. From Pyongyang's standpoint, the optimum strategy would be to accept limits on its nuclear programme in exchange for political and economic benefits, while preserving a small nuclear hedge to deter and intimidate potential enemies.

While the US argues that giving in to the North Korean ploy would constitute acceptance of blackmail, it recognises that threats of military or economic pressure would not result in the desired outcome. It too has been ameliorating its harsh, and originally very rigid, positions. The result has been a not very stately dance: a series of multinational meetings so that the US can hold to its position of refusing to discuss the problem with North Korea bilaterally and so that North Korea can maintain that it is meeting the US on the periphery of multilateral talks. The latest round in February 2004 did not produce any significant breakthroughs, but they did lower

---

* For further details on North Korea's weapons programmes, based on the most authoritative attainable open-source material, as well as prospects for resolving related international security problems, see *North Korea's Weapons Programmes: A Net Assessment*, an IISS Strategic Dossier (January 2004).

tensions and hold open the possibility that an agreed further round might lead to progress towards a satisfactory agreement. On the other hand, neither Pyongyang nor Washington seems prepared to make fundamental concessions. Pyongyang is content to let the talks play out while it continues to enhance its nuclear capabilities and waits for the outcome of the US presidential elections. The Bush administration remains preoccupied with Iraq and deeply divided over the terms of an agreement with North Korea. At the same time, both sides have an incentive to continue the talks, if only to avoid blame for blocking a diplomatic solution. As a consequence, the talks may stagger along for the time being, but without making any significant progress towards a solution.

Creation of a problem

North Korea and the United States in the opening days of 2003 faced the most serious crisis in their relations since 1993–94. The threat that North Korea was intent on developing nuclear weapons was the catalyst for both crises. President Bill Clinton had concluded in 1993 that diplomacy could achieve a satisfactory result without bloodshed and this judgement proved sound in the short term. But that result was not easy to achieve. It required at least five major, often frustrating, negotiating sessions spread out over a 17-month period after May 1993, accompanied by and interspersed with many more informal meetings, before the Agreed Framework was reached in October 1994. At one point, in June 1994, negotiations appeared so stymied that the US president seriously contemplated military action to counter the continuing threat of proliferation on the peninsula. A face-to-face meeting between former US president Jimmy Carter and then-DPRK president Kim Il Sung was required to defuse this standoff and smooth the way for a final agreement.

The Agreed Framework traded North Korean promises to freeze and eventually dismantle its nuclear weapons efforts and allow International Atomic Energy Agency (IAEA) inspections to verify that it was doing what it promised to do in exchange for US, South Korean and Japanese promises of economic and technical aid. South Korea and Japan promised to construct two light-water reactors that could produce electricity but were inefficient for the production of weapons-grade plutonium, while the US would provide 500,000 tonnes of oil per year for North Korea's energy needs until the new reactors began production. Although neither side lived wholly up to the spirit of the agreement, the Framework did calm the atmosphere for several years and opened the way for negotiations between the four nations that appeared to hold the promise of relieving one of the world's most serious flashpoints.

Evidence had been accumulating, however, that North Korea was surreptitiously trying to resurrect its drive for a nuclear arsenal, this time based on technical knowledge and materials acquired from Pakistan. By October 2002, the US had gathered enough evidence to confront North Korea with its hardened suspicions that the communist regime was constructing a gas centrifuge facility that could soon produce enough enriched uranium to make at least two nuclear bombs a year. According to Assistant Secretary of State James Kelly, his North Korean interlocutor had privately admitted that the regime was indeed working on such a programme. Publicly, however, the North Koreans immediately denied that they had ever conceded the US charges and accused the US of lying about this confession and about the evidence it claimed to have. The putative talks – the first that the Bush administration had agreed to hold with North Korea – broke up at once and Pyongyang reverted to vituperative propaganda assaults and vague nuclear threats, claiming that it was entitled to have nuclear weapons because it was surrounded by intractable enemies armed with such weapons. Nevertheless, it acknowledged its willingness to settle the 'nuclear issue' if the United States would agree to legally binding assurances of non-aggression, including the use of nuclear weapons.

While Washington insisted it had no plans for military action against North Korea, it refused to hold direct talks with Pyongyang or to agree to any kind of non-aggression treaty. Hoping that it could bring North Korea around by creating some economic pain, the US announced in November 2002 that it intended to cancel the oil supply programme after the November delivery. In response, North Korea moved to reactivate its 5-megawatt reactor, and at the end of December 2002 insisted that the IAEA withdraw its inspectors and in addition remove its surveillance equipment. The situation was speeding toward a familiar descending spiral.

Searching for a solution

In the opening months of 2003, Washington faced the same dilemma that it had in 1993–94. As then, using military force was an unpalatable choice for North Korea would be certain to unleash what it colourfully called a 'sea of fire' against Seoul. Its army may have been weakened by years of economic frugality, but it still possessed almost 10,000 artillery pieces, rocket launchers and long-range guns, ready to devastate Seoul and other cities well within their range. Though North Korea would undoubtedly lose in the end, no one willingly contemplated facing the deadly interim period when thousands of lives would be lost and the destruction in the South would be high. In addition, the US was gearing up for an attack on Iraq, and did not want to begin wars on two fronts simultaneously. Its preferred choice was to gather behind it the east Asian nations – Japan and South Korea – that would be most immediately threatened to impose economic penalties on North Korea, including, if necessary, an economic embargo.

Asia and Australia

To its chagrin, neither were wholeheartedly behind such actions. Rather, they each encouraged Washington to enter into negotiations with Pyongyang, suggesting that it would return to the status quo ante in exchange for economic and technical aid.

In January 2003, North Korea withdrew from the Nuclear Non-Proliferation Treaty (NPT) arguing that this action was a result of hostile actions previously taken by the US and the IAEA, while at the same time asserting that it had no intention of producing nuclear weapons. Following a Pyongyang announcement in early February that it was restarting its nuclear facilities 'for the production of electricity' the Board of Governors of the IAEA formally found North Korea in violation of its NPT safeguards and forwarded the matter to the Security Council for action. Despite US hopes that a condemnation of North Korea would encourage firmer action, it was clear that neither China nor Russia, both veto-wielding members, were inclined to encourage such action; both felt that this would be provocative. The US decided that it would be useful, both to show the flag and to prepare for any worst-case eventuality, to deploy additional stealth bombers to the area, leading Pyongyang to warn that it might engage in a pre-emptive strike of its own if opposing offensive forces were enlarged and alerted. In a typical show of North Korean bravado, on 1 March 2003 four North Korean fighter planes buzzed a US RC-135 reconnaissance aircraft over international waters. Later in March, the US increased its deployment of bombers to Guam and sent a few stealth bombers to South Korea.

Tensions were once again getting out of hand. US Secretary of State Colin Powell used the opportunity afforded by his trip to represent the US at the 25 February 2003 inauguration of the newly elected President of South Korea, Roh Moo Hyun, to stop off in Beijing. He hoped to encourage China to persuade North Korea to take part in five-power talks, involving North and South Korea, the US, China and Japan, to seek an accommodation on the nuclear question. China had been publicly backing a peaceful dialogue between the US and North Korea as the best way forward; privately it had been telling the US that it had little or no influence over North Korea. This humble stance was creative with the truth. China's economic aid to North Korea, particularly its food and energy aid, gave it some clout; its status as the last government to act in a reasonably friendly way added to its stature vis-à-vis the DPRK. In any event, Beijing soon changed its position. Although China would have felt more comfortable playing a role on the sidelines, it apparently had concluded that tensions in the area had begun to reach such dangerous levels that a more direct role was called for. Both the language being used by the two antagonists, and their actions, were seriously rocking the stability in east Asia that China desired and needed to allow its domestic political and economic transition to proceed without regional distractions.

In early March, China proposed to North Korea that it join with Beijing in three-party talks on the nuclear question. This compromise of Washington's suggested five-party talks was probably a realistic acknowledgment that Pyongyang, which had been insisting on direct two-party talks with Washington, would balk at a radical departure from its position. China sweetened the suggestion by noting that since it was hosting the talks in Beijing, there would be opportunities for the two antagonists to talk privately outside the formal sessions. Apparently to make it clear how seriously it viewed the initiative it had presented, China reportedly temporarily halted 'for technical reasons' its shipment of oil supplies that Pyongyang could hardly do without. Then, in conjunction with Russia, China blocked any move towards action by the Security Council to pressure North Korea.

This adroit set of manoeuvres had the desired effect. On 12 April, Pyongyang announced that it would be flexible about the format and would take part in the three-party talks Beijing had proposed. The United States, pleased that Beijing had decided to play a mediating role, felt that it could not now turn down the opportunity, even if it did not include South Korea and Japan (though before it agreed, Washington had cleared the decision to participate with those two nations). The talks, held from 23 to 25 April 2003, got off to a bad start. On 18 April, Pyongyang, broadcasting an English translation of a government statement, declared that it had begun reprocessing its spent nuclear fuel into weapons-grade plutonium. Only after US and South Korean analysts deconstructed the original statement in Korean did it become clear that what was being said was that Pyongyang was ready to begin producing plutonium, not that it had already begun to do so. The kerfuffle, however, triggered a renewed argument in Washington between the State Department and hardliners in the Pentagon and Vice-President Cheney's office over how to deal with North Korea. Powell argued that the US should have no conditions for talks, but insist that Pyongyang get no aid until it agreed to dismantle its nuclear programme. The hardliners were against any talks, and wanted to use the swift victory in Iraq to put pressure on North Korea until it dropped its programme or until its economy, and thus its regime, collapsed.

Although the talks proceeded, they did nothing to clear the air. The North Koreans had come to Beijing expecting to meet the US in informal bilateral meetings; the US delegation was under instructions not to do so under any circumstances. In the formal sessions there were reiterated exchanges of the basic positions held by both sides without a hint that negotiation was possible. Pyongyang put forward the notion of a phased settlement of the impasse: in four stages, the US, Japan and South Korea would be expected to provide a renewal of aid, then a non-aggression pact, then normalisation of relations in exchange for a series of North Korean promises with regard to its nuclear programme. Only in the last stage,

Asia and Australia

which would not occur until the two light-water reactors were up and running, would Pyongyang dismantle its nuclear weapons facilities. The US dismissed this proposal contemptuously and restated its own basic position. It would be prepared to provide economic and diplomatic benefits only after North Korea disarmed 'completely, irreversibly and verifiably'. Not surprisingly, the talks broke up without a communiqué.

Acrimony reigned for the next three months. Washington decided it would resume talks only if South Korea and Japan were included. It also moved to impose a blockage of the movement of goods that could be used for proliferation purposes. This effort, while ostensibly worldwide, was developed with North Korea primarily in mind; it resulted in President Bush's proclamation of the Proliferation Security Initiative at the end of May 2003. In July, North Korea informed the US that it had reprocessed the 8,000 fuel rods that had been kept under surveillance by the IAEA since 1994. US intelligence had picked up indications that some activity of this kind had been underway in May and June, but there was some doubt that Pyongyang had completed the processing as it claimed.

While the two antagonists were trading unpleasantries in word and deed, China was working hard to find a way to bring them back to the negotiating table. At the end of July 2003 it succeeded: Pyongyang agreed to attend six-party talks (North and South Korea, US, China, Japan and Russia) and Washington agreed to meet North Korea in informal bilateral talks alongside the formal multilateral sessions. China had burnished its bona fides with Pyongyang by joining Russia in blocking an attempt in the UN Security Council in mid-July to condemn North Korea for its flouting of non-proliferation norms.

The six-party talks, which took place on 27–29 August 2003, could hardly be considered a resounding success, but they did represent a glimmer of a beginning towards a peaceful solution. Although there is no indication that the bilateral US–North Korea meeting which took place on the first day of the formal sessions made much progress, the two nations at least did meet and talk. The formal sessions provided only the barest of change in substance. North Korea iterated its proposal of simultaneous steps, but intimated that it could move a freeze on its nuclear activities to the first step. In its usual method of mixing threats with any sign of compromise, it said that if no solution were reached soon it would publicly proclaim its possession of nuclear weapons and conduct a nuclear weapons test. It also expressed surprise and displeasure that the US had not responded to its April proposals with a counter-proposal. For its part, the US maintained that its proposals contained a concept of moving forward in stages, thus hinting that it was conceivable that it could find a way to provide aid before Pyongyang arrived at complete and irrevocable disarmament. But again neither side felt that it could sign a closing joint communiqué despite China's best efforts.

Instead, China took it upon itself to issue a chairman's statement that summarised its sense of what had been achieved. This included a purported agreement among the parties on a peaceful solution based on a denuclearised Korean Peninsula that would be arrived at through 'stages and through synchronous or parallel implementation in a just and reasonable manner' – a usefully woolly diplomatic statement that either side could read as it wished. China also noted that there had been agreement for the six-party talks to resume as soon as possible. It hoped to arrange for this second round to take place around mid-October 2003. In the interim, it took it upon itself, through consultations with each side, to create a statement of principles that would form the basis for the discussions to come.

This proved a thankless task. North Korea balked at joining another meeting in October; perhaps believing that the US, now deeply embroiled in Iraq, would be willing to buy its attendance with a relaxation of its demands. Having turned down China on the question of a meeting, Pyongyang instead announced on 2 October that it had completed reprocessing its 8,000 spent fuel rods and had added the resultant plutonium to its bomb-making potential. US intelligence estimated that this would be enough for a few nuclear devices, although it still could not be sure that Pyongyang had in fact successfully finished the job. President Bush used a meeting with Chinese President Huo Jintao in Bangkok on 19 October to announce a slight easing of the US position: he intimated that the US was willing to sign a written multinational security guarantee for North Korea if Pyongyang was prepared to abandon its nuclear ambitions. At the end of October, North Korea announced that it was willing to accept such a multinational guarantee if it were part of a package for a solution to the nuclear impasse. China hoped these small signs of accommodation from both sides would pay off. It floated a draft of principles and tried to set up another six-party meeting for mid-December 2003. The US, South Korea and Japan countered with their own draft, arguing that China's leaned too far in North Korea's favour, but this was quickly discounted by Pyongyang. The new year dawned with both sides apparently as much at loggerheads as they had been throughout 2003.

This public perception masked more salutary behind-the-scenes activity. In early January, North Korea announced a 'bold' concession. It would freeze its construction and testing of nuclear weapons and in addition shut down all of its nuclear reactors, even those engaged in the peaceful energy production, in exchange for a non-aggression pact with the US, along with many other things. Although no one knew of any power-generating nuclear plants in North Korea, this did suggest some movement. Pyongyang then invited an unofficial five-person group from the US and showed them what it claimed was bomb-usable plutonium, perhaps believing that this would buttress its position in future talks. China, trying to lubricate the rails to a meeting in February, developed a somewhat more accommodating position

Asia and Australia

based on the possibility that North Korea did not have a programme of uranium enrichment – against American claims and in line with North Korean contentions. South Korea, whose new president Roh Moo Hyun had never backed away from the 'sunshine policy' of his predecessor, Kim Dae Jung, towards the North but had little political space in which to carry it forward, weighed in with a suggestion that it was prepared to offer more inducements to improve the prospects for better relations.

Specifically, Seoul would offer economic aid in return for a North Korean pledge to freeze its nuclear weapons activities and eventually to dismantle them. South Korea was reported ready to resume the fuel oil shipments that had been suspended at the end of 2002. China was also ready to provide new economic aid: it was reported that Beijing had offered to set up a bottle manufacturing plant in honour of Kim Jong Il's birthday to entice the North to join renewed talks. The US, which had been adamant about not rewarding North Korea just for a freeze, was willing to use these offers as a screen for what in effect was a considerable change in its long-held positions. Powell maintained that the US would not offer any economic aid, though it might agree to support the security assurances it had earlier mentioned. Still, it was clear that South Korea could not have made its offer without firm, if informal, agreement from Washington. The upshot was renewed six-party talks, which opened in Beijing on 25 February 2004 and ended late on 28 February.

Yet again the talks concluded without a formal communiqué, despite China's holding open the last session for hours after it was to have ended in the hope of hammering one out. But the tone of these talks was far more conciliatory than at any time since the crisis had broken. Both the US and North Korea said that they were dedicated to deepening their negotiations over nuclear weapons and they pledged to meet in smaller working groups, aiming at another six-party meeting before the end of June. Both senior US officials and North Korea's top negotiator, Kim Kye Kwan, said that while deep disagreements remained, the talks had been useful. Kim noted that there had been substantive discussions concerning the nuclear issue and that his delegation had 'adopted a businesslike attitude with the intention of resolving the issue peacefully through dialogue and negotiations'.

The most significant advance came through agreements reached by North and South Korea regarding what China labelled the first stage in dismantling North Korea's nuclear programme. The North offered to freeze its nuclear developments in exchange for aid; the South then offered energy assistance with the proviso that the freeze was recognised as the first step toward disarmament. China and Russia stepped in with promises of additional aid in support of the South. Although such a deal smacked of what the US had been characterising as submitting to blackmail, the US, joined by Japan, said that while it would not itself provide aid at this time it 'understood and supported' plans by others to make energy supplies available even before North Korea's nuclear programme was completely dismantled. However, the main stumbling block was US (and Japanese) insistence that the freeze must include North Korea's clandestine enrichment programme, as well as its known plutonium production facilities, and North Korea's refusal even to acknowledge the existence of the enrichment programme, despite the Pakistani government's public admittance that its nuclear scientists had provided enrichment technology to North Korea in the late 1990s.

The US was also encouraged by what it saw as sufficient flexibility on the part of the North Korean negotiators early in the talks, with some North Korean delegates giving the impression that they might accept the US formula of 'complete, irreversible and verifiable' nuclear disarmament. In the event, Pyongyang turned this step down, but the US claimed that it was pleased that everyone else had accepted the formula and that it was therefore now firmly on the agenda. The Chinese chairman said in his closing statement: 'Differences, even serious differences still exist. The road is long and bumpy. But time is on the side of peace'. All five other nations – including North Korea – acknowledged that this comment reflected their own views. Although South Korea's leadership was thrown into uncertainty when Roh Moo Hyun was impeached in March 2004, and his presidential authority assumed on an interim basis by Prime Minister Goh Kun pending a ruling on the impeachment by a constitutional court, Goh stated that he would seek to maintain Roh's policies on North Korea.

Getting there from here

It is too early to judge whether the rickety bridge that is being built between both sides will support mutually acceptable substantive agreements. A major stumbling block is whether North Korea is prepared to acknowledge its programme for the production of fissile material through uranium enrichment in addition to its admitted plutonium enrichment programme. The US claimed that it had solid intelligence pointing to the existence of uranium-enrichment efforts even before Pakistan's leading nuclear scientist, A.Q. Khan, confessed that he had supplied uranium-enrichment technology to North Korea. Yet US officials noted that they had not presented any evidence at the Beijing talks because intelligence agencies were still analysing the information. North Korea publicly denies the existence of any such programme, and has done so consistently since October 2002, when Kelly claimed that a senior North Korean diplomat had confessed to such a programme. At the same time, the North readily admits it has had a long history of cooperation with Pakistan, including selling missiles to that country.

Until this difference of positions is sorted out, arranging a mechanism for verifying a final agreement will be impossible. Although the US insists

Asia and Australia

that it knows that the North Koreans have an enrichment effort underway, it also admits that it has been unable to pinpoint where it is or what the status of the programme is. The US is aiming to develop a verification regime built on teams of nuclear experts drawn from the nations now engaged in the negotiations who will be allowed to perform follow-up challenge inspections whenever and wherever they wish. It is difficult to see the suspicious and entrenched North Korea regime allowing them such wide-ranging freedom, as they would be sure to uncover other military facilities that Pyongyang would want to keep secret. Even if North Korea agreed to declare and open its nuclear facilities to inspectors – as Libya has done – unless the US or other countries were certain, from their own intelligence sources, that these were all of North Korea's facilities they would not be willing to accept Pyongyang's assurances. The failure to uncover weapons of mass destruction in Iraq shows how difficult it is for the US to be sure about carefully hidden activities abroad. With regard to North Korea specifically, the US admits that it knows little with any certainty about its nuclear activities. Briefing Congress on 2 March 2004, Kelly said that it was quite possible that North Korea had turned all of the 8,000 spent fuel rods into plutonium for nuclear weapons, but that the US had not changed its formal intelligence assessments of North Korea's arsenal because 'we don't know for sure'.

This uncertainty concerning North Korea's capabilities parallels uncertainty about its intentions. At each step along the threatening path that Pyongyang has been following through 2003, it has been careful not to completely foreclose the option of reversing course if inducements were big enough. It may feel that only possession of nuclear weapons will protect it from the enemies that surround it. Yet it is difficult to resist the notion that North Korea is a mouse that roared (albeit probably one with nuclear weapons): one that is prepared to accept constraints on its nuclear arsenal for more aid and pledges of non-aggression. Even if some important members of his administration do not agree, Bush has apparently accepted that negotiations, however long and difficult, constitute the most attractive option available to the US. If nothing else, the US must demonstrate that a negotiated solution is impossible before it can appeal to other countries to apply economic and political sanctions designed to pressure or even remove the North Korean regime. The concept of graduated steps, with each side giving enough for the other to be willing to go on to the next step, appears to have become the operative mode, but the details of a staged approach remain highly contentious within Washington. North Korea is not likely to upset the present equilibrium, or to give too much ground, until it sees how the US election is decided, and Bush is unlikely to countenance a new initiative during an election campaign. Whether a diplomatic solution is possible will likely remain unclear until the next US administration takes office.

China's Anxious Activism

By March 2003, the leadership transition that had so preoccupied Beijing throughout the preceding year had formally been accomplished. Hu Jintao, long ago anointed by late paramount leader Deng Xiaoping for eventual succession to the highest offices, had been appointed both Secretary-General of the ruling Chinese Communist Party and President of the People's Republic of China. His predecessor Jiang Zemin's success in retaining command of the armed forces through his chairmanship of the Central Military Commission, and his facility in populating all of the main decision-making bodies with close associates and protégés who could anticipate his wishes, underlined the partial and anomalous nature of this transition. But its outcome, while pointing to a more cumbersome administration, ultimately did not excite sufficient controversy to threaten fundamental alignments within the Party, whose factions continued to be bound together by a collective sense of political insecurity expressed in a common desire to project confidence and unanimity. Against this backdrop, China's first manned spaceflight in October 2003, which saw the astronaut Yang Liwei orbit the planet in the *Shenzhou*-5 module and achieve heroic status in China, provided a welcome patriotic rallying point and an undiluted a success with which the leadership could – and did – associate itself. The mission was characterised as a 'coming of age' moment, and as providing the plainest demonstration of China's increasing modernity, technological prowess and ambitiousness.

Such feats apart, and as much as Beijing's leaders may have hoped for a period of relative tranquillity in which fully to digest and settle into the new political dispensation, they have over the last year been tested by a variety of domestic and foreign policy challenges. At home, the leadership's inadequate early handling of the outbreak of Severe Acute Respiratory Syndrome (SARS), which reached its peak in the spring of 2003, threatened to inflict lasting damage on public confidence and China's international reputation. In July 2003, efforts to incorporate strict anti-subversion legislation favoured by Beijing into Hong Kong's constitution brought half a million of the territory's citizens onto the streets in protest at this perceived threat to civil liberties. Hong Kong's pro-Beijing administration was plunged into some disarray, and has remained on an unsteady back foot ever since.

Abroad, Beijing found itself drawn ever more intimately into efforts to resolve the crisis sparked by North Korea's resumed nuclear activities, both by hosting multilateral talks between regional powers and attempting to construct a framework for substantive negotiations. If Beijing had little expectation that Pyongyang and Washington would quickly be cajoled into creating a new species of settlement to replace the failed Agreed Framework of 1994, there was nevertheless the hope that talks, if they could be sustained, would lessen the risk of an unmanageable escalation of tensions.

By late 2003, Beijing's attention was increasingly absorbed by political developments in Taiwan, where presidential elections were to be held on 20 March 2004. An emboldened Taiwanese President Chen Shui-bian, seeking both to placate disaffected grassroots supporters from the pro-independence wing of the political spectrum – many of whom resented his initial tepidness in asserting Taiwan's identity – and to divert attention away from his administration's unimpressive record on economic management and other facets of domestic policy, made the military threat from China the centrepiece of his re-election campaign. His decision to call an unprecedented 'defensive referendum' on this issue to coincide with the presidential election, and his plans to push ahead with the drafting of a new constitution whose eventual promulgation – also by plebiscite – Beijing would regard as a step perilously close to a formal declaration of independence, unleashed a furious but ultimately futile campaign by China to mobilise international pressure against Taipei. It caused significant discomfort in the triangular relationship between the United States, China and Taiwan. Chen's extremely narrow – and disputed – re-election victory exasperated China and held out the prospect of a prolonged period of tension, with all the attendant military risks this entailed.

In Beijing's calculations, these various crises and distractions helped to confirm the importance of keeping the crucial relationship with the United States on track, even when differences – some related to the looming US presidential election – over China's trade policy, human-rights record and proliferation behaviour began to resurface from mid-2003. Indeed, as cross-Strait tensions had grown more bitter, and recognising its own lack of effective levers of influence over Taiwan's leadership, Beijing increasingly looked to the United States to exert pressure on Chen Shui-bian not to take further steps that China would consider provocative. Yet, at the same time, a lingering apprehension regarding America's global strategic predominance, and its perceived tendency to exert this in ways detrimental to China's interests, gave Beijing a powerful incentive to hedge by seeking out new partners and expanding its international influence. All of this was evident in China's increasingly vigorous embrace of the European Union (EU) and its continuing overtures to the ten-member Association of Southeast Asian Nations (ASEAN).

Under new management?
Although the Communist Party suffers from factional tensions between groupings led by Jiang Zemin and Hu Jintao, respectively, these have not taken the form of a brutal confrontation. Nor has the contest been one

focused on fundamental matters of policy. There appears to be broad agreement on the need to ensure social stability by deepening reforms to an economy that has shown worrying signs of overheating and imbalance; to give particular attention to problems in distressed rural areas; and to make the Communist Party more appealing and relevant to an increasingly demanding and sophisticated urban entrepreneurial class. To this last end, the Communist Party, having already agreed to admit businessmen to its ranks, in March 2004 enacted constitutional revisions that afford protection to private property.

The factional dispute is primarily one about relative position and influence. At issue has been the extent to which Hu has succeeded over the last year in establishing himself in the face of a dominant Jiang faction that is disproportionately well-represented in the highest decision-making body, the Politburo Standing Committee. The evidence is mixed. In the Kremlinological manner still relevant to China's political system, Jiang's continuing high visibility in the state broadcast and print media, where his speeches and public appearances are prominently reported, appears designed to underline his continuing pre-eminence. Personnel changes instigated by Jiang within the People's Liberation Army (PLA) in January 2004, which involved the reshuffling of 24 senior generals, witnessed the elevation of Jiang loyalists and were seen as consistent with his ongoing efforts to consolidate power. Moreover, Hu Jintao has himself been notably deferential in his public references to various ideological precepts, principally the 'Three Represents' theory, which are closely associated with Jiang, and whose somewhat opaque terms now provide much of the vocabulary of official political discourse in China.

Yet there were also indications that Hu Jintao has been able to engineer the appointment of allies to a number of provincial positions, from where they might in time migrate to the political centre in Beijing. In addition, Hu is thought to have assumed chairmanship of several important policy committees, including the Leading Small Group on Foreign Affairs and the Leading Small Group on Taiwan Affairs. Although such advances are comparatively slight, Hu has begun to carve out a distinct public persona that stands in contrast to the stuffy, status-conscious and elitist tendencies for which his predecessor was criticised. Hu has also manifested a limited concern for greater openness and transparency in the conduct of government. Meetings of the Politburo, its Standing Committee and of the State Council (cabinet) are now regularly reported in the press. In 2003, Hu took the further step of abolishing the annual August leadership conclave in the coastal resort of Beidaihe – deflecting charges that the leadership enjoyed unusual privilege and usefully depriving Communist Party elders of an informal mechanism through which to oppose Hu's interests. None of these initiatives, however, indicated an appetite for more thoroughgoing political reform and pluralism.

Hu and Premier Wen Jiabao both emerged reasonably well from the SARS outbreak, a problem initially exacerbated by attempts to conceal its full extent from domestic and international publics. In April 2003, Hu and Wen's sacking of the health minister and of the mayor of Beijing, who had been associated with the cover-up, combined with a resort to draconian state powers to halt the spread of the virus, reflected firm leadership against accusations of cynicism and incompetence. Hu and Wen's public visibility, moreover, contrasted with the conspicuously low profiles adopted throughout the crisis by Jiang (who had decamped to Shanghai) and his chief lieutenant, Vice-President Zeng Qinghong, (Jiang's closest lieutenant and the man seen as the most credible future challenger to Hu).

Meanwhile, the debacle surrounding the attempted introduction in Hong Kong of a new state security law (the so-called Article 23) to protect the Chinese state from acts of sedition, treason and subversion committed in the territory, proved troublesome to Jiang and Zeng, whom the public most closely associated with it. Mass protest in July 2003 forced the territory's Beijing-appointed chief executive, Tung Chee-hwa, to shelve the legislation indefinitely pending further consultations. The bill galvanised and animated pro-democracy groups, who characterised its terms as an egregious infringement on civil liberties as well as an affront to the promise of a 'high degree of autonomy' that China had made Hong Kong under the 'one country, two systems' formula enshrined in its Basic Law. With its faith in Tung's abilities shaken, and public disapprobation having already led to the punishment of pro-Beijing political parties in District Council polls held in November 2003, Beijing grew increasingly alarmed at the prospect that the pro-democracy parties would capture control of the Hong Kong Legislative Council in the September 2004 elections, and then permanently impede passage of Article 23 and agitate for political reforms permitted under the Basic Law from 2007–08. Such reforms would include the direct election of all Legislative Council seats as well as the chief executive, implying a loss of Beijing's capacity to shape developments in the territory. Beijing anticipatorily began to argue that the pace at which constitutional reforms could take place would be for the central authorities in China to decide. The scene was thus being set for greater tension between Hong Kong and the mainland in 2004 and beyond.

Taiwanese travails

As Taiwan prepared for presidential elections in 2004, Taiwan President Chen Shui-bian saw developments in Hong Kong as a cautionary tale, with Beijing's interventionism providing a warning to those in Taiwan who might be tempted by China's standing offer to reunify with the island on the basis of a 'one country, two systems' formula similar to that granted Hong Kong in 1997 and Macao in 1999. Meanwhile, having seized on the

SARS outbreak to again argue the case for Taipei to be granted observer status within the World Health Organisation (WHO), Chen characterised Beijing's vehement resistance to this proposal as callous. China retorted that Chen was motivated only to expand Taiwan's diplomatic space, and had no real medical agenda. Thus rebuffed, Chen in May 2003 announced his determination to hold a referendum that would allow the population of Taiwan to voice its support for WHO membership, adding that plebiscites would also provide a suitable mechanism for deciding contentious matters of domestic policy, such as the construction of nuclear power plants. Fearing that a referendum on even comparatively mundane matters would set a precedent for a plebiscite on the status of the island and lead to a formal declaration of independence, Beijing treated these developments with increasing seriousness and alarm. Its sense that the Chen administration was marching towards more radical and dangerous policy positions appeared essentially correct.

By the middle of 2003, it seemed reasonable to assume that Chen faced defeat in the presidential election. Whereas he owed his narrow victory in the 2000 poll to a split in the opposition vote between Lien Chan's Kuomintang (KMT) and James Soong's People First Party (PFP), these forces were now ranged against him on a joint ticket. Obstructed in its domestic policies by an opposition-dominated legislature, and with an unenviable record on economic policy, the Chen administration had few notable successes to advertise and had disappointed his grassroots supporters by the cautiousness of his administration on domestic as well as cross-Strait policy. Chen thus seemed liberated to focus his re-election campaign on the issue of Taiwan's international identity and its relationship to China.

In June, Taipei announced that passports would in future carry the word 'Taiwan' in English (having been restricted to the island's formal name of 'Republic of China'), with the first of these being issued in September 2003. Much more significantly, the Chen administration began to elaborate plans for a new constitution, to be drawn up between 2005 and 2007 and promulgated by May 2008 – coinciding with the end of what Chen hoped would be his second term. Beijing saw this plan for a new constitution, to be adopted by plebiscite rather than growing organically out of the 1940s-era Republic of China charter, as approaching a de facto declaration of independence – and not an attempt, as some in Taipei claimed, to correct longstanding bureaucratic anomalies. Moreover, the timetable for constitutional reform left Beijing in no doubt that Chen was attempting to exploit a window of opportunity to assert Taiwan's identity, capitalising on China's still limited military options towards the island, as well its aversion to conflict pending the 2008 Olympic Games in Beijing. For a trip to Panama for its 100th anniversary celebration, Chen secured a transit visa from the US that allowed him to hold high-profile meetings in New York.

Asia and Australia

In Panama itself, Chen on 3 November scored the symbolic success of shaking the hand of US Secretary of State Colin Powell. This move further incensed Beijing. On 7 November, Taipei induced the Pacific island state of Kiribati to switch diplomatic recognition from China to Taiwan, thus depriving Beijing of a valued satellite tracking facility it had stationed there. In the game of diplomatic competition, this partly offset Liberia's decision in October 2003 to recognise Beijing.

On 27 November, a bill to allow referenda was approved by Taiwan's legislature. While opposition parties had succeeded in diluting its provisions so as to make it difficult to hold a referendum on independence, they had conceded scope for a 'defensive referendum' in the event that Taiwan faced an imminent external threat to its security and sovereignty. Subsequently, Chen announced his intention to proceed with such a referendum, citing China's build-up of hundreds of short-range missiles opposite the island and its refusal to renounce the use of force in settling their dispute as providing more than sufficient grounds. Other Taiwanese politicians countered that this threat was neither new nor particularly imminent.

Having initially been comforted by the prospect of Chen's defeat at the hands of the KMT and PFP, both of which were seen as favouring better ties with China, Beijing began to feel an urgent need to respond to the changing scene. Recognising that sabre-rattling alone would play into Chen's hands, Beijing asked Washington to use its influence to rein him in. This parlay highlighted a US role in the cross-Strait dispute that had become more complicated and problematic in the preceding two years. The Bush administration had come to office pledging to expand arms sales to Taiwan to correct an emerging military imbalance, and offered explicit rhetorical support in the form of a commitment to do 'whatever it takes' to defend the island. These actions reflected the Bush administration's impatience with the limitations of the 'strategic ambiguity' on which US policy towards the cross-Strait dispute had traditionally rested. In essence, this approach theoretically deterred rash action by either side by leaving both Taipei and Beijing guessing as to the nature of Washington's precise involvement in any conflict between the two. The Bush administration instead aspired to a 'strategic clarity', in which the scope for miscalculation by all sides would be narrowed. The change of policy has been troubled at best. Through its early statements on Taiwan, the Bush administration may have emboldened sections of the pro-independence lobby who sensed that Washington's sympathies lay with Taipei. At the same time, however, increasingly vehement protestations by Beijing and Washington about the new strength of their bilateral relationship induced fears among some Taiwanese that Washington might trade concessions over the island for China's continuing acquiescence in the war on terror and efforts to address North Korea's resumed nuclear activities.

In early December, President George W. Bush sent James Moriarty, then Senior Director for Asia at the National Security Council, to Taipei for secret talks with Chen. Moriarty is understood to have conveyed a personal request from Bush for Chen to abandon the referendum on the grounds that it was unnecessarily provocative. Chen rebuffed this appeal, and on 8 December publicly set out the basis and focus of the planned referendum. This invited a public rebuke by Bush on the following day, uniquely during the course of a press conference at the White House with visiting Chinese Premier Wen Jiabao. Bush stressed that 'we oppose any unilateral decision by either China or Taiwan to change the status quo ... and the comments and actions by the leader of Taiwan indicate that he may be willing to make decisions unilaterally, to change the status quo, which we oppose'.

In Beijing, these reproaches were taken as an unqualified diplomatic triumph; in Washington, conservative opinion lambasted the Bush administration for its alleged hypocrisy in championing democracy in the Middle East while seeking to prevent Taiwan from exercising its right to test public opinion on a major issue. For other commentators, however, the circumstantial and presentational aspects of Bush's remarks had obscured their full content, particularly insofar as the strengthened American attachment to the 'status quo' in the Taiwan Strait seemed to preclude reunification with China just as much as it did a declaration of independence. Although Chen did not retreat from the referendum, scheduled to coincide with the presidential election on 20 March, the questions he unveiled in mid-January were less alarming and more anodyne than the Bush administration – and Beijing – had initially feared. The first question sought approval for steps to acquire (presumably from the United States, if Washington was indeed minded to cooperate) 'anti-missile weapons' in the event that China did not withdraw missiles deployed opposite the island and renounce the use of force. The second question invited views on whether Taipei should seek negotiations with China for the purpose of establishing a 'peace and stability framework'.

As election day drew nearer, it became apparent that support for Chen Shui-bian and Lien Chan was finely balanced, with a sizeable proportion of the electorate undecided. A sense of crisis descended on the eve of the election on 19 March, when Chen and Vice-President Annette Lu were shot by an unidentified gunman while campaigning in the southern city of Tainan. Lu was only grazed and Chen suffered a relatively minor stomach wound. Speculation about the precise electoral impact of this incident assumed considerable significance, as the tally showed that Chen had been re-elected by a slender margin of 30,000 votes. Lien Chan called for a recount while also pledging to challenge the legality of the election, and implied that Chen may have staged an assassination attempt to attract sympathy votes. Other electoral irregularities were also alleged. Meanwhile, in a significant reversal for Chen, the referendum that had caused so much controversy and

Asia and Australia

had been pushed through at immense diplomatic cost to his administration was formally pronounced a failure, as less than 50% of the electorate had seen fit to participate in it. Many of those who did not vote believed the refereundum to be a contrived and unenessary partisan ploy.

The election quickly poisoned the political atmosphere. Under pressure from opposition parties, whose supporters staged a series of mass demonstrations, and with Washington deafeningly silent on the result, Chen conceded a recount of the vote. As *Strategic Survey* went to press, the modalities of the recount had yet to be agreed upon, and the opposition parties were still pushing hard for an offiical inquiry into the shooting of Chen and Lu in the expectation – or the hope – that this would uncover foul play. A period of political upheaval appeared inevitable. On one hand, if the poll result was invalidated, there seemed no immediate reason to suppose that a new tally or even fresh elections would necessarily yield a more decisive or accepted outcome. On the other hand, if the 20 March result were upheld, Chen's legitimacy would continue to be challenged by the KMT and PFP, which would seek to strengthen their grip on the legislature in general elections scheduled for December 2004 and then enfeeble Chen's administration to the point of collapse.

Observing developments from afar, Beijing largely maintained a studied silence, acutely aware that any rhetorical intervention would have to be timed and calibrated correctly. At one point, its officials suggested darkly that China would not stand by if Taiwan descended into political and social chaos. But no action followed. For its part, China may have drawn some comfort from the relative weakness of Chen's overall position and particularly the fate of his referendum, which provided neither a satisfactory precedent for future plebiscites nor a basis for further policy departures. Nonetheless, Beijing recognised that Chen, if re-appointed, could be expected to advance his plans for constitutional reform and assert Taiwan's identity over the next four years. Nor could it ignore the fact that his share of the vote had virtually doubled between 2000 and 2004. Chen's willingness to defy Washington in the period leading up the election, thus souring the relationship between Bush and Chen, was also troubling to China. Doubts arose about the true extent of America's restraining influence over Taipei. And while Beijing hoped that the KMT–PFP alliance would act as a domestic constraint on Chen, it had also to entertain the possibility that this marriage of convenience might subside into bickering and divorce. At the very least, a question mark would continue to hover over Lien's future as leader of the KMT. In consequence, there continues to be a risk that, in the face of further 'provocation', Beijing might conclude that it has no choice but to resort to coercive measures towards Taiwan. The issue of Taiwan's status has become intimately bound up in the Chinese Communist Party's domestic legitimacy and is a key determinant of its political survival. Accordingly, it would be imprudent to assume that the risks of military failure, economic dislocation and damage to China's international reputation would be sufficiently powerful to deter Beijing from precipitate action if it believed a declaration of independence was imminent. In these circumstances, the importance of continuing American engagement of both Taipei and Beijing became obvious.

Living with North Korea

Washington and Beijing were each preoccupied by other foreign and domestic policy matters, and recognised that there were certain issues on which one side was of use to the other. Thus, China and the United States exhibited a strong desire to prevent such differences as did arise from unbalancing the relationship as a whole. The tensions produced by the resumed nuclear activities of North Korea, which in 2003–04 claimed to have reprocessed nuclear material formerly under International Atomic Energy Agency inspection and to be near fabricating it into nuclear weapons, provided a focus for much Sino-American diplomatic interaction. Beijing found itself in the unaccustomed position of interlocutor between Washington and Pyongyang: an 'honest broker' role for which it seemed uniquely qualified in northeast Asia.

China's unusual activism was partly a by-product of the Bush administration's reluctance to be drawn into an exclusive bilateral dialogue with Pyongyang, arguing that the regional dimensions of the crisis demanded a multilateral diplomatic approach. An internally divided Bush administration also had trouble settling on an agreed policy towards Pyongyang. Beijing feared that the absence of contact between Washington and Pyongyang would only harden positions and create a greater risk of escalation towards war or a regionally destabilising collapse of the neighbouring North Korean regime as Washington tilted towards a sanctions- and pressure-based strategy. Nevertheless, China initially saw a strictly limited role for itself. In convening trilateral talks in Beijing on 23–25 April 2003, China believed it was kick-starting and providing a fig leaf for direct negotiations between Pyongyang and Washington. Indeed, it was on this implied basis that Beijing was able to convince North Korea, which initially had no interest in multilateral discussions, to take part. Yet the acrimonious tone of the April talks – in which Washington restated its demand for North Korea's complete, irreversible and verifiable disarmament and Pyongyang threatened to advance its capabilities unless provided with security guarantees and abundant economic and political benefits – persuaded China that it would have to do much of the diplomatic heavy lifting if further discussions were to come about. In the months that followed, Beijing threw its energies into convening six-party talks (involving North and South Korea, Russia, Japan, China and the United States), with the first round taking place in late August. Beijing was again crucial in bringing North Korea to the table, having probably convinced Pyongyang that the expanded format was not necessarily threatening to its interests; indeed, Pyongyang began to realise that Washington might come under pressure from other participants to dilute its maximalist demands in favour of more limited and achievable goals.

China sought to reinforce such reassurances, and increase its influence in Pyongyang, through more regular and senior-level contacts between Chinese civilian and military leaders and their North Korean counterparts. A few days before the April talks, President Hu Jintao had received Vice-Marshal Jo Myong Rok, the deputy chairman of North Korea's Defence Commission, in Beijing. In mid-July, Hu sent Vice-Foreign Minister Dai Bingguo to Pyongyang, reportedly bearing a personal letter encouraging North Korean leader Kim Jong Il to allow his negotiators to participate in the six-party talks. Then, shortly prior to the August meeting, Xu Caihou, a vice-chairman of China's Central Military Commission, led a delegation to Pyongyang for talks with both Kim Jong Il and Vice-Marshal Jo. This pattern was sustained into late 2003 and early 2004, as China's second most senior leader, Wu Bangguo, travelled to Pyongyang at the end of October, and Li Zhaoxing in late March 2004 became the first Chinese foreign minister to visit North Korea in five years.

The cordiality demonstrated on such occasions only partially obscured China's increasing impatience with North Korea's antics, and in the course of 2003 Beijing also sent less agreeable signals to Pyongyang: the temporary 'technical fault' that cut off Chinese energy supplies to North Korea ahead of the April talks and the subsequent supposedly 'routine' deployment of sizeable PLA forces to the Sino-North Korean border to replace non-military guards were both construed as subtle pressure on Pyongyang to behave cooperatively. But Beijing continued to sympathise with core aspects of North Korea's substantive position. It stressed that any diplomatic solution would have to reflect legitimate North Korean security concerns, and worried that Washington's demand that Pyongyang immediately denude itself of its principal military assets for no immediate rewards was not credible. On occasion, Chinese officials gave the impression that they saw Washington as the primary obstacle to a solution. In the meantime, China worked with Russia to prevent the North Korean crisis from being referred to the UN Security Council, fearing that Pyongyang would – as it had threatened – regard any sanctions levied by the UN as tantamount to an act of war.

The mere fact that the six-party talks were held as planned in August was a diplomatic success for which China secured much of the credit. Yet the failure to achieve a substantive breakthrough convinced Beijing of the need to devise, in the form of a communiqué, a clearer framework for the ongoing dialogue. Beijing aimed to have this in place by December 2003, when it hoped a second round of talks would be held. But even the additional negotiating time granted by the slippage of this round to 25–27 February 2004 did not enable Washington and Pyongyang to overcome differences on the terms of the communiqué. The two sides differed in particular on what sequence North Korea's disarmament might follow. North Korea offered limited disarmament steps that would be matched by simultaneous and substantial rewards, whereas Washington favoured significant disarmament steps followed by the delivery of limited benefits, with the most important withheld until North Korea's disarmament could be verifiably established. Nor did the February talks achieve progress on the issue of North Korea's offer to freeze elements of its nuclear weapons programme in return for energy assistance. Although Beijing and Seoul appeared tantalised by this offer, Washington argued that any freeze would have to extend to North Korea's clandestine uranium-enrichment programme (whose existence Pyongyang continued to deny) as well as its plutonium-based facilities and would have to be properly verified, lest North Korea be able to advance its nuclear programme under cover of negotiations. The talks did, however, result in a commitment to meet again in July or August 2004, and to establish working groups that would meet in the interim to address specific issues.

The six-party talks established China's credentials as a responsible and constructive regional power. Beijing's role has become increasingly pivotal. North Korea recognises that it cannot take steps, such as missile or even nuclear tests, intended to put pressure on the United States without inviting the severe disapproval of Beijing, on which it depends for food and fuel aid. Even those in Washington who favour a tougher approach to North Korea recognise that the six-party talks cannot be withdrawn from lightly on account of China's heavy diplomatic investment in them. But as it looked ahead, Beijing worried that this delicate balance might yet be upset. There was a risk that North Korea would sense an opportunity in the run-up to the US presidential election to stir up a crisis intended to dim Bush's chances for re-election and favour a less hostile Democratic nominee; alternatively, if Bush's re-election seemed inevitable, North Korea might decide to press ahead with its nuclear programme so as to confront a second Bush administration from a position of greater strength. Beijing was also concerned that a re-elected Bush might see himself as freer to adopt a more coercive approach towards Pyongyang – one to which China was expected to subscribe. In these circumstances, Beijing and Washington's conflicting priorities – with the US focusing primarily on the threat of proliferation, and China on averting regime collapse in North Korea – might be thrown into sharper relief.

The broader Sino-American relationship

Away from the issue of North Korea, the bilateral relationship between

Asia and Australia

China and the US continued to make steady progress. In September 2003, Secretary of State Powell remarked that Sino-American ties were better than at any time since President Richard Nixon's visit to China in 1972. This buoyant mood was supported by a series of successful high-level exchanges. At the start of June 2003, Presidents Bush and Hu met at the G-8 summit in Evian, where China was present at the special invitation of the French hosts. They met for a second time in late October, during the Asia Pacific Economic Cooperation (APEC) summit in Bangkok, while Chinese Premier Wen Jiabao was treated to a 19-gun salute during his December visit to Washington. Vice-President Dick Cheney, meanwhile, was scheduled to visit Beijing in mid-April 2004.

Bilateral defence diplomacy loomed particularly large in 2003 and early 2004, signalling an effort to recover from the angry suspension of military-to-military contacts that had followed the collision in April 2001 of a US surveillance aircraft and a Chinese fighter off southern China. In October, China's defence minister, Cao Gangchuan, visited Washington for meetings with Defense Secretary Donald Rumsfeld, National Security Advisor Condoleezza Rice, Powell and others. General Richard Myers, chairman of the US Joint Chiefs of Staff, travelled to China in mid-January for talks with Liang Guanglie, chief of the General Staff of the PLA. The following month, Undersecretary of Defense for Policy Douglas Feith was in the Chinese capital for discussions with his counterpart, General Xiong Guangkai, deputy chief of staff of the PLA, in the sixth round of US–China Defense Consultative Talks. North Korea, Taiwan and US plans to reconfigure military deployments in the region featured on the agenda. Although these meetings were generally characterised as positive and useful, the Pentagon's official pronouncements on Chinese military developments remained guarded. In its congressionally mandated Annual Report on the Military Power of the People's Republic of China, published in July 2003, the Pentagon again drew attention to what it saw as the rapid progress being made by the PLA in accumulating the means to coerce Taiwan and deter any intervention by the United States in a cross-Strait conflict. The report estimated that the number of short-range missiles deployed opposite the island had reached 450, assessing that the annual rate of increase had risen from around 50 to around 75 missiles. The report also charged that official Chinese data on defence expenditure considerably understated actual outlays. Such claims were rebuffed by Beijing. Even so, China announced in March 2004 that spending that year would increase by 11.6% to 21.8 billion renminbi, compared with a 9.6% increase in 2003.

Proliferation issues emerged as a source of bilateral friction in the first half of 2003, as the Bush administration imposed a series of sanctions against several state-linked Chinese entities, including the leading Norinco conglomerate, for their alleged involvement in the transfer of missile-related and other sensitive technologies to Iran. While these measures invited bad-tempered diplomatic protests, Beijing subsequently took steps to burnish its non-proliferation credentials. It did so in recognition of the Bush administration's tendency to treat adherence to non-proliferation norms as a decisive factor in determining the tone and direction of America's bilateral relationships. On 3 December, shortly before Premier Wen Jiabao's visit to Washington, Beijing published its White Paper on non-proliferation. This document set out in some detail the terms of China's evolving non-proliferation and export control mechanisms, and proclaimed China's support for international non-proliferation regimes. To support this claim, China on 26 January 2004 applied to join the voluntary Nuclear Supplier Group. Yet Beijing continued to decline invitations to join the Proliferation Security Initiative, an enterprise vehemently denounced by Pyongyang as an attempt to blockade North Korea. Meanwhile, Beijing was mildly embarrassed by US media reports in mid-February which suggested that Chinese designs for an implosion-type nuclear device had been uncovered in Libya during the voluntary dismantling of that country's weapons of mass destruction programmes. The implication was that these 1960s designs, having been passed to Pakistan by China in the 1980s, had been transferred to Libya by the network of disgraced Pakistani scientist A.Q. Khan.

China's human-rights record and trade policies were two further bones of contention. In April 2003, the Bush administration announced that it would not sponsor a resolution critical of China at that year's meeting of the UN Human Rights Commission in Geneva. However, by July US Deputy Assistant Secretary of State for East Asian and Pacific Affairs Randall Schriver was complaining publicly that specific quid pro quo commitments on human rights made by China had not been acted upon, and that Beijing appeared to be retreating from them. Then, on 21 March 2004, Washington announced that it would pursue a resolution at the 2004 UNHCR meeting, prompting Beijing angrily to suspend bilateral dialogue on human rights and to summon US Ambassador Clark T. Randt in order to lodge a protest. Within days, China produced a timely policy document outlining its claimed successes on enhancing human-rights standards.

On trade policy, US Treasury Secretary John Snow was among several of Bush administration officials who throughout 2003 and early 2004 argued that the burgeoning US trade deficit with China, which by the first quarter of 2004 had reached a staggering $125bn, was the product of an artificially undervalued Chinese currency. US officials called for Chinese capital controls to be relaxed, allowing the currency to appreciate to a level which would not only moderate the flow of exports to the US but also draw in more imports from the US to China. Beijing resisted these calls, arguing that many exports to the US were in fact manufactured by US-invested firms taking advantage of low Chinese cost structures, and that any premature liberalisation of capital controls might destabilise China's fragile financial

Asia and Australia

system. On the whole, however, this issue was handled reasonably politely by Beijing, which suspected that the Bush administration was posturing on the job-creation issue ahead of the November 2004 presidential election.

Chinese Europhilia

If China's relations with the United States waxed and waned throughout 2003 and early 2004, Beijing's ties with the European Union (EU) were much less fraught and showed every sign of brightening. Ahead of the Sixth EU–China summit in Beijing on 30 October 2003, both sides published somewhat gushing strategy papers intended to provide a conceptual framework for their relationship, articulate aspirations for its future direction and establish a wide variety of declaratory positions on economic, social and political issues. China's interest in strengthening its ties with the EU is grounded in a number of economic and political calculations. On the economic side, the incentives for engagement are obvious. Beijing has been impressed by the pace and scope of the EU's expansion and integration. After the next round of enlargement, the EU will not only have a population numbering considerably over 400 million, but a GDP of around $10 trillion (accounting for 25% of global output and matching that of the US). The EU has emerged as a leading source of foreign investment into China, and is expected to become the principal destination for Chinese exports in reasonably short order. The introduction of the euro and the launch of European Central Bank, meanwhile, has boosted Europe's influence over global monetary policy and therefore the health of the international economy in a way that China cannot ignore.

Political considerations have lately emerged as equally important to Beijing. China no longer sees the EU simply as a trade bloc. Instead, the EU is recognised as an increasingly political entity that aspires to be a major force in world affairs and is developing some of the paraphernalia of a major global power. Beijing has taken note of the Strategy Paper unveiled by EU High Representative Javier Solana at the Thessaloniki summit in June 2003, which constituted an attempt to formulate a 'National Security Strategy' and to provide a conceptual basis for the Common Foreign and Security Policy and the European Security and Defence Policy. China has also followed closely the vigorous debate in Europe concerning the development of European defence capabilities and planning facilities that are either independent of or complementary to those organised under NATO. The prospective – or, perhaps, imagined – emergence of the EU as a major global actor chimes with China's long-stated preference for the development of an international system based on the principle of 'political multipolarity and economic globalisation' (framed in the opening paragraphs of China's 'EU Policy Paper'). Although China has in recent years given the impression of having reluctantly resigned itself to the international primacy of US, apprehensions about the extent of American power and its perceived use in containing China's rise have continued to preoccupy strategists in Beijing. In the transatlantic divisions over the Iraq war and, more broadly, America's perceived penchant for unilateral action, Beijing has sensed a Sino-European convergence in strategic perspectives that seems worth investigating further.

Many of these questions about the trilateral relationship between China, the United States and Europe came into sharp focus in late 2003, as French President Jacques Chirac and German Chancellor Gerhard Schröder began to lobby publicly for the lifting on the EU ban on arms sales to China (imposed in 1989 following Tiananmen Square). In doing so, Chirac and Schröder appeared to be running ahead of their own more cautious foreign ministries and wider European opinion. But the vehemence of the French and German case made it difficult for smaller European states to dissent without fearing diplomatic retribution from China. Among the sceptical larger powers, Britain was reluctant to wage a diplomatic guerilla campaign at precisely the moment when its relations with Paris and Berlin had undergone some improvement following the Iraq trauma. London also sensed that its energies would be better used in pursuit of successes on interal EU policy matters.

Paris and Berlin argued that human-rights developments in China, while still generally unsatisfactory, were at last moving in the correct direction; that the lifting of the ban would be consistent with the new 'maturity' in Sino-European relations; that Europe was more likely to influence China through engagement than by imposing a form of pariah status on it; and that an existing EU Code of Conduct on arms transfers would severely limit the practical and military significance of lifting the ban. The Code does contain several restructive provisions: Criterion Two of the ban prohibits transfers of defence items in cases where these may be used in human-rights abuses; Criterion Three denies any transfers that may exacerbate internal tensions and armed conflict; while Criterion Five demands that full account be taken of the extent to which any transfers would be inconsistent with the preservation of 'regional peace, security and stability'. The Code's Operative Provisions, nonetheless, concede that 'the decsion to transfer or deny the trasnfer of any item of military equipment will remain at the national discretion of each Member State [i.e., member of the EU]'.

Washington derided these arguments as either flawed or cynical, and privately tended to regard them as 'protest' foreign-policy initiatives undertaken mainly because they were independent of and contrary to US wishes. In US defence circles, there was outrage that formal European allies were willing to contemplate the transfer of defence technologies to a PLA that was being configured for the possibility of a contingency involving US forces. The charge of commercial opportunism was also laid at the door of the French and Germans, who were seen as currying favours that could

Asia and Australia

be cashed in on non-military transactions in the event that military transactions did indeed prove impossible top push through. In its public remarks, the Bush administration contended that recent reversals in China's human-rights record should not be rewarded; that a lifting of the ban would send an unhelpful signal to Beijing at a time of acute tension in the Taiwan Strait; and that any future ending of the embargo would have to be preceded by efforts to make the Code of Conduct more strict and less ambiguous. On 26 January 2004, European foreign ministers agreed to set up working groups to examine the issue. Paris and Berlin wished to sustain their momentum, recognising that the accession in May of new EU members thought not to favour lifting the ban would introduce a major diplomatic hurdle.

Asian engagement

China's careful efforts over the last year to enhance its influence and standing in Europe were matched by similar endeavours closer to home. In November 2002, China reached agreement with the Association of Southeast Asian Nations (ASEAN) to establish a loose code of conduct regarding disputed territories in the South China Sea as well as a free trade agreement. These initiatives appeared to be intended not only to calm regional perceptions of any Chinese threat, but also to wean southeast Asia away from US-centric foreign policies. Further formal agreements followed in October 2003. Issuance of a 'Joint Declaration on Strategic Partnership for Peace and Prosperity', setting out scope for cooperation on economic and security matters, was accompanied by China's formal accession to ASEAN's 1976 Treaty of Amity and Cooperation, which commits parties to renounce the use of force and resolve disagreements through multilateral consultation.

At the same time, China continued to promote its proposals, aired in June 2003, for the establishment of a Security Policy Conference under the auspices of the ASEAN Regional Forum, designed to bring together, probably at the deputy defence minister level, military officials from across the region. The initiative underlined China's stated preference for multilateral approaches to security issues, and demonstrated a more proactive regional policy. Moreover, China probably sees distinct advantages in being 'present at the creation' of new security forums, giving it greater leeway to shape the terms of reference and ensure that Chinese interests are reflected in them. From Beijing's perspective, multilateral security forums may also present an alternative to an Asian security architecture that has traditionally been dominated by US bilateral alliances. Meanwhile, Beijing's approach to India reflected Chinese flexibility and diplomatic outreach, as the two powers held their first joint naval exercises in November 2003.

By contrast, China's relations with Japan remained distinctly cool. Although August 2003 marked the twenty-fifth anniversary of their Treaty of Peace and Friendship, and interaction at the defence and foreign minister level was stepped up to reflect this occasion, there was little evidence of a celebratory mood. On the Chinese side, this reflected not only customary irritation with Japanese Prime Minister Junichiro Koizumi's annual visit to the Yasukuni Shrine, but also increasing misgivings about the direction that Tokyo's defence and security policy was taking in response to the demands of the campaign against terror and developments on the Korean Peninsula. The Japanese Diet's passage of bills providing the defence forces with greater powers to respond to a terrorist attack, Tokyo's decision to press ahead with the deployment of missile-defence systems in closer collaboration with the US and its December 2003 deployment of non-combat ground troops to Iraq proved discomfiting to Beijing. Having in the past tended to see the US–Japan alliance as inhibiting Japanese 'remilitarisation', Beijing began to fear that America's post-11 September encouragement of greater Japanese activism would alter the nature of the alliance and make it a more credible instrument for containing China.

Year of living dangerously?

By April 2004, Beijing could with some satisfaction look back over three years of major foreign-policy accomplishments. Its initially antagonistic relations with the Bush administration had undergone a transformation. Its activity on the Korean Peninsula had been applauded. And its strategy of 'diplomatic diversification' had achieved better relations with Europe, southeast Asia and south Asia. All of this provided a more favourable setting for domestic economic development and the maintenance of social – that is, political – stability. Yet, for the remainder of 2004 and into 2005, China's dexterity and skill in foreign policy will be challenged repeatedly. Developments on Taiwan (an issue into which the Communist Party has sunk immense political capital) will absorb much of its energy, presumably to the detriment of the attention it can devote to the North Korean crisis. If situations in the Taiwan Strait and on the Korean Peninsula do begin to unravel, China's relations with the US could be sorely tested, with uncertainties exacerbated by the onrush of the US presidential election.

India and Pakistan: Towards Greater Bilateral Stability

As India and Pakistan prepared to resume their official-level dialogue in May–June 2004 after a three-year hiatus, prospects for greater bilateral stability loomed larger than they had for years. The past year had shown how complicated it was to manage and sustain the fledgling peace process, initiated in April 2003. There remains deep mistrust between the two countries, as well as considerable confusion and misunderstanding – some of it deliberate – between the two sides on the pace and content of the peace process. Nonetheless, since the 6 January 2004 joint press statement in Islamabad, Indian Prime Minister Atal Behari Vajpayee and Pakistani President Pervez Musharraf have had a significant political stake in the future of the peace process. At the same time, the outcome rests on two individuals and their ability to deliver.

Within Pakistan's highly charged and volatile politics, there are legitimate concerns over Musharraf's personal safety – highlighted by two assassination attempts in 11 days in December 2003. His reputation and influence is increasingly under question in light of the proliferation activities of key scientists in the nuclear weapons establishment. They are expected to decline further when he retires as army chief at the end of the year, even though he is slated to continue as president until 2007. In India, the level of commitment to the peace process by the broader political and administrative leadership is also not clear. India goes to the polls on 20 April 2004, with a new government expected to be sworn in at the end of May. Although Vajpayee could return to power as head of a coalition government, age and health are not in his favour.

Nuclear stability in the region is also a major concern. Both states fought a limited conflict in Kargil after their respective nuclear tests in the summer of 1998. Following the terrorist attack on the Indian parliament on 13 December 2001, India and Pakistan between them mobilised over a million armed personnel and came to the brink of war, which carried inherent risks of nuclear escalation. Although Delhi and Islamabad are examining the border confrontation, they may well be learning contradictory lessons, which would have serious implications for a future crisis. But the fact that the US is revitalising relations with both countries holds out the possibility that Washington will act as a 'facilitator' for easing tensions between the two nuclear-armed states.

Resumption of the peace process

In early April 2003, prompted by a 24 March attack in Nadimarg, Indian-administered Kashmir reportedly by the Lashkar-e-Toiba (LeT) Islamist terrorist group that left 24 dead – Indian Foreign Minister Yashwant Sinha asserted India's right to take 'pre-emptive' military action against alleged terrorist training camps in Pakistan-administered Kashmir. On 26 March, India and Pakistan flight-tested nuclear-capable short-range ballistic missiles within hours of each other. Delhi denied Islamabad's allegation that it had not provided advanced notification of the test, in accordance with existing practice. Thus, it came as a surprise that Vajpayee chose to announce to a public gathering in Srinagar, capital of Indian-administered Kashmir, on 18 April that problems with Pakistan could not be resolved through the barrel of the gun but only through dialogue. Emphasising that the time had come to usher in a sea change in bilateral relations, he stated that 'we again extend the hand of friendship, but it has to be a two-way road'. This address – the first by an Indian prime minister in 15 years – revived the India–Pakistan peace process. It resulted in considerable confusion in both Delhi and Islamabad as to whether India was prepared to give up its existing preconditions for resuming bilateral talks.

Vajpayee made it clear that this was his 'third and final' effort at improving relations with Islamabad. But his subsequent statement in parliament – that a meaningful dialogue could only begin once cross-border terrorism had ended and terrorist infrastructure had been dismantled – obfuscated the point as to whether junior-level talks could begin unconditionally, even as a summit or high-level dialogue was ruled out. Foreign Minister Sinha elaborated a month later that a halt to terrorist attacks was a precondition of a 'successful outcome' of the talks rather than a requirement for the talks to begin, but no formal proposal for bilateral talks materialised. Indeed, India once again test-fired its *Prithvi* short-range ballistic missile, though this time it unambiguously provided Pakistan advance notice. Nevertheless, the Indian High Commissioner to Pakistan, withdrawn after the December 2001 terrorist attack on the Indian parliament, was sent back to Islamabad. Delhi announced the resumption of the Delhi–Lahore bus service, and technical talks began with Islamabad on the restoration of civil aviation links. India released a number of Pakistani fishermen and civilian prisoners from Indian jails, and Islamabad promptly reciprocated the gesture. By mid-July, exchanges of media, business and parliamentary delegations had also resumed. The plight of Noor Fatima, a two-year old Pakistani girl who successfully underwent open-heart surgery in India in July, also caught the imagination of the two publics and demonstrated the goodwill among the people. In early October, both countries agreed to marginally increase the strength of their diplomatic missions, and, for the first time, a Pakistani team was permitted to visit the Baglihar hydroelectric project in Indian-administered Kashmir to ascertain whether it violated provisions of the Indus Water Treaty (1960).

Asia and Australia

By the middle of October, however, progress had stalled and the peace process appeared to be winding down. The first round of technical talks on air links had failed following a terrorist attack in Mumbai, India's financial capital, on 25 August that left 52 dead and 149 injured. President Musharraf's television interview in early June – where he did not rule out another Kargil-like operation – was deeply disappointing to Delhi. Delhi also rejected Musharraf's conditional offer in mid-August of a ceasefire on the Line of Control (the de facto border dividing Indian- and Pakistan-administered Kashmir) and the Indian-administered Kashmir valley was also rejected by Delhi as offering 'nothing new'. A public spat at the UN General Assembly session in New York in September 2003 made matters worse. Restless over the absence of official talks, Pakistan flight-tested three nuclear-capable ballistic missiles.

Confidence-building measures

In an attempt to bolster the peace process and deflect US pressure on talks with Pakistan, Delhi unexpectedly proposed 12 confidence-building measures (CBMs) on 22 October, four days before Diwali, the major Hindu festival of lights. These included the second round of technical talks on air links, follow-on discussions on the resumption of rail services, forbearance from arresting fishermen in certain designated areas, expansion of diplomatic missions and a new bus service between Srinagar and Muzzafarabad, the capitals of divided Kashmir. Delhi also offered free medical treatment for a group of Pakistani children. Earlier, Islamabad had proposed two CBMs – on the resumption of sporting links and Coast Guard interaction – in private diplomatic communications. Thus, Delhi's direct media appeal to the Pakistani public was seen as one-upmanship. But India's mooting of CBMs came without any offer of official bilateral dialogue at any level. Communicated in kind through the media, Islamabad's reaction a week later was largely positive. But it added a thirteenth CBM to provide 100 scholarships for Kashmiri graduates and medical treatment for disabled Kashmiris 'and those affected by the various operations launched by security agencies'. India predictably responded by stating that Kashmir was 'not a disputed territory', and pointing to Pakistan's 'illegal occupation of a portion of the state'.

Notwithstanding these differences, both Delhi and Islamabad began implementing proposals acceptable to both – the most important being the second round of talks on air links, subsequently scheduled for 1–2 December, and the resumption of all sporting links. This set the stage for a more pronounced thaw in India–Pakistan relations initiated by Pakistan, probably at the behest of the United States. In a televised address to mark his first year in office on November 23, Pakistani Prime Minister Zafarullah Jamali offered a unilateral ceasefire on the Line of Control, subsequently encompassing the international border and the Actual Ground Position Line in Siachen. This was immediately accepted by Delhi, and a mutual truce began on midnight 25 November – the holy Muslim day of Eid ul-Fitr, marking the end of Ramadan. The Eid ceasefire dramatically ended the daily exchange of artillery shelling and small arms fire across the Line of Control, which Delhi had perceived as a cover for infiltration into Indian-administered Kashmir. As of April 2004, this ceasefire continued to be scrupulously observed by both sides.

Two additional developments eased tensions. Within a week of the ceasefire, Musharraf unilaterally announced the lifting of Pakistan's ban on Indian overflights, leading to the resumption of air links on 1 January 2004 and technical talks on rail links, which in turn resulted in the restoration of rail passenger and cargo links from 15 January. Vajpayee promptly confirmed his participation in the 12th South Asian Association for Regional Cooperation (SAARC) Summit in Islamabad in the first week of January. In mid-December 2003, Musharraf also publicly offered to drop a traditional demand for a UN plebiscite in Kashmir, and meet India 'half-way' in a bid to resolve the Kashmir issue. Delhi was impressed with Musharraf's candour. While the UN plebiscite – requiring both sides to withdraw their forces from divided Kashmir – could not realistically have been implemented, Pakistan's insistence on it was a major psychological irritant to Delhi. Most important, perhaps, was the fact that all of these developments took place as infiltration across the Line of Control declined markedly – even allowing for the usual seasonal diminutions due to snow.

Joint India–Pakistan statement

Vajpayee's strong personal desire for a peaceful relationship with Pakistan and credit for forging it, along with subtle US pressure, fuelled India's preparations for a bilateral meeting on the sidelines of the SAARC Summit. For Islamabad, Vajpayee's rising popularity, reflected in the results of the December 2003 assembly elections, buttressed the view that it would be advisable to deal with Vajpayee himself. The two assassination attempts on Musharraf in December 2003 – the second traced to the Jaish-e-Mohammad (JeM) Islamist terrorist group active in Indian-administered Kashmir – reinforced Islamabad's determination to deal with terrorism in all its facets. The emergence in October 2003 of the nuclear proliferation scandal centring on Pakistani nuclear scientist Abdul Qadeer Khan – the 'father' of Pakistan's bomb – increased US leverage for pressuring Islamabad on this score.

The Vajpayee–Musharraf meeting on the sidelines of the SAARC Summit yielded a dramatic joint press statement. Issued on 6 January and based on unprecedented compromises on previously rigid positions, the statement by its terms satisfied Islamabad's demand for the resumption of official talks

Asia and Australia

and the recognition of its role in the resolution of the Kashmir dispute. Bilateral dialogue was to commence in February 2004 and the Kashmir problem was to be settled 'to the satisfaction of both sides'. Not only was the resumption of talks unconditional – not dependent on ending cross-border infiltration or dismantling terrorist infrastructure – but Delhi formally recognised Islamabad's role in the future of divided Kashmir. In addition, Delhi implicitly appeared to agree that Kashmir was disputed territory – which it had refused to do less than three months earlier. The joint statement also met Delhi's requirement of a pledge by Islamabad to prevent cross-border infiltration and terrorism. Musharraf explicitly undertook to Vajpayee, personally and in writing, that he would 'not permit any territory under Pakistan's control to be used to support terrorism in any manner'. In addition, Islamabad for the first time implicitly appeared to acknowledge a Pakistani role in cross-border infiltration and terrorism, and to refrain from characterising Kashmir as a 'central' or 'core' issue or a 'freedom struggle'.

On 13 February, Vajpayee personally intervened in an internal Indian debate to permit the Indian cricket team to tour Pakistan in March and April – for the first time in 13 years – which was a hugely popular decision in both countries. Five days later, the senior officials of the two countries agreed to resume a structured bilateral 'composite dialogue' – for the first time in three years – in May–June 2004, soon after the Indian general elections. The talks are to tackle the eight disputes on which 1997 talks had foundered. These include: peace and security, including CBMs; Jammu and Kashmir; Siachen; the Wullar Barrage/Tulbul Navigation project; Sir Creek; terrorism and drug-trafficking; economic and commercial cooperation; and the promotion of friendly exchanges. In August 2004, the two foreign ministers are to meet to review progress.

Crisis stability and nuclear doctrine

Soon after the withdrawal of the Indian and Pakistani armed forces from the international border in October 2002, both governments began examining the nuclear-related lessons of the ten-month border confrontation. Islamabad believed that at the peak of the crisis in the summer of 2002 its nuclear weapons – along with conventional forces – had deterred India from using force across the Line of Control. Furthermore, the confrontation illustrated to Pakistan that the Kashmir dispute was a 'nuclear flashpoint' that required the involvement of the international community for its resolution. Delhi's position was that Musharraf's commitment to the US to end cross-border infiltration 'immediately', and not Pakistan's nuclear weapons, had reduced tensions. According to the Indian Permanent Representative to the UN in New York, an 'artificial nuclear scare' had been created during the border confrontation for political purposes. Thus, not only do both nuclear-armed states hold contradictory views on the viability and applicability of nuclear deterrence in a crisis, but they also have a limited understanding of nuclear responsibilities and obligations. These concerns raise the possibility of serious misperceptions and miscalculations by Delhi and Islamabad in another crisis.

Both countries have continued to provide glimpses of their nuclear command-and-control systems to satisfy international concerns and gain credibility for respective nuclear postures, and tolerance for the conduct of flight-tests of nuclear-capable ballistic missiles. Pakistan's nuclear proliferation scandal increased American pressure on Islamabad to revamp its nuclear weapons establishment, but the US stopped short of imposing strictures for fear of weakening Musharraf, who was already under pressure as a result of India's order for sophisticated airborne radar systems from Israel. Although Pakistan has yet to formally publish its nuclear doctrine, its military leadership and former senior leaders have indicated a posture contemplating the first use of nuclear weapons.

Islamabad believes that intense and multiple nuclear signalling during the border confrontation in 2002 – through flight tests of nuclear-capable ballistic missiles, public speeches, press briefings and interviews by its leadership – paid rich dividends. Its assessment is that it has been able to convince Delhi of the credibility of its threat to use nuclear weapons to counter a conventional Indian attack across the Line of Control, and kept the nuclear threshold deliberately vague but adequately low. Two Italian physicists reported that in January 2002, Lieutenant-General Ahmed Kidwai, the Director General of Pakistan's Strategic Plans Division of the National Command Authority, had briefed them on four fairly broad and ambiguous 'thresholds': conquest of a large part of its territory (space threshold); destruction of a large part of land or air forces (military threshold); economic strangulation of Pakistan (economic pressure); and domestic political destabilisation or large-scale internal subversion (domestic destabilisation). An official denial was issued that these were ever considered thresholds for the use of nuclear weapons, and were 'purely academic'. But on 11 March 2004, Pakistan's Defence Committee of Cabinet (DCC), to demonstrate its resolve in the wake of the nuclear proliferation scandal, reportedly stated that nuclear weapons would be an 'unavoidable part' of Pakistani defence policy, that 'minimum nuclear deterrence' would be maintained, that imbalances in conventional arms were to be erased to decrease nuclear risks and that the 'expansion of conventional and non-conventional weapon systems' was to continue.

This statement illustrates the centrality of nuclear weapons in Pakistan's military policy. In contrast, the broad contours of India's official nuclear doctrine, finally unveiled in January 2003 reiterate the posture of 'no first use' of nuclear weapons, with the aim to 'build and maintain a credible minimum deterrent'. Thus, nuclear retaliation to a first strike is to be 'massive and designed to inflict unacceptable damage'. The 'no first use' posture has two important caveats. First, nuclear weapons will not only be used in retaliation against a nuclear attack on Indian territory, but also 'on Indian forces anywhere', which remains undefined; theoretically, it could imply nuclear first use on Pakistani territory. Second, India retains the option of retaliating with nuclear weapons in the event of a major attack against India, or Indian forces anywhere, by 'biological or chemical weapons'. Strict control is to continue on the export of nuclear and missile-related materials and technologies, and the unilateral moratorium on nuclear tests is to be observed.

For Pakistan, then, deterrence is essentially a 'military' concept, relating to both nuclear and conventional forces. By refusing to formally define its nuclear red lines, Pakistan seeks to hold India's superior conventional forces at bay in addition to deterring its use of nuclear weapons. For India, deterrence is essentially a 'political' concept, relating primarily to deterring other nuclear forces. But, with the two elaborations of the conditions of India's nuclear use, it appears to be moving towards a 'military' concept of nuclear forces. This movement serves to create some confusion, and uncertainty, over Delhi's own nuclear red lines. While Pakistan's nuclear doctrine is also wholly directed towards India, India's nuclear doctrine is not specific to Pakistan.

Delhi appeared convinced that Pakistan's nuclear signalling during the border confrontation was largely bluff and bluster, and that in the event of a conventional attack across the Line of Control, Islamabad would not use nuclear weapons until a major city were under siege or its sovereignty threatened. Accordingly, Delhi perceived, and continues to perceive, that it could credibly threaten the limited use of force – including 'surgical' strikes on alleged terrorist training camps in Pakistan-administered Kashmir – without crossing Pakistan's red lines. This is based on three assumptions. First, escalation dominance favours India, so Pakistan's most prudent response to a 'limited' use of force would be limited and conventional. Second, India's numerical superiority in nuclear weapons will deter Pakistan from a nuclear response. Third, India's larger geographical size renders the state far better able to survive a nuclear exchange. But there are major problems with such reasoning. For one, it is not clear that escalation can be easily controlled in battle conditions. Furthermore, asymmetry in nuclear forces has less operational significance than it does in a conventional context as long as nuclear weapons can reach their targets and neither of the opposing nuclear forces can be destroyed in a 'first strike'. The costs of a nuclear conflict for India as well as Pakistan would be devastating. Third, India tends not to distinguish 'first use' as a product of escalation from 'first strike' as pre-emptive strategic attack; it is not clear that in the former context the threat of massive 'unacceptable' retaliation would be credible. The credibility of an Indian nuclear response to a biological or chemical attack also appears weak.

India, then, may well have been more concerned over its ability to control escalation than it is willing to reveal. While there should be little doubt that India would use force across the Line of Control if faced with a major assassination or a radiological weapon attack, it might focus largely on special operations to reduce the risk of escalation. The fact remains that both countries engaged in nuclear brinkmanship during the border confrontation – India, by threatening the use of force across the Line of Control despite the risk of nuclear escalation, and Pakistan by signalling a 'low' nuclear threshold and concomitant risks of misperceptions and miscalculations. Nevertheless, both countries have attempted to enhance the credibility of their nuclear command-and-control systems. In February 2000, Islamabad established a National Command Authority to manage its nuclear forces. Chaired by Musharraf, it exercises control over all strategic forces and organisations. Despite symbolic civilian membership, control over the use of nuclear weapons lies in the hands of the military, led by Musharraf as army chief. In India, the use of nuclear weapons rests firmly with the civilian political leadership. In January 2003, Delhi publicly revealed its Nuclear Command Authority (NCA). The NCA comprises a Political Council and an Executive Council. Whereas the Political Council, chaired by the prime minister, is the sole body which can authorise the use of nuclear weapons, the Executive Council, chaired by the national security advisor, provides inputs for decision making by the NCA and executes the directives given to it by the Political Council. The NCA is also concerned with the state of readiness, the targeting strategy for a retaliatory attack, operating procedures for various stages of alert and launch, and arrangements for alternate chains of command.

Both Delhi and Islamabad remain engaged in flight-testing nuclear-capable ballistic missiles. Since 2003, India has carried out four tests of its short-range *Prithvi* (150–250 kilometres) and a test of its medium-range *Agni*-1 (700km) ballistic missile; it plans to test the longer medium-range *Agni*-3 ballistic missile (3,000km) in 2004–05. This flight test would be significant, as it would be the first missile with a range sufficient to reach Beijing; in this case, the diplomatic advantages of testing to a shorter range would outweigh the strategic. In addition, four of the six tests of the Indo-Russian joint venture *Brahmos* supersonic cruise missile, with nascent nuclear capability, were carried out in 2003. Meanwhile, Pakistan tested its longest-range missile for the first time – the *Shaheen*-2, with a range of 2,000km, on 9 March 2004. This solid-fuelled two-stage nuclear-capable ballistic missile, based on the Chinese M-18, was first displayed during the Pakistan Day military parade in Islamabad on 23 March 2000. This was also the first Pakistani missile test in the direction of the Arabian Sea, and the fifth overall since 2003. The other tests involved the short-range *Hatf*-2 (180km) and *Hatf*-3 (300km), and medium-range *Shaheen*-1 (700km).

Asia and Australia

Pakistan's nuclear proliferation scandal

In late 2003, Pakistan became the centre of a growing nuclear scandal revolving around the proliferation activities of pre-eminent Pakistani nuclear scientist A.Q. Khan. Khan was reportedly the head of an international network which clandestinely supplied nuclear technology and equipment to North Korea, Libya and Iran. These allegations emerged with the interception of a Libya-bound merchant ship loaded with Malaysian-made centrifuge components in October 2003, and subsequent declarations by Iran to the International Atomic Energy Agency (IAEA) and Libya to US and British intelligence officials. Reportedly, Khan supplied Iran with gas centrifuge designs and components to enable it to produce its own enriched uranium, and Libya with designs of nuclear warheads (of Chinese origin provided to Pakistan in the 1970s), centrifuge casings and nuclear materials. In addition, it was widely suspected that a government-sanctioned deal with Pyongyang in the 1990s involved the exchange of North Korean *No-dong* ballistic missiles and production technology for Pakistani gas centrifuge technology and perhaps other assistance for North Korea's covert nuclear weapons programme.

While it was clear that financial considerations dominated Khan's (and probably others') motivations, the revelations raised a number of questions about to what extent successive Pakistani governments were aware of these activities. The key question, of course, was whether Musharraf was personally aware of the activities. Although Musharraf immediately denied any knowledge of Khan's activities – as did Khan in his televised confession on 4 February 2004 – Khan's subsequent 'conditional pardon' by Musharraf added to international concerns. The reasons for Musharraf's dismissal of Khan as head of the former Khan Research Laboratories in early 2001 have not been made public. Currently, a 'cleansing' of the labs (renamed Kahuta) is being carried out. Khan and some 25 of his former associates were questioned, and a number arrested. But Khan's transgressions – along with the alleged involvement of two retired Pakistani nuclear scientists with the Taliban and al-Qaeda in Afghanistan in late 2001 – raise more questions than answers about the extent of 'leakage' of nuclear technology and components from Pakistan. Juxtaposed with Khan's financial motivations, Pakistan's continuing economic difficulties and political instability suggest that these questions will remain open.

Pakistan's struggling polity

Pakistan's economy – though improving – remains wracked with major structural problems and a lack of confidence by the foreign investor. Notwithstanding robust growth of 5% in 2002–03 and record foreign exchange reserves of $12 billion, foreign direct investment was limited, and improved debt management related largely to financial assistance from the international financial institutions and the US stemming from Pakistan's post-11 September cooperation in the anti-terror campaign. Domestic political stability remains fragile amidst Islamic extremism, terrorism and sectarian violence – strained by assassination attempts on Musharraf. Although Musharraf's position in Pakistan's polity improved in the short-term, his influence appears likely to decrease. On 29 December, the constitutional deadlock between the government and parliament was finally resolved with the latter's passage of the 17th Constitutional Amendment. This provision essentially ratified Musharraf's Legal Framework Order (LFO) of 2002, allowing Musharraf to continue as president till 2007, with enhanced powers – including the power to dismiss the government and parliament, and to name judges, military service chiefs and provincial governors. However, there were two curtailments of the powers prescribed by the LFO. First, any move to dissolve parliament must be referred to the Supreme Court within 15 days. Second, the National Security Council (NSC) was to be authorised by ordinary legislation, not a constitutional amendment. Accordingly, the National Security Bill 2004 was approved by parliament in April 2004. Furthermore, in exchange for the amendment's enactment, Musharraf had to agree to give up his post of army chief at the end of December 2004.

Musharraf's fight against Islamist extremists appeared to acquire renewed vigour following the peace moves with India and the two attempts on his life. In mid-November 2003, Musharraf re-banned three renamed Islamist terrorist groups (which had already been banned under their earlier names in January 2002). These included the Khudam-ul-Islam (formerly JeM) and the Jamaat-ul-Dawa (formerly LeT). In one of his strongest statements against Islamist extremism, Musharraf – during his first address to the joint sitting of parliament on 17 January – appealed to the Pakistani nation 'to wage jihad against extremism'. Nevertheless, violence between militant Sunni and Shi'ite groups continued. In Quetta, on 2 March, 47 Shi'ites were killed and more than 150 injured in a suicide attack. It occurred on Ashoura, the Shi'ites most holy day.

Pakistan has become a close ally of the US in its war on terror. Pakistani paramilitary and armed forces have continued to battle Taliban/al-Qaeda-linked terrorists on Pakistan's border with Afghanistan, with US intelligence and logistical support. In October 2003, it set up a quick-reaction team to hunt down the al-Qaeda leadership. But Islamabad has remained hesitant to involve US forces in confronting al-Qaeda operatives for domestic political reasons. Thus, while Pakistan launched a major operation in South Waziristan in March 2004 – the first of its kind in the loosely controlled tribal areas – it insisted that US assets were not directly involved. This resulted in considerable opposition from tribal leaders and a call for Musharraf's overthrow, allegedly by Ayman al-Zawahiri, the al-

Qaeda second-in-command. On a visit to the region, US Secretary of State Colin Powell granted Pakistan 'major non-NATO ally' status – subject to congressional approval – in March 2004. Although this gesture appeared to be largely symbolic, to provide additional support for Musharraf under trying conditions, it created consternation in Delhi because it had not been informed earlier, and increased Islamabad's prospects for acquiring US military equipment, ammunition and defence research-and-development cooperation – previously denied to Pakistan.

Stabler India

The marked exuberance in India in the health of its economy remains a dominant factor in Indian polity. It is largely the result of a decade of reform. The economy grew by 8% in 2003–04, double the previous year's growth, and the stock market reached an all-time high as the Sensex (30-stock index) crossed the 6,000 mark. Inflation and interest rates stayed low. Foreign exchange reserves reached $100bn in December 2003 – in contrast to the low of $1bn during the 1991 economic crisis. Other economic indicators were not so rosy. Foreign direct investment at $4.7bn was less than a tenth of China's $50bn. Though the thirteenth-largest economy in the world, India still accounted for less than 2% of global GDP and 1% of world trade. Moreover, over a quarter of India's one billion-plus population remained below the poverty line. With nine million new entrants to the job market annually, unemployment remains high; the challenge will be to sustain high economic growth along with the creation of jobs. India's infrastructure – roads, electricity, water – remain inadequate for systemic structural reform. Corruption continues to impede sound administration. Although at 10% of GDP the public sector budget deficit is high, it continues to be financed by a high savings rate and therefore does not, yet, have a negative impact.

On balance, considerable optimism is justified for the future of the Indian economy. Not surprisingly, the governing Bharatiya Janata Party (BJP)-led National Democratic Alliance (NDA) has made economic success – a 'Shining India' – the centrepiece of its general election campaign, which began soon after the early dissolution of parliament on 6 February. Having done better than expected in provincial assembly elections in December 2003 – winning three of four states – the NDA is in a favourable position to win, with the new government expected to be in place at the end of May 2004. The chief opposition party, the Congress Party led by Sonia Gandhi, is weak and divided, increasing the NDA's prospects for victory. While the political consensus appears to favour reforms, the implementation of second-generation reforms – especially of the huge and unproductive public sector labour force – will be a challenge for the new government. But, this is essential if a high growth rate is to be sustained.

Post-11 September, India and the US have worked hard to establish a 'strategic relationship' in spite of Pakistan's importance to the US as a counter-terrorism partner. Notwithstanding India's refusal of the United States' request in mid-July to send troops to Iraq due to the absence of a UN mandate or UN forces command, India–US trade and military ties progressed considerably. In January 2004, a joint agreement on a 'quartet' of issues – civilian nuclear and space programmes, high technology trade, and dialogue on missile defence – provided the framework for significantly enhanced bilateral relations.

India has also tried to improve ties with Beijing. Defence Minister George Fernandes' successful visit to China in April 2003, amid the SARS crisis, set the tone and the pace for Vajpayee's June visit, which was the first by an Indian prime minister in 10 years. While the joint declaration that emerged referred to the 'Tibet Autonomous Region', marking India's explicit recognition of Tibet as an integral part of China, the quid pro quo appeared to be China's implicit recognition of Indian sovereignty over Sikkim – through the designation of trading posts on the Sikkim–Tibet border – in the accompanying Memorandum of Understanding. Progress seemed closer on the resolution of the Sino-Indian territorial dispute – in spirit if not substance – through two meetings of the new special representatives on the issue. The first joint naval exercises off Shanghai in November 2003 was followed by the visit of Chinese Defence Minister Cao Gangchuan to Pakistan and India in March 2004.

India's other key bilateral relationship is with Israel. Ariel Sharon's visit to India in September 2003 was the first by an Israeli prime minister. It took place against the backdrop of growing military and intelligence ties – especially in areas of sophisticated technology and hardware – between the two countries. In late February 2004, Delhi finalised its largest-ever arms deal with Israel: the $1.1bn acquisition of three sophisticated Phalcon Airborne Warning and Control System (AWACS) units mounted on modified Russian Il.-76 aircraft, scheduled for delivery in 2005. US approval had been provided earlier. Selling India an estimated $3bn in defence-related items annually, Israel has become India's second largest military supplier, after Russia – with which Delhi signed a $1.5bn deal for the aircraft carrier *Admiral Gorshkov* and its complement of combat aircraft in January 2004. In March 2004, Delhi signed a Memorandum of Understanding with Britain for the $1.45bn purchase of 66 *Hawk* advanced jet aircraft.

Maintaining momentum towards peace
Notwithstanding the significance of the 6 January and 18 February 2004 statements, to call them 'historic' would be to overreach, and the India–Pakistan peace process remains fragile. Clearly there are good signs.

Asia and Australia

The ceasefire is holding, Musharraf is hardening his stance on terrorists, and Delhi has accepted Islamabad's role in the resolution of the Kashmir dispute and is inclined towards negotiation. But if the peace process is to endure, it needs to be carefully managed by both Delhi and Islamabad, with a few quiet nudges behind the scene from the US in the form of facilitating communication, sharing ideas and anticipating pitfalls.

Substantively, there are several major challenges to regional stability and security. First, the commitment to the peace process needs to be broadened to the wider political, bureaucratic and military leaderships in both countries. A series of CBMs could help in this regard, especially in Kashmir. For example, a Srinagar–Muzzafarabad bus service – proposed by Delhi in October 2003 – would serve a humanitarian purpose by facilitating contact among divided Kashmiri families and politically symbolise the legitimacy of the Line of Control as an international border, which has been strongly opposed by Islamabad. Notwithstanding Islamabad's initial response – that passengers must carry UN documents and that checkpoints on both sides must be manned by UN personnel – and Delhi's well known opposition to any UN role in Kashmir, talks on this bus link were to begin in mid-2004. In addition, Delhi needs to prioritise the fledgling talks between Indian Deputy Prime Minister L.K. Advani and Kashmiri leaders of the separatist amalgamated Hurriyat Conference for greater state autonomy, and to ensure that Indian security forces do not commit human-rights violations during current counter-terrorist operations in Indian-administered Kashmir.

Second, Musharraf will at least have to make a demonstrably good faith effort to prevent the use of Pakistani territory by terrorists and dismantle their infrastructure. Early indications are that cross-border infiltration has decreased from a similar period last year, which is significant. Violence in Indian-administered Kashmir, including the valley, has also decreased. But evidence of the dismantlement of terrorist infrastructure is scarce. India has alleged the existence of over 80 terrorist training camps in Pakistan-administered Kashmir and the presence of some 1,500 militants already in Indian-administered Kashmir. The critical test will take place in April–May, when the snow melts and the customary season for cross-border infiltration into Indian-administered Kashmir begins. This could have an impact on the Indian general elections scheduled in the same time frame. Although the multi-layered fencing of nearly 600km of the 740km Line of Control is expected to be completed in July–August 2004, it will not completely block infiltration. The fence also has problematic political implications, owing to Pakistan's fear that it could turn into a de facto border.

Third, any resolution of the Kashmir problem will be in the distant future, which underlines the need for diplomatic commitment and stamina. Several fraught 'solutions' are already in the public domain. One is the conversion of the Line of Control into an international border – with minor modifications due to terrain – along with greater autonomy to divided Kashmir; this is favoured by Delhi, but unacceptable to Islamabad in that it does not take into account the wishes of the Kashmiri people. It also requires an amendment of a politically sensitive Indian parliamentary resolution on Kashmir. A second possibility is the division of Kashmir based on the Chenab River, ceding all Muslim-majority areas, including Srinagar and most parts of the valley, to Pakistan, with Hindu and Buddhist-majority areas remaining under Indian sovereignty; this is flatly unacceptable to Delhi. Another solution mooted is independence for Kashmir, which neither India nor Pakistan want. A variation – independence for the Kashmir valley – is a non-starter for India. Political autonomy under joint Indian and Pakistani control – an idea advocated by the US-based Kashmir Study Group – is not acceptable to Delhi. Moreover, dialogue will also be complicated by the need to resolve the status of a sixth of the former territory of Jammu and Kashmir – comprising the Shaksgam valley and Aksai Chin – controlled by China.

Better short-term prospects for bilateral stability – which would help preserve longer-term commitments to bilateral diplomacy on Kashmir – may lie in the basket of euphemistically named 'peace and security issues', especially those that amount to nuclear CBMs. Clearly, nuclear deterrence in both countries needs to be made more stable, with far greater understanding and thinking on critical issues such as nuclear doctrine, force development, command-and-control, deployment and readiness, survivability and nuclear safety. A useful beginning could be made by concluding a bilateral agreement on the advance notification of ballistic missile flight tests. While each government has unilaterally undertaken the obligation of notice in 'spirit', it needs to be formalised, especially as missile flight times to major targets is less than ten minutes. The substance of such an agreement could include the following: advanced notification of the type of ballistic missile tested; mutually agreed minimum period of notification; process of communication between the Foreign Ministries in Delhi and Islamabad; directional constraints (i.e., no launching of test missiles towards each other); designation of test sites; annual exchanges of lists of flight tests and test sites; verification measures; and a precise consultation mechanism.

In addition to the dispute over Kashmir's governance and sovereignty and the challenges of nuclear stability, there are several other potentially destabilising bilateral disputes over territory. The armed conflict related to the Siachen dispute is actually taking place further to the west, on the Saltoro glacier, where Indian and Pakistani troops have been engaged in mortar and small arms fire at an operationally taxing altitude of 7,000 metres since 1984. Although the strategic value of the glacier is unclear, the rigid positions symbolise national honour. Notwithstanding several rounds of talks, there has been little progress towards disengagement – though a

Asia and Australia

ceasefire has been in effect since November 2003. Neither country even agrees to a common name for the Kashmir-based dispute that Pakistan calls the Wullar Barrage project and India the Tulbul Navigation project. The core of the dispute is whether or not India's construction of a barrier on the Jhelum River commenced in 1984 (suspended three years later) at the mouth of the Wular Lake violates the 1960 Indus Water Treaty. Delhi claims that barrier is intended to make the river navigable, while Islamabad contends that it is for water storage in violation of the Treaty. Eight rounds of talks have been held since 1989, and an agreement was close in 1992. Recently, Islamabad also objected that India's Baglihar hydro-power project would violate the Treaty. As noted, however, in October 2003 Delhi permitted a Pakistani team to visit and examine the construction taking place. The Sir Creek dispute involves differences over defining the land boundary in Sir Creek (a 38km-long estuary in the marshes of the Rann of Kutch) on the Gujarat–Sindh border, potentially rich in oil and gas deposits, and differences over demarcating the maritime boundary. Six rounds of talks have yielded no progress. In August 1999, India shot down a Pakistani naval Atlantic aircraft in this area, increasing sensitivities over this dispute.

It remains unclear whether progress on any of these other territorial disputes can be made in the absence of movement on Kashmir. It is plain, however, that progress on Kashmir remains key to overall bilateral stability, and that ongoing dialogue on Kashmir will enhance prospects for reducing virtually all other India–Pakistan tensions. Accordingly, notwithstanding the considerable problems and difficulties that lie ahead, the bilateral dialogue process between the two nuclear-armed neighbours is a highly salutary development. But for the peace process to bear fruit, it needs to be understood as a long-term process, as there are no quick solutions. The key, therefore, will be to sustain dialogue beyond practically inevitable moments of disruption. With unprecedented and simultaneous influence over both Delhi and Islamabad, Washington's facilitation, and therefore its close attention, would increase the likelihood of success on this score. Whether the tentatively greater stability in south Asia can be consolidated therefore depends, to a significant degree, on whether the US can muster the diplomatic resources and staying power to look beyond counter-terrorism and crisis management on the subcontinent.

Central Asia: Dilemmas of Security and Democratisation

Although overshadowed by events in Iraq, Central Asia (Afghanistan in particular), has continued to present a series of problems for the international community, especially the US, during 2003. Few of these are likely to be fully resolved in 2004. On the ground, the continuing low-intensity conflict with Taliban and al-Qaeda loyalists in Afghanistan shows no sign of letting up. Often the military priorities of the coalition have cut against various multilateral peace-building initiatives. As a consequence, many of the most important post-war reconstruction programmes remain frustrated, and the prospects of installing a government with genuine democratic legitimacy in the elections scheduled for June 2004 remain slim. On a political level, the US government is coming under increasing pressure to examine its relationship with regional allies such as Uzbekistan, whose human-rights record remains poor, and to use its leverage to promote rapid and genuine democratisation in these states. Finally, the region's security dynamics are likely to impact on broad strategic decisions made in the US government's looming Base Realignment and Closing (BRAC) programme, which intends to reconfigure US basing postures in the light of new security threats.

Although Tashkent was briefly convulsed by a series of suicide bombings and gun battles in late March 2004 that left at least 40 people dead, the preceding year had been one of domestic quiescence in the former Soviet Central Asian republics (CARs). All five presidents have been in situ for over a decade and, health permitting, are likely to remain so in 2004. Most spent 2003 assiduously manoeuvring to co-opt or sideline rivals and to secure their legacies. The region's internal security dynamics are complex. Until the Tashkent events, the threat of Islamist terrorism was thought to have receded from its high water mark of 2000. In 2004, there will have to be a fundamental rethink on how to manage radical Islamism in the region, particularly as the use of suicide bombers in Uzbekistan is a new departure for Central Asia. Apart from the 'soft' security threats posed by illicit trafficking of narcotics, arms and people, disputes over border demarcation and resource sharing are the other issues with the greatest potential to destabilise inter-state relations during 2004, in the absence of a comprehensive regional security institution equipped with conflict resolution mechanisms.

One common but largely unnoticed policy thread that emerged during 2003 was that, a dozen years after the collapse of Soviet power, there has been a quietly positive reappraisal by Central Asian leaders of their

Asia and Australia

bilateral relations with Russia. Now that their sovereignty appears to be more secure, particularly in light of the US/NATO military presence in the region, the CARs have proven more willing to accelerate military and economic cooperation (and even integration) with Russia. Russian President Vladimir Putin's more coordinated and nuanced approach to the region has also encouraged this tendency.

Persistent conflict in Afghanistan

The two direct security challenges faced by both the US-led coalition forces and International Security Assistance Force (ISAF) personnel in Afghanistan during 2003 stemmed, firstly, from the ongoing insurgency of resistance fighters loyal to, or allied with, the Taliban regime, and secondly, from internecine feuds between warlords that have their roots in the period prior to the coalition's arrival in 2001. Those militias ranged against the coalition forces in Afghanistan in 2003 fall in to three overlapping groups. The largest is the Taliban itself, followed by remnants of al-Qaeda forces of multiple nationalities and, finally, Gulbuddin Hikmatyar's Islamic Party of Afghanistan (Hikmatyar).

The Taliban is able to call on residual support in two Afghan–Pakistani border regions, Pakistan's North West Frontier Province and Baluchistan, both of which are governed by the Muttahida Majlis-i Amal (MMA), a coalition of six radical Islamist parties. The MMA has permitted the Deobandi madrassas, from which the Taliban emerged, to continue to operate in these two regions. They are producing fresh recruits to rejuvenate the Taliban's ranks. The fact that Pashtuns perceive themselves to have been excluded from Hamid Karzai's Afghan Transitional Administration (ATA), provides an additional motive for a minority of local Afghans to support the Taliban's guerrilla campaign. Moreover, elements within Pakistan's Inter-Service Intelligence (ISI) agency appear to have maintained links with the Taliban. While some of the ISI's support for the Taliban may still be ideological, another key factor is the practical calculation that the US, for whatever reason, might leave the Afghan theatre altogether. Having a client with some military capability is therefore perceived to be a useful insurance policy for Pakistani security interests. In addition, the Taliban provides an important vehicle for the ISI to contain and direct potential Pashtun ethno-nationalist sentiments, which may threaten Pakistan's own territorial integrity.

Although the Taliban continued to operate in the border districts of Kandahar, Zabul and Paktika in 2003, it was unable to pull off any major operations and, indeed, was weakened by coalition forces through *Operation Mountain Viper* in August 2003, and in *Operation Avalanche*, which prevented disruption of the constitutional Loya Jirga in December 2003. Despite its former pan-Islamic rhetoric, the Taliban is now more of a revanchist ethno nationalist grouping whose ability to function in 2004 is likely to hinge largely on how effectively it can exploit notions of Pashtun solidarity. A critical challenge to the government elected in the June 2004 presidential and parliamentary elections, therefore, will be to form an administration with a sufficiently broad base as to undercut the Taliban's constituency.

There is much less local support for foreign al-Qaeda militants holed up in the Afghan–Pakistani border regions, although these are likely to be better organised and trained than new Taliban recruits. Al-Qaeda forces are also much more expendable from the standpoint of the ISI and Pakistani military. Notably, after the visit of US Secretary of State Colin Powell to Pakistan in mid-March 2004, Pakistani armed forces moved quickly to surround and attack a suspected al-Qaeda base in Waziristan, which reportedly contained numerous foreign fighters.

Hikmatyar, Pakistan's most favoured client warlord prior to the Taliban, has apparently spent much of 2003 operating in mountainous border areas in eastern Afghanistan around Jalalabad. Removing him and his forces from the military equation would be an important boost to the coalition. Although Hikmatyar is not considered, by himself, to have the capacity to fatally disrupt the broad political reconstruction of the country, he does, acting in concert with other wings of the resistance, have sufficient experience and standing to cause trouble for the ATA.

Ongoing bloodshed between warlord factions continued to plague Afghanistan in 2003 and early 2004. In early October 2003, General Abdul Rashid Dostum's mainly Uzbek militia clashed with Tajik forces loyal to Atta Mohammed, close to the northern city of Mazar-i-Sharif, leaving at least 60 dead. Further serious fighting claimed over 100 lives after the assassination on 21 March 2004 of Civil Aviation Minister Mirwais Sadiq, son of Herat-based warlord Ismail Khan, by forces loyal to rival commander Zahir Nayebzada. Both incidents appear to have originated in local disputes – for example, over the right to extract tolls from road users or the status of certain commanders. Given the potential rewards involved (Ismail Khan is reputed to rake in up to $80 million per year from road tolls and the trafficking of contraband), the militarised nature of Afghan society, and the lack of an effective government writ in the outlying areas, it is unsurprising that these conflicts swiftly escalate. They also underscore the reality that the ATA can at best function as a broker, but not enforcer, of civil peace and, at worst, carries almost no weight in the outlying provinces. That said, the ATA announced on 26 March 2004 that a detachment of 1,500 troops from the fledging Afghan National Army (ANA) will be deployed in Herat at Nayebzada's former barracks. If the ANA can establish a semi-permanent foothold in the city, it may be able to incrementally erode the influence of Ismail Khan and provide a foundation for the return of the city to central government control.

Asia and Australia

Afghan warlordism also illustrates the differing priorities accorded the country's security situation by the coalition forces on one hand, and ISAF peacekeepers and the ATA on the other. The coalition does not intervene in incidents of so-called 'Green on Green' (that is, Muslim versus Muslim) violence, and has utilised the services of warlords and mid-level militia commanders for intelligence purposes when fighting Taliban forces. This policy has served to alienate many ordinary Afghans, with whom warlords tend to be unpopular, while undercutting the objective of ISAF and the ATA – to remove or demobilise commanders in order to build a framework of civil law. This anomaly has been accentuated by the coalition's proposal in January 2004 to create an Afghan Guard Force (AGF) by converting militia groups into counter-insurgency units used by coalition special-operations forces in anti-Taliban operations. The AGF risks sending mixed messages to Afghans by undercutting demobilisation programmes and drawing potential recruits away from the ANA, which will be essential to the long-term stabilisation of the country.

During 2003, the coalition forces undoubtedly forfeited some goodwill on the ground. Not only have they become identified with local warlords, but heavy-handed search and arrest tactics have offended local sensibilities in the south and east of the country. A decisive defeat of Taliban recusants, and the capture of Mullah Omar and/or Osama bin Laden in 2004, would obviate the need for such tactics and do much to clear the political way for an expansion of the reconstruction programme and eliminate the ambiguities in the international community's current objectives. The US administration appears to have recognised this with the decision on 25 March 2004 to dispatch an additional 2,000 US Marines to Afghanistan.

Afghanistan's political reconstruction

The cornerstone of political reconstruction during 2003 was the Loya Jirga held in December 2003, which agreed to the adoption of a new national constitution. The previous Emergency Loya Jirga of 2002 had been strongly criticised for failing to accommodate sufficiently the demands of Pashtun representatives for a transitional administration with a broader ethnic base, and for according to regional warlords an elevated political status that their behaviour over the previous decade scarcely merited. The Loya Jirga of 2003 redressed this imbalance only partially. However, no final document was ever likely to please all the conference's participants, and the compromise reached at least provided a basis to move into an electoral cycle. One interesting ambiguity in the new constitution is that it establishes the primacy of civil law, and yet the country is designated an Islamic republic and Article 3 of the constitution states that 'no laws can be contrary to the sacred religion of Islam'. Although designed to satisfy both religious conservatives and secularists, this provision has the potential to store up divisiveness and create the kind of conflict between different branches of the judiciary and executive seen in recent years in Iran.

Karzai rescheduled presidential elections from June 2004 to September 2004, as there was scant evidence that the country was well prepared for the poll. Less than 15% of voters had been registered by March 2004. Although the UN Assistance Mission to Afghanistan (UNAMA) promised a further grant of $9.7m to assist with preparations, this sum appeared to be woefully inadequate. Notwithstanding a planned 'national mobilisation' campaign set for May 2003, the prospects of achieving the 70% voter registration target by election day appear slim. Some NGOs recommended that the election timetable be put further back than September. Yet there were compelling reasons to stick to a September 2004 date. Many Afghans perceive Karzai to be an aloof 'palace ruler' proceeding hand-in-glove with the US, so he requires swift electoral legitimisation (assuming he wins) to shore up his authority. An early presidential election victory would also give Karzai a mandate to curb leading Northern Alliance figures, such as Defence Minister Mohammed Fahim, who continue to control the 'power' ministries and are perceived to elevate the interests of ethnic Tajiks above other groups. Another important factor is that the legal authority vested in Karzai's administration by the Bonn Agreement of 6 December 2001 and subsequent Loya Jirgas unequivocally expires in June 2004. Unilaterally extending that mandate a second time, beyond September 2004, is likely to prove extremely unpopular. There will also be external pressure from the US government to adhere to a September 2004 election date. With foreign policy shaping up to be a key issue in the 2004 US presidential election in November, President George W. Bush would like to be able to demonstrate that Afghanistan is a functioning democracy during his re-election campaign.

Whatever the timing of the Afghan presidential election, it is vital that parliamentary elections be held soon afterwards in order to balance Karzai's authority and ensure a broad range of representation. Yet genuine political parties are still at an embryonic stage of development, to say the least, and early elections risk entrenching existing militias, in the form of pseudo-parties, in the political system, thus reducing the likelihood that a truly pluralist multiparty framework will be able to develop in the medium term.

Local reconstruction initiatives

The UN-mandated ISAF changed substantially during 2003. On 1 February 2003, the 1st German/Netherlands corps assumed command of ISAF, and on 16 April 2003, it was decided that, rather than rotating individual states as lead members of ISAF, NATO itself would offer to assume the permanent lead role, a proposal the UN subsequently endorsed. This made good sense for several reasons. It would provide continuity and stability, avoid the twice-yearly search for new states to lead ISAF and allow smaller nations, several of which have specialised peacekeeping skills, to contribute more fully. NATO has had extensive experience in complex multinational peacekeeping operations in the Balkans, and its institutional commitment is more likely to be long-term. Indeed, Canadian Major-General Andrew Leslie, deputy commander of ISAF, confirmed on 6 February 2004 that NATO's commitment would be 'for five to ten years, or even as long as it takes'.

NATO formally assumed the lead role in ISAF on 11 August 2003, and on 6 October 2003, announced that ISAF intended to expand its operations beyond Kabul to Kunduz. As of 1 April 2004, ISAF force strength is approximately 6,100 troops, but this number is expected to increase to between 8,000 and 12,000 troops in the course of the year, with some Spanish troops being shifted from Iraq by the new socialist government in Madrid. There is pressure from the UN and NGOs to expand ISAF beyond Kabul and Kunduz. On 7 January 2004, ISAF assumed command of a German-led Provincial Reconstruction Team (PRT) in Kunduz. ISAF contemplated this undertaking as a pilot project for the further expansion of the force. However, neither NATO nor the coalition wishes the ISAF mission to be confused with, or hinder, coalition forces' counter-terrorism efforts and, given the responsibilities of several leading NATO members in Iraq and Kosovo, there may be a lack of political conviction and military resources in the North Atlantic Council to deploy further personnel in substantially less secure areas of Afghanistan. Yet NATO cannot really afford to perform ineffectively in a country of 26m, most of whom are broadly supportive of its mission. Were NATO to fail, as out-of-area deployments are increasingly mooted as part of its post-11 September mission, NATO's raison d'être would be seriously questioned.

The main products of reconstruction activities developed by coalition forces and ISAF, in conjunction with the ATA's New Beginnings Project (ANBP) launched by Karzai on 16 April 2003, were the PRTs, the Disarmament, Demobilisation and Reintegration (DDR) programme and the creation of the ANA.

PRTs are small civilian–military units originally phased in by coalition forces during 2003 to supervise the reconstruction of civic amenities and strengthen local security. They are often co-located with coalition firebases and have a 'synergistic relationship' with special-operations forces based on the PRTs' ability to gather intelligence from local people. ISAF will gradually assume command and control of the PRTs in 2004, expand their number from 12 to 16 by late summer and develop their functions to include oversight of DDR programmes and brokering local ceasefires, which a UK-led PRT already accomplished with distinction in the dispute between Dostum and Atta in Mazar-i-Sharif during October 2003. Nevertheless, it is difficult to envisage how the complex relationship between PRTs and local warlords will evolve satisfactorily. PRTs are intended to elicit and use intelligence supplied by local commanders on Taliban movements, and mediate disputes between armed factions; yet they are also charged with dissolving these very same militias through the ANBP and DDR mechanisms. This anomaly will be further accentuated should the PRTs be required to liaise with the Coalition's new AGF.

The three-year DDR programme was launched in October 2003 and aims to disarm, demobilise and reintegrate soldiers from warlord factions by targeting mid-level commanders, in the hope that they can then deliver the men under their control. In exchange, each soldier will receive a $200 one-off payment, a voucher for 130 kilograms of food, and either employment with PRTs or an assistance package, such as access to tools or grants for livestock. The aim is to dismantle the 'pyramids of power' that sustain warlord militias. Notwithstanding the generosity of the overall package by local standards, early take-up was reportedly still very low and, by mid-February 2004, only 2,246 soldiers had been demobilised. Many of them may have returned to the land within a couple of months. The DDR programme also still leaves unaddressed the issue of heavy artillery and, with the Russian government having admitted to supplying the Northern Alliance with tanks and helicopters in 2003, the task of disarming militias at command level is likely to take several years. On 26 March 2004, Karzai set a target for the demobilisation 40% of militia soldiers and the cantonment of 100% of heavy weapons by the September 2004 elections. This objective will require serious external support, and much will hinge on whether promises of aid made at the Berlin donors' conference on 31 March–1 April 2004 are honoured.

US, UK and French officers are training the ANA, with Germany assuming responsibility for police training. The US battalions have a heavy preponderance of Tajiks, while the European battalions are more ethnically balanced, creating the residual risk that the US will again become identified with non-Pashtun elements in the national administration. Russia's and Iran's patronage of their respective client warlord factions continues to undermine efforts to create a governmental monopoly on force.

Depending on perspective, the glass in Afghanistan is either half full or half empty. There have been discernible signs of progress during 2003. The overall security situation has improved, a constitution has been agreed and elections are still on track. Yet Taliban forces remain active across swathes of southern and eastern Afghanistan. Substantive reconstruction work has barely begun and can make only limited progress in any event while an armed conflict is still being fought. Warlords like Rashid Dostum and Ismail Khan are as entrenched as ever in their fiefdoms. Weary Afghans undoubtedly want to see the back of the warlords but, as long as these commanders are able to control significant weaponry and resources, and can provide some form of rudimentary security and employment, they will be difficult to dislodge.

Asia and Australia

Central Asia's domestic landscape

By all outward appearances, there was continued political stagnation in the post-Soviet Central Asian states in 2003, and there is little evidence to suggest that the authoritarian veil over the region is about to be lifted over the coming year.

President Askar Akayev of Kyrgyzstan won a constitutional referendum in March 2003 that effectively gave both him and his family immunity from prosecution after he steps down, which he is scheduled to do in March 2005. As of early 2004, there was considerable jockeying for position among Bishkek's elite to succeed Akayev, who may yet decide to continue in power. In Kazakhstan, Dariga Nazarbayeva, the daughter of President Nursultan Nazarbayev, entered the political fray in January 2004 by launching her own political party, Asar, which is expected to do well in the November 2004 parliamentary elections. Her father enjoyed a smooth year at the helm in 2003, as oil prices remained buoyant and the moderate political opposition either melted away or was skilfully co-opted by the regime. In Tajikistan, President Imomali Rakhmonov won a June 2003 constitutional referendum that revised presidential term limits, thereby effectively enabling him to stay in power until 2020. Still, there is a touch of hubris about Rakhmonov that may yet prove his undoing. In January 2004, he sidelined important allies from the civil war in the 1990s, and by doing so risked alienating key personnel in the power ministries. He has also undercut the spirit, if not the letter, of the 1997 peace agreement by arresting leading figures in the opposition Islamic Renaissance Party on non-political charges.

President Saparmurat Niyazov of Turkmenistan announced to the nation's Council of Elders in mid-August 2003 that he would step down in 2008. Given that he is not only president for life, but also notoriously unpredictable, little weight can be attached to this statement of intent. Niyazov continues to change policy course and rotate or dismiss ministers and officials with bewildering frequency, making the political contours of his regime almost impossible to discern. The only certainty is that Turkmenistan's continued stance of isolationist neutrality will continue as long as Niyazov remains in power.

The labyrinthine machinations in the domestic Uzbek scene are often hard to fathom but, although President Islam Karimov often appears in public looking unwell, he remains securely in control. The US made some half-hearted representations to Tashkent about the need for democratisation in 2003, but little real progress was made. The government did allow the opposition party Birlik to meet at the same time as the European Bank of Reconstruction and Development conference was held in Tashkent in early April 2003. It also released from custody 62-year old Fatima Mukhadairova, who has been campaigning for an investigation into the death of her son, reportedly by police torture, prior to the visit of US

Defense Secretary Donald Rumsfeld on 25 February 2004. When asked about Mukhadairova's high-profile case at a Tashkent press conference, Rumsfeld evinced little knowledge of, or interest in, the matter. This blankness, coupled with minimal US pressure with respect to democratisation, would appear to reflect an American approach to Uzbekistan in particular and Central Asia in general that is, at least in the short term, instrumental rather than reformist.

The eruption of violence in Uzbekistan at the end of March 2004 came as something of a shock, especially given the apparent use of suicide bombing tactics, hitherto unknown in post-Soviet Central Asia. The fact that the bombers struck local rather than Western targets indicates that resentment is primarily directed at Karimov's regime, which has cracked down on all political and religious dissent over the past decade. Although the immediate temptation would be to link the attacks to al-Qaeda or Chechen militants, there may be a sufficient number of desperate locally based activists to mount such operations. The Islamic Movement of Uzbekistan (IMU) tended to operate as a seasonally active rural guerrilla movement in the late 1990s, and was thought to have been fatally damaged during *Operation Enduring Freedom* in late 2001. The IMU, or a linked group, could have reconstituted and switched tactics, recognising the high international profile that women suicide bombers can yield, or it may have been superseded by a previously unknown group. Nevertheless, many in the region will continue to believe that the bombings were an 'inside job' perpetrated by the regime at a critical juncture to forestall democratic reform and remind the US of the dangers of political liberalisation.

US policy in Central Asia

Since late 2001, as it prepared to intervene militarily in Afghanistan following the 11 September terrorist attacks, the US has usurped Russia's self-appointed role as Central Asia's principal security manager. The Uzbek airbase at Khanabad was used by US forces as a command centre for the air war in Afghanistan and as a base for search-and-rescue operations. About 1,000 American troops remain there, alongside a further 700 NATO personnel at Manas airbase, outside Bishkek in Kyrgyzstan. Should the conflict in Afghanistan wind down during 2004, the US government will face the task of deciding what to do with these bases in the context of the BRAC programme. Neither a Bush nor a Kerry administration is likely to abandon such sensitive and salient strategic locations lightly, in view of their proximity to China and the northern tier of the Middle East. The most likely possibility is that Khanabad and Manas will be converted to Forward Operating Bases (FOBs) with a limited fixed infrastructure and semi-permanent troop deployments. A more cost-effective alternative would be to retain the bases as Forward Operation Locations (FOLs) with a skeletal

Asia and Australia

infrastructure that could be occupied intermittently as local circumstances dictated. However, FOLs carry political risks in that part-time deployment of troops could, with some justification, be interpreted by the Central Asian states as merely a provisional and perfunctory commitment to their security.

The long-term commitment of the US to Uzbekistan will be further tested by the decision of the US Congress to insert conditions to the Foreign Operations, Export Financing and Related Programs Appropriations Act for Fiscal Year 2004 that would terminate aid and training programmes on 1 July 2004 unless Tashkent makes tangible progress towards the democratisation goals embodied in the bilateral cooperation and partnership agreement reached in 2002. The Bush administration would probably be unwilling to have its hand forced by domestic opponents on this issue, but is likely to insist on some cosmetic gestures at least from Karimov in order to continue the relationship and demonstrate that the US government takes democratisation seriously.

The US position in western Central Asia appeared to be consolidated further on 13 March 2004 when General Charles Wald, Deputy Commander of US European Command, and Admiral Gregory Johns, Commander-in-Chief of NATO forces in southern Europe, each spoke separately of conducting anti-terrorism exercises with the Azerbaijani naval forces in the Caspian Sea. The announcement drew a predictably hostile response on 19 March 2004 from Viktor Kalyuzhni, Russian President Valdimir Putin's special envoy on Caspian issues, who sarcastically suggested that the Russian Navy might conduct similar exercises in the US Great Lakes. An enhanced US military presence in the Caspian region will seek to improve the security of the Baku–Tbilisi–Ceyhan (BTC) oil pipeline, which is scheduled for completion in early 2005, and facilitate the movement of Kazakh oil across the Caspian seabed in due course. On the downside, US policy runs the risk of ratcheting up tensions in a region that has undergone steady militarisation over the past decade, and where legal ownership of the Caspian Sea itself remains under dispute.

Russian policy in Central Asia

Russia's Central Asian policy has become far more coherent during Putin's presidency. The economic and security dimensions of Putin's regional objectives have been carefully defined and calibrated. For example, although the concept of a formal Eurasian gas alliance proposed by Putin in January 2002 has not materialised, a series of bilateral deals with the CARs has made it a de facto reality. The largest of these was signed with Turkmenistan on 12 March 2003. On very advantageous terms for Moscow, Russia will take the vast majority of Turkmen gas produced over the next 25 years. This will be resold to western Europe by Gazprom – Russia's largest oil company, 38% government-owned – at a much higher price and alleviate Russia's need to develop its Arctic gas fields in the short to medium term. Moreover, several Russian companies, many state-owned, have been swallowing up strategically important plants and factories across the former Soviet states in 'debt for assets' deals. This restores a considerable amount of economic leverage lost after the collapse of the Soviet Union and chimes with the concept of a 'liberal Eurasian empire' promoted in Moscow by, amongst others, Anatoly Chubais – a former first vice-premier and finance minister and now a prominent member of the Union of Rightist Forces party.

Although attempts to develop economic cooperation through an institutional framework sputtered during 2003, the Shanghai Cooperation Organisation (SCO), comprising Russia, China, Kazakhstan, Kyrgyzstan and Tajikistan (with Uzbekistan as an observer), has developed into a regional security organisation of serious content, conducting two sets of joint military exercises during August–September 2003 in eastern Kazakhstan and Kyrgyzstan. The SCO provides a non-negligible counterweight to US influence for Russia and China, and is attractive to the CARs because it focuses practically on issues such as Uighur separatism in China and Islamic radicalism more broadly, which are perceived to be significant local security threats.

There are also indications that, during 2003, the CARs felt sufficiently confident in their statehood to positively re-evaluate their relationships with Moscow. Both Putin and Niyazov have shown a willingness to move on after their row over the phasing out of joint Russian–Turkmen citizenship in summer 2003. Nazarbayev has been a consistent advocate of regional integration initiatives and in May 2003 called for a common currency to be established between Russia, Ukraine, Kazakhstan and Belarus. Though largely symbolic at this stage, the establishment of the Russian-manned airbase at Kant, near Bishkek as well as the coalition base at Manas, in 2003 indicates that Akayev views Russia as an indispensable component of Kyrgyzstan's security (and a bulwark against Uzbek designs). Even the hitherto rather frosty Uzbek–Russian relationship showed distinct signs of warming after Putin's visit to Tashkent in February 2004 to sign agreements on economic and security cooperation. Perhaps surprisingly, the partial exception is Tajikistan, which has functioned as a de facto Russian protectorate since independence. Rakhmonov has stalled over renewing the treaty confirming Russian command over the Tajik border service, which expired on 25 May 2003, and authorisation for the permanent deployment of the 201st Motorised Division of the Russian Army in Tajikistan. Rakhmonov is conducting the sort of bargaining the other Central Asian leaders did with President Boris Yeltsin over a decade ago. But Putin likely understands that Rakhmonov can do little to prevent Russian forces remaining, and that even the US would prefer that the Tajik–Afghan border be patrolled by Russian armed

Asia and Australia

forces than by Tajiks alone or – as would likely to be the case in the absence of the Russians – not at all.

Geopolitical equilibrium

Elements of the Moscow political establishment regard the US military presence in Central Asia as an intrusion into their backyard. But while Russia's reaction to perceived Western encroachment on its interests in Eurasia has been awkwardly unilateral and confrontational, Putin's response to similar challenges in Central Asia has been to play a weak hand well by developing Russia's economic influence and maintaining a military presence. Russia is bound to the region by geographical proximity and embedded infrastructural linkages. Ironically, its preferences for Central Asia are not dissimilar to those of the US administration: stable, secular regimes with developing market economies able to contribute to their own security, but not sufficiently so as to emerge as wholly independent regional players. The real disagreement is over who wishes to be the region's principal security manager. Should a new US administration seek to impose uncomfortable aid conditionality related to good governance and human rights, the post-communist sultans of Central Asia may well turn their gaze back to Moscow and consider that their erstwhile Russian masters were not so bad after all. It is more likely, however, that irrespective of who is in the White House, Washington will in the short and medium term continue to favour security relationships over political reform, and that a somewhat tense but manageable geopolitical equilibrium between Russia and the US will therefore be maintained in the region.

Weak Regionalism in Southeast Asia

In 2003 and early 2004, southeast Asian states faced more serious and diverse security challenges than at any time since the end of the Cold War. Internationally linked regional terrorism remained a particularly serious threat across much of the region. However, member governments of the Association of Southeast Asian Nations (ASEAN) made little progress towards closer or more substantive multilateral security cooperation, notwithstanding their embrace at the Bali summit in October 2003 of an 'ASEAN Security Community' (ASC) as a long-term goal. The Indonesian-inspired ASC was apparently intended in part to emphasise ASEAN members' aim of managing their domestic and intramural security affairs without external interference, particularly in the face of Beijing's drive to increase China's regional influence. Yet, though inspired mainly by a drive to secure southeast Asian support for the campaign against terrorism and the US-led coalition's role in Iraq, President Bush's regional tour soon after the Bali summit underscored the continuing relevance of the United States as a balancing factor in southeast Asian security affairs.

Domestic security concerns

Indonesia and the Philippines were challenged by continuing armed separatist rebellions, to which they responded with new military offensives that were represented as similar in aim to the US-led campaigns in Afghanistan and Iraq. In the Indonesian province of Aceh, a ceasefire agreed in December 2002 broke down; in May 2003, the Indonesian government imposed martial law and launched a major 'integrated military operation' intended to eradicate the 5,000-strong armed separatist Free Aceh Movement (GAM). After six months, Jakarta claimed that operations by the 35–40,000 Indonesian troops and police in Aceh had resulted in 1,000 GAM rebels killed and more than 1,800 others captured. In early November 2003, the operation was extended for a further six months, despite a joint statement by the United States, the EU and Japan – all concerned over the potentially counterproductive impact of Jakarta's strategy in the longer term – urging Indonesia to seek a political solution. During 2003, evidence emerged that GAM was involved in piracy (including the abduction of ships' crewmembers for ransom) at the northern end of the Malacca Strait, though the separatist group denied it.

Only days after the Indonesian offensive against GAM began in May, the Armed Forces of the Philippines (AFP) started *Operation Enduring Peace*, the latest phase of a wider military operation that had begun against the 12,500-strong Moro Islamic Liberation Front (MILF) on the southern island of Mindanao in February 2003. The declared objective was to dislodge 'embedded terrorist cells' that had allegedly executed a series of bombings (for which the MILF denied responsibility), but the broader aim was evidently to force the MILF to re-engage in peace talks. In mid-July the two sides agreed to a ceasefire that, despite occasional clashes, they have broadly respected. In February 2004, Malaysian-brokered exploratory negotiations resulted in agreement by Manila and the MILF to resume formal peace talks in Kuala Lumpur in April. The agreement also mandated the March deployment to the southern Philippines of an 'advance survey team', a precursor to a Malaysian-led international monitoring team that would supervise the ceasefire once formal talks began.

Though the July 2003 natural death of Hashim Selamat, the MILF's long-serving hardline chairman, and a US offer of $30 million in development aid for MILF areas in the wake of an eventual settlement may have facilitated the revival of dialogue, rapid progress seemed unlikely. While the MILF continued to demand a referendum to decide the future of Muslim-populated areas, Manila ruled out any solution that might undermine the Philippines' national integrity. Another obstacle was the government's insistence that the MILF relinquish its alleged links with the pan-southeast Asian terrorist group, Jemaah Islamiah (JI), which the rebels repeatedly denied in the face of considerable evidence to the contrary.

Meanwhile, the AFP continued to engage the Abu Sayyaf Group (ASG), a Muslim splinter group that has financed itself through hostage-taking for ransom, and the communist New People's Army (NPA). During 2002, more than 1,000 US troops had been involved in supporting AFP operations that reduced ASG strength from around 800 to 450. However, following the withdrawal of all but 200 US troops who stayed on to train AFP units, the AFP failed to meet a 90-day deadline imposed by Philippine President Gloria Macapagal-Arroyo in late February 2003 for the ASG's eradication. Controversy surrounded plans to deploy a 750-strong US unit whose role would have included participation in combat patrols, leading to the idea's deferral. In early 2004, the ASG still numbered approximately 250–500 fighters, but the group had been demoralised by factional fighting, according to one of its leaders, 'Commander Robot' (Ghalib Andang), who was captured in December. However, there were also signs that the beleaguered ASG was turning to large-scale terrorism. In late February, the group claimed responsibility for killing more than 100 people in an explosion and fire on a ferry close to Manila. A month later, President Macapagal-Arroyo announced that the arrest of four ASG members and the seizure of explosives had prevented 'a Madrid-level attack' on Manila.

In late February, the ASG claimed responsibility for an explosion on a ferry that left 180 people missing. NPA activity was relatively subdued during the second half of 2003, but escalated significantly during February 2004 as peace talks between the National Democratic Front (NDF), the NPA's political wing, and the government resumed in Oslo. In late February, the NDF rejected a draft settlement that required it to provide a list of all NPA members and a full weapons inventory, but talks continued. While Manila is an enthusiastic US counter-terrorist partner, US forces have been frustrated by operational lapses on the part of Philippines forces.

In Thailand, a major upsurge in violence in the four Muslim-dominated southernmost provinces in January 2004 created a security crisis for the Bangkok government. Four soldiers were killed in an attack at the beginning of the month on an army base in Narathiwat, during which the raiders stole more than 300 weapons. Over the next three months, as many as 60 government officials, security personnel, Buddhist monks and other civilians were killed in shooting and bombing incidents. The government responded firmly, declaring martial law in Yala, Pattani and Narathiwat provinces and dispatching more than 1,000 additional troops (including special-operations forces) to the region. In February, Thailand began survey work for a security fence along sections of the southern border to prevent infiltration from Malaysia which, Bangkok has long alleged, provides sanctuary for Thai Muslim militants and criminals. Nevertheless, given that the separatist rebellion in the south mounted by the Pattani United Liberation Organisation (PULO) and other groups had apparently withered a decade previously, with only isolated incidents occurring in recent years, the scale of the violence during 2004 apparently puzzled the Thai authorities.

While some senior Thai security officials blamed a combination of separatist remnants and young Thai Muslim militants inspired by media coverage of the Palestinian intifada and Iraqi resistance to coalition forces, others claimed that the Acehnese GAM had sponsored the initial attack on the Thai army in order to bolster its own weapons inventory, and that JI involvement was possible. According to Thai Prime Minister, Thaksin Shinawatra, separatists linked to a 'network of international terrorists' were responsible. However, Thaksin acknowledged that discrimination against Thai Muslims had exacerbated militancy in the south and there was consensus in Bangkok that a long-term 'hearts-and-minds' strategy focused on providing more responsive governance and delivering economic and social development was necessary to defeat Muslim militancy. But such measures will not be sufficient. The insurgent raids of early January 2004 showed that the Thai government's adversaries were more numerous and capable and better organised than any notional criminal gangs previously assumed to be the culprits, and that government intelligence on them was severely wanting. Of particular concern are the largely Thai Buddhist security apparatus's ignorance of the Muslim minority's Malay dialect and culture, mutual mistrust between the two groupings and stove-piped Thai intelligence organisations. Thaksin has acknowledged the attacks as a 'wake-up call' and in February ordered a 'new security order' established. But correcting decades of cumulative inadequacy will require more than public admonitions and a few bureaucratic adjustments.

In March 2004, the cabinet secretariat proposed that the government should spend 32 billion baht (US$810 million) on reducing poverty through job creation, infrastructural projects, and providing better access to schools and hospitals. Seeking a less heavy-handed approach by the security forces, Thaksin replaced his defence and interior ministers, and then – after the disappearance of a leading Thai Muslim human-rights lawyer provoked a wave of arson attacks on government buildings in the south – the national police chief and the regional army commander. In late March, though, bombings and the ominous theft of more than a tonne of industrial explosives exacerbated southern Thailand's atmosphere of insecurity.

In Myanmar, the State Peace and Development Council (SPDC) military regime faced continuing domestic and international pressures for political

Asia and Australia

reform. The regime caused international outrage in May 2003 when its supporters attacked opposition leader Aung San Suu Kyi's motorcade in northern Myanmar, killing as many as 75 opposition activists. The military authorities took Suu Kyi, whose National League for Democracy (NLD) won a landslide victory in the 1990 general election, into 'protective custody' and she was held incommunicado. The international response was forthright, with the United States and EU imposing heavy economic sanctions and Japan suspending its aid. In response to the Thai government's announcement in July 2003 of a 'road map' for resolving Myanmar's political deadlock, in late August the regime responded with its own plan for national reconciliation, which will involve reconvening a national constitutional convention during 2004 as a first step. The challenge was to reconcile the interests of not just the military and the NLD, but also Myanmar's ethnic minority organisations, many of which remained armed despite having entered into ceasefires with Rangoon since 1988. A positive development from the regime's viewpoint was a Thai-brokered ceasefire in December 2003 with the Karen National Union, one of the last ethnic minority rebel movements to continue fighting.

Jemaah Islamiah: a continuing challenge

JI, probably the largest regional terrorist network aligned with al-Qaeda, remained prominent among the security challenges faced by several southeast Asian states. Though based primarily in Indonesia, JI's activities extend into Malaysia, Singapore, Thailand, Cambodia, the Philippines and Australia. Revelations in the aftermath of the March 2004 terrorist bombings in Madrid regarding links between Spain-based al-Qaeda cells and JI training camps in Indonesia highlighted the extent of JI's wider international connections.

A car-bomb attack on the JW Marriott Hotel in the Indonesian capital, Jakarta, in early August 2003 killed 14 people and demonstrated the continuing regional threat that JI posed. Nevertheless, security forces in the region scored significant successes against the organisation. After the mass-casualty Bali bombings of October 2002, the Indonesian authorities were demonstrably more willing to take active measures against terrorism, and to cooperate more closely with Western and other southeast Asian intelligence and law-enforcement services. During 2003, Indonesia detained more than 100 alleged JI terrorists and by March 2004 Indonesian courts had convicted more than 30 people for involvement in the Bali attack, including three who were sentenced to death. Technical support from Australia helped the Indonesian security forces to intercept and track JI's mobile phone communications. One effect of Indonesia's more aggressive counter-terrorism stance may have been to deepen a schism within JI's leadership between those favouring an immediate resort to action, and those preferring a longer-term strategy involving efforts to build JI's organisational strength before mounting large-scale attacks on Western targets in the region.

After failing to act, apparently for fear of jeopardising the economically vital tourist trade, on evidence that had been accumulating since 2001 that its southern provinces (particularly Narathiwat) had become sanctuaries for JI, in 2003 the Thai government at last began to take the threat from Islamic terrorism seriously. Having arrested and repatriated a Singaporean JI suspect in May, on the eve of Thaksin's June meeting with President Bush in Washington, Thailand yielded to sustained US pressure. Using intelligence supplied by Singapore, Thai authorities arrested three Thai citizens suspected of being significant JI operatives. With a fourth suspect who surrendered in July, they went on trial in November for conspiring to attack the Bangkok embassies of Australia, Britain, Israel, Singapore and the United States. The need to improve security in Thailand ahead of the October 2003 Asia-Pacific Economic Cooperation (APEC) summit in Bangkok – attended by 20 heads of government including President Bush – led to a joint US–Thai operation days after the Marriott bombing. This resulted in the capture in Ayuthaya, 80 kilometres north of Bangkok, of the key JI fugitive Riduan Isamuddin, better known as Hambali. Hambali, an Indonesian, was believed to have been part of Osama bin Laden's inner circle as well as JI's operational commander. In that capacity, he was alleged to have masterminded the Bali attacks (for which planning discussions were held in Thailand), the Marriott bombing and a string of lethal explosions in the Philippines. Thai authorities quickly transferred Hambali to US custody and received a $10m bounty from Washington. Hambali was held and interrogated at a secret location (possibly the US base on the British Indian Ocean Territory island of Diego Garcia). Within two months of his capture, US interrogators claimed that he had revealed extensive details of JI's operational methods and funding arrangements. Plans disclosed by Hambali included attacks in Bangkok, possibly involving surface-to-air missile strikes on airliners, to coincide with the APEC summit. Furthermore, Thai authorities in 2003 identified Malaysian Islamist links (some by virtue of dual nationals) to the Thai insurgency and believe that some of Thailand's 400-plus Muslim schools ('pon-ohs') have been used for paramilitary training. Potential al-Qaeda or Jemaah Islamiah connections are suspected, and have concerned Western and regional as well as some Thai intelligence officials that transnational Islamists outfits are trying to recruit Thai 'clean-skins' without arrest records or conspicuously Islamic names, appearances or provenances. These concerns are likely to spell sustained pressure on the Thai government to enhance hard counter-terrorism capabilities.

Hambali's interrogation led to the arrest of other significant JI figures. In late September, Pakistani authorities arrested his brother, Rusman

Gunawan, who was also linked to al-Qaeda in Karachi. Others arrested in Karachi soon afterwards included more than 20 Malaysian, Singaporean, Myanmarese and Indonesian madrassa students who were allegedly undergoing terrorist training. The Malaysian authorities subsequently claimed that those arrested, including some who were the sons of JI suspects already detained, were being groomed as future JI leaders. Meanwhile, in September, Malaysian authorities extended the detention of nine members of the Kumpulan Mujahidin Malaysia, which it claimed was a militant organisation aligned with JI. In November and December, they arrested small numbers of alleged JI members in the eastern state of Sabah. In the Philippines, in mid-October, security forces killed Fathur Rohman al-Ghozi, a leading Indonesian JI figure who in July had escaped from custody in Manila where he was serving a 12-year sentence for terrorist bombings in December 2000.

Despite these instances of successful counter-terrorism enforcement and their damaging impact on JI's overall operational capacity and internal cohesion, as well as on its communications and financial links with al-Qaeda, JI and other violent Islamist groups continued to pose serious threats to the security of Indonesia and other southeast Asian states. Part of the problem is Jakarta's ambivalent posture on counter-terrorism. Notwithstanding its moves against the Bali culprits, Indonesian President Megawati Sukarnoputri's government remained unwilling to act decisively to dismantle JI. Significantly, despite retrospective anti-terrorist legislation approved by parliament in April 2003, Jakarta would not declare JI a terrorist organisation, which in turn would justify banning it and facilitate the conviction of terrorist suspects under arrest. Megawati's government faced domestic political constraints. Outlawing Jemaah Islamiah – which translates as 'Islamic community' – might alienate large numbers of devout Muslims and boost support for Islamist parties and their leaders in advance of the 2004 elections. The government's ambivalence stemming from this reality was reflected in an Indonesian judicial decision in early March 2004 to halve the three-year prison sentence for immigration offences and forgery imposed on alleged JI spiritual leader, Abu Bakar Bashir, raising the prospect that he could be freed on 30 April. As the US and Australian governments pressed Jakarta to re-open the case against the cleric in order to prevent his release, in late March new evidence emerged to support claims that he was JI's 'emir'.

In late 2003, at least 10 alleged senior JI figures, including Malaysian bomb-makers Azahari bin Husin and Noordin Mohammed Top, were believed to be among at least 2,000 members of the organisation still free in Indonesia, provoking fears of a terrorist bombing campaign there over Christmas and the New Year. While these short-term fears were unrealised, in early 2004 concern remained high throughout the region. The Indonesian authorities expressed concern that JI might attempt to disrupt the parliamentary and presidential elections scheduled for April–September 2004. In addition to evidence that JI leaders based in madrassas were still recruiting and training new potential terrorists, another cause for concern in Indonesia was the existence of aggressive and impatient JI splinter factions, now operating freelance. These groups included Laskar Mujahidin Kompak (which in October 2003 attempted to re-ignite conflict between Christians and Muslims in Central Sulawesi), Laskar Jundullah based in South Sulawesi and Kelompok Banten in West Java.

In the Philippines, concern centred on JI's use of sanctuaries in areas controlled by its apparent ally, the MILF. In January 2004, six Indonesian JI members were caught attempting to infiltrate from the southern Philippines into the Malaysian state of Sabah, but at least 15 new members reportedly graduated in mid-February from a JI training camp within the MILF's main stronghold, Camp Abu Bakar. By March 2004, the Philippine authorities were more urgently investigating the relationship between the MILF and JI, and sent investigators to interrogate JI members detained in Indonesia and Malaysia.

Even in Singapore, where the local JI structure was effectively smashed in 2001–02 by two waves of arrests that led to the detention of more than 30 local JI members, the security apparatus remained on high alert, particularly in relation to the perceived serious threat from air and maritime terrorism. In October, *Lloyds' List* reported that terrorists might be training in the Malacca Strait in order to seize merchant ships with the intention of detonating them in a regional port or maritime chokepoint.

Regional counter-terrorism cooperation

Despite the continuing region-wide challenge from JI, counter-terrorism cooperation among southeast Asian governments and between southeast Asian states and non-regional governments remained patchy rather than comprehensive. Reasons included incapacity as well as domestic political constraints such as those faced by Jakarta. Despite some notable successes, individual ASEAN members' intelligence and law-enforcement bodies were often poorly paid, ill-trained, lacking in specific counter-terrorism capability and focused on other pressing concerns including separatist insurgency. Thus, Fathur Rohman al-Ghozi was able to escape easily from a 'top security' Philippine prison in July 2003. In Indonesia, documents revealing potential JI targets were captured in July, but not acted on in time to prevent the Marriott hotel bombing. Moreover, despite their neighbours' growing fears over the risk of maritime terrorism, the Indonesian security forces failed to interdict pirates operating in the Malacca Strait and other national waters, where almost one-third of the attacks on vessels recorded worldwide by the International Maritime Bureau's Piracy Reporting Centre occurred during the first three quarters of 2003.

At the ASEAN level, cooperation against terrorism remained under-developed, in spite of the ASEAN Declaration on Joint Action to Counter Terrorism agreed by the Association's 10 members in November 2001 and the Agreement on Information Exchange and Establishment of Communications Procedures, often referred to as the Trilateral Agreement, signed by Indonesia, Malaysia and the Philippines in May 2002. Thailand and Cambodia subsequently joined the Agreement, followed in October 2003 by Brunei. Singapore declined to sign this wide-ranging but rather ill-defined pact (aimed at other types of international crime as well as terrorism), preferring to concentrate on developing bilateral and trilateral intelligence exchanges and other practical counter-terrorism measures with partners in southeast Asia and further afield.

On the wider regional stage, delegates from 25 Asia-Pacific nations met in February 2004 in Indonesia for the Bali Regional Ministerial Meeting on Counter-Terrorism, organised jointly by Canberra and Jakarta. The conference involved working groups on legal harmonisation, and on improving intelligence and investigative cooperation. The two convening countries, Australia and Indonesia, announced the impending establishment of the Indonesia Centre for Law Enforcement Cooperation (ICLEC). Expected to be operational by the end of 2004, ICLEC will be headed by a senior Indonesian police officer and largely funded by Australia at a cost of almost US$30m over five years. It will possess both regional capacity-building and operational mandates. The new centre's remit 'to provide operational support and professional guidance in response to specific terrorist threats or actual attacks' distinguished it from the existing US-financed Southeast Asian Regional Centre for Counter-Terrorism in Kuala Lumpur and the International Law Enforcement Academy in Bangkok, which were both restricted to training and research activities. ICLEC held clear potential utility in terms of institutionalising Australia's role in galvanising Indonesian counter-terrorism efforts, but substantive results were likely to come slowly.

An ASEAN security community

Like previous years, 2003 featured intra-ASEAN distrust and tension. After anti-Thai riots in Phnom Penh, the Cambodian capital, in January 2003, triggered by rumours that a Thai actress had suggested that Cambodia's Angkor Wat temples should belong to her country, Thailand closed its border crossings and both sides withdrew their ambassadors. Bangkok mobilised military units for possible intervention in Cambodia to evacuate Thai nationals. Full relations were not restored until April 2003, after Cambodia compensated Thailand for damage to the Thai embassy. Bilateral frictions between Singapore and Malaysia intensified in 2003, despite the close economic and social links between the two sides, as they clashed over issues ranging from the pricing of Singapore's long-term water supplies from the Malaysian state of Johor to the disputed islet of Pedra Branca, and Malaysian politicians warned of the potential for armed conflict with Singapore. It was only after Abdullah Badawi replaced Mahathir Mohamad as Malaysia's prime minister in November 2003 that the tone of bilateral relations began to improve. Another fraught relationship was that between Malaysia and Brunei, whose dispute over maritime territory containing significant oil and gas reserves escalated in June 2003 when a Malaysian patrol boat chased away an exploration vessel. Occasionally, in the past, tensions between ASEAN members have erupted into border clashes. Several bilateral disagreements, such as that over Pedra Branca, have been referred to international bodies for arbitration because the governments involved do not trust the impartiality of the ASEAN High Council, established by the Association's 1976 Treaty of Amity and Cooperation, as a mechanism for dispute resolution.

This is not to say that ASEAN has been an abject failure. By 1997, ASEAN had achieved its long-held objective of expanding to include all ten southeast Asian states. There is a sense of community amongst southeast Asian political elites, based on a rudimentary underlying regional culture, on shared interests in regime survival and on avoiding the costs of outright conflict. Since ASEAN was established in 1967, there has been no major armed conflict between any of its members, and the Association's role in developing a sense of common interest amongst them should be given credit for helping to mitigate intra-regional tensions. But ASEAN movement towards closer economic cooperation has been glacially slow, and its responses to the East Timor crisis of 1999 were conspicuously weak. Flagrant regional problems like Indonesia's widespread disarray – including religious and ethnic conflict costing thousands of lives, and uncontrolled forest fires causing large-scale seasonal air pollution across southeast Asia – suggest that the Association has lost momentum and direction. It is particularly unsettling, given the increased saliency of transnational Islamist terrorism and southeast Asia's status as the demographic centre of Islam, that ASEAN has also essentially failed to deepen its members' proactive security cooperation. Intramural tensions, compounded by the increased diversity of ASEAN's members since 1995 and Indonesia's effective abdication of its previous role as the Association's low-key leader after Suharto was ousted in 1998, have impeded efforts to intensify such cooperation.

In the late 1990s, the diversity and seriousness of the security challenges facing the region – including terrorism – provoked renewed debate over ASEAN's security role. Southeast Asian policymakers began to question the desirability of revising the Association's core principle of non-interference, and to entertain the possibility of allowing more assertive supranational responses when members' domestic problems threatened

Asia and Australia

neighbours' interests. In December 1999, after the East Timor crisis, the debate over non-interference led ASEAN to adopt the idea of 'enhanced interaction', including activation of an 'ASEAN troika' and resuscitation of the long-dormant High Council to adjudicate bilateral disputes. In practice, however, these measures did little to strengthen ASEAN's security role. The problem of ASEAN's ineffectiveness as a security institution was particularly obvious in the case of Myanmar, where conflict between the Yangon authorities and ethnic minority rebels continued to impinge on Thailand. Large numbers of Karen, Karenni and Shan refugees fled across the border, and by early 2004 approximately two million had settled semi-permanently on Thai soil. Occasionally, Myanmar security forces' pursuit of rebels directly challenged Thailand's security, leading to military clashes between the two countries in February 2001. Illegal drugs from Myanmar also contributed to large-scale social problems in Thailand, leading Thaksin's government to mount a violent 'war on drugs' in which more than 2,000 suspected traffickers were killed. Within and outside the region, the problem of Myanmar was widely seen as a test-case for ASEAN's stated determination to assert itself more vigorously on political and security issues, and Malaysia's then-Prime minister, Mahathir Mohamad, indicated that Myanmar risked expulsion from the Association if it failed to release Aung San Suu Kyi. However, ASEAN acquiesced to Rangoon's August 2003 proffer of a 'road map' lacking a timetable or any mention of Aung San Suu Kyi or her party the following month.

Such persistent evidence of ASEAN's declining credibility provoked a radical initiative from Indonesia. Apparently motivated by its wish to reassert itself as a regional power through ASEAN in the face of perceived challenges from the US and Australia on the counter-terrorism front, Japan over energy security, and China and possibly India's potentially wide-ranging regional security roles, Indonesia proposed that the Association become a 'security community' by 2020. Indonesia's goal of an ASC was adopted as a component of the Declaration of ASEAN Concord II (which also included the objectives of establishing economic and socio-cultural communities) at the group's annual heads of government summit meeting on Bali in October 2003. The initiative focused on using ASEAN's own existing mechanisms – notably the High Council – for resolving intramural disputes, and much closer cooperation on transnational security challenges, including terrorism, narcotics and people trafficking, and maritime security issues. As envisaged in the Declaration, the ASC reflected ASEAN's established collective emphasis on both comprehensive security and the principle of non-interference, explicitly ruling out an ASEAN defence pact, military alliance or joint foreign policy.

The Association's retained axiomatic insistence on non-interference may be a firm impediment to robust conflict resolution, but it does not rule out vastly improved security cooperation. In the coming years, the ASC concept may help ASEAN members to develop their cooperation against terrorism and other transnational threats, provided that they also strengthen their national capabilities and – particularly in Indonesia's case – somehow overcome political obstacles to firmer action. But the recent evidence of ASEAN members' management of bilateral disputes, where recourse to international arbitration is apparently becoming normal, suggests that ASEAN's main instrument for resolving intramural problems – the High Council – will remain fundamentally compromised unless it becomes a judicial rather than a political mechanism

Major powers and southeast Asian security

As noted, Indonesia's promotion of the ASC is partially explained by Jakarta's interest in retaining its status as ranking regional power – despite its domestic disarray since 1998 – by promoting regional self-management of security matters to balance China's assertiveness. Beijing, trying to break out of what it perceived to be strategic encirclement by the United States and its allies, has increasingly flexed its economic and diplomatic muscle in southeast Asia. Since the region-wide economic recession of 1997–98, when it won kudos for not devaluing its currency (which would have further damaged southeast Asian economies), China's regional influence had steadily increased. Most other ASEAN states, of course, were acutely interested in developing closer economic relations with their giant neighbour through the proposed ASEAN–China free trade area (agreed in principle in 2001 and intended to become effective by 2010) to soften the potentially calamitous impact of its rapid growth on their prosperity. At the same time, they were wary of China's potential dominance as well its recent inclination to challenge ASEAN members' territorial claims in the South China Sea. Combining economic leverage with a relaxed diplomatic style that contrasted favourably with the US fixation on security issues and human rights, Beijing still hoped to encourage ASEAN members to take greater account of China's political and security interests.

At the ASEAN–China meeting that followed ASEAN's Bali summit in October 2003, new Chinese premier Wen Jiabao underscored Beijing's benign posture by signing ASEAN's Treaty of Amity and Cooperation (TAC), the basic code for peaceful intra-regional relations. China and ASEAN also agreed on a Strategic Partnership for Peace and Security. Described as 'non-aligned, non-military and non-exclusive', this cover-all document was essentially a regionally focussed expression of China's 'new security concept' that had first been enunciated in 1997, and called for cooperation on political, economic, social, security and regional affairs in the most general terms. While the Strategic Partnership lacked specifics, it nevertheless seemed to represent an early step towards incorporating southeast Asia in an East Asian economic, political and security community

Asia and Australia

led by China, the economic dimensions of which could include ASEAN–China, northeast Asian and pan-east Asian ('ASEAN plus three') free-trade areas.

ASEAN and its members, however, appear to have no intention of acquiescing in China's rise to regional hegemony and remain open to developing closer ties with the other major powers. Also at Bali, the Association signed framework agreements covering comprehensive economic cooperation at summit meetings with both Japan and India. In the security sphere, India signed the TAC. At a subsequent special Japan–ASEAN summit in December, Japan also agreed to sign the TAC, and the two sides agreed the Tokyo Declaration for a Dynamic and Enduring Japan–ASEAN Partnership in the New Millennium, which mirrored the China–ASEAN Strategic Partnership and included a 'political and security cooperation' element stressing the need for enhanced collaboration on counter-terrorism, anti-piracy and non-proliferation.

The United States' security role in southeast Asia showed no signs of diminishing, despite widespread resentment among Muslims in the region over the war in Iraq and Washington's complicated relationships with the Indonesian and Malaysian governments. Sandwiched between visits to Japan and Australia, President Bush's whistle-stop tour of southeast Asia following the APEC meeting in Bangkok in October 2003 carried greater immediate significance for the region's security than either the ASC idea or the ASEAN–China Strategic Partnership. While also seeking to boost US economic links with key southeast Asian partners, Bush reinforced security and defence relations with Thailand, the Philippines and Singapore, cementing their support for the US-led war on terrorism and strengthening US forces' access to southeast Asian staging posts and logistical support. Singapore agreed to deploy minor naval and air units in support of the occupation of Iraq, to which Thailand and the Philippines had already committed troops. The US designated Thailand a 'major non-NATO ally' (MNNA), allowing wider access to American arms and military technology. Under a new bilateral Framework Agreement on Defence and Security signed in October, similar benefits will accrue to Singapore. The Philippines had already been granted MNNA status and was promised at least $356m in US security-related assistance when President Arroyo visited Washington in May.

Economic incentives – such as the plans for a bilateral free trade agreement announced when President Bush visited Bangkok – may help explain these ASEAN members' tightening security relationships with Washington. Yet the reinforcement of Washington's key alliances in southeast Asia also highlighted the continued use by regional states of bilateral security arrangements with the United States to hedge against a widening array of security challenges. China's rising regional assertiveness and influence is likely to intensify this already strong tilt towards close bilateral security relationships with the US. Insofar as the US will be all the more confident in close relationships with effective counter-terrorism partners, the ongoing need among southeast Asian nations to hedge against Chinese ambitions in the region may increase their incentives to strengthen both national and regional security capacities.

Japan: Dynamism Abroad and at Home

Japan's foreign and security policy during 2003–04 has been dominated by three issues: its relations with the United States and planning for the post-conflict reconstruction of Iraq; North Korea's multiple security challenges, and in particular its potentially expanding nuclear capability; and attempts by Japan to enhance its security preparedness through a variety of means, most notably its substantially expanded commitment to developing and acquiring an advanced missile defence capability. Each of these concerns has reflected the underlying trend in Japan's post-Cold War foreign policy towards a more proactive security stance closely aligned with US policies. Equally significant domestic changes are under way. Japan finally appears to be developing a genuine two-party system, shifting away from the fractured multiparty structure that has hampered coherent policymaking. Further evolution could present the Japanese electorate with a clearer and more distinct choice of policies and administrations. Whether this will be sufficient to restore public confidence in the political process or to enable government to devise an effective response to the country's persistent economic difficulties remains open to debate. What seems highly likely is that ongoing diplomatic and political changes will fundamentally reshape the character of the Japanese state.

Washington–Tokyo amity

Throughout 2003 and early 2004, policymakers from the US and Japan expended considerable energy in promoting regular dialogue and consultation. Senior US officials visiting Tokyo included Vice-President Dick Cheney, Secretary of Defense Donald Rumsfeld, Deputy Secretary of Defense Paul Wolfowitz, Deputy Secretary of State Richard Armitage and Assistant Secretary of State James Kelly. In May 2003, Japanese Prime Minister Junichiro Koizumi travelled to the US for a summit meeting with US President George W. Bush, and Bush made a brief visit to Japan in mid-October. Koizumi has consistently demonstrated Japan's strong

Asia and Australia

commitment to the United States and, although the country is constitutionally prohibited from participating in combat operations, Koizumi's government has supported the war against Iraq. This support has involved considerable political risk, given firm Japanese popular criticism of the war as well as resistance from members of the governing Liberal Democratic Party (LDP) and, especially, from the Democratic Party of Japan (DPJ), the main opposition party. Japan, of course, has some self-interested economic and diplomatic motivations for proactive involvement in Iraq. Japan receives 90% of its oil supplies from the Middle East and is therefore eager to promote regional stability there. Support for Washington in Iraq has also been viewed by some as a tradable commodity, useful for securing active American backing for Japan's diplomatic objectives vis-à-vis North Korea. Nevertheless, aligning Japan so unequivocally with the US does appear to constitute a fundamental shift away from Tokyo's longstanding 'dual-hedge' of tilting towards both Washington and the UN to a closer and more cooperative relationship with Washington on a variety of fronts.

In both the run-up to war and its aftermath, however, Japan attempted to position itself as a mediator between the US and key European and Middle Eastern countries. Koizumi engaged in active telephone diplomacy in support of a second UN resolution expressly supporting armed intervention. In early March 2003, Koizumi dispatched Yukio Okamoto, his private advisor, to Kuwait and Jordan and Foreign Minister Yoriko Kawaguchi to the United Kingdom, France and Germany to explore ways of planning for a UN, rather than a US-run, administration in post-conflict Iraq. In a series of visits to Britain, France, Germany and Spain in late April and early May 2003, Koizumi pushed, ultimately unsuccessfully, for an international, UN-led post-conflict reconstruction initiative. At the end of May, having announced a $5 million emergency plan for Iraq on 21 March and a $25m assistance package on 9 April, Koizumi met the president at his ranch in Crawford, Texas – a privilege reserved for the closest US allies. He was also given a CIA intelligence briefing – a first for a Japanese leader and another indication of Washington's strong desire to cultivate its bilateral relations with Tokyo. For his part, Koizumi underlined his continuing support for the US by expressing his government's intention to introduce legislation allowing for the dispatch of Japan's Self-Defence Forces (SDF) to post-conflict Iraq to provide humanitarian, engineering and infrastructure support, and to back the two-year extension of key 2001 anti-terrorism legislation authorising Japan to deploy ships to the Indian Ocean to provide surveillance and logistical support for US and UK naval vessels.

Japan's national parliament approved the SDF deployment legislation on 26 July and the anti-terrorism legislation on 10 October 2003. Sharp opposition from the DPJ and Japanese government fears that SDF casualties in Iraq would expose it to damaging political criticism at home delayed the deployment of an advance SDF investigative team until December 2003. But a staggered deployment of up to 1,000 personnel to Samawah in southern Iraq began in February 2004. The SDF deployment was highly significant. For the first time in its 50-year history, the SDF, albeit nominally restricted to serving in non-conflict areas in Iraq, had been sent to an occupied country without an invitation from an indigenous sovereign government and placed at risk of hostile attack. The fatal shooting of two Japanese diplomats in late November 2003 in Tikrit and the abduction of two Japanese aid workers and one Japanese journalist in April 2004 drove home the considerable dangers faced by Japanese personnel. In the latter case, an Iraqi militia demanded that the Japanese government withdraw its 550 combat troops from Iraq within three days or the civilian captives would be killed. Nevertheless, Tokyo maintained a strong commitment to state-building in Iraq. In October 2003, Tokyo announced that it would provide $5 billion in direct grants and soft loans for reconstruction assistance – almost 10% of an estimated $55bn bill. This amount is less than the $13bn it provided after the first Gulf War, but Japan's additional operational contribution is viewed in Washington as more than offsetting. US officials have spoken of a new 'global alliance' with Japan, and likened bilateral ties to the Anglo-American 'special relationship'.

The US has more concretely reciprocated with reassurances that any minor adjustments in the US military presence in Japan will not lead to a major build-down of US forces deployed there. The two countries agreed in February 2004 to revisions of the bilateral Acquisition and Cross-Servicing Agreement (ACSA) to allow the US military and SDF to better share goods and services. On 2 April 2004, they also concluded a revised US–Japan Status of Forces Agreement. The revision is intended to facilitate the pre-indictment rapid transfer to Japanese authorities of US military personnel suspected of criminal activities. In return for a US willingness to give 'sympathetic consideration' to such transfers, Japan has agreed to allow American third parties to be present during Japanese police interrogation of US suspects. Such an understanding is politically important, as a number of serious crimes (including murder, rape and assault) involving US service-personnel (particularly US Marines based at Futenma in Okinawa) against Japanese nationals have occurred. Improvement of conditions in Okinawa is also important in light of reports of a fractious meeting in November 2003 between Rumsfeld and Okinawa Governor Keiichi Inamine, who called for a reduction of US forces in the prefecture. The American military presence on the island is unlikely to change dramatically in the immediate future. But the new agreement, as well as the relocation subsequently urged by Rumsfeld of the Marine base to a less problematic site at Nago, should ease tensions.

Cooperation with the United States over security has not prevented friction in other areas. The two governments have clashed over economic

Asia and Australia

matters, with Tokyo experiencing considerable frustration over Washington's apparent willingness, despite public statements to the contrary, to exploit a weak dollar harmful to Japan's export prospects. Further, in November 2003, the Koizumi government threatened retaliatory trade sanctions in an effort to persuade the Bush administration to withdraw steel safeguards designed to protect US steel producers from foreign competition. But the US relented. Overall, bilateral cooperation has far outweighed the few points of disagreement.

Confronting North Korea, countering WMD

Japan is directly threatened by North Korea's plutonium-reprocessing efforts and its covert highly enriched uranium programme, as well as by the North's estimated inventory of around 100 *No-dong* medium-range ballistic missiles and an unspecified number of longer-range *Taepo-dong* missiles. There have also been suspected North Korean espionage activities in Japan, efforts to smuggle counterfeit currency and large amphetamine shipments into Japan, and attempts, through companies based in Japan, to illegally export dual-use technology to enhance North Korea's programmes for weapons of mass destruction (WMD). Tokyo has demanded that Pyongyang allow the relatives of Japanese nationals abducted by the North in the 1970s and 1980s to rejoin their families in Japan. The US has vocally supported this demand. In early March 2004, France, the UK and other European countries joined Japan in submitting a resolution at the United Nations Human Rights Commission condemning North Korea's human-rights violations and its past abductions of Japanese citizens.

Japan has participated in international negotiations on North Korea's nuclear programme, via the tripartite April 2003 talks and the six-party discussions in August 2003 and February 2004. Japan has also been very active on a number of other non-proliferation or counter-proliferation fronts. Since May 2003, Japan has been a member of the US-led Proliferation Security Initiative (PSI), which involves the selective application of export and import controls as well as naval interdiction of ships carrying cargo suspected of including illicit WMD-related materials. From Japan's point of view, the PSI is most acutely aimed at North Korea. Japan's Coast Guard (JCG) and Maritime SDF participated in September 2003 in a series of training drills off the Australian coast with French, US and Australian ships. As a collaborative initiative, the PSI represents a step-change in Japan's security activism, although there remain a number of complex legal issues – not least of which is the restriction on Japan's ability to fire on or board non-Japanese vessels – which need to be resolved before Japan can be fully integrated into such activities. Japan's Construction and Transportation Ministry has also imposed tighter inspections on North Korean-registered ships entering Japan. As a result, the number of such vessels entering Japan in 2003 dropped by 29% and the volume of Japan's North Korean imports fell by 32%. On 8 February 2004, the Diet also enacted revisions to Japan's Foreign Exchange and Foreign Trade Law empowering the government to suspend financial remittances to North Korea. In March, the government introduced new draft legislation providing for government authority to ban North Korean ships from calling at Japanese ports.

The high-profile pressure tactics cater to the 80% of the Japanese public that favours economic sanctions against North Korea. By contrast, any government official advocating discussion and engagement with Pyongyang risks exposing himself to public opprobrium or worse, in the case of Deputy Foreign Minster Hitoshi Tanaka – the official responsible for negotiating with North Korea – who was the target of a bomb attack by a Japanese nationalist in September 2003. Underlying the Koizumi's government willingness to adopt tough measures against North Korea, however, is a basic pragmatism. The administration has characterised its North Korea policy as 'pressure and dialogue' ('atsuryoku to taiwa'). Prime Minister Koizumi was careful in early 2004 not to rush to apply the more punitive legislative tools at his disposal, and two groups – one of senior officials (Hitoshi Tanaka and Mitoji Yabunaka), and another of prominent politicians (Taku Yamasaki and Katsuei Hirasawa) – travelled to Pyongyang in February and April, respectively, for important, albeit inconclusive talks with the North Korean government.

Security safeguards, missile defence and regional challenges

Notwithstanding the potential opportunities offered by diplomatic give-and-take with North Korea, Japan's policymakers have had to retain a realistic sense of their country's vulnerability and plan accordingly. One reflection of this has been the passage in June 2003, with near unanimous cross party support, of three key pieces of long-discussed legislation to strengthen the government's ability to respond to security emergencies unencumbered by obstructive local and national regulations. As of April 2004, seven related bills were being debated by parliament. The government had hopes that they would be enacted by early May. At the same time, Japanese leaders are acutely aware that legislation alone is not enough to safeguard Japan's security. A major increase in Japan's willingness to participate in missile defence development with the United States signals perhaps the most important change in Japanese security policy in recent years. In August 2003, Tokyo announced that it would deploy an advanced missile defence system by 2007. The system is a two-tier structure composed of *Patriot*-3 missiles designed to intercept cruise and ballistic missiles close in and upper-tier *Standard*-3 missiles deployed on *Aegis*-equipped destroyers. The missile defence project is expensive.

The initial cost for the 2004 fiscal year is $1.23bn, but when the project is fully expanded by 2011 to cover all four of Japan's *Aegis* destroyers and 16 of Japan's 27 *Patriot* batteries, it will have cost some $4.6bn. These outlays are likely to siphon resources away from other elements in Japan's defence planning.

The missile defence deployment is significant for a variety of reasons. It signals a broader departure from Japan's past cautious approach to missile defence and will involve much more active co-development and co-testing with the US as well as the sharing of critical technology. In this connection, there are indications that the Japanese government, encouraged by the Japan Defense Agency (JDA), will lift its ban, dating from 1967, on arms exports. While Tokyo is free to share arms technology with the US under an existing 1983 bilateral agreement with Washington, the Bush administration is pushing for greater flexibility so that advanced Japanese technology for composite materials, missile nose-cone fabrication and lightweight solid rocket motors can be licensed and sold on to other countries as part of a wider set of US-sponsored missile-defence collaborations. Co-development with the United States raises important interoperability issues and the practicalities of coordination and collaboration when dealing with potential threats. The latest development in this regard has been Japan's decision at the end of March 2004 to share with the US information derived from it new FPS-XX radar systems developed to support new missile defence. It is now possible to envisage a scenario in which Tokyo might inform Washington of a potential North Korean ballistic missile attack on the United States – an interesting inversion of the putative hypothetical, wherein Washington warns Japan. At the same time, the new technology has important constitutional and legal implications adding pressure for a further clarification of the limits on Japan's non-offensive defence policy and potentially challenging the country's long-standing ban on the military development of outer space.

Looking farther out, Japan's decreased vulnerability to potential missile attacks from North Korea or China may prompt a more robust defence posture. Shigeru Ishiba, head of the JDA, suggested publicly that Japan could launch pre-emptive strikes against North Korea to forestall a missile attack on Japan. He subsequently qualified his remarks, making it clear that Japan would have to rely on the US for any such action, but even a qualified pre-emption option for Japan confirms a substantial attitudinal shift. But missile defence may raise concerns among Japan's neighbours, most notably China, which worries that the mobile component of Japan's missile defence plans might allow *Aegis* destroyers equipped with *Standard* rockets to be redeployed to provide protective cover for Taiwan. Chinese Defence Minister Cao Gangchuan has already warned Japan of the dangers of a possible regional arms race prompted by Japan's new missile plans.

Overall, Japan's relations with China have been generally improved in 2003 and early 2004. In the first half of 2003, Sino-Japanese trade grew by almost 34%; Japan now imports more from China than it does from the US. Generational change in the Chinese leadership has encouraged President Hu Jintao and Prime Minister Wen Jinbao to adopt a forward-looking approach to diplomatic relations with Japan and to place relatively less emphasis than their predecessors on contentious historical issues, including controversial visits by Koizumi to Japan's Yasukuni shrine. The shrine issue still matters, but it did not prevent Koizumi from meeting with Wen at the Association of Southeast Asian Nations (ASEAN) summit on 7 October 2003, and two weeks later with Hu at the Asia-Pacific Economic Cooperation (APEC) meeting in Thailand. Moreover, there was a steady stream of official meetings between senior Japanese and Chinese leaders, both in Japan and China, throughout the year in part to mark the twenty-fifth anniversary of the Japan–China Peace and Friendship Treaty. These meetings have facilitated cooperation on issues such as SARS prevention, illegal immigration, disposing of residual Second World War Japanese chemical weapon stocks in China and re-establishing bilateral defence discussions and military-to-military contacts.

Such progress should not obscure significant difficulties in the bilateral relationship. China is now widely seen as having stolen a march on Japan in trade negotiations with ASEAN countries. Japan made up some ground in hosting the Japan–ASEAN summit on 11–12 December (the first time such a meeting has taken place outside the ASEAN region) and by signalling its intention to sign ASEAN's Treaty of Amity and Cooperation (TAC). But this commitment merely followed China and India's signing of the TAC in October 2003, and many believe that intramural disagreements and resistance from powerful agricultural groups in Japan will prevent Tokyo from developing a confident and leading role in the regional integration process. Other sources of Japan–China friction include the dispute over the status of the Senkaku/Daiyoutai Islands, Japanese corporate sex tourism, inflammatory anti-Chinese statements by Japan's more nationalistic politicians (notably Tokyo Governor Shintaro Ishihara) and Chinese public resentment of Japan fuelled by propaganda.

There remain troublesome issues between Japan and South Korea, including territorial disagreements over the status of Takeshima/Tokto Island and the persistent issue of Japan's wartime responsibilities. But bilateral relations have improved. There is some evidence of close, behind-the-scenes coordination (particularly among civil servants) between the South Korean and Japanese governments in seeking to restrain the more hawkish instincts of Washington when dealing with Pyongyang. A more public demonstration of a nascent Japan–South Korea entente was the visit to Japan in June 2003 of South Korean President Roh Moo Hyun and both countries' stress on a future-oriented dialogue. An end to the longstanding

Asia and Australia

ban on Japanese cultural exports to South Korea, an agreement to exempt South Korean students from visa requirements when visiting Japan, the introduction of regular flights between Tokyo's Haneda and Seoul's Kimpo airports, and the launch of extensive negotiations to establish a Free Trade Agreement between the two countries by 2005 further improved the bilateral mood music.

Koizumi's domestic political agility

On the domestic font, 2003–04 has been a broadly successful year for Koizumi, punctuated by his re-election as party president in September 2003 and victory for the LDP-led coalition government in the Lower House parliamentary elections of 9 November 2003. Initial political and economic indicators had suggested a less promising and more unpredictable year for a Japanese leader often characterised as impulsive and at odds with his party colleagues. At the end of the fiscal year in March 2003, persistent deflationary pressures, unemployment in excess of 5%, an apparently stagnant Nikkei stock average at less than 8,000 points and public approval ratings of 42% – the latter two measures being half the level Koizumi enjoyed when first elected LDP president in spring 2001 – had prompted a barrage of criticism from conservative rivals within the LDP. Traditional party barons such as Makoto Koga and Hiromu Nonaka (both former LDP Secretary Generals) echoed the chorus of the Japanese business community calling for the replacement of key cabinet economic policymakers and a reorientation of government policy away from structural reform in favour of expansionary fiscal policy. However, Koizumi refused to bow to such pressure and, buoyed in part by the LDP's strong showing in March 2003 nationwide local elections, positioned himself against the party's old guard as a reformist. This strategy appealed to an electorate widely disillusioned by and distrustful of traditional politics.

Specific national policies and internal party initiatives further bolstered his reputation as a decisive and uncompromising leader. These included: commitments to privatise Japan's national postal system and the four road-related public highway corporations; emphasis on structural reform and resistance to deficit-expanding reflationary initiatives; and a pronounced unwillingness to defer to party factions in making cabinet appointments. Koizumi also shrewdly used the media to appeal to public opinion and to stave off internal LDP revolt by hinting – without promising – that members willing to back him in the leadership election might be rewarded with posts in any post-election cabinet reshuffle. Koizumi's ability to stay ahead of his rivals has also been a product of long-term systemic changes and the specific political context in which the LDP leadership contest was played out. In the Lower House, the replacement in 1994 of multi-member districts with first-past-the-post single-member constituencies has weakened the power of party factions and strengthened central LDP party authority. In particular, the once decisively important Hashimoto faction has been compromised. The allocation, in 2000, of 300 of the 657 votes required in the Diet for the election of the party president to rank-and-file party members, among whom Koizumi is especially popular, has also helped him.

Koizumi's tactics were also very sound. In announcing before the leadership election that he would dissolve parliament and hold a general election in November, he forced many of his rivals to moderate their criticism and line up behind a leader who, despite a dip in his popular standing, was still seen as the individual most likely to attract support for the party from Japan's key floating voters – some 40% of the electorate. This electoral logic became increasingly important following the merger in September of Japan's two largest opposition parties, the Democratic Party of Japan (DPJ) and the smaller, conservative Liberal Party (LP). This long-awaited consolidation – seen by many as the start of a genuine two-party system - was important not only numerically (giving the newly expanded DPJ 136 lower house seats to the 247 held by the LDP in the 480-seat Lower House), but also ideologically in giving a more distinctly conservative tinge to the DJP, which has long sought to attract support from traditionally minded backers of the government. Against this background, Koizumi coasted to a comfortable victory in the LDP presidential contest on 20 September, securing 399 of 657 votes over his conservative rivals Shizuka Kamei (139 votes), Takao Fujii (65) and Masahiko Komura (54).

Koizumi moved quickly to capitalise on his success. In a swift cabinet reshuffle, he unambiguously rebutted his conservative critics by retaining controversial Economic and Fiscal Affairs Minister, Heizo Takenaka, Foreign Minister Yoriko Kawaguchi and JDA head Shigeru Ishiba. Sadakazu Tanigaki, former head of the National Public Safety Commission and an active supporter of structural reform, replaced Masajuri Shiokawa as Finance Minister. Most dramatically and unexpectedly, Koizumi's chose Shinzo Abe to take up the prominent post of LDP Secretary General. As the grandson of former Prime Minister Nobusuke Kishi and son of Shintaro Abe, and a leading LDP politician in the 1980s, Abe has an impeccable conservative pedigree that endears him to many of Koizumi's traditional opponents. His hawkish position on foreign-policy issues, most notably on relations with North Korea, also accounts for his high standing in the eyes of a public vociferously critical of Pyongyang. This public popularity, and his relative youth at 49, has also positioned Abe to challenge the DPJ leaders Naoto Kan and Ichiro Ozawa. Early opinion polls have already ranked Abe behind Koizumi but ahead of Kan as a suitable head of government.

Asia and Australia

A close parliamentary contest

Nimble appointment tactics, coupled with a recovery in share prices and a gradual but steady decline in corporate bankruptcies, helped to boost the standing of the government in the run-up to the Lower House election. By the end of September, the cabinet's approval ratings had jumped dramatically in one month by 20 points to 65%. But the electorate remained concerned by the government's apparent inability to resolve the country's fundamental economic problems. Despite this, the government could take some comfort from divisions among its political opponents. The DPJ, in particular, continued to grapple with internal policy and personality tensions that reflect its heterogeneous political origins – made up as it is of former socialist and conservative politicians. The Lower House elections were also marked by a degree of political novelty. Both the DPJ and the LDP sought to appeal to the electorate by adopting the British political practice of submitting relatively detailed campaign manifestos. Yet Japan's political sociology has yet to evolve to the point of producing post-election adherence to such pledges: many candidates interviewed during the campaign indicated that they would not feel bound by them.

The election campaign itself focused on domestic rather than foreign-policy issues, with little of substance to separate the two principal parties dramatically in the eyes of the electorate. The LDP, together with its two small coalition partners (Komeito and Hoshushinto – the New Conservative Party), reiterated its message of structural reform. In addition to the key issues of postal and highway corporation privatisation, the government presented detailed proposals for tackling the vexed question of pension provision, as well as plans for administrative consolidation and cost-cutting initiatives to enhance the tax-raising autonomy and policy independence of local government. An unexpected, but important political wild card emerged with the government's commitment to constitutional revision by 2005, timed to coincide with the fiftieth anniversary of the founding of the LDP. Specific reforms in this respect include a revision of Article IX, the long-standing clause defining the non-offensive defence doctrine of the SDF, as well the possible removal of the prohibition on SDF participation in collective security initiatives. For its part, the DPJ sought to sell itself as both a more populist and also more radical alternative to the government. This portrayal involved proposals for the abolition of highway toll charges, a guarantee of small classroom sizes, ambitious plans to reduce central government subsidies to local authorities and possible increases in the politically sensitive consumption tax to fund pension reform.

In line with the substantive closeness of the parties, the election outcome was somewhat ambiguous. Including the 34 seats of its Komeito coalition partner and the seven prevailing independent candidates and former members of Hoshushinto (which disbanded in the wake of a poor electoral performance), the LDP actually secured 277 seats, from which it could claim a clear mandate to govern, albeit a reduction on the 287 total it had enjoyed before the election. Koizumi could take comfort from the success of candidates affiliated with his faction and the relatively poor performance of those associated with his conservative rivals within the LDP. The DPJ could also claim a victory of sorts, having boosted its seat total from 137 to 177 (the largest tally for an opposition party since 1955) and having captured 56% of non-aligned voters (compared to 21% who voted for the LDP). This positive outcome represented more a psychological than a practical success, allowing the DPJ to present itself as a potential credible alternative to the government. The unambiguous losers were the small Japan Communist Party and particularly the now even smaller Social Democratic Party of Japan (SDPJ), which suffered the indignity of having its leader, Takako Doi, defeated. Voter turnout was only 60%, 2.5 points down on the 2000 Lower House contest, and a sign of continuing disenchantment with the political process.

Post-election challenges

Koizumi's strategy of running against the LDP party machine, while electorally seductive, has practical drawbacks. One is the growing reluctance of once influential interest groups – medical doctors, dentists, agricultural workers and forestry-owning cooperatives – to support the government. In addition, Koizumi has been forced to compromise with some of his internal party opponents, agreeing in late December to allow road tolls to be used to fund continuing highway development – a sharp departure from his earlier commitment to halt wasteful pork-barrel construction projects and potentially undermining his reformist credentials in the eyes of the public. Cooperation with Komeito has also raised serious policy coordination problems and ideological difficulties for the LDP. Komeito's 24 members in the Upper House of the parliament, when added to the LDP's 115 seats, give the government a majority in the 247-seat second chamber that is often critically important in securing the passage of key pieces of legislation. Yet Komeito and the LDP lack any well-developed joint policymaking mechanism and often differ over basic policy issues. Komeito has, for example, had strong reservations about the government's effort to develop a more proactive security policy and has resisted recent efforts by LDP politicians to promote educational reforms that downgrade individual rights in favour of the development of a broadly conservative set of civic values. Some of this tension has been resolved by political horse-trading. The Komeito leadership has grudgingly supported the Koizumi cabinet's decision to send SDF personnel to Iraq in exchange for the LDP's agreement to consider rescinding income tax cuts to fund the government's pension reforms. Second, Komeito, via its close ties with the controversial lay Buddhist organisation Soka Gakkai, has powerful vote-mobilising

Asia and Australia

power during elections that is often wheeled out in support of conservative candidates. However, Komeito's religious links are viewed with suspicion by many Japanese voters, and the DPJ has seized on this in criticising the government for being overly dependent on support from a non-secular organisation.

The logical solution for the government, particularly in the face of the forthcoming July 2004 elections to the Upper House, is to secure its own independent majority in both houses of parliament. Yet it is not clear that this will be possible. Policy decisions have undercut Koizumi's image as an uncompromising reformer. By late December, popular support for the cabinet, according to a *Nihon Keizai Shinbun* poll, had dropped precipitously to 43%, while the LDP's overall approval rating was at 38%, giving it a 10% lead over the DPJ, but less than half the margin it had enjoyed in August 2003. The budget for the year beginning 1 April 2004 has been criticised for lacking serious reform measures, and highway and postal privatisation are at best only partial, incomplete initiatives. Moreover, the potential for more Japanese deaths in Iraq and the possibility – made more salient by the Madrid bombing – that Japan's support for the United States' Iraq policy could make it a more prominent terrorist target are ongoing political risks. Koizumi himself is committed to a decisively more extroverted Japanese foreign and defence policy. A succeeding government might not be. While Japan's plans for more robust regional security cooperation with the US would likely survive Koizumi's political decline, its tentative global assertiveness – and mission in Iraq – are more in doubt. Yet Japan's regional and global extroversion are dynamically linked, and may be difficult for any political successor to separate. Washington increasingly sees Japan's global activism in support of broader US security goals, and not just Asian ones, as a benchmark for the health of the alliance.

Australia: Rising Regional Power or US Proxy?

Due to the international coverage of the military intervention in Iraq by the 'coalition of the willing' – essentially, the United States, Britain, Australia and Poland – John Howard has probably become the best known Australian prime minister ever. The Australian Defence Force (ADF) was involved in the 1990–91 Gulf War when Australia deployed a naval contingent.

But because there was broader international participation in the first Gulf War, this commitment, undertaken by Labor Prime Minister Bob Hawke, did not attract the same attention as that devoted to Australia a decade later.

Howard, the leader of the Liberal Party–National Party Coalition – the conservatives in the Australian political spectrum – was on an official visit in Washington DC when the terrorist attacks on the World Trade Center and the Pentagon occurred on 11 September 2001. The attacks had a profound impact on Howard, and he was quick to realise how significantly they had affected international security. Australian foreign policy changed accordingly. On his return to Australia, John Howard invoked the alliance provisions of the ANZUS Treaty – signed by Australia, New Zealand and the US during the Cold War, but effectively abrogated by New Zealand in 1995 – as authorisation for Australia to extend broad security cooperation and assistance to the US in the global campaign against terrorism.

The Howard government's foreign policy

Before Australia's 1999 leadership of the UN-sanctioned International Force in East Timor's intervention – arguably the most successful international peace-enforcement/state-building enterprise to date – John Howard had not demonstrated intense interest in foreign policy, preferring to focus on economic issues and national politics. He was conspicuously absent at a number of meetings of the South Pacific Forum, now known as the Pacific Island Forum. From the time of Australia's involvement in East Timor, however, his government has taken a greater interest in the Pacific region. This interest increased dramatically following 11 September 2001, and sharpened further after the bombing by Jemaah Islamiah – an al-Qaeda affiliate – of a nightclub in Bali on 12 October 2002, in which 88 Australian tourists were killed and many others injured.

The Howard government's decision generally to involve Australia in the war against terrorism in Afghanistan enjoyed bipartisan domestic support. Canberra committed the ADF to the war in Afghanistan, and Australian Special Forces played a significant role in several battles – in particular, *Operation Anaconda* in April 2002. To send a self-sufficient force, the ADF upgraded the equipment of Australia's Special Forces before they were deployed in Afghanistan. Only three nations had special-operations troops in Afghanistan that were equipped to operate completely independently of the US military: the UK, Australia and Italy. The Labor Party opposition argued against the commitment of the ADF to the Iraq intervention on the grounds that military action had not been sanctioned by the UN Security Council. In spite of this, the Howard government's decision to join the US and the UK enjoyed majority support within the electorate. Over 2,000 Australian military personnel played important long-range reconnaissance and other roles in early hostilities in the western Iraqi desert in March 2003.

Asia and Australia

Australian assets in theatre included: an Australian Special Forces Task Group with an Australian Special Air Service squadron, which engaged in combat with Iraqi units early in the war; elements of an aviation regiment with three CH-47 *Chinook* helicopters; a squadron of 14 F/A-18 *Hornet* attack fighters; a nuclear and chemical defence detachment of specialist troops drawn from the newly established Incident Response Regiment; a quick-reaction support force drawn from the 4th Royal Australian Regiment (Commando); two P3-C *Orion* maritime patrol aircraft ;and three warships.

Howard's activism and close alignment with Australia's traditional allies, the US and the UK, was broadly consistent with a century of Australian foreign policy. Successive Australian governments – conservative and social democrat alike – have seen cause to support them in conflict. The ADF was involved in the First World War, the Second World War, the Korean War, the Malayan Emergency, the 'konfrontasi' (in support of the newly created state of Malaysia), the Vietnam War and the first Gulf War. Since the end of the Vietnam War, Australia has also involved the ADF in various forms of peacekeeping or peace-enforcement – including Cambodia, Bosnia, Somalia, Bougainville, the Sinai, Rwanda, East Timor and, most recently, the Solomon Islands.

The logic behind such robust commitments centres on Australia's unique economic, political and geographical place in the world. Australia is situated on a vast land mass to the south of southeast Asia. As an immigrant and trading nation, Australia has a vested interest in secure sea and air lanes, which require relative region-wide security. Australia has 60,000 kilometres of coastline, and is the closest 'Western' nation accessible by sea to potential Islamic terrorists in southeast Asia: Australia's maritime security, therefore, is integral to its homeland security. In addition to terrorism, the country faces maritime challenges in the form of illegal immigration, illegal fishing, drug smuggling, threats to biosecurity (e.g., introduction of diseases and pests) and the proliferation of weapons of mass destruction (WMD). Starting on 7 August 2003, an Australian fisheries patrol boat demonstrated the country's relentlessness in protecting maritime interests when it began the 'hot pursuit' of a Uruguayan vessel – its crew had poached rare Patagonian toothfish in Australia's exclusive economic zone – that lasted 21 days and spanned 7,200 kilometres, from the Heard and McDonald Islands across the Indian Ocean to the southern Atlantic. It was the longest hot pursuit in maritime history. But its protracted nature was in part the result of the Australian craft's inability to force the suspect vessel to heave-to due to lack of firepower; ultimately, help was required from British and South African ships. Overstretch of Australia's coercive maritime assets, then, is a concern – especially given the increased salience of maritime threats. Accordingly, Australia has joined the US-led Proliferation Security

Initiative – and joint maritime interdiction programme focused on WMD – and hosted the first exercise under its auspices (*Pacific Protector*) in the Coral Sea in September 2003.

Australia has a population of 20 million, which is very small relative to its physical size, and cannot afford armed forces – in particular, naval ones – of sufficient size to render it capable of ensuring regional security on its own. Nevertheless, as of 2002 Australia spent about 2.0% of GDP on defence – less than the US (3.3%) and the UK (2.4%), but significantly higher than Canada (1.1%) and New Zealand (1.2%). This level of expenditure, coupled with an activist and multilateral foreign policy, is premised on the prevailing view that Australia's security needs are best served by cooperation with traditional allies so as to reinforce their perceptions of Australia as a highly engaged and exemplary international citizen, and their disposition to act in Australia's regional interests.

In 2003–04, Australian foreign policy showed both steady resolve and measured restraint. John Howard noted that the intention in Iraq was for the ADF to assist at the 'sharp end' of the conflict. About 1,000 Australian military personnel remain in and around Iraq in a peace-support role, but Australian troops have not played a major part in Iraq following the defeat of Saddam Hussein's regime. Thus, Australia supported the US and Britain in the principal military engagement, but did not become heavily involved in the aftermath. Australia also continued its peace-enforcement role in East Timor.

Regional challenges, proactive policy

Australia's high-profile involvement in the Iraq war has focused regional scrutiny on the Australian–American alliance and Australia's activities within its sphere of interest in the immediate region. Their concern reached a head following the Bali bombing. On 1 December 2002, Howard was interviewed on the influential Channel 9 programme *Sunday*. Asked whether Australia would take 'pre-emptive' action based on solid intelligence that terrorists in a neighbouring country were planning to attack Australia, he replied, 'Oh yes, I think any Australian prime minister would'. He went on to say that the situation in question has not arisen 'because nobody is specifically threatening to attack Australia'. While these off-the-cuff comments caused momentary consternation in the region, they also showed how Australia's attitude to security issues had changed since 11 September and Bali. Less provocative but notably proactive regional policies confirmed this change.

In particular, heightened Australian concern about failing states in Australia's vicinity reflects new concerns about terrorist threats, which amplify traditional worries about the security of its sea lanes and air lanes. Once these routes were vulnerable only to a substantial state possessing sea

Asia and Australia

or air military power. Increasingly, however, terrorist movements are capable of threatening Australia's security by disrupting, or preventing, the entry or exit of individuals or goods and services. In addition, Australian defence planners are legitimately worried that transnational terrorists might co-opt weak neighbouring states and use them to draw recruits or to plan and stage terrorist operations – potentially against the Australian homeland. At the very least, failed states in the region could also lead to an increase in people smuggling, money laundering, gun running and drug trafficking – all of which support terrorist movements.

In July 2003, in leading the Regional Assistance Mission to the Solomon Islands (RAMSI), Australia demonstrated its intention to fulfil a broad regional-security role by strengthening weak states. This commitment was undertaken in cooperation with all of Australia's Pacific neighbours and at the invitation of the government of the Solomon Islands, where ethnic tensions and economic decline had produced unmanageable lawlessness. In *Operation Anode*, a military deployment led by 1,500 ADF soldiers provided security cover for a 155-strong police contingent of the Australian Federal Police (AFP). AFP Commissioner Mick Keelty reported in January 2004 that some 800 people had been arrested for crimes ranging from professional misconduct to murder. In addition, some 3,700 weapons were seized along with some 350,000 rounds of ammunition. Key gang leaders Harold Keke and Jimmy Rastas were arrested. Australian Foreign Minister Alexander Downer observed that this combined military and police operation had enabled the Solomon Islands government to operate and deliver services to its people free of intimidation for the first time in three years. Australian aid to the Solomon Islands has almost trebled over the past four years and was expected to total $36.2 million in the 2002–03 financial year. The large development assistance component of RAMSI will involve the placement of expatriate advisers in line positions in the judiciary and the prison service, and in key financial institutions to eliminate corruption and create opportunities for economic revitialisation. RAMSI is expected to cost the Australian government between A$200-300m annually for up to ten years.

The Solomon Islands are over 1,500 kilometres northeast of Australia, and their insecurity does not pose a direct threat. But there was concern in Canberra that the collapse of legitimate authority in the Solomon Islands could not only imperil Australia's maritime security but also lend momentum to comparable state deterioration in Papua New Guinea – Australia's nearest neighbour, a mere 160 kilometres from its northern coast. A ceasefire to a long-running secessionist conflict there was established in 1997, and a peace agreement signed in 2001, but disarmament has not been completed and the peace process remains politically fragile. A failed state so close by would pose a major threat to the Australian homeland. Thus, in 2003 Australia entered into an agreement with Papua

New Guinea to provide security assistance to its government. The pact covered a wide range of functions – including economic management, public sector reform, border security, law and justice and, most significantly, policing. In addition to this assistance, Australia extends bilateral aid of roughly A$300m per year and led the Peace Monitoring Group in Bougainville from 1997 until it terminated in June 2003.

Canberra is also acutely concerned about terrorist activity in southeast Asia, particularly in Indonesia. There was considerable focus on counter-terrorism in the run up to the 2000 Olympic Games in Sydney. Australia was then aware of the activities of such organisations as the Moro Islamic Liberation Front and the Abu Sayyaf Group in the Philippines, but it was only after the Bali attack that the range of Jemaah Islamiah's activities, and its links to the al-Qaeda network, were more fully appreciated. Australia has provided substantial counter-terrorism assistance to Indonesia and, to a lesser extent, the Philippines. In the aftermath of the Bali terrorist attack, the AFP worked closely with Indonesian police to identify the terrorists involved and establish evidence that could be used to bring about convictions. In February 2004, Canberra announced the opening of the Indonesia Centre for Law Enforcement Cooperation (ICLEC), to which Australia pledged A$35m over five years. Scheduled to begin operations by the end of 2004, the ICLEC is mandated both to provide operational support for counter-terrorist activities and to build regional counter-terrorism capacity through training and professional guidance. But Australian officials concede that standing regional counter-terrorism cooperation remains inchoate, which will keep the premium on Australia's homeland and maritime security measures high.

Asian perceptions

The strongest argument for opposing Australia's participation in the coalition of the willing in intervening in Iraq turned on Australia's location within the Asian region. Some critics of the Howard government maintained that Canberra's unalloyed support ignored Australia's commitment to multilateralism in that the intervention was not authorised by the UN; and that the problems of the Middle East/Persian Gulf area did not sufficiently implicate Australia's security to warrant direct involvement. Underlying this argument was the view that the prime focus of Australian foreign policy should be Australia's relations with its Asian neighbours – especially Indonesia, which has the world's largest Muslim population, and Malaysia, in which political Islam is influential. Howard did not accept that argument. Nor did Labor's Bob Hawke in 1990–91, when the ADF was deployed during the first Gulf War.

The counter-argument was also strong. Australia was not the only nation in the Asian region to support the decision to invade Iraq and overthrow

Saddam Hussein's regime. So did Japan, South Korea, the Philippines and Singapore. Other Australian governments have demonstrated that it is possible for Australia to maintain its close alliance with the US while enjoying friendly relations with many Asian nations. After all, Japan, South Korea, the Philippines, Thailand and Singapore have security arrangements with the US – and the US regards all of them as major non-NATO allies save for Singapore, which is nonetheless considered a very close partner. Furthermore, the US relationship with China in 2003 was as healthy as it had been for some time. And, for the first time in three decades, a US Navy ship had visited Vietnam. Thus, there was a case that Australia's closeness to the US on Iraq could actually improve its standing in the Asian region – particularly among nations that were not US allies – by presenting Canberra as a potential channel to Washington. The fact that in November 2003 US President George W. Bush and Chinese President Hu Jintao visited Australia, and addressed Parliament on successive days, suggests that this position may be valid. Furthermore, Canberra's stance on Iraq does not appear to have damaged its economic relations with Asian capitals. In 2003–04, Australia agreed in principle with Thailand to negotiate a free-trade pact, and commenced discussions with China to examine the possibility of a similar arrangement.

Balancing Australia's bilateral relationships

Nevertheless, a perception among some Asian countries persists that Australia has become an American regional functionary. This may reflect some maladroit Australian diplomacy and journalism, but does not seem to describe the actual situation. In September 1999, *The Bulletin* magazine ran a cover story titled 'The Howard Doctrine', in which it described the Howard government's foreign policy as that of a 'deputy sheriff' to the US in the Asian region. The article followed an interview with Howard in which there was no reference whatsoever to 'sheriff' in the entire discussion. On several occasions, however, the journalist put it to the prime minister that Australia was a 'deputy' to the US in the region – and Howard unfortunately did not deny the assertion. John Howard has since expressed regret that he did not immediately correct this mischaracterisation. The issue re-emerged on the eve of President Bush's Australian visit. In Washington, on 16 October 2003, an Australian journalist asked George W. Bush: 'Does the United States actually see Australia as its deputy sheriff in southeast Asia?' President Bush, evidently unaware of the context of the question, lightheartedly responded, 'No. We don't see it as a deputy sheriff, we see it as a sheriff'. Following mutual laughter he continued: 'No, equal partners and friends and allies; there's nothing deputy about this relationship'. Bush's first comment had the unintended consequence of providing ammunition to

Australia's critics in the region. But Howard subsequently entered the debate, declaring that 'Australia behaves in the region as Australia; we are not derivative of anybody and we don't seek to imitate anybody'.

It is true that Australia's security relationship with the US is particularly close – and has been since the two countries fought together during the Second World War in the Pacific theatre in 1941–45. This does not mean, however, that Australia has proceeded or will proceed in lockstep with the US. A few examples illustrate the point. Unlike the US, Australia has diplomatic relations with North Korea. Unlike the US, Australia signed up to the International Criminal Court. And, unlike the US, Australia has continued to enjoy cordial relations with Libya and Iran – even when the US had imposed sanctions on both, and even after Bush branded Iran part of the 'axis of evil'. For the moment, of course, the Howard government's foreign policy is basically in line with that of the Bush administration. But disagreements do exist between the two nations, and they tend to focus on trade – in particular, the entry of Australian agricultural products into US markets. These problems will be alleviated, to some extent, by the Australia–United States Free Trade Agreement agreed in February 2004. While the agreement, which as of April 2004 still required approval by the US Congress, should benefit both nations, Australia will continue its campaign for freer trade access to the US in the agricultural area through the World Trade Organisation.

Australia's relationships with Asian governments, with the exception of Malaysia's, are generally cordial. In 2003, Australia negotiated a commercial agreement to sell liquefied natural gas to China. Australia has played a role – involving discussions with China, Japan and South Korea – in the multilateral effort to secure a resolution of issues relating to North Korea's apparent nuclear capability. Attitudes towards Australia within the government of Indonesia are erratic. Australia's central military and political role in East Timor's independence and its close alliance with the US has produced some lingering resentment. But the Bali bombing and broader Western pressure on Indonesia to ramp up its counter-terrorism capability and activity have provided a platform for restoring warm relations – which are economically and politically important to both countries – through security cooperation and institutions such as ICLEC.

Like many Western democracies, Australia experienced difficulties with former Malaysian Prime Minister Mahathir Mohamad, who stepped down in October 2003. It is true that these problems reflect, to some extent, Australia's close relationships with the US and the UK. Given these ties as well as Australia's racial and cultural provenance, Mahathir viewed Australia's pretensions to being a southeast Asian nation with deep scepticism. He also had little patience for Australia's concern for human rights in southeast Asia, and offended Australian governments by citing its own treatment of the aboriginal population to highlight what he

Asia and Australia

considered hypocrisy. It is likely that the relationship between the two countries will improve – though within limits – now that Abdullah Ahmad Badawi has succeeded Mahathir.

Malaysia's opposition remains the primary obstacle to Australia's joining the Association of Southeast Asian Nations (ASEAN) + 3 grouping – that is, the ASEAN nations plus China, Japan and South Korea. New Zealand faces a similar exclusion. This means that Australia's multilateral involvement in the region turns primarily on its participation in the Asia-Pacific Economic Cooperation (APEC) forum and the ASEAN Regional Forum (ARF), the regional security group established in 1994. Through no fault of Canberra's, neither organisation has proven particularly effective, with APEC so large as to be unwieldy and the ARF hobbled by ASEAN's stringent non-interference principle.

Australia's internal foreign policy debate

Australia's next general election will probably occur towards the end of 2004 – but possibly not until early 2005. John Howard is the favourite to win the next election, but electoral results in Australia are usually close. A re-election of the Howard government would probably yield more of the same on strategic issues. Projecting farther out, Howard's age is a possible factor. He turned 65 in mid-2004, and even if successful he could step down before the following election. If so, he would probably be replaced by his deputy (and finance minister) Peter Costello. Costello's policies on economic and foreign policy are close to Howard's. If he becomes prime minister, however, it is possible that Costello would give a higher priority to increasing Australia's role in the Asian region. During his tenure as treasurer, Australia was one of the two countries (the other was Japan) that contributed in the late 1990s to the IMF rescue packages for Indonesia, South Korea and Thailand – all of which were seriously affected by the Asian economic downturn.

It is unlikely that foreign policy will play a key part in the election campaign, though border protection might. When travelling overseas John Howard sometimes makes the point that there is a bipartisan approach to border protection, including mandatory detention, in Australia. This is substantially correct. At home, however, Howard tends to say that Labor is weak on border protection. The issue of asylum-seeker management played a small part in the November 2001 election campaign – which was conducted against the background of the war against terrorism. However, the Howard government was essentially returned to office on its record of presiding over economic prosperity at a time of relatively high growth and relatively low inflation. National security issues, which tend to favour the incumbent, also had a high profile owing to the 11 September attacks. They will continue to resonate.

Kim Beazley, who was strong on national security issues and was a firm believer in the Australian–American Alliance, led Labor to narrow electoral defeats in October 1998 and November 2001. He then resigned from the leadership and was replaced by Simon Crean who, in December 2003, stood down for Mark Latham. In early 2003, Latham made a controversial entry into the Iraq debate when he described Bush as 'the most incompetent and dangerous president in living memory' and referred to Howard as an 'arselicker' with regard to the American president. Following his election as Labor leader, Latham has attempted to improve relations with US representatives in Australia and has promised to remove all 'crudity' from his language. Kevin Rudd, Labor's able shadow minister for foreign affairs, remained in this position following the leadership change. Rudd too is a strong backer of the Australian–American Alliance, but he is also a fluent Mandarin speaker with a deep interest in Australia's involvement in the Asian region.

The Australian Labor Party (ALP) has never adopted the absolutist attitude towards the US taken by the New Zealand Labour Party two decades ago, when New Zealand bailed out of the ANZUS Treaty due to its opposition to the visits by nuclear-armed or nuclear-capable US Navy ships to New Zealand ports. The election of a Latham government would not affect the fundamentals of the Australian–American Alliance or Australia's commitment to the war against terrorism. However, as Rudd has made clear, a Labor government would place greater emphasis on Australia's involvement in multilateral organisations and on Australia's relationships with Asian countries. It would discontinue the Howard government's support for US initiatives on ballistic missile defence. Furthermore, the closeness of the relationship between a Latham government and Washington would turn, to an extent, on whether Bush won a second term in November 2004 – and, perhaps, on the short- to medium-term outlook in Iraq.

Continuity on the horizon

With the trauma of 11 September and Bali still fresh, there will be relative consistency in Australian foreign policy. Irrespective of whether the Liberal/National Party Coalition or Labor is in office, Australia will be intimately involved in the war against terrorism. And Australia's relationships with the United States, the United Nations and the Asian region will continue more or less as previously. However, the nature and intensity of these relationships will depend, to some extent, on who is prime minister in Australia and president in the United States.

Asia and Australia

Africa

Immediately after the US-led intervention in Afghanistan in late 2001, the demonstrated capacity of radical Islamic groups like the Taliban to hijack failed or failing states, and host transnational Islamic terrorist organisations like al-Qaeda, seemed to dictate more proactive Western efforts to prevent such outcomes by rescuing and helping to develop such states. Several were in Africa. Somalia, the continent's most chronic failed state, was considered a prime candidate to be al-Qaeda's next host after the Taliban and al-Qaeda's leadership were removed from power in Afghanistan. But the US and its European allies, seized of more urgent strategic and security matters, merely adopted a preventive counter-terrorism posture in East Africa and the Horn, mainly through the Combined Joint Task Force–Horn of Africa, based in Djibouti. More than two years after the Afghanistan intervention, however, Africa may have acquired greater strategic resonance.

The US, the UK and Norway, along with regional powers like Kenya, sharpened their focus on brokering peace between the Islamist Sudanese government and the Christian/animist southern rebels, and a formal peace deal looked close in April 2004. Other factors make it likely that close American and European strategic attention to East Africa and the Horn will continue. Khartoum, though perhaps more controllable, probably will not abandon either its expansionist Islamist vocation or its violent resistance to political change in other parts of the country, notably Darfur. Further, while Somalia and other weak African states did not prove immediately susceptible to wholesale terrorist co-optation, radical Islam is increasing in Somalia; this development and the absence of effective central government authority there has allowed weapons to flow over the Somali border – especially to Kenya, where they have been used by Islamic terrorists. The modest rise of Islam in Rwanda – many of whose citizens feel Christianity let them down in light of the 1994–95 genocide – is also likely to keep major-power interest piqued. American concern about transnational terrorist threats farther west is reflected in the US Pan-Sahel Initiative, a $100 million counter-terrorism train-and-equip programme for the security forces of Chad, Mali, Mauritania and Niger. Western authorities are also worried about al-Qaeda and Lebanese Hizbullah's illicit fundraising and money-laundering operations in East, Central and West Africa.

Furthermore, democracy and good governance in Africa are slowly advancing. Notwithstanding Rwandan President Paul Kagame's old-style

Map Africa

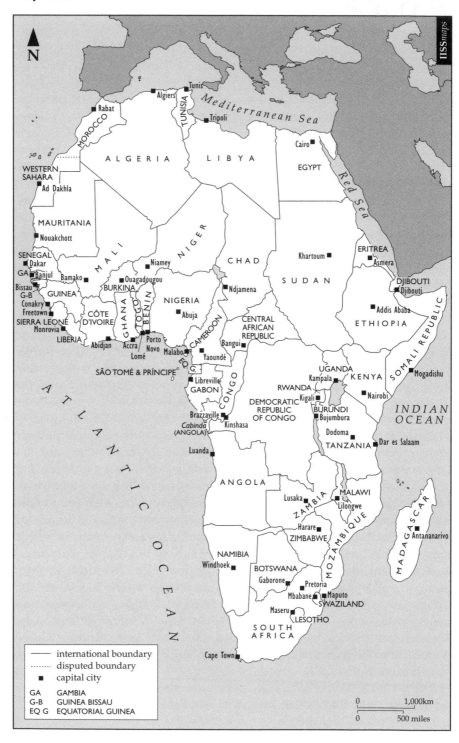

95% victory in August 2003 elections, Kenya's competitive December 2002 elections raised expectations that African countries would merit international aid. Nigeria's April 2003 elections proceeded less hectically than anticipated, and Ghana has held comparatively clean national elections. In South Africa, the ruling African National Congress (ANC) was certain to retain power in April 2004 national elections, which were likely to involve less violence than the 1999 poll – though the relationship between the ANC and the Inkatha Freedom Party remained toxic. Most importantly, regional powers in Africa are taking greater charge of their own problems. Spearheaded by South Africa and Nigeria, the New Partnership for Africa's Development (NEPAD), while seeking investment of $64 billion mainly from the West to achieve a 7% growth rate, in February 2004 announced plans for largely African-financed peer reviews to be completed by March 2006. South African President Thabo Mbeki has effectively abandoned his obdurate notion that HIV does not cause AIDS, a particularly counterproductive stance when South Africa has more HIV-afflicted people - 5.3m - than any other country. In November 2003, the South African Cabinet approved a comprehensive AIDS strategy, including free medicine for all who need it within five years, to combat an epidemic that has continued to spread in sub-Saharan Africa, which as of early 2003 was home to about 30m of the world's roughly 42m HIV/AIDS victims. Since late 2002, South Africa and Nigeria have also adopted more energetic and assertive foreign policies that hold promise for resolving conflict and strengthening states. In Congo, South Africa's proactive diplomacy resulted first in a series of ceasefires and agreements between the Kinshasa government and opposing state and non-state actors, then, in July 2003, in a landmark comprehensive power-sharing settlement. Implementation has been fraught, the rule of law has a long way to go and fighting has continued in the Ituri region, but the level of violence in Central Africa has remained relatively low and in April 2004 a return to all-out civil war appeared unlikely. Effective regional diplomacy was instrumental in inducing Liberian President Charles Taylor to step down and leave Liberia. Nigeria, for its part, provided the leading contingent of peacekeeping troops for Liberia in mid-2003 under the auspices of the Economic Community of West African States. The residue of Central Africa's 'Great War' and West Africa's interlinked conflicts in Liberia, Côte d'Ivoire, Guinea and Sierra Leone still pose daunting challenges that will require sustained diplomatic attention and substantial long-term deployments of peacekeeping troops – some of which would ideally come from major powers with professional armies. Still, sub-Saharan Africa's regional management is arguably better than it has ever been.

The most conspicuous failure of African regional diplomacy involves Zimbabwe, which President Robert Mugabe has ruled with increasing brutality, economic recklessness and disregard for the rule of law. A country

Africa

once able to feed itself, Zimbabwe in early 2004 faced the prospect of famine. Non-interference has been as strong a principle in sub-Saharan Africa as it has been in southeast Asia, and it is dying hard. In May 2003, South Africa, Nigeria and Malawi did respond to outside pressure in attempting to broker a deal between Mugabe and the opposition Movement for Democratic Change. Pretoria later proposed a new constitution and fresh elections, with an eye towards affording Mugabe an opportunity for a graceful exit. But these efforts at 'constructive engagement' were insufficient to move him towards better governance, let alone relinquishment of power. Sanctions imposed by the European Union and the US, suspension from the Commonwealth and the suspension of Zimbabwe's IMF voting rights have also been unavailing. But international futility only places a greater onus on Mugabe's African neighbours to rein him in. Inevitably, NEPAD support has been linked to more effective regional efforts on this score.

Finally, the development of Africa's oil resources remains an important, if sometimes overrated, dimension of its strategic identity as well as its potential for alleviating poverty. Along with Europe, the US is interested in diversifying its sources of supply away from the Middle East. Oil could transform Chad – expected to produce 250,000 barrels per day profitably with the advent of a new pipeline through Cameroon to the Atlantic, owned and built by Western oil companies – from one of the world's poorest countries into a middle-class one. The World Bank is overseeing Chad's development of an oil-based economy. Sub-Saharan Africa accounts for 15–18% of US oil imports. Non-OPEC African oil production – led by Angola, Equatorial Guinea, Chad and South Africa – could double to over 10m barrels per day by 2010, depending on the pace of Western investments. Angola, after OPEC member Nigeria, has the most abundant oil reserves in sub-Saharan Africa, and in 2002 supplied about 6% of US oil imports. Angola alone could produce up to 3.2m barrels per day by 2020. However, optimism about the end of the prolonged civil war in Angola has yet to translate into rapid development of the country's oil and gas sector, which has been hindered by intermittent residual disturbances in the oil-rich Cabinda province. The Angolan government has been slow to approve new development deals, holding out for more lasting onshore investments in facilities that would create jobs in the country. But the oil companies generally prefer cheaper and more secure offshore facilities that are less likely to be affected by unrest in the host country. West and Southern Africa were only expected to offer an additional 100,000 barrels per day of oil production in 2003, despite much greater potential. In the short term, this underachievement compromises Africa's status as a major new oil supply region. In the longer term, however, oil development could dovetail with Africa's growing political maturity to help extricate the continent from the difficulties that have plagued it since decolonisation.

Liberia After Taylor: Watershed for Regional Stability?

Since the death of Liberian President Samuel Doe in 1990 and the end of the Cold War, the United States has kept Liberia at arm's length. The country lost its strategic significance as Charles Taylor's rebellion gathered pace in the 1990s and, though the United States was the only Western country to maintain an embassy in Monrovia throughout the civil war, Washington did not want to get too deeply involved. This has been a huge disappointment to the Liberian people, whose historical ties with the US date back to the founding of the republic by the American Colonization Society in 1817 as a haven for freed slaves. During the civil war, the US military stepped in to evacuate foreigners at intervals when security became especially perilous, but US policymaking on Liberia was largely left to the US ambassador – a powerful figure in Monrovia, but not in Washington. When the rebels reached the capital in 1996, the US sent a couple of warships to the Liberian coast, but deployment on the ground was limited to boosting US embassy security.

Taylor's 1997 election victory won the approval of international observers. Former US president Jimmy Carter, leading a team from the Carter Center, said there had been 'small irregularities' which did not affect the final outcome. But the international community soon found that engaging with Taylor as president was no more successful than ignoring him as a rebel leader, and a consensus gradually developed that regime change was the only way to extricate Liberia from chronic internal instability. This was, however, a narrow view of the problem. Until the 11 September terror attacks, the remedies applied consisted mainly of US and UN sanctions and the Kimberley diamond certification scheme, which slowed the flow of illegal diamonds through Liberia but did little to ameliorate internal unrest.

Taylor remained the central player in the illicit 'conflict diamond' trade, however, and after 11 September it transpired that al-Qaeda was using Taylor's networks to finance its operations and shield its assets. In fronting the sale of Sierra Leonean diamonds through Liberia, Taylor also supported the Revolutionary United Front (RUF)'s brutal rebel campaign in Sierra Leone. In mid-2003, Washington stationed Marines off Monrovia and encouraged the Economic Community of West African States (ECOWAS) to initiate peacekeeping missions, as well as conditioning its operational involvement on Taylor's exile. This posture was sufficient to induce Taylor to relinquish his leadership and leave the country in early August. In mid-August 2003, 200 US Marines disembarked amphibious assault ships and

Africa

entered Monrovia to assist ECOWAS forces already deployed. US forces resumed a sea-based posture in late August, remaining close at hand as a quick-reaction force. Both deployments were sanctioned by the UN, but neither was adequate for the state-building task that was evidently at hand. When British troops went into Sierra Leone in mid-2000 and French troops into Cote d'Ivoire in late 2002, it was to support an elected government. In Liberia, the international consensus was that the elected president had to go and a new government to be legitimised. At its full strength of 15,000, the UN peacekeeping operation in Liberia would be the largest UN deployment in the world.

Towards normality

The International Monetary Fund sent a delegation to Monrovia in December to discuss what can be done to restore some semblance of order to the economy, and a donors' conference, co-chaired by UN Secretary-General Kofi Annan and US Secretary of State Colin Powell, was held in New York in February 2004. The interim government, authorised by a peace agreement between the government and the two rebel groups signed in August 2003, sought $500 million for the first two years – the price tag established by the UN and the World Bank – excluding the existing requirements for the humanitarian investment outlined in a November 2003 appeal for $170m. A minor boon for infrastructure contractors can be expected. The presence at the Liberia donors' meeting of French Foreign Minister Dominique de Villepin was significant, especially as he did not attend a similar gathering held in 2003 for Iraq. The fate of former French colonies in the region hinges on whether the instability spreading outward from Liberia can be halted, and there are potential business opportunities to be considered, too. Conflict resolution and reconstruction comparable in type and scope to what is under way in Liberia, of course, have been mounted before. This time, however, there may be enough momentum and strategic interest to produce a better result. The US has pledged $35m to help build a new Liberian army, and may provide training for Liberian officers. The US has also earmarked $200m for post-conflict assistance.

Some key figures are staying out of the interim government and preparing for new elections. Interim leader Charles Gyude Bryant has asked Taylor opponent Ellen Johnson-Sirleaf to chair a commission on good governance, which will put her in a strong position for a run at the presidency. Johnson-Sirleaf has an international financial background and spent much of the civil war in comfortable exile in Cote d'Ivoire, but came a creditable second to Taylor in the 1997 elections and has played an important role in representing Liberian civil society at successive rounds of talks on the country's future.

Elections are scheduled for October 2005 (as they are in neighbouring Cote d'Ivoire), with the new government due to take office in January 2006. Bryant, a businessman who in 1997 tried to unite the main opposition parties behind a single candidate, will not be permitted to run for the presidency.

As of February 2004, the UN had assembled a force of 5,000 troops and more than 1,000 civilian police in Liberia, with an extraordinarily strong mandate encompassing not only Chapter VII enforcement powers but also the disarmament, demobilisation, reintegration and repatriation of former combatants, a role for the UN in monitoring and restructuring the Liberian police force, and UN assistance to the transitional government in re-establishing 'national authority throughout the country'. The UN Mission in Liberia (UNMIL) is slightly smaller than the biggest force ever deployed in Africa, the UN force in Sierra Leone, which had a maximum strength of 17,500, some of whom are being redeployed in Liberia. The UN force is expected to reach its full authorised strength of 15,000 by mid-April 2004.

The Liberia peacekeepers' early attempts at disarmament were a victim of their own success. A cantonment site on the outskirts of Monrovia was swamped by fighters hoping for cash in exchange for their weapons. The process resumed in February 2004 with more sites and more soldiers. While there was general optimism among UN officials that most fighters would disarm, a hard core were likely to remain in the bush. Experience – especially in Sierra Leone – indicated that there will be a residual risk of rebellion by disillusioned fighters from various factions who did not get what they wanted from the war and do not improve their position during peace.

In early 2004, as the peacekeepers gradually deployed deeper into Liberia's interior, the rebel Liberians United for Reconciliation and Democracy (LURD) seemed to implode. There were calls to sack the movement's discredited political leader Sekou Conneh and replace him with his wife Aisha. She became a key spiritual adviser to Guinean President Lansana Conté, the LURD's most important backer, after apparently foreseeing the 1996 army rebellion in Conakry in a dream. The LURD has always suffered tensions along the usual Liberian ethnic faultlines between its Krahn and Mandingo wings, as well as between battlefield commanders and political leaders.

The regional dimensions

The peace process this time around has an unprecedented amount of international support, but unless the initiative can take in all the region's interlinked conflicts, the same fighters are likely to provoke insecurity somewhere else. The international community has been pursuing the narrow goal of regime change in Monrovia, which has obscured the

Africa

substantial regional dimensions of the conflict. With Taylor apparently out of the way, this may be about to change, and the UN has started to consider ways of addressing the region's problems more widely. There is a UN office for West Africa in Dakar, Senegal, but it keeps a very low profile. As is often the case with the UN, personality clashes and office politics have marred coordination between the UN missions in Liberia and in Sierra Leone and the French and West African force in Cote d'Ivoire. There is, for instance, a real risk that those Liberian weapons being stashed safely over the border in Cote d'Ivoire will be returned to Liberia once Ivorian disarmament begins, thus evading the attentions of peacekeepers on both sides. Controlling the region's remote and porous borders is famously difficult.

Guinea could well be the next West African state to crumble. President Lansana Conté is in poor health. In the December 2003 presidential election, Conté scored an improbable 95.25%, despite being too ill to campaign, thanks partly to a boycott by his opponents who did not want to lend credibility to a patently unfair election. Conté's government has been kept going partly through the support of the United States and the United Kingdom, who initially saw in the LURD a credible alternative to Taylor. The United States has trained Guinean troops in border security, who in turn allowed the LURD to operate along the border. The LURD's patronage prompted Taylor to back anti-Conté rebels, who have not melted away with Taylor's departure. The net effect of US support, then, was increased insecurity. But Conté's backing for the LURD is likely to be less enthusiastic now he has achieved his aim of removing Taylor, and Washington in late 2003 began putting pressure on Conté to stop supporting the LURD. These developments are probably behind the movement's internal rift: Sekou Conneh was a vital link to the Guinean leader, and is now no longer as useful. At the same time, without strong Western backing, Conté is politically more vulnerable. A coup by junior military officers seems a likely method of regime change, and he has no obvious credible successor.

Sierra Leone is now fairly peaceful, though the border area remains a concern and a relatively weak government is being kept in place by large amounts of international aid and support. Cote d'Ivoire's civil conflict is a more acute regional problem, despite the stabilising presence of 4,000 French soldiers. The Liberian civil war was launched from Cote d'Ivoire, and Sierra Leone's RUF rebels came from the Liberian border area. Cote d'Ivoire managed to escape any spillover from the Liberian conflict until 2002, when Liberian and even Sierra Leonean mercenaries appeared on both the rebel and the government side. Even with peacekeepers maintaining an arms-free security zone next to the border, western Cote d'Ivoire remains troubled and lawless. In early 2003, Ivorian rebels tried to end their ties with Sam Bockarie, the leader of the Liberian and Sierra Leonean mercenaries. In the resulting clashes, Felix Doh, leader of the Mouvement Populaire Ivoirien du Grand-Ouest (MPIGO), was killed and

Bockarie had to flee back to Liberia, where he was reported to have been killed by Liberian troops after a heated dispute with Taylor. With Taylor's support, Liberians and Sierra Leoneans fought alongside the Ivorian rebels of MPIGO and the Mouvement pour la Justice et la Paix – apparently opportunistic movements that sprung up in the west of the country with a far less considered political agenda than the main rebel group, Mouvement Patriotique de la Cote d'Ivoire. Ivorian President Laurent Gbagbo in turn was sponsoring Liberian forces backing Ivorian loyalists. Recruited mainly from refugees, they formed a militia called Lima, while others crossed back into Liberia to form The Movement for Democracy in Liberia (Model). Model is made up largely of former fighters from the ULIMO-J militia loyal to ethnic Krahn leader Roosevelt Johnson who were driven out of Monrovia in September 1998. After a string of successes, Model was reining in its military activities by mid-2003, settling into illegal, and profitable, logging.

Model's quiescence, to be sure, indicates that Cote d'Ivoire reduced its support under pressure from France. Yet many of Gbagbo's supporters oppose the January 2003 French-brokered Marcoussis power-sharing peace accord, seeing it as an unconstitutional formula imposed by the former colonial power, and consider France to be biased towards the rebels. Thus, France's position as an honest broker in Cote d'Ivoire is far from assured. The United States initially expressed reservations about Annan's proposals for 6,240 UN peacekeepers to be sent to oversee disarmament in Cote d'Ivoire. This has as much to do with US–French tensions on the Security Council following French opposition to the war in Iraq as it does with US opposition to expensive UN peacekeeping operations, but the UN presence will be vital. France has said its 4,000 troops will stay until after the elections planned for October 2005, but they will not oversee disarmament or provide security for the polls. Nevertheless the peacekeeping contingent – the UN force in Cote d'Ivoire (UNOCI) – was authorised by UN Security Resolution 1528 on 27 February, and began deploying on 31 March 2004.

Faced with armed activity on several fronts, ECOWAS was managing regional security as of early 2004. Ghana is in its second year of the organisation's rotating presidency, and Secretary-General Mohamed Ibn Chambas, halfway through a four-year term, is a former Ghanaian deputy foreign minister, a highly experienced diplomat and a veteran of numerous past Liberian peace processes. Another vital component is the forthright UN Special Representative Jacques Klein, a Bosnia veteran happy to describe Taylor as a psychopath. Klein has high ambitions for Liberia, premised on a highly interventionist UN presence over the next three years, with an army of international civil servants providing technical support to local and central administration and reforming Liberia's institutions and bureaucratic infrastructure. Its role would be similar to that of Britain's Department for International Development in

Africa

supporting the government of Sierra Leone. But to consolidate peace and stability in Liberia, hence in the region, ECOWAS, the UN, France and the US will have to ensure that Cote d'Ivoire's peace process enjoys sustained diplomatic support. The same players would also do well to pay close diplomatic attention to Guinea's domestic politics, and to attempt to forestall any traumatic change of regime thereby encouraging Conté to groom a suitable successor.

The Special Court

One of the key reinforcements to West Africa's recent relative – and highly provisional – stability will be a strengthened rule of law. The UN-backed Special Court for Sierra Leone was, as of early 2004, the key institution. But it is not universally respected. The court has been widely condemned for the crass way it handled Taylor's indictment for his role in backing Sierra Leonean rebels. The indictment was originally issued on 3 March 2003 but sealed, to be announced at a later date. On 4 June, when Taylor was attending a regional summit in Ghana, prosecutor David Crane unsealed the indictment, served an arrest warrant on the Ghanaian authorities and transmitted the warrant to Interpol. This profoundly embarrassed Taylor's Ghanaian hosts, who had not been consulted in advance and were expected abruptly to arrest their guest. In the event, Ghana used diplomatic efforts to bring about Taylor's departure from Liberia and the Special Court acquiesced. Conversely, this 'African solution' has not been entirely to the liking of American officials, who want to see the Liberian leader brought before the Special Court, rather than tucked away in a comfortable villa in Calabar, Nigeria. The US Congress has threatened to cut aid unless the former Liberian leader is handed over, and in October approved a $2m reward for his capture. Northbridge Services Group, a UK-based private security company, then emerged, looking for a backer to fund an operation to go into Nigeria and grab him. As of April 2004, no sponsor had been forthcoming.

One key weakness of the Special Court in Sierra Leonean terms is that it is seen very much as a US creation. Chief prosecutor David Crane is a former US Defense Department lawyer, and Washington has made no secret of its enthusiasm for this model of war crimes court rather than the ex-Yugoslavia and Rwanda courts that are based in another country, and indeed the International Criminal Court (ICC) in The Hague, which it vehemently opposes. Crane has carefully spoken of the Special Court as an institution different from the ICC but potentially complementary to it, rather than in direct competition with it. However, the Sierra Leone government has signed a so-called Article 98 agreement with the United States, undertaking not to hand over US nationals to the ICC. The agreement was signed in March 2003 during a visit to Freetown by then US

Undersecretary for African Affairs Walter Kansteiner, along with a $25m investment guarantee from the US Overseas Private Investment Corporation (OPIC) to support the reopening of the Sierra Rutile titanium minerals mine, once the country's biggest export earner.

The Special Court has indicted 13 main players in the conflict (including RUF leaders Foday Sankoh and Sam Bockarie, who have since died). The process is moving slowly, and most Sierra Leoneans are more interested in the grassroots community activities of the Truth and Reconciliation Commission. The Ivorian parliament passed an amnesty law in August 2003 covering crimes against state security since September 2000, but it specifically excludes economic crimes and 'serious violations' of human rights. Atrocities like the killing of 57 northern Muslims whose bodies were found dumped on the outskirts of Abidjan after the October 2000 presidential election have never been fully investigated. Nor have the abundant abuses of Taylor and his adversaries. The issue of how to deal with those responsible for wartime atrocities remains, and will have to be tackled in Cote d'Ivoire and Liberia.

A daunting task of reconstruction

Liberia's nearer term prospects will depend centrally on the integrity of the new Liberian government. The historical record is not encouraging. Previous interim administrations installed amid much fanfare at intervals during the 1990s crumbled ignominiously, as politically neutral figures from civil society had no leverage against warlords. Furthermore, Taylor himself cannot be trusted to stay out of Liberian politics. Key Taylor lieutenants such as Defence Minister Daniel Chea remain in their posts in the new interim government and his followers have yet to be disarmed. Taylor has already been rebuked by Nigerian President Olusegun Obasanjo for keeping in close telephone contact with his friends back home.

Bryant's administration is a collection of representatives from various factions who may prove more interested in carving out political fiefdoms than in uniting to bring the country out of 14 years of conflict. The 21 cabinet posts are to be shared between representatives of Taylor's government, the LURD and Model, as well as political parties and civil society. There has been substantial horse-trading over the many deputy and assistant minister posts, and some of the appointments are less than reassuring. As well as naming its leader Thomas Nimely as foreign minister, Model has control of the Forestry Development Authority and the Bureau of Maritime Affairs, which will enable it to continue to profit from state resources exactly as it did as a rebel group. LURD has named Kabineh Janneh as justice minister, Luseni Kamara to the finance portfolio, Vamba Kanneh for transport and Lavalla Supuwood for labour. UNMIL has expressed concern that the factions are concentrating more on getting their

Africa

cronies into positions of power than on nominating people who might do a good job.

Despite the installation of the new government, UN sanctions will remain in force until the security situation is calmer. The measures imposed under UN Security Council Resolution 1343 in May 2001 include a travel ban on senior members of the Taylor government, a ban on direct and indirect imports of rough diamonds, and an arms embargo. Sanctions on timber exports were added in May 2003. The sanctions were renewed in December and are due for review again in May 2004, and Annan has commissioned another follow-up mission by the UN panel of experts that has doggedly tracked Taylor's use of false end-user certificates to circumvent the arms embargo. Another enforcement issue is that of ensuring that revenues paid to the Liberia Ship and Corporate Registry for the use of the Liberian flag of convenience are used for legitimate purposes.

The arms embargo will probably stay until a broadly trustworthy and stable government is clearly in place. In April 2004, Liberian government ministers were doubtful that elections could be held as early as October 2005. Registering voters while refugees are still returning home poses practical difficulties, and the refugees themselves are in turn encountering logistical and financial obstacles in making this transition.

A gradual lifting of economic sanctions is likely, provided the interim government regains control of logging areas and is able to operate and enforce a certification scheme for diamonds. The resumption of diamond and timber exports would provide a badly needed revenue stream for the government, which faces a gruelling task in rebuilding the economy. Liberians are hoping peace will bring a revival of mining and rubber tapping, and there are also prospects for the licensing of offshore acreage for oil and gas exploration. Liberia is unlikely to be another Angola in terms of oil, but neighbouring Sierra Leone is attracting interest from international oil companies. Under plans drawn up with the Taylor government, Liberia's offshore is currently divided into 17 unusually small blocks, presumably to maximise the potential income from signature bonuses. In any event, revenues from external sources are sorely needed. The interim government inherited just over $2m in the national treasury, and debt of $2.8bn. Relations with donor institutions are hampered by unpaid debt arrears. On 12 March 2004, however, the UN Security Council passed a unanimous resolution – proposed by the US – freezing Taylor's assets to prevent them from being used to destabilise Liberia. The resolution also provided that those assets should eventually be transferred to a future elected government in Monrovia.

The interim Monrovia government has already shown some flair for financial opportunism. Liberia had cut diplomatic relations with Beijing in 1989 after Taiwan promised $200m in aid for education and infrastructure. When Taylor went into exile in Nigeria, he took with him $3m donated by the government of Taiwan to disarm and demobilise his private militias. In January 2004, however, China deployed 500 troops to the Liberian force, its biggest ever commitment to a UN peacekeeping operation. One of the interim government's first acts was to cut the ties with Taiwan forged by Taylor's government and establish diplomatic relations with Beijing in exchange for pledges of substantial aid. But a long stream of assistance will be needed. More than 80% of Liberia's population are unemployed, 74% have no access to safe drinking water and 60% lack access to sanitary facilities. Life expectancy is 48 years and infant mortality a striking 157 deaths per 1,000 births.

The international stage?

Liberia's tragedy is that in order to attract a high level of international commitment, it had to fall apart completely. A generation has grown up knowing nothing but civil war. Communities and even families have fractured, and basic but vital skills like childrearing are no longer being handed down. There are few schools. Foreign investment is limited to those companies that were happy to deal with Taylor, who may not always have the best interests of Liberia in mind. Child soldiers get a great deal of publicity, and hopefully therefore lots of aid, but now all of the former combatants have to find new lives and livelihoods, and cannot live indefinitely by donor initiatives, however well designed. Estimates of the number of fighters vary widely, but there could be up to 58,000, including women and children.

Nigeria, the ranking regional power, is playing a key role in Liberia, which became particularly important for establishing regional peacekeeping and crisis-management credibility when Nigeria's help in the Cote d'Ivoire crisis was rebuffed. Liberia presents an opportunity to show how regional diplomacy under an elected, civilian government can yield a far better result than the chaotic one in Sierra Leone that followed Nigeria's intervention under late military leader Sani Abacha. ECOWAS – whose manpower and political clout derive primarily from Nigeria – has been playing a strong and effective role in the region's interlinked conflicts. But especially as several of its member states are implicated in them, and if more regional states start to crumble, ECOWAS is not likely to be able to stretch itself further. Outside military and diplomatic help will be needed to sustain UNOCI in Cote d'Ivoire, and could be needed in Guinea. In addition, Sierra Leone will require a strong, if diminished, UN presence – down to 10,000 in early 2004 – to ensure that gains achieved there are consolidated and that a shift of focus to Liberia and Cote d'Ivoire does not allow Sierra Leone to slip back into conflict.

Africa

Congo: A Landmark Year, but Problems Persist

The Democratic Republic of Congo (DRC)'s civil war was five years old on 2 August 2003. Less than three weeks earlier, a new power-sharing government had been established in Kinshasa after months of tortuous negotiations and arm-twisting among rival factions. Politicians and diplomats triumphantly declared that the war was over, and the World Bank said the government's performance was good enough to warrant the writing-off of much of its $10 billion in foreign debt. The country does have a better chance of stability and economic improvement in 2004 than it has had for more than a decade. But the security and political agreements remain fragile. Several hours of shooting in the capital city of Kinshasa in late March was followed by Congolese President Joseph Kabila's claims that former soldiers from the late Mobutu Sese Seko's regime had attempted to overthrow the new government. More broadly, fighting continued throughout 2003 and into early 2004 along the country's eastern axis, from Ituri district in the northeast to Bukavu in the southeast. There has been little sign of a peace dividend outside the tiny political and bureaucratic caste running the new order.

The establishment of the transitional government in July 2003 did not mean the end of violent conflict: many of the factions negotiating in Kinshasa also covertly sponsored local proxies in still-simmering mini-wars in eastern Congo. But it was a landmark insofar as it showed a shared commitment by rival factions to settle their differences by political negotiation rather than resort to arms. As a product of the inter-Congolese dialogue which started in South Africa in April 2002 and subsequent political accords, the transitional government aimed to bring the armed and non-armed factions into a cooperative arrangement. At the apex, Kabila remained president, a post he has held since the death of his father in January 2001. There are four vice-presidents, each representing a different political faction: Yerodia Abdoulaye Ndombasi, for Kabila's appointees; Jean-Pierre Bemba, for Mouvement pour la Liberation du Congo (MLC); Azarias Ruberwa, for the Rassemblement Congolais pour la Democratie (RCD-Goma); and Arthur Zahidi N'goma, for the non-armed opposition. In a complex scheme, the vice presidencies, cabinet posts, state company directorships and 500 parliamentary seats are shared among Kabila's extant government in Kinshasa, five rebel movements, civil society groups and the non-armed opposition. The government is designed to stand for two years, whereupon national elections will be held. During this time, the national army is to be rebuilt, drawing on the assets of all the contending factions, and the rebel-held provinces are to be brought back under national control.

In spite of the ongoing hostilities in eastern Congo, progress in establishing new administrative and political structures – including those for Ituri – encouraged multilateral bodies such as the UN, the World Bank and the European Development Fund to increase financial and technical support for post-conflict reconstruction in the DRC, and to improve the administrative capacity of the new government.

Beyond paper agreement

Negotiations to share out ministerial positions took most of the first half of 2003. Reaching consensus on the structure and functioning of the new government was a considerable achievement, given the level of mutual distrust and political division. Each party joined the government with a differing perspective; within each party there were varying degrees of enthusiasm and commitment. Many in President Kabila's camp believed they were merely widening their previous government to include erstwhile opponents without any substantial surrender of their own power. In the opposition camp, the MLC was the most enthusiastic and RCD-Goma the most sceptical. These differences have been less important than the calculation that drove the parties into government: that they gain more negotiating within the new government than fighting outside it. Thus, their sticking to the agreement will depend on the government working well and delivering benefits to the factions' leadership and their support bases.

The main political factions reached broad agreement on the core structures for power-sharing at the centre, but there were disagreements about how these could be made more accountable and representative. For example, it remained uncertain whether parliament would have the power to review and change mining contracts signed by the mines minister or cabinet. At the end of 2003, the president's office was still making many of the key decisions on security and the economy, although it had to negotiate a little more energetically, taking into account some of its new partners. At the same time, some government ministers who were not affiliated with Kabila were asserting themselves constructively. Foreign Minister Antoine Ghonda – from Bemba's MLC – vigorously defended Kabila and Congo's transition at the African Union summit in Mozambique in 2003. There were also some signs immediately after the formation of the new government that each faction was keeping its erstwhile rivals usefully under scrutiny, and that the new administrative structures facilitated these checks and balances. The core 'money' functions of the government, for instance, were spread among the various factions: economy, finance, budget and planning were all given to different parties, each understudying the other. No one party or faction had total control of an economic sector.

Africa

Such elaborate structures may have impaired administrative efficiency somewhat. But it was more important, in the context of a fledgling government in a war-torn country, that they provided a check on revenues and spending with each faction.

The next major hurdle will come in 2005 or, more likely, 2006, when national elections are to be held. Initially, the prospect of an electoral test exerted some discipline in the government. No party wanted to be held responsible for breaking up the government, lest they lose support. In late 2003, both Kabila's Parti Populaire pour le Reconstruction et le Developpement and Bemba's MLC started preparing for elections, glad-handing supporters across the country and appointing fundraisers. By early 2004, however, growing doubts emerged about the election timetable and preparations. These required censuses to be taken, voter registration to be implemented and an independent electoral commission to be established – none of which had occurred as of April 2004. Opposition politicians tended to believe that Kabila would delay elections in order to further entrench his rule. Recognising that political inertia would spark new discontents threatening the stability of the transition, parliamentarians started to scrutinise government policy more effectively. If parliament is able to develop an oversight role, it would earn itself some popular credibility and lay the basis for a more dynamic relation between executive and legislature after the elections. But parliament's legitimacy is limited, as it has been configured by appointment on the same power-sharing basis as the cabinet and the quartet of vice-presidents.

A national army?

Unsurprisingly, security cooperation among the factions has been an especially knotty problem. Its crux is that all three of the main armed groups – RCD-Goma, MLC and Kabila's clique – are disinclined to disband independent armed forces or relinquish arms caches and military financing, which they feel they may need as fall-back options should power-sharing fail. The major points in contention after the July 2003 power-sharing agreement was reached were: the distribution of military high command posts in the new unified national army, control of the 11 military regions, and the relationship between central government and provincial administrations. The military region and command issues were referred to the 'comite de suivi' (follow-up commission) established to resolve disputes in implementing the accord. Rival claims to senior posts and regional commands of a national army dominated negotiations in 2003. The composition of the officer corps and the regional background of the foot-soldiers were likely to dominate negotiations through 2004.

RCD-Goma's Ruberwa, who runs the defence and security ministry, announced that the new national army would have some 150,000 soldiers.

Given that the aggregate number of combatants was around 350,000, this meant that some 200,000 additional soldiers would have to be disarmed, demobilised and rehabilitated. In the original timetable for the transitional government, by the end of 2003 they were all meant to have joined a new national army under a new joint command, trained by teams of military experts from the European Union (EU). But progress on disarmament, demobilisation and rehabilitation (DDR) was held back by political disputes, mainly over which fighters and commanders would run the new national army and which would take retirement, as well as a shortage of funds.

Belgium, France and the United Kingdom have offered to help finance the building of the new national army. But with an estimated cost of more than $1bn (including retirements and pensions), they cannot foot the bill alone. At an international fundraising meeting in Paris in December 2003, the World Bank said it was willing to raise a special fund for demobilised fighters, but raising adequate funding was likely to take until mid-2004 or longer. Military reform and building a new national army that would take many of the die-hard fighters out of circulation was to have been a key task of the transitional government; its failure to make reasonably swift progress caused it to lose credibility. Similarly, its failure to establish a new professional national police force to tackle the growing number of criminal attacks has eroded support for the Kinshasa government.

Political and economic reform
Congo was reunified on a de jure rather than a de facto basis. Thus, the political arrangements agreed in July 2003 charged the new transitional national government with fulfilling a key ground-level prerequisite to post-war reconstruction: the reform and rebuilding of state institutions. The first major indication of its capacity to accomplish this task was the attempt to rebuild a national customs and excise service. The formerly rebellious RCD-Goma administrations agreed to the principle of surrendering revenue to the centre. In practice, however, they were reluctant to do so in the absence of alternative revenue sources, which were needed to preserve political patronage. Amplifying the problem, the Kinshasa-based transitional government was unable to pay its own functionaries, let alone the provincial governments. But other efforts to reintegrate the national economy were less contentious. These included reunifying the monetary system and establishing uniform exchange rates for the Congolese franc, as well as re-establishing the national authority of the Banque Centrale du Congo (BCC) in Kinshasa as the only institution able to issue money, both of which were essential to the government's ability to control the money supply and inflation. BCC officials were included in the new government's first joint delegation to eastern DRC – which included Kisangani, Goma and Bukavu – in August 2003.

Africa

In the inter-Congolese dialogue, participants agreed on devolving some central government functions to the provinces. Efforts to do so faced formidable administrative and practical difficulties because provincial and local governments were even more under-resourced than the central government in Kinshasa. Further, the conflict-torn parts of eastern Congo have lost most of their qualified administrators, who were either killed in the fighting or chose to depart for reasons of comfort and opportunity. There were also political obstacles to devolution. Congo was one of post-independent Africa's first failed states but there was still little consensus about how the state should be rebuilt – that is, as to how much power should be allocated to the centre, how much to provincial and local structures, and how much shared concurrently. Proponents of devolution sought a balance between accountable structures at local and provincial level with rebuilt central authority. But opponents of devolution argued it would further weaken the authority of the state in Kinshasa and promote secessionism, defeating the very purpose of the new political arrangements.

As of April 2004, there had been little substantive progress on establishing a workable balance of authority between the central government and the provinces. The main sticking points were financial. Former rebel authorities in Gbadolite, Goma and Bukavu remained reluctant to surrender even a proportion of locally collected revenues to the Kinshasa, claiming that they had not received any subvention from the Kinshasa government and needed all monies to finance their rudimentary provincial and local government structures. During the civil war, local revenue collection was often arbitrary and extortionate – sometimes reaching millions of dollars a week in each province – but, unsurprisingly, little was used to finance public projects or pay local civil servants. Vice-President Bemba, who has overall responsibility for economic policy in the power-sharing government, has stated that the national budget for 2004 would be premised on the full integration of provincial and national revenue collections into a national tax and excise authority. But making that system work is critically dependent on better relations between provincial authorities and central government. These relations were on hold pending the Kinshasa government's announcement of new governors and senior civil servants in the provinces. Though these appointments were due by early 2004, as of early April the new governors had not been named.

Pressure for de facto political and economic devolution remains a potent threat. Figures such as Kyungu wa Kumwanza, former governor of Katanga province, General Nathaniel Mbumb, who led the Kolwezi rebellion in 1979, have re-emerged to demand a strongly federal form of government. Some activists in RCD-Goma and their allies, including veteran oppositionist Etienne Tshisekedi, who has a substantial power base in Kasai, have also demanded that greater powers be devolved to the provinces. Such calls from leaders in the mineral-rich zones of Katanga and Kasai represent a powerful challenge to Kinshasa. RCD-Goma's Eugene Serufuli, backed by a local militia of some 10,000 fighters in Kivu-Nord province, has also railed against interference from Kinshasa. Through April 2004, Kabila preferred to buy off dissenting politicians in the provinces by offering them jobs in the capital rather than making concessions on devolution or federalism.

Residual conflict in Ituri

Lack of trust held back progress on power-sharing at the centre mainly because of disputes about control of resources. Such problems were even more acute at the provincial and local level, where armed factions still threatened public security. In Ituri in the northeast, some 50,000 people were killed in factional fighting between 1999 and early 2003, and a further 500,000 fled the district to others regions of Congo or to neighbouring states. The conflict shaped up as a proxy war, with sponsors from Kinshasa, Goma, Rwanda and Uganda backing rival factions, shipping in weapons and shipping out the area's deposits of gold and diamonds. By April 2003, the fighting was intensifying and UN officials were predicting mass slaughter, perhaps genocide. Both the rate and the mode of killings were horrific: women and children were gunned down or hacked with machetes, then mutilated. As predictions grew more dire, the UN grew increasingly uneasy. Its Mission d'Observation des Nations Unies en Republique Democratique du Congo (MONUC) was chronically under-manned and under-supplied. It was also legally impotent, as its weak Chapter VI mandate discouraged armed intervention on the part of participating troops.

Tensions mounted again after Uganda withdrew its troops from Ituri district, leaving a power vacuum the local militias were fighting to fill at a growing cost of civilian lives. MONUC had no battle-hardened soldiers to send into Ituri. Instead, in May 2003 it dispatched a battalion of Uruguayan soldiers who had been on guard duty in Kisangani. The 700-man Uruguayan contingent proved too small, and security in Ituri continued to deteriorate. UN Secretary-General Kofi Annan was then able to focus the UN Security Council on Congo's war. To the surprise of some, in June 2003 France agreed to lead a European intervention force – with a robust Chapter VII mandate, giving troops the right to intervene to stop killings wherever they occur – in Ituri. At the same time, the MONUC force was to be expanded to 10,800 as the French-led force was deployed. In part, it seemed that President Jacques Chirac's government wanted to prove that the French Army still could and would take on important roles – justifying its permanent seat on the UN Security Council – even though it had declined to join the Anglo-American invasion of Iraq. It also helped Paris to shore up its regional relations with both DRC and Uganda, which had completed a strategic shift in favour of Kinshasa in 2002, while keeping the Rwanda government, which viewed the DRC as both a strategic threat and a source of wealth, guessing. But French generals were less enthusiastic than Paris' diplomats, and insisted the deployment in Ituri would last no longer than three months, by which time the UN was expected to have deployed enough troops in Ituri under a stronger mandate.

The French force was unable to pacify the entire district, which is about the size of Belgium and the Netherlands combined, but it did secure the capital city, Bunia, and surrounding areas and greatly reduced the frequency of violent confrontations. Thus, the security operation in Ituri was a qualified success: while almost 2,000 deaths occurred there in May 2003, ten times that number had been predicted. Political efforts there were also at least partially successful. The new International Criminal Court made it clear that it had investigators in the field gathering information to be used against the Ituri faction leaders in a possible trial. This concentrated minds, reduced the clashes and prompted several faction leaders to travel to Kinshasa in search of a more conventional political role – as ministers or advisors – or funds to bankroll a new political party. Moreover, the UN and local civilian leaders established a special interim administration – the Administration Speciale Interimaire de l'Ituri (ASII) – in which all of the district's political and military factions were represented, and which elected an executive body to implement policy. In addition, the ASII included an assembly and several commissions to handle reconstruction and ceasefire negotiations with the local militias. The old militia-controlled local administration was dismantled and the new authority started to disburse some of the funds allocated to it from the EU and the World Bank. Part of the French force's mandate, and subsequently that of the Bangladeshis, was to protect and underpin the ASII.

The ASII was held up as a foray into local conflict resolution that might work in other areas. Given the recent history of mass killing and material deprivation in the district, however, credible security guarantees and the capacity to disburse development funds for short-term repairs after the conflict and for longer-term investments in clinics and schools were essential to the empowerment of the assembly in Ituri. These evolved, but far more slowly than hoped. Like the national power-sharing government in Kinshasa, Ituri's multi-party order was fragile and venal. The central conflict in Ituri was between Thomas Lubanga's Union des Patriotes Congolais, drawing support mainly from the Hema people and backed by Rwanda, and Ndjabu Ngabu's Front des Nationalistes et Integrationistes, constituted mainly from the Lendu and backed by the Kinshasa clique around Kabila and Mbusa Nyamwisi, who leads the RCD-Mouvement de Liberation (RCD-ML). Uganda spread its largesse across several of the smaller militias, including Commandant Jerome Kakwavu's Forces Armees du peuple Congolais (FAPC) and Chief Kahwa Mandro Parti pour l'Unite et la Sauvegarde de l'Integrite du Congo (PUSIC). All of the militias pledged their allegiance to ASII while also striving covertly to undermine it and confine its authority to the main city, Bunia.

Bangladesh agreed to send three battalions of peacekeepers to Ituri to take over in September 2003. The Bangladeshi battalions gradually fanned out up-country to try to bring the more remote militia-controlled fiefdoms under control. Their success has been mixed. Generally, the Bangladeshis have been able to hold the line in Bunia, despite some clashes. But farther away there have been several more massacres, one of the worst being an apparently random slaughter of passengers disembarking from a ferry on Lake Albert in February 2004. But some of the fighting has been tactical and strategic, according to the dictates of a proxy war. Some aggression has also been aimed at positioning forces to control resources. In 2002, Chief Kahwa of PUSIC wrote to Heritage Oil, whose board includes the military-business entrepreneur Tony Buckingham, explaining that he controls the area around the company's exploration sites and would collect the appropriate taxes. Then, in mid-2003, Kahwa visited Libya, where he had discussions with the Libyan affiliate of Tamoil about operations in Ituri. Data on the oil reserves in Lake Albert is scarce, but some Heritage officials believe that it could be one of Africa's biggest offshore fields. Ituri's gold reserves are impressive too, though none of the interested companies (which included South Africa's Anglo-American Gold Investment Co., Ghana's Ashanti Gold Co. Ltd. and Canada's Barrick Gold Corp.) have been able to start industrial-scale production.

Recalcitrant conflict in the Kivus

With the advent of the ASII, there was at least a road map to resolution of the conflict in Ituri, even if some of the militias didn't choose to read it. But no such plan materialised in the equally war-torn Kivu-Nord and Kivu-Sud, which were racked by violence between RCD-Goma and its Rwanda-backed scions, on one hand, and local Mom groupings supported by RCD-ML and Kabila's circle. Violence in the Kivus was also more intractable and intense than that in Ituri. The battle lines are more clearly drawn in the Kivus because of the military and political dominance of the RCD-Goma, which controlled rebel administrations in Goma (capital of Kivu-Nord) and Bukavu (capital of Kivu-Sud). That primacy came under strong attack in 2003 from a combination of Mayi-Mayi fighters and Rwandese rebel fighters (including some drawn from the Interahamwe groups and former government army linked to Rwanda's 1994 genocide).

Although the initial pretext for Rwanda's military intervention in the Kivus in 1998 was to establish a security bulwark against the Interahamwe and ex-Forces Armees Rwandaise fighters, by 2002 the conflict had

Africa

become resource-driven. In 2001, the frantic pace of coltan exploitation by RCD-Goma and its Rwandan allies drove the provinces' brutal militarisation and social degradation. As the coltan price crashed in 2003, RCD-Goma diversified its revenue sources to include gold trading, local taxes and cattle. The RCD-Goma chieftains in the Kivus were ambiguous about support for the organisation's relations with the Kinshasa government – even after RCD-Goma won national representation in the transitional government, and indeed, RCD-Goma officials were still commonly accused of having real allegiance to Kigali. For Rwanda, engagement in the Kivus offers a neat conflation of security, strategic and commercial imperatives.

Notwithstanding Rwanda's spoiler role, Kivutian civil society groups pushed for a multi-dimensional peace deal with regional, national and local components. They wanted the transitional government to address Kivutian nationality, ethnic and land-use issues, which they claimed lay at the root of the fighting. To do this, the writ of the Kinshasa government would have fully to extend to the Kivus. RCD-Goma leaders there countered these pressures in two ways. First, they co-opted local Mayi-Mayi leaders by entering into local treaties with them. This effectively isolated RCD-Goma's other opponents, the Rwandan rebel groups that were sustained by elements of Kabila's clique. Second, RCD-Goma helped negotiate the return and surrender of several Rwandan rebel leaders – most notably, Paul Rwarakabije in November 2003. Based in eastern Congo, Rwarakabije had led the Forces Democratiques de Liberation du Rwanda (FDLR), which included a mixture of younger generation rebels and 'genocidaires'. Rwarakabije's surrender was evidently a long-prepared gambit and reflected the extent of Rwanda's intelligence network in Congo. Official documents obtained by the UN also revealed that Rwandan intelligence had secured the free passage of the Hutu fighters by paying off senior members of the RCD-Goma administrations, including the RCD-Goma governor of Kivu-Sud, Xavier Chiribanya.

Rwandan officials claim the Rwarakabije defection – he has been promised a high ranking post in the Rwandan Defence Force – has decapitated the Rwandan rebel group based in Congo. This assertion has some credence. Another 4,000 ex-rebels returned to Rwanda's Mutobo demobilisation camp from the DRC at the end of January 2004. The remaining Rwandan rebels in Congo – about 12,000 according to UN estimates – no longer represent a serious threat to the Kigali regime, according to an assessment provided by Rwandan Army Chief of Staff James Kaberebe to Aldo Ajello, the EU Special Envoy to the Great Lakes. William Swing, the UN Secretary-General's Special Representative to the DRC and head of MONUC, has stated that most of the remaining rebels are being held hostage by FDLR commanders who refused to negotiate with Kigali.

Criminal and commercial activity

Criminal networks have become as serious a threat to Congo's stability as militant political opposition. Criminal organisations have raised money through exploitation and smuggling of Congo's gold, diamonds and cobalt and organised arms shipments, as well as smaller criminal operations such as smuggling and car-jacking. Successive reports by a UN panel on illegal exploitation in Congo confirm links between criminal networks and politicians and military officers from all the main factions. In many cases, criminal networks have also served as financiers and organisers of rebel militias.

Working closely with the World Bank, the power-sharing government announced a series of economic and judicial reforms, including the establishment of a new legal and regulatory framework. Prior to the formation of the power-sharing government in July 2003, there was a spree of looting and illicit contract awards in both government and rebel-held zones. Those contracts and all others signed during the war were meant, under the terms of the power-sharing accord, to come under scrutiny by parliament and the ministerial commissions. The corruption and politicisation of the judiciary, however, have obstructed efforts for greater accountability, and the theft and smuggling of state-owned resources continued unabated after the power-sharing government was formed.

The government's official evaluation estimated in late 2003 that up to 50% of Congo's diamond production was smuggled across the Congo River to Brazzaville. There were also reports that individuals named in UN reports as arms and mineral traffickers – such as Viktor Bout, Yuri Sidrov and Sanjivan Ruprah – had resumed business operations in Kinshasa. Without progress on judicial reforms and the re-establishment of a national police force with a serious investigative capacity, the criminal networks' power and influence are likely grow and undermine efforts to restructure the economy and attract legitimate investment.

From war to disorder

By early 2004, the central African security landscape had changed sharply. Both Uganda and Rwanda had essentially dropped their national security arguments for intervention in eastern Congo. Both had announced their commitments to the new power-sharing government in Kinshasa, and both had resumed full diplomatic ties to Kinshasa. Rebel fighters based in Congo, opposing the Rwandan government, had been militarily marginalised. These diplomatic developments did not, however, preclude covert security interventions in Congo by Rwanda, Uganda or indeed Angola or Zimbabwe, which had all deployed several battalions of troops to Congo's war fronts between 1998 and 2002. But the primary battlefield had become a political one again, and involved Congo's rival factions

Africa

struggling for dominance rather than outside actors with their own regional agendas.

There remained much distrust among the Congolese political leaders and their supporters, and the potential for a resurgence of war was reinforced by large quantities of arms cached around the country as hedges against the failure of the new power-sharing order. But violence in Congo has become linked to crime and commercial interests as much as political ambition. As of April 2004, a return to the all-out civil war splitting the western and eastern regions of the country looked improbable. But worsening criminal violence has the capacity to erode much of the country's recent civil progress unless the government can reach agreement quickly on a new national security service – including both a reshaped army command and a police force – to tackle the insecurity. Even with a consensus among factions on the composition of these forces, financial and technical support from major powers and multilateral institutions will be required for them to be brought to bear quickly and effectively.

Zimbabwe: Waiting for an Endgame

The subversion of domestic laws and increase in localised disorder continued apace in Zimbabwe in 2003–04 – a situation exacerbated by government policy and lack of food security and healthcare as well as general economic collapse. Negotiations between the government and opposition – officially denied by sources on both sides – sputtered on and off inconclusively. But for the vast majority of Zimbabweans the hardships of daily living occupied every moment. President Robert Mugabe's intransigence and the widening divisions within the Zimbabwe African National Union–Patriotic Front (Zanu-PF) over his succession, coupled with the opposition's inability to mobilise sufficient support to effect a change of government, all contributed to a sense of political stalemate and social anomie within the country. Punitive action taken by the Commonwealth (and individual member states), the EU and the United States against the government's systematic abuse of human rights contrasted strongly with the backing offered by regional leaders in southern Africa to the regime in Harare. At a time when Africa was engaged in a public renewal of its commitment to good governance and sound economic management, the ongoing crisis in Zimbabwe seemed a stark reminder to African leaders eager to demonstrate reinvigorated foreign policy that efficacious regional diplomacy required them to back fine words with concrete deeds.

In 1980, fresh from the Lancaster House Agreement establishing Zimbabwean independence and the transition to majority rule, Mugabe was viewed by some as a pragmatist. The constitution enshrined property rights, adopted the 'willing buyer, willing seller' model for land reform and, as part of a negotiated compromise, guaranteed 20 parliamentary seats for the defeated white settlers. Mugabe deliberately de-emphasised the issue of land reform, which had been much discussed at Lancaster House, and the acquisition of 8% of the country's commercial farmland by party and bureaucratic elites seemed to signal further that Mugabe was not serious about drastic land reform and redistribution. It has since become clear that Mugabe is in fact an ideologue enamoured of power. He brutally suppressed dissent in Matabeleland in the early 1980s, and bullied potential political rivals into submission. These included Zimbabwe African People's Union (Zapu) leader and later Vice President Joshua Nkomo (in 1987 Zapu merged with Zanu under the 'Unity Accord'), as well as significant figures within Zanu-PF itself, such as General Josiah Tongogara. Mugabe also abrogated the ten-year clause prohibiting changes to the constitution, later attempted to formally establish a one party state – a move thwarted only by the election of ex-Zanu-PF dissenters to parliament and changing international circumstances – and re-introduced land as a campaign issue in the 1990 elections. In 1995, Jonathan Moyo, Zimbabwe's current Minister for Information, was quoted as saying that 'Zanu-PF has no political philosophy beyond the desire to stay in power by hook or by crook'. Over the course of nearly ten years, the party's obsession with regime security at all costs has only intensified.

Constitution and judiciary under pressure

The government's assault on the constitution and its institutions is rooted less in Mugabe's commitment to addressing the land question specifically and more in his frustration with the limits on action it imposes across all areas. Indeed, the re-emergence of land as a defining question in Zimbabwean politics underscores the centrality of the constitution as a bulwark against Zanu-PF excesses. Starting in 1990, the government passed a series of bills whose main thrust was to give it the legal means to expropriate land from the commercial farming sector without recourse to financial compensation. Until 1998, the land issue was primarily employed as a means of mobilising an increasingly disenchanted electorate to support Zanu-PF on polling day and, invariably, was put back on the shelf once the governing party was securely back in office. The slow pace of land acquisition by the government, its redistribution to party apparatchiks and regime favourites rather than landless peasants, served to fuel further discontent within Zimbabwean society. The 1998 UN Development Programme conference on land to reach an agreement between the donors, international financial institutions and the Zimbabwean government foundered on Mugabe's wish to administer the proposed donor resources with minimal accountability. Thereafter, the government moved towards a more overtly aggressive position on land. This was brinkmanship designed to force the hand of the international community. It failed for two reasons: the staunch unwillingness of donor countries – the United Kingdom in particular – to finance land reform without transparency and other safeguards; and the Zimbabwean judiciary's rulings against the government's challenges to property rights and due process.

With the constitution itself increasingly seen by the government as an obstacle to addressing the land issue, Zanu-PF officials began a campaign to harass and intimidate the judiciary, the independent media and other elements of civil society. The ruling party has pressured judges, forced the resignation of those deemed inimical to Zanu-PF and replaced them with friendlier ones. Mugabe has remarked dismissively, 'If judges are not objective, don't blame us if we defy them'. The passage of the Access to Information and Protection of Privacy Bill, which established a media commission to implement onerous defamation, libel and 'privacy' standards of which violation carries heavy penalties, in early 2002 raised vehement protest among independent media organisations. The government's summary closure of the independent newspaper, *The Daily News,* and persecution of its editors highlighted the importance it placed on controlling the media and its willingness to dispense with rule of law when it was seen as detrimental to Zanu-PF. Again, recourse to the beleaguered Zimbabwean courts resulted into a brief re-opening *The Daily News* in January 2004, but the government shut it down a week later.

Mugabe and the 'Third Chimurenga'

Mugabe's nepotism and cronyism have distanced him from the party rank and file. His second wife Grace and nephew Leo Mugabe have been involved in numerous dubious business deals involving government contracting and have outraged Zimbabweans by their ostentatious lifestyles. Corruption charges have routinely arisen against senior members of the Zimbabwe government, which has simply blocked court-mandated action against perpetrators through presidential pardons and 'creative' legislation passed by the Zanu-PF majority. Nevertheless, Mugabe has an acute sense of history and, however buried beneath tactics driven by the requirements of personal and regime survival, it remains a guide to his conduct and ultimately actions. The turning point for Mugabe, moving him out of his relative torpor, was the looting of the War Victims Compensation Fund by senior party officials, exposed by a judicial inquiry. This transgression inspired a series of demonstrations by angry war veterans that culminated in a humiliating public standoff with the president in 1997.

Profoundly shaken by the inaction of his security forces in quelling these demonstrations, Mugabe belatedly recognised his own political vulnerability and at the same time the potential of war veterans as a movement outside of party interests open to his control as well as the saliency of the land issue as a way of re-establishing his authority within the party and securing his position in history.

The establishment of the Movement for Democratic Change (MDC) in September 1999 introduced into the Zimbabwean political landscape what was arguably the first substantive challenge to Zanu-PF rule since independence. Inspired by growing dissatisfaction with government corruption and slipping standards of living, exacerbated by the imposition of a structural adjustment programme in 1992, the leader of the Zimbabwe Congress of Trade Unions, Morgan Tsvangirai, led a series of strikes against price hikes imposed by the government in late 1997. Fresh from this success, a broad-based coalition of NGOs, church groups, the labour movement and commercial interests united to establish the National Constitutional Assembly with the purpose of ensuring that any post-Lancaster House constitution would reflect democratic values, retain property rights, and limit executive powers and presidential terms in office. Its constituency was drawn, ironically, from the urban-based beneficiaries of the post-independence expansion in education and social services. At the same time, the prominence of a few white Zimbabweans in the MDC, as well as the financial support that it received from commercial interests, suggested to government officials that the relative political quiescence of the remaining settler community had come to an end and that it was actively testing Zanu-PF capacity to hold onto power. The surprise defeat of the government's referendum on the proposed constitution in February 2000, followed by the polling success of the MDC in parliamentary elections in June that year despite irregularities, made it clear that the opposition enjoyed broad support, especially in the urban municipalities.

In response to these multiple challenges to his position, Mugabe drew upon his revolutionary past for inspiration. The approach he adopted towards reclaiming the support of the population had distinctively Maoist characteristics. Sidelined by the Communist party in the aftermath of the disastrous 'Great Leap Forward', Mao Zedong mobilised the youth and the army in a virulent campaign against his own government and party under the putative claim of returning to the ideological purity of the liberation period. Mugabe, for his part, has utilised the metaphor of the 'Third Chimurenga' (the 'First Chimurenga' having been the armed opposition to colonialism in the nineteenth century and the second being the liberation struggle itself) as a way of rekindling the ideological fervour of the liberation era among the disaffected elements of society. In so doing, he has sought to frame the parameters of political choice between Zanu-PF and any form of opposition to his rule in terms that paint all his opponents (and

Africa

any 'wavering' friends at home and abroad) as supporters of colonialism and racism. The land question, which remained a festering sore for Zanu-PF's key rural constituency, provided Mugabe with an issue around which he could mobilise support, while the war veterans became a personalised instrument for asserting authority and striking terror among his opponents. Thus, in late 2001 he established a youth militia, under the cover of vocational training centres sited on the outskirts of key urban centres, to serve as 'shock troops' for the regime.

The 'storm that destroys everything'

The Shona word 'gukurahundi' – meaning 'the storm that destroys everything' – was invoked by Zanu-PF in the final days of the liberation struggle and again in the suppression of dissent in Matabeleland in the early 1980s. The term bespeaks a kind of wilful nihilism, whereby the economic devastation wrought by the land occupations, the systematic abuse of human rights and famine in the wake of the general collapse of the Zimbabwean economy are not just accepted as by-protects of regime security but promoted as means of advancing it. They are products of a new 'gukurahundi' instigated by the regime. Schooled in a violent course of Zanu-PF ideology, deification of Robert Mugabe himself and subject to military discipline as well as selected training in techniques of violence and torture, the 'Green Bombers' (as the youth militia is more colloquially known) provided Mugabe with the requisite instrument to embark upon an extra-legal campaign against the 'enemies of the state'. Former members of the youth militia have admitted their involvement in the torture and killing of opposition supporters, as well as being brutalised themselves and forced to carry out attacks on their own families. Poor conditions within the camps have reportedly begun to cause some of the young Zimbabweans to desert their posts, as has the increasingly hostile reception of the population as a whole.

The land issue, which had triggered the onset of the crisis, has taken on a new shape as a consequence of the virtual collapse of the agricultural sector. The 'fast-track' approach to land redistribution, as the wholesale occupation of white-owned farmland came to be called, was done without reference to proven farming skills by occupants or provisions for technical expertise or financial credits by the government. The result, predictably, has been reduced planting, a failed harvest and the outbreak of foot and mouth disease among cattle, all culminating in a slow abandonment of farms and return to the urban areas or communal lands by occupants. Concurrently, the seemingly irrepressible impulse of senior Zanu-PF members to use the process as a means of obtaining title to commercial property – even if it meant driving black small-holders off the land again – caused consternation among putative government supporters. While Mugabe declared in July

2003 a 'One Man One Farm' policy in an effort to respond to these accusations, the burning of hundreds of homes and eviction of newly settled tenants by police at the behest of government officials intent on taking ownership continued. Indeed, a report produced by the Presidential Land Review Committee in November 2003 found that while less than 5% of the country's arable land remained in white hands out of over 30% before the invasions, only 127,200 black families had actually been resettled as opposed to the 300,000 claimed by the government. Beyond the issue of who benefited from the redistribution and how to return the land to productive use, there remains the difficult question of who is responsible for settling the not inconsiderable debts held by ex-farmers.

The collapse of an economy once seen as a regional 'breadbasket' and, with that, the spectre of famine dominated the lives of ordinary people over the last year. By the end of 2003, inflation was running at 622%, unemployment was estimated at 70% and there were critical shortages of basic foodstuffs, petrol and medicine. The currency had been devalued a number of times, and its tumbling worth was reflected in the scarcity of notes in high enough denominations to pay for nominal items such as bread. Government action has been ineffective. In December 2003, Mugabe appointed Gideon Gono governor of the central bank. He proceeded to raise interest rates roughly to the level of inflation, pushing some financial institutions to the verge of failure. In March 2004, two local banks collapsed, triggering a run on currency. With an estimated six million Zimbabweans threatened by starvation, international donors, NGOs and the World Food Programme (WFP) assumed a crucial role in providing emergency food to newly vulnerable communities. Shortages of government-held grain provisions (apparently due to internal theft) and accusations that local officials manipulated food distribution to favour Zanu-PF supporters moved the WFP to insist that the government recommit itself to allowing direct emergency assistance without government constraints.

Internal disarray in both parties

The opposition MDC and its supporters continued to be harassed, intimidated and even murdered by Zanu-PF militants and the state apparatus. The trials of Morgan Tsvangirai and other key personnel in the movement dragged on well after it was established that the government's key witness and evidence were not credible. Tsvangirai was forced to endure a two-week stint in jail in June. Elections remain flashpoints. During the run-up to presidential elections in March 2002, municipal elections held in September 2003 and a bi-election in the Kadoma Central district in December 2004, orchestrated acts of violence occurred against the MDC and its supporters. The MDC itself has expanded its contacts abroad and has become adept at arguing its case to a wider international audience.

Africa

However, efforts by Tsvangirai to mobilise his supporters in a series of nationwide strikes in March and June 2003, designed to topple the regime, failed to garner the expected crowds. This revealed the thinness of the MDC's political strategy and ultimately forced the MDC back to the negotiating table the following month.

While criticism of Mugabe and Zanu-PF's gross violations of human rights, handling of the land issue, corruption and economic mismanagement is fully deserved, the MDC itself has some shortcomings. Though a broad coalition of interests bound together by a shared desire to unseat Mugabe and his party, the MDC has yet to provide a clear articulation of how it would address the deeply rooted structural problems facing the Zimbabwean economy. The launching in January 2004 of 'Restart: Our Path to Social Justice – the MDC's Economic Programme for Reconstruction, Stabilisation, Recovery and Transformation' was an important step towards addressing some of these deficiencies and preparing the MDC for a role in government. But in certain respects it also demonstrated the uneasy coalition politics within the organisation. The 'Restart' document states that both the pre-2000 land-ownership situation and the current situation is unacceptable, and advocates the creation of an independent land audit commission 'to establish the physical and legal status of all land-holdings'. The document adds that 'where people are found to have been settled legitimately according to the commission's criteria, or are subsequently legitimately settled, they will be fully supported'. Nevertheless, the party's position on the return of land illegally seized during the 'fast-track' process remains unclear and is therefore potentially destabilising. More broadly, there are disputes within the MDC leadership between Tsvangirai's 'trade union' wing and Deputy Leader Welshman Ncube's 'intellectual' wing. In July 2003, Tsvangirai faced criticism within the MDC when he publicly characterised South African President Thabo Mbeki's representation to US President George W. Bush that political reconciliation talks had begun between Zanu-PF and the MDC as 'false and mischievous' and 'without foundation'.

Within Zanu-PF, tensions grew over the succession issue and the absence of any clear political heir. In January 2003, a tentative approach by two senior Zanu-PF figures, Emmerson Mnangagwa and General Vitalis Zvinavashe, to the MDC prompted heavy criticism from Mugabe loyalist (and party outsider) Jonathan Moyo. Zvinavashe's unexpected resignation as army commander in November 2003 was interpreted as reflecting his desire to engage in fulltime politics and, perhaps, to distance himself from the government. Mnangagwa is reportedly seen to be Mugabe's choice as a replacement, but he is deeply unpopular with the party rank-and-file and younger members of the party are worried that their future is being compromised by the older generation of leaders. In April 2003, Mugabe said, 'We are getting to a stage where we shall say fine, we settled this matter [the land issue] and people can retire' In May, he called for a debate on succession. These moves seemed to indicate an intention to step down in an orderly fashion. But discussion of the issue was quashed at the Zanu-PF party congress in June 2003. In September 2003, Vice-President Simon Muzenda died, but Mugabe did not name a new vice-president. His apparent intention was to keep internal opposition divided. Indeed, the president subsequently launched an anti-corruption campaign aimed at party and government officials who profited from the land invasions or black market activities, targeting a number of younger contenders for party leadership. Whether this 'clean-up' constituted a purge of Zanu-PF dissenters by Mugabe, a move to clear the ground for his chosen successor or merely an effort to keep party followers off-balance and allow him to cling longer to power remains to be seen. Parliamentary elections are scheduled for March 2005.

Africa faces Zimbabwe

As of early 2004, the persistent failure of the government and the opposition to overcome their mutual distrust and rancour and begin serious negotiations on transitional arrangements seemed understandable. Tsvangirai, having been subjected to a treason trial, incarceration and a personal assault, appeared to be in no mood to abandon the MDC's court case challenging the veracity of the 2002 presidential elections. For his part, Mugabe insisted that the opposition had to recognise him as president as a precondition for talks. Efforts by South Africa, Nigeria and Malawi to encourage talks in May 2003 had fallen apart and despite rumours of contact between the two Zimbabwean parties no significant progress had been made by April 2004.

At the time that Africa is seeking to reinvigorate continental institutions and promote a development strategy grounded in democracy and market economics, the crisis in Zimbabwe stands as a serious challenge to the commitment of African leaders to realising these values in practice. At the heart of this conundrum has been the position of South Africa, whose leadership under Mbeki has been crucial to opening a new dialogue with the Group of Eight (G-8) in support of the New Partnership for Africa's Development (NEPAD). While Mbeki has been adamant that the deteriorating situation in Zimbabwe should not influence the G-8's position on NEPAD, the salience of Zimbabwe's problems makes linkage politically unavoidable. South Africa's policy of constructive engagement, characterised as 'quiet diplomacy', has been widely discredited at home and abroad as ineffectual even on its own terms. In spite of this, it remains the touchstone of Pretoria's approach towards its neighbour, in part due to the African National Congress' vulnerability on the land question in South Africa and its concern over future domestic challenges rooted in local trade unionism.

Africa

Southern African governments, with some notable exceptions like Botswana, have been relatively supportive of their fellow leader in Harare despite the considerable cost in terms of lost commercial activity and refugee flows. In part this is a legacy of the solidarity politics of the liberation era, but it also reflects the fragile compromises between liberation movements and settler communities that ushered in democracy in southern Africa. Mugabe himself has been quick to exploit the emotive power of land in neighbouring countries – for example, calling on the people to follow the Zimbabwean example and occupy commercial farmland in Namibia and South Africa. Indeed, the Namibian government has itself implemented some land seizures.

Divisions within the rest of Africa were evident, however, in the run up to the December 2003 Commonwealth meeting in Abuja, as Kenya, Senegal and Nigeria put forward critiques of the Zimbabwean government. South Africa's bungled bid to unseat New Zealander Secretary-General Don McKinnon in a vote of no-confidence was roundly defeated by 40 to 11, unambiguously indicating that the supposed solidarity of African (not to mention Asian and Caribbean) states was illusory. After the organisation's decision to indefinitely extend Zimbabwe's suspension on 7 December, Mugabe pulled the country out of the Commonwealth altogether. A bitter response by Southern African Development Community followed. Mbeki swiftly visited to Harare in an attempt to salve Mugabe, voicing sympathetic comments regarding the parallels between South Africa and Zimbabwe. This rhetoric only served to confirm Pretoria's biased position towards the crisis.

The limits of international action

The EU, after its own divisive scuffle over France's wilful breaking of travel sanctions in the name of its all-Africa diplomacy the previous year, recommitted itself to 'smart sanctions' against the regime in February 2004 which involved travel bans and the freezing of assets owned by Zanu-PF officials. The United States followed suit, widening its sanctions programme to include measures against seven Zimbabwean government businesses in which senior government officials like Moyo and Zvinavashe were involved. The suspension of Zimbabwe's voting rights by the International Monetary Fund (IMF) in June 2003, and subsequent initiation of procedures for expulsion in December, brought about a belated recognition of the costs to the state and business by the Central Bank and the Treasury in late February 2004. Faced with the IMF's unwillingness to provide short-term loans to cover balance of payment requirements (and given its status as the proverbial 'lender of last resort', the consequential negative impact on all government borrowing), Zimbabwean officials have scrambled to come up with the $270 million in back payments it owes the organisation. Nevertheless, international pressure has not yet moved Mugabe to change his ways.

Mugabe's ability to dominate the politics of Zimbabwe, even in the face of the severest challenges to his leadership from within and outside the country, speaks for his canny political instincts and ruthless determination. Unencumbered by those elements that had acted as moderating influences upon his behaviour in the past – from his first wife to the international community – have perversely afforded Mugabe greater freedom of action: he believes he has little to lose. The appointment of a number of top military officers to senior posts in the government, from the governorship of Manicaland province to the electoral supervisory commission, is a sure sign that as long as he can rely upon the army as a loyal source of support, Mugabe is capable of pursuing regime security to the point of wholesale violent repression. As of early 2004, it appeared that only concerted action between senior figures within Zanu-PF and the military, on one hand, and the MDC, on the other, would be able to produce a smooth transition from power. It appears doubtful that a corrupt and divided ruling party stubbornly intent on the righteousness of its claim to power, and an understandably mistrustful and defiant opposition, can recognise and act upon this reality before more damage is done to Zimbabwe.

Sudan's Deceptive Transformation

The Sudanese government knew it was in Washington's sights well before 11 September 2001. Sudan was implicated in the 1995 assassination attempt on Egyptian President Hosni Mubarak and as al-Qaeda's host and abettor, and targeted when the US bombed the Al-Shifa pharmaceutical factory in 1998 in retaliation for the Islamist terrorist bombings of the US embassies in Nairobi and Dar-es Salaam. As a regime holding power by force, Khartoum understood Washington's message to be that it could effectively destroy the regime at will. The Sudanese government also knew that Arab states as well as the West perceived the need to contain Sudan's ruling party, which many regard as the world's most efficient Islamist organisation. As a consequence, Khartoum launched a charm offensive, toning down its support for international terrorism and becoming more open to peace negotiations with the Christian/animist southern Sudanese with whom Khartoum has fought, since 1983, Africa's longest ongoing civil war. Subsequently, George W. Bush was elected, and his administration faced pressure from America's religious right – an important element of Bush's

Africa

constituency – which had learned that over two million civilians had died in a civil war against overmatched Christians that had 'gone on too long'.

Only five days before the 11 September terrorist attacks, Bush appointed a personal envoy for Sudan, Senator John Danforth. This factor, and later heightened US attention to Islamist extremists following the 11 September attacks, moved Sudan to appear even more conciliatory. But Khartoum's less obvious conduct suggests that Sudan is uninterested in being a genuine part of a pluralistic international community but would prefer – consistently with al-Qaeda – to establish a new Islamist one. Sudan's National Islamic Front (NIF) restyled itself the National Congress Party (NCP) in 1998, but the party is controlled largely by the same Islamic fundamentalists who overthrew a democratic government and seized power in a 1989 coup d'état. Indeed, Sudanese still commonly refer to the ruling party as the NIF.

An end to civil war?

However deceptive the Sudanese transformation may be, the regime's need to keep the US off its back is real enough and has produced some tentatively positive changes on the conflict-resolution front. The central issue in the civil conflict is the degree of political autonomy to which the non-Muslim southern majority, represented by the Sudan People's Liberation Movement/Army (SPLM/A) is entitled. As the largest element of the umbrella National Democratic Alliance (NDA), the SPLM/A is in alliance with northern Muslims who oppose Islamist rule as well as rebels fighting the government in the Nuba Mountains and the western province of Darfur. They too want enhanced political rights – in particular, freedom from government-imposed sharia law.

The current peace process began in Machakos, Kenya in July 2002, when the Machakos Protocol according the southern Sudanese their own government and acknowledging their right to self-determination was signed. This development led to a ceasefire monitored by international observers (the US, UK, Norway, Italy, the African Union and the UN), though the Sudanese government continued bombing villagers and obstructing UN food deliveries for months after talks had begun. On 25 September 2003, Khartoum and the SPLM/A signed a framework agreement on security arrangements, negotiated directly between Sudanese Vice-President Ali Osman Mohamed Taha and SPLM/A Chairman John Garang, which will involve the deployment of joint or integrated units of government and SPLM/A soldiers to sensitive areas and calls for nationwide elections.

The main regional sponsor of the peace process is the Inter-Governmental Authority on Development (IGAD), which includes Djibouti, Eritrea, Ethiopia, Kenya, Somalia, Sudan and Uganda.

Political negotiations have been built on two principles enshrined in the IGAD Declaration of Principles (DOP): the separation of state and religion, and self-determination. The NIF grudgingly agreed to these in 1995. They are seen as the key issues of the north–south conflict and were later adopted as fundamental principles of NDA. But although Kenyan General Lazaro Sumbeiywo has been a proactive and effective mediator of the Machakos dialogue, the African players in IGAD have gradually been sidelined by the US and European powers, including the 'troika' of the UK, Norway and Italy, which formed the IGAD Partners Forum (IPF). American interest in the peace process is mainly political and strategic insofar as re-engaging with Sudan is a political dimension of its campaign against terrorism (though oil is a secondary factor). But the US approach pivots on autonomy for the southern Christian population, which the State Department believes will drive political reform and isolate the Khartoum regime's Islamist kingpins. The European powers' interest is essentially economic, and pivots on oil development.

These foci, coupled with IGAD's marginalisation and the Islamist government's conditioning movement towards southern autonomy on leaving northern Sudan a sharia-governed Islamic polity intact, has largely taken the first element of the DOP – separation of state and religion – off the table. The resulting emphasis on self-determination has advanced southern separation, but at the cost of consigning northern Sudan to the Islamists' grip in presumptive perpetuity. One consequence of this development is that the SPLM/A views the US and the UK as non-neutral players who favour the government, in spite of their efforts to appear even-handed. Even so, southerners remain optimistic about the peace process because they are convinced that it will ultimately yield independence. There is no doubt, in any case, that in a free referendum an overwhelming southern majority would vote in favour of independence.

A salutary wealth-sharing agreement was signed on 7 January 2004. It provides that the north and south evenly divide oil and non-oil revenues, and jointly manage the oil sector, and that a dual banking system and new national currency be established, during a six-year interim period followed by a self-determination referendum. But a comprehensive agreement remained at risk due to the inability of the parties to agree on terms for power-sharing and for broader political and security arrangements in three other disputed areas: the Nuba Mountains, Abyei and Southern Blue Nile. All are in the centre of Sudan, near the historical north–south border. As of April 2004, negotiations on the outstanding issues were under way in Naivasha, Kenya. The parties seemed close to a compromise over the Nuba Mountains and Southern Blue Nile, whereby these areas would enjoy autonomy, with a review of their status after four years. But the government remained wary of any deal of potentially broad applicability that could imply the right of self-determination of all minorities in Sudan –

Africa

which would, to Khartoum, amount to acquiescing to the dismemberment of Sudan as a country. Such an outcome would also be unacceptable to Egypt, which fears that another independent African state would ally with Kenya and Uganda and threaten Egypt's control of the Nile waters. Egyptian strategic priorities have thus produced a pragmatic convergence of positions on the southern Sudan question between the Arab nationalist Mubarak government and the Islamist Khartoum regime.

In February 2003, Khartoum launched a ground and aerial assault on Darfur in the far western part of the country. Darfur is the base of two other rebel groups: the Sudan Liberation Army (SLA), which is part of the SPLM/A-dominated NDA; and the Justice and Equality Movement (JEM), whose leader, Khalil Ibrahim, is a veteran Islamist. Both groups seek greater political and economic rights, but it will be easier for the government to compromise with JEM because both are Islamist. Over the course of a year of fighting, hundreds or people were killed, 750,000 displaced and 100,000 more forced to flee over the Chadian border. The international players initially acquiesced in the government's aggression in the interest of preserving momentum in negotiations with the SPLM/A. When the government and SPLM/A failed to conclude a 'final deal' in time for Bush's State of the Union address in late January 2004, however, Washington publicly protested Khartoum's show of force in Darfur, with Oslo echoing the complaint. The Sudanese government's willingness to undertake such a blatant provocation with key negotiations pending cast doubt on its good faith. In early 2004, a succession of reports and interviews detailing mass slaughter perpetrated by the Sudanese government were issued by organisations such as Human Rights Watch and Amnesty International. Indeed, what has been characterised as 'genocide' in Darfur moved Washington to step up pressure on Khartoum for a final peace deal by 21 April 2004, the date for the semi-annual presidential assessment of the Sudan Peace Act. On 8 April, the Sudanese government and the two Darfur-based rebel groups agreed to a 45-day ceasefire and to allow relief groups access to war-torn areas of Darfur.

Sudan's entrenched Islamism

Conspicuous but relatively painless gestures by Khartoum over the past several years have conditioned Europe and the US to believe that the ruling party was reforming itself. Sudan began in earnest by handing over notorious Venezuelan terrorist-for-hire 'Carlos the Jackal' to French authorities in 1994. The quid pro quo was a change of attitude in Paris, a couple of million dollars and, allegedly, satellite imagery of SPLM/A troop movements. Similarly, immediately after 11 September, Sudan gave up suspects and information to the US State Department. Given Sudan's résumé as a terrorist sponsor, failure to do so could have resulted in punitive American action. Nevertheless, it may have produced a more sanguine view about the durability of Sudan's apparent cessation of terrorist sponsorship than the facts warrant.

Unlike, say, the Taliban, Sudan's ruling elite is not a cabal of traditionalist clerics with little secular education or experience of the outside world. Rather, it is a highly organised party in possession of doctorates from Western universities and a clear assessment of their own strengths and their enemies' weaknesses. In the 1970s and 1980s, when computers were virtually unknown in Sudan and psychology scoffed at, the NIF paid for students to do advanced computer and psychology studies in the West. One of the favourite dictums of Sorbonne-educated NIF spiritual leader Hassan Abdulla el Turabi, who transformed Sudan's branch of the Muslim Brotherhood into the NIF, is: 'we know you better than you know us'. In 2001, the government jailed Turabi for two years, reinforcing the impression that Khartoum had jettisoned its 'terrorists'. Mubarak, who publicly blamed Turabi for the 1995 attempt on his life, has vouched for the genuineness of Khartoum's conversion. Accordingly, American and European officials have cited the apparent marginalisation of Turabi as a sign of positive change in Sudan. Paradoxically, Turabi is more popular than his former government colleagues in Khartoum and now claims to be in favour of democratisation and self-determination. The US Department of State's Country Report on Human Rights Practices, dated 25 February 2004 begins: 'Sudan has an authoritarian government in which all effective political power is in the hands of President Omar Hassan al-Bashir'. The report accurately describes the NIF as having instigated and supported Bashir's 1989 coup, but sees Bashir as having ousted Turabi.

The actual state of affairs may be more complex. Many regional analysts see Bashir as a figurehead, noting that he has always been flanked by NIF 'gatekeeper' ministers to ensure he toes the party line. Vice-President Taha, who has close links to the military, the intelligence agencies and the party apparatus, appears to be the national leader with the real power. In 1999, the NIF split, with Turabi leading the Popular National Congress party (since renamed the Popular Congress Party, or PCP) in opposition, and Taha the ruling NCP faction. Genuine disputes exist. Turabi takes issue with the NCP's venality, corruption and lack of transparency, and the loss of its appeal to women, students and the young professional elite, and favours democratic reforms. He also has a substantial support base in Khartoum, and is a formidable political rival for Taha. To gain opposition support for peace negotiations with the SPLM/A, however, the NCP made a commitment to democratisation and, in October 2003, released Turabi from prison. Taha is likely to constrain any overt reunification of the Islamist movement in order to limit Turabi's political power. Furthermore, from the Sudanese government's point of view, Turabi's ostensible decline as a political force bolsters disarming appearances of Khartoum's shift

Africa

away from anti-Western Islamism and of the NCP's political weakness. Thus, the government had little compunction about re-arresting Turabi on 31 March 2004 – purportedly in connection with a coup plot involving Darfur rebels, for which at least ten Sudanese military officers had been arrested two days earlier.

Yet the NCP's crowning achievement has been to retain power for 15 years against an array of challengers in Africa's largest country while reinforcing a potent international Islamist network and arguably nurturing al-Qaeda through its growing pains. Sudan hosted Osama bin Laden, other core al-Qaeda members and his nest of commercial front companies and 'Islamic' charities from 1992 to 1996. Those achievements are still bearing fruit, and the man most responsible for them is Turabi. His 2003 release remained a strong indication of his overall value to Sudanese Islamism on account of his charisma, his understanding of Islam and of the West, and above all, his ability to use his religious authority to carry the less erudite zealots with him when making tactical compromises with the West or Arab governments. The government cited Turabi's willingness to apply sharia law on an individual basis in the north to justify his arrest to its Islamist domestic constituency. But the arrest may in part be a coded message to the US to pressure the SPLA/M to sign the NCP's version of a peace deal – which would involve, among other things, a highly qualified species of power-sharing – if it wants to keep hardline Islamists out of power in Khartoum. In any case, Turabi is not likely to stay in jail for long.

There may also be less to Sudan's economic reform than meets the eye. The government has privatised the large state sector, with International Monetary Fund and World Bank blessing. But Khartoum also put the new private assets, at well below market value, largely into the hands of shell companies fronting government interests and linked to international Islamist financiers in the Gulf states and Malaysia. A number of prominent, established non-government companies were allowed to thrive on condition that they work within government strictures. Most of the 'infrastructure investments' are oil-related and therefore directly or indirectly government-controlled. In a number of cases, their implementation has involved ethnic cleansing. Furthermore, the government has increased the commission charged on inputs imported for government use and inflated contracts with overseas partners, either by creating an extra layer of companies (routinely exempted from state taxes and customs duties) or by directly utilising government firms to fill NCP coffers. While sometimes dismissed abroad as routine corruption, it could also constitute an NCP effort to build up and shield its assets by getting them out of the country in case the post-11 September counter-terrorism crackdown – which has already dried up the financial flow into Sudan from Arab donors – intensifies its focus on Sudan. Khartoum regards a final peace deal as economically instrumental, insofar as it would eventually mean the lifting of US sanctions and an international aid package. Multilateral lending could not resume until Sudan reduces its huge arrears to institutions like the IMF and the African Development Bank. Meanwhile, however, the Khartoum government can raise additional cash through loans secured against future oil production. The upshot is that Sudan perceives its oil to give it a hedge against Western co-optation.

Nevertheless, the West has chosen, on balance, to diplomatically support the Sudanese government on the basis of its recent reformist image in the hope of transforming it into a secular, or at least non-radical, party. Among the considerable factors that comes into Western calculations is the fact that alienating the West would leave Sudan to rely on China and India as the purchasers of its oil, which would be less lucrative. Even so, 'constructive engagement' may also run the risk of underrating Sudan's value to the transnational radical Islamist movement. Counter-terrorism analysts, especially in justifying the US-led Combined Joint Task Force's search for Islamists in the Horn of Africa and Sahel belt, have understandably focused on the threat of Islamists' taking over 'failed states'. This term usually alludes to Somalia, where radical Islamists – though certainly on the rise – have not achieved dominance. It remains significant, however, that the NIF took over an intact state that had not failed.

Future problems

Since 1991, the government has signed a string of agreements with the SPLM/A or with its splinter groups pledging non-aggression and the recognition of varying degrees of self-determination. All the while, the government has enhanced its military capabilities. Defence expenditures rose from 2.9% of GDP in 1985 to 4.9% of GDP in 2002. This expanded military power has severely curtailed the SPLM/A's ability to use force to take control of the government's southern oilfields, which yield Khartoum 250,000 barrels a day (to rise to 500,000), netting $1–2 billion a year. For the time being, Khartoum has an interest in appearing to cooperate in conflict-resolution, and to refrain from sponsoring terrorism. The former has operationally freed the NCP to use force in other areas, such as Darfur, while the latter has placated Washington. The fact remains that, although the SPLM/A itself is far from purely democratic, the SPLM/A would win free and fair elections in the south. In the north, a free vote would probably leave the NCP in single figures. Thus, the government cannot afford to implement the plan for nationwide free elections contained in the framework agreement with the SPLM/A. Absent sustained external pressure on the government, it is only slightly less unlikely to relinquish actual control of southern Sudan or to share power on anything approximating co-equal terms.

Africa

The NCP is also in all likelihood loath to give up its radical Islamist vocation. Sudan is distinguished in being the only Sunni Muslim country ruled by a modern Islamist party. Sudan would logically be a source of inspiration and optimism to the transnational Islamist movement led by al-Qaeda – a source of status and power that Khartoum would not easily forsake. This consideration also cuts against genuine self-determination – that is, by referendum – in the south, which would legally result in independence. Such a loss of southern territory would mean not only foregone oil, but the removal of a springboard for Islamist penetration of the Central African Republic, Democratic Republic of Congo, Ethiopia, Kenya, Uganda and points south.

Accordingly, Khartoum is likely to continue to temporise in the peace process. In early 2004, to be sure, a 'final' peace agreement between the government and SPLM/A looked reasonably likely. Signalling a broadly conciliatory attitude, the Sudanese government began face-to-face talks with the Darfurian rebel groups on 6 April. Under pressure from the troika, Khartoum seemed inclined to sign a written agreement which by its terms would require a notional referendum in the future. The government would, in all probability, find a reason not to honour such a commitment. Real peace, therefore, is likely to remain elusive. Rogue behaviour on Khartoum's part may remain constrained by international pressure for Sudanese peace and against terrorism, and by NCP/PCP political infighting, which also motivates each faction episodically to curry favour with the SPLM/A. But in contrast to Libya, Sudan courts support rather than rivalry from radical Islam, and therefore has less to gain and more to lose from a rapprochement with the US. Thus, a thoroughgoing Libya-style conversion for Sudan is unlikely.

Prospectives

As 2004 got under way, the strategic 'dissensus' over Iraq certainly was persisting in the sense that neither the original proponents nor the original opponents of coercive regime-change were willing to admit error. At the same time, the United States and the United Kingdom were recognising that they could not do the job of state-building by themselves, and needed both allies and the UN. The governments that most vehemently resisted intervention – France, Russia and Germany – were coming around to the view that, for better or worse, Saddam Hussein had been ousted and Iraq now needed a new government that outside actors had no choice but to midwife. France contemplated contributing troops to Iraq, and the UN assumed a more prominent role in determining the details of the United States' handover of sovereignty to the Iraqis. Transatlantic counter-terrorism cooperation continued to be robust, and US–Europe dialogue on matters such as defence burden-sharing and trade moved back towards normality. On the strategic appropriateness of the US-led intervention, ongoing rancour was giving way to an agreement to disagree – to let consequences and historians make the determination.

Yet there remained some questions that required more urgent answers. Chief among them, perhaps, was whether intervention in Iraq in 2003 was legally proper and, more broadly, what new legal standards had to be entertained and established to manage the new international security environment in a principled way. The Bush administration – in its insistence on half-baked theories as to the legal status and rights of over 600 prisoners held at Guantanamo Bay, in its reluctance to confront sharpening doubts about the legality of the Iraq intervention occasioned by the failure to find weapons of mass destruction (WMD) there – seemed uninterested in looking for answers. How quickly and thoroughly they are formulated, as well as other key strategic developments, will depend on who is elected president in the US elections in November 2004.

Beyond election 2004

Although most non-Americans now take a generally dim view of the Bush administration's foreign policy, it does have the virtue of clarity. Bush foreign policy is intolerant of dissent or incomplete allegiance; unabashedly seeks to export American political values and economic standards; insists on a full mobilisation against global terrorism that extends to potential state sponsors and proliferators of WMD; and features the threat of the use of force more prominently than previous US policies in the belief that the existential fact of overwhelming American military superiority can change state behaviour. In substance, however, each of these components has perverse aspects.

Abhorrence of dissent over Iraq may have hastened a highly risky intervention, and in any event seems to have amplified the political consequences of coalition discord. Indeed, virtually every Democratic presidential candidate impugned the White House for squandering the good will generated by a near-global sense of outrage over the 11 September attacks by adopting a 'go it alone foreign policy' that ignored the advice and preferences of allies and partners. Aggressive entrepreneurship with respect to American values has alienated many of those – especially Muslims – to whom they are meant to apply. As for the broad construction of terrorist activity and full mobilisation against it, European critics contend preventive action against the Iraqi regime increased the terrorist impulse of non-state actors, while American political rivals argue that the Iraq war diverted attention and resources from a homeland-security effort that was of more immediate importance and far from complete. Although Bush administration supporters have claimed that the prospect of US military intervention induced Libya to abandon its WMD programme, other current and former US officials have credibly asserted that Libya's reform was rather the last step of a happy evolution that began with discreet and candid dialogue during Clinton's second term. Certainly whether the omen of regime change will tame perennially roguish regimes in Iran, North Korea and Syria remains to be seen. Indeed, in December 2003, John Kerry – now a US Senator for Massachusetts and the most likely Democratic presidential nominee – cast Libya's move as an example of what dialogue in lieu of force and threats could achieve.

After branding Bush foreign policy 'inept' and 'reckless', in February 2003, Kerry intoned that the Bush team was 'intoxicated with the pre-eminence of American power' and had abandoned fundamentals like 'belief in collective security, respect for international institutions and international law, multilateral engagement and the use of force not as a first option but truly as a last resort'. While Europeans and others have exaggerated the Bush administration's stress on pre-emption and prevention, Kerry foreign policy would pointedly de-emphasise it. Kerry would also pay more attention to the wishes of bilateral partners (e.g., France and Russia) and the UN, especially when contemplating military action. More particularly, he has said he would resume bilateral negotiations with North Korea, and he would be more likely than Bush to take steps towards a rapprochement with Iran. A more hands-on approach to the Middle East peace process – and more pressure on the Israeli government to ease aggressive security policies, including the construction of the security barrier – would be on the cards.

Furthermore, Kerry foreign-policy adviser Rand Beers, who resigned from Bush's National Security Council as Senior Director for Counter-terrorism in June 2003, has indicated that intervention in Iraq orphaned the state-building effort in Afghanistan and drained an uncompleted domestic-security overhaul of manpower, money and intellectual support. 'We are asking our firemen, policemen, Customs and Coast Guard to do far more with far less than we ever ask of our military', he remarked. A Kerry administration, then, would probably reallocate defence expenditures away from high-end military capabilities and missile defence and towards state-building (to include Afghanistan) and homeland security. Following the lead of a US judiciary increasingly impatient with the Bush administration's dilatoriness in fully confronting legal questions raised by the campaign against terrorism, Kerry would be far more likely than Bush to carry forward a wholesale review of the USA PATRIOT Act, the legalities of military intervention and the law of armed conflict as it relates to terrorists – in particular, the detainees held at Guantanamo Bay.

Whoever is elected, however, will regard failure in Iraq as non-optional and keep US troops and advisers committed until Iraq is a functioning unitary state. Any president also could not fail to appreciate the strategic priority of Iraq, its heavy claim on US military resources and, consequently, the need to conserve military resources and leverage – as indeed the Bush administration has begun to do with respect to North Korea and Iran. The Bush team has also come to acknowledge more readily its operational and diplomatic need for the UN in the state-building arena, and – given the highly critical White House-commissioned study on the inadequacies of US public diplomacy – unacceptable American insensitivity in dealing with the Muslim world. Furthermore, any US administration would be risk-averse as to the Israeli–Palestinian conflict in an election year. The problems that the 'road map' has encountered, coupled with widespread pressure for deeper US involvement after January 2005, portend a reinvigorated American commitment to conflict resolution in the Middle East. On balance, therefore, the difference between Bush's second term and Kerry's first one might be more rhetorical than substantive. That alone, however, could improve US standing overseas – especially in Europe.

Unappealing contingencies

Any US president will have to handle difficult challenges to preclude several ominous strategic outcomes. The most dire involve nuclear proliferation. While the Bush administration has used the threat of pre-emption or prevention to gain leverage – for instance, over Syria immediately after intervening in Iraq – it seems to recognise the risk of its abuse in practice. In early 2004, the US was pursuing diplomatic options with Iran and North Korea. In the case of Iran, its nuclear programme is not yet conclusively illegal, let alone militarily operational. By contrast, North Korea's missile threat to its neighbours is substantial and possibly nuclear, while its conventional artillery threat would pose undue risk to South Korea were the US to attack. The United States' operational judgement, then, is that it is too soon for any pre-emptive or preventive attack on Iran and too late for one on North Korea. This does not reflect the mindset of a 'rogue superpower', and doubtless comes as a relief to many who feared that Iraq signalled a policy (rather than just an extraordinary option) of pre-emption. Yet the slow pace of the respective diplomatic processes, as well as evidence of both Iranian and North Korean duplicity, raises an even more disturbing possibility: that of the failure of counter-proliferation in Iran and North Korea, and a multipolar nuclear world.

Another unattractive prospect is a prolonged stalemate in the Israeli–Palestinian conflict. Palestine is not the source of America's or its partners' problems in the region, but it must be part of the solution. More robust US involvement is required. The disincentives are strong: the parties remain far apart; militarily, the two societies are fatigued but not wrung out; and politics in both camps remain stagnant. The Bush administration is unlikely to take risks before a potentially close election. At the same time, it is indispensable that Washington be perceived to promote conditions that will favour a successful Palestinian state: territorial contiguity and borders close to the Green Line, with sensible adjustments. The US must also do its utmost to nurture a less corrupt and repressive Palestinian Authority able to take care of the needs of the Palestinian people in a nascent state, and to ensure that religiously motivated Palestinian terrorist groups are militarily neutralised before they have a chance to destabilise that state by challenging their secular rivals and ultimately the state of Israel. Failure to do so will not only produce near-term diplomatic costs, but in the longer-term lead to a stunted, violent Palestinian state that is a source of instability in the region and beyond.

Finally, a failed Iraqi state would be a strategic nightmare for the US and the West. The deeper strategic justification for regime change and post-conflict state-building in Iraq is the wider political remaking of the Gulf region. The original idea was that the 'demonstration effect' of democracy in Iraq would stimulate liberal political reform in other illiberal, authoritarian regimes. With a formidable indigenous insurgency – possibly penetrated by foreign jihadists – having developed in Iraq and complicated the transfer of sovereignty to an Iraqi government, the trajectory for this policy has become flatter. Nevertheless, it is key to regional security – and the stability of the international system – that the US and its allies get Iraq right. The region's political centre of gravity is shifting from the west – Egypt and Syria – to the east. Politics in Iran are turbulent but arguably democratic. In Saudi Arabia, Crown Prince Abdullah, though facing an insurgency, talks about elections. In several of the smaller littoral states, genuine participatory democracy is beginning to replace sham practices. Iraq's evolution will have an enormous impact on these trends. If the state succeeds, the regeneration of the region may indeed occur. If Iraq fails, or reverts to a dictatorship, positive recent developments may fade. In that case, the US would be seen as an unredeemed aggressor, and the warmer relations between Islam and the West that intervention was supposed to start would be all the harder to engender.

Invidious perspectives

Since Bush took office, and especially since the Iraq intervention, the United States' world image has hit rock-bottom. In many quarters, the US is viewed with suspicion on account of its perceived unilateralism. In a December 2002 survey report entitled 'Global Gloom and Growing Anti-Americanism', the Pew Research Center found that while majorities in most of the 27 countries surveyed felt favourably towards the US, ratings had fallen in 19 of the 27 since 2000. Most people broadly supported the campaign against terrorism, but those in Europe, Africa, Asia and Latin America tended to believe that US foreign policy was inordinately self-interested and 'unilateralist'. There were large-scale public protests in each continent after military operations against Saddam Hussein's regime began in March 2003. These negative perceptions at least have an arguably rational, empirical basis: they started with the US' rejection of the Kyoto Protocol on global climate change and its renunciation of the Anti-ballistic Missile Treaty and were crystallised by coercive regime change in Iraq without a specific authorising resolution from the UN Security Council. Accordingly, Washington has the ability to ameliorate or reverse negative views of the US by adjusting US foreign policy. The situation in the Middle East and Persian Gulf region, however, is less straightforward and more unsettling. There the United States has come to be seen as an implacable enemy.

The Pew Global Attitudes Project survey released in June 2003 found that only 27% of Moroccans, 15% of Lebanese and Turks, 12% of Pakistanis and 1% of Jordanians and Palestinians had a favourable view of the US. Primarily due to the invasion of Iraq, these results reflect a marked drop from 2002: the Lebanese and Turkish figures registered a decline of 50%, and the Jordanian figure 96%. Moreover, the antipathy has spread beyond the Middle East to other Muslim countries. In 2003, only 38% of Nigerians held positive views of the US, down from 71%; in Indonesia the figure dropped to 13% from 60%. In seven of the eight Muslim populations surveyed, 50% or more believed that the US posed a serious threat to Islam. According to the Arab Public Opinion Survey in early 2003, large majorities in the region also believe that oil and Israeli interests drive US policy. These perceptions are grounded in reality. On the other hand, the US has never tried to hide its policy preferences. Nevertheless, the survey results indicate that the US is viewed with deep suspicion and even hostility. Remarkably, significant majorities in seven of the eight – and a near majority in Morocco – worried about a potential US military threat to their countries. Thus, Muslims seem to need a powerful figure to stand up for their interests. In six of the populations studied by Pew, 40% or more had confidence that Osama bin Laden would do the right thing in world affairs, with a majority of Jordanians (56%) and Palestinians (72%) placing their trust in his leadership.

Improving Muslim perceptions of America will require not merely adjusting existing policies but building some new ones from the ground up. The most important new policies will be in the areas of trade and foreign aid. One of the reasons that Muslims react so viscerally to the US is that, while it is the prime mover of the globalised economy, they have seen few of its benefits. Unemployment in the region is already between 12% and 35%, depending on the country. On average, real wages in the region have remained unchanged for 30 years. To complicate the supply-side problem, most Arabs and Iranians are literate enough to make unskilled labour an unacceptable alternative, but not sufficiently educated to constitute a labour force capable of competing in an increasingly competitive global market. On the demand side, GDP growth has lagged behind the rest of the world for at least two decades. To amplify the problem, over the next 12 years, the total population of the Middle East will grow by 32%. Despite declining fertility rates in some countries (Iran, Egypt, Tunisia), demographic momentum will continue to yield high population growth. Moreover, 50% of Arabs and 54% of Iranians are under the age of 20 (versus 25% in high-income Organisation for Economic Cooperation and Development countries); over 60% are under 30. The Middle East has the fastest growing labour force in the world: 3.4% per year from 1990 to 1998. Some countries, such as Syria at 4.8%, Algeria at 4.9% or Yemen at 5.6% (compared to 0.4% for the US, 0.8% for the European Union) face especially acute pressures.

The region has in effect disengaged from the global economy. Rapid urbanisation without commensurate infrastructural improvements has added to the overall misery in the region. This is because rent-seeking behaviour by distributive states cut against transparency and accountability, in favour of corruption and unsustainable subsidies. States dominated national economies, became employers of last resort and adopted import substitution policies. In some countries, military procurement added to dead weight losses. These policies and practices are difficult to reverse, and have discouraged foreign direct investment. Thus, Middle Eastern populations tend to regard the US as either propping up corrupt or incompetent governments or undermining regional regimes' ability to improve living conditions. If the US is to reach a better accommodation with the Muslim world in the hope of outflanking radical Islam, it will have to change Muslim perceptions of America by helping to improve those conditions and winning credit for doing so.

Grand strategy: new requirements

Whereas in the 1990s the US was criticised for not using its power more proactively, during the Bush administration it has drawn fire essentially for using it too zealously and insensitively. A grand strategy of disengagement is infeasible in a world with threats that are many and ubiquitous, and in which the US has assumed myriad security responsibilities. Thus, Washington has little choice but to remain extrovert in its foreign policy. Increased global confidence in its execution of that policy will come with more palpable global benefits and greater US accountability. These results, in turn, call for more incisive approaches to regional problems than have materialised so far. This inadequacy was hard to avoid: after 11 September, the priority was necessarily self-protection and 'hard' counter-terrorism; second-order tasks aimed at attenuating the root causes of terrorism had to wait. Since 11 September, however, North America and Europe, at least, have got a provisional operational grip on hard security. They cannot, of course, let their guard down, as the Madrid bombings in March 2004 horrifically demonstrated. And there remain essential primary security problems – such as insurgency in Iraq – that have yet to be satisfactorily resolved. But with enhanced counter-terrorism regimes in place, and thickened inter-governmental cooperative links established, Western capitals can start to turn to second-order tasks.

One of the essential tasks is state-building. There is an oft-noted inconsistency between the Bush administration's reluctance to embrace state-building as a central element of US foreign policy and its assumption of one of most daunting state-building challenges in recent history in Iraq. Washington ought to give up the pretence of the magisterial approach and concede that state-building and the strategic problems that it addresses – saving failed states, strengthening weak ones, promoting democratisation – are too important to be neglected by the world's lone superpower. Implicitly, the US has already relented on this score with respect to Iraq. But a fuller embrace could motivate an extension of US policy in Afghanistan and central Asia beyond counter-terrorism into state-building, and perhaps a more multi-faceted approach to supporting development in Africa.

Democratisation is a paramount component of both state-building in particular and Western diplomacy in general. But Washington has tended to cast it as a panacea, when poor and illiberal democracies or Islamist, anti-Western ones probably would not produce net diplomatic or security gains. Democratisation, then, may have to occur slowly and deliberately. The Bush administration's Middle East Partnership Initiative is focused on key objectives: empowerment of women, support for civil society and enhancement of education. The EU has been pursuing these objectives for a number of years at a somewhat more modest level. The potential synergy of US–EU work in these areas would serve shared interests in the region well. These programmes, however, are not enough. Pressure on governments to open up political space is essential. But the West must have patience, and accommodate potential conflicts between democratisation and security.

Financial assistance will also remain necessary for a number of states that without it would be more vulnerable to terrorism and instability. The Millennium Challenge Account, until a large portion was re-allocated for use in Iraq, makes sense except for its substantial adherence to 'Washington Consensus' neo-liberal economic standards for largesse. They are too exacting to be diplomatically useful in failed or failing states, where even nascent democracy and financial transparency will constitute major achievements. Yet such states pose the most urgent threats to Western interests. A successful strategy would have to channel funds to the doctrinally challenged poor as well as the compliant poor. On the economic diplomacy front, of course, trade is a systemically superior way to help societies help themselves, in that it shifts resources from authoritarian regimes to the middle class, empowering civil society and setting the table for democratic transition. The US has finally adopted this policy toward Pakistan's textile industry and – with celebrated exceptions – made pursuit of free trade arrangements an important part of its foreign policy. Here the harmonisation of US and EU policies could yield positive results. While direct aid is needed in the medium term, trade should be favoured over the longer haul.

The US and its partners must also perform conflict resolution more effectively. While it is incumbent on Washington to re-immerse itself in the Israeli–Palestinian conflict, it must do so in a way that balances conflicting priorities. For example, the US wants to promote pluralism because it is conducive to democratisation and demonstrates a kind of value-neutrality that is key to American credibility; yet religious pluralism in the Israeli–Palestinian context means recognising the political legitimacy of radical Islamic groups like Hamas, Hizbullah and Palestinian Islamic Jihad. Although these groups perform valuable charitable functions, those roles – insofar as they involve fundraising – are also integral to their terrorist and paramilitary operations. Accordingly, for the US to promote both peace and pluralism without undermining one or the other, it must find a means of neutralising the terrorist capabilities of religious groups that have significant political constituencies. In re-engaging in the Israeli–Palestinian conflict, therefore, the US should consider how best to impel the Palestinian Authority to disarm Hamas, and how to persuade Israel to re-engage with Syria, which would then be more open to restraining Hizbullah.

A grand strategy for the Middle East entails coordinated, firm control over the trajectory of Iraq's development as a state, perceptions of the American threat, and the potential diplomatic and economic costs of proliferation. Notwithstanding Iran's flirtations with nuclear power, whether Tehran concludes that a weapons capability is necessary or desirable will depend on how seriously it perceives the threat of a reconstituted Iraq. Few regional states are now interested in a nuclear capability, and most support non-proliferation goals. But risks – including potentially those of a remilitarised Iraq – remain, and managing them calls for a higher level of inter-alliance respect and cooperation than the large-scale US occupation of Iraq allows. A discreet over-the-horizon US military presence will be needed to reassure the Arab states in the Gulf, on one hand, while discouraging anti-Western public opinion, on the other.

Talking to Islam

As of early 2004, transnational Islamic terrorism remained the most serious strategic concern. The aforementioned components of Western grand strategy do not amount to a comprehensive prescription for marginalising it. But even if terrorism's root causes are not easily susceptible to Western measures, terrorists will have to be rooted out. As al-Qaeda evolved from a relatively small group of Egyptian revolutionaries and Saudi mystics into a widely shared ideology, this will be increasingly difficult. The presence of insurgents in Saudi Arabia and other countries in the region will compel the US and UK to foster close ties to regimes whose politics spurred the Islamist insurrection in the first place. Although this enforced dependence cannot be avoided entirely, a grand strategy will require that it be balanced by nuanced pressure on autocratic regimes transmitted openly. The balance is extremely delicate and the risk of perversely worsening the climate for effective counter-terrorism will be high. But the pliancy of the governments whose cooperation is needed would be enhanced and the risk decreased – by better American public diplomacy.

The West – primarily the US – needs to find a way to talk at once more candidly and more agreeably to opposition movements. In commissioning the blue-ribbon Djerejian Panel to produce a report on US public diplomacy and showing concern over its damning findings, the Bush administration appears seized of the challenge. While US policy – despite the religious embroidery of much of its rhetoric – is governed by secular concerns, and Europe has expunged religion from the public sphere, the language of the only organised and credible oppositions in the Muslim world is self-consciously Islamic. The US, in particular, needs to explain itself better to conservative Islam in the hope of keeping it from falling into the radical camp. Perhaps even more importantly, the US needs to enhance the quality and flow of its communications with the young, regional technocratic elite, which is most likely to move society into modernity and render it more compatible with the West. With US credibility at an all-time low, improved dialogue will come hard. Yet a grand strategy demands that the US and its allies be perceived as partners, predators or ideological or religious adversaries.

Transatlantic strategic conversation

While talking more constructively to Islam may be the top priority, transatlantic dialogue also needs work. Though improved by virtue of the passage of time, it remains strained over Iraq. Because Iraq is a sticky problem that will not go away quickly, residual friction will probably persist. In this connection, the Spanish electorate's ouster of the ruling Popular Party in the national elections that occurred three days after the Madrid attacks was ominous. The result appeared to reflect, at least in part, a collective judgement that outgoing Prime Minister José Maria Aznar's government was rash to support the US in Iraq because the intervention needlessly antagonised Islamist terrorists and made Spain a more inviting target, and derogated the democratic process by ignoring the 90% majority of the Spanish people who opposed Spain's participation in the intervention. Incoming Socialist Prime Minister José Luis Rodriguez Zapatero has vowed that Spain will loosen its alliance with the US, and withdraw troops from Iraq by July.

Given that the UK and Italian governments are vulnerable to comparable anti-American domestic backlash, the Madrid bombings may prompt Washington to exercise greater foresight as to the effects that US diplomacy may have on the counter-terrorism coalition's stability. Washington could not be expected to cease urging European governments to back controversial American counter-terrorism initiatives simply because domestic populations are antsy about them. But the US may find it prudent to provide more political support to governments that have taken risks on the coalition's behalf. For example, had the US been publicly more confessional about intelligence failures with respect to Iraq's WMD, and more candid about the unexpected difficulties of the occupation – thus willingly taking more of the international community's heat – the Spanish people might have forgiven Aznar his perceived transgression. Even before Madrid, the fallout over the Iraq crisis seemed to be slowly pushing the US towards a more consultative diplomatic approach. In increasingly seeking partners on the ground and the UN's diplomatic expertise and political imprimatur, the Bush administration had implicitly begun to moderate any perceived American unilateralism on Iraq, suggesting that it was less than sanguine about the capacity of European allies to get the political cover they needed to tighten the bilateral relationships with Washington – politically if not operationally weakened by Iraq – on which the global counter-terrorism coalition rests.

Nevertheless, particularly if Kerry is elected – and even if Bush gains a second term – Europe for practical reasons is likely to resolve simply to turn over a page and re-establish warm, normal relations with Washington. The more vexing question is whether it will engage with Washington merely from issue to issue, on an ad hoc basis, or at strategic level in a way that enshrines joint priorities and moves towards a shared strategy. The latter would be preferable, but there are substantial obstacles in its way. As the European ructions over the Iraq crisis suggested, European capitals may be too divided as to their own respective interests to develop the common approach that is prerequisite to a unified transatlantic strategy. There may be some common principles in some substantive areas – such terrorist financing and certain aspects of non-proliferation – that can be hammered out under the auspices of the G-8 or NATO. But neither side would make either of those forums its top choice as a vehicle for generating strategic consensus. The US generally views both the G-8 and NATO as diplomatically subsidiary to bilateral avenues, while European countries are not about to give up on the EU as Europe's single foreign-policy voice. Given the EU's increasingly sharp growing pains and Washington's wariness towards Brussels, European reticence with respect to a coordinated transatlantic grand strategy is likely to persist for some time, with Europe defaulting to a case-by-case dispensation that delays its achieving co-equal status with the US.

Bumps in the road

Even if grand strategy materialises in some form, few years go by without significant interruptions. While transatlantic minds are concentrated on terrorism, WMD, and the Middle East and Gulf, problems could arise in other areas that shift priorities. North Korea's leadership, having been assiduously managed and currently a diplomatic preoccupation, is famously erratic and could suddenly jump the diplomatic track and turn bellicose again. If Taiwanese President Chen Shui-bian continues to press the issue of Taiwan's independence, China could resort to the threat of force across the Taiwan Strait. In that event, the US would almost certainly feel compelled to intervene, as it did in 1996 – and divert some of its attention from the pressing matters that topped its priority list in early 2004. State collapse in Africa – for example, Côte d'Ivoire – or the rise of Islamic radicalism in an already-failed state like Somalia could make a major state-building effort a strategic obligation.

Regime change of an undesirable kind among counter-terrorism's 'partners of concern' could also produce abrupt and serious security challenges. A coup in Pakistan – whether bloodless or by the assassination of Pakistani President Pervez Musharraf – could potentially leave nuclear weapons in the hands of Islamic extremists and prompt a crisis-mode decision about pre-emptive military action by the US and its European allies, not to mention India. An Islamist victory in the Indonesian elections could yield a regime more friendly to Jemaah Islamiah, producing high anxiety among southeast Asian members of the counter-terrorism coalition. The implosion of the House of Saud's regime in Saudi Arabia – though unlikely – could provide al-Qaeda with the state host that it has lacked since the Afghanistan intervention, and necessitate another Western intervention in a region already stirred by the one in Iraq. Russia could pose another problem, though less severe. If President Vladimir Putin's government becomes appreciably more autocratic – and perhaps more violent in countering Chechen rebels – Washington might have little choice but to criticise him. This could loosen Russia's partnership in the counter-terrorism coalition, reduce its counter-proliferation cooperation with respect to Iran and possibly stoke Putin's instigation of a standoffish attitude towards the US among Russia's European partners.

A sudden genocide in Africa or a massive civil war in a large state could reawaken humanitarian impulses and both divert resources from the strategic priorities of WMD, terrorism and the Middle East towards prevention of future state failure and open opportunities for multilateral coordination. Strategic surprises are more likely in the prevailing environment than they were during the Cold War or before. America's unilateral strategic entrepreneurship will not be enough to deal with such surprises. Whether Europe can break out of its present moment of strategic arthritis remains doubtful. Between America's grandiose attempt to shape the strategic future, and Europe's uncertain acquiescence to it, a better way forward will need to be found.

The fact that strategic relationships are now heavily determined by controversial WMD, terrorism and Middle East problems may translate into a relatively high capacity for strategic partners to reach consensus on less divisive difficulties that arise. In dealing with them, the challenge is likely to be not so much substantive as bureaucratic and logistical. For all its resources and power, the US is having a hard time bearing the security burdens that it has assumed and had thrust upon it. What seems certain is that if still more strategic crises occur, international coordination and cooperation will be at a high premium.